THE GERMAN OFFICER-CORPS

THE
GERMAN OFFICER-CORPS
in Society and State
1650 – 1945

KARL DEMETER

Translated from the German by Angus Malcolm

Introduction by
MICHAEL HOWARD

FREDERICK A. PRAEGER, *Publishers*
NEW YORK · WASHINGTON

BOOKS THAT MATTER

Published in the United States of America in 1965
by Frederick A. Praeger, Inc., Publishers
111 Fourth Avenue, New York 3, N.Y.

Library of Congress Catalog Card Number: 65–14178

Printed in Great Britain by
Western Printing Services Ltd. Bristol

Contents

Contents

Introduction

Interest in the German officer-corps and in the part which it has played in the history of Germany reached its peak during the decade following the end of the second World War. During that conflict the Allies had been fascinated in spite of themselves by the almost melodramatic combination of social archaism and superb military efficiency which seemed characteristic of their adversaries. The *coup râté* of 20th July 1944 gave to the world the first glimpse of the moral and political dilemma in which some of its foremost members found themselves. The subsequent War Crimes Trials enabled us to study in detail the total lapse by many of them from the standards of honour and soldierly conduct which they had proclaimed for the best part of two hundred years, and in virtue of which they had demanded – and to a great extent achieved – a privileged status vis-à-vis not only the rest of the German people but the dynasty, and the successor governments, which they had professed to serve.

Today our concern to understand the behaviour of the Germans during the second World War has abated. But enough has occurred elsewhere in the world to remind us how universal and how recurrent are the problems of civil-military relations of which the German experience provides only one, if possibly the best documented, example. How, in an age of great social fluidity, can anything so rigid as a corps of officers be created and preserved? How can it remain responsive to social and political development, yet maintain its essential cohesion? What control should it have over its own recruitment? What factors should be stressed in its education? What degree of political autonomy is permissible? There can hardly be a State of significance in the world where some or all of these problems do not arise. In States where the authority of the civil power is either traditionally weak or has recently been violently shaken they can arise in a particularly disagreeable form. The German officer-corps should therefore properly interest not only the historian of Germany and her wars, but the political and social scientist concerned with a recurrent problem of human organisation.

It is significant that the first edition of Dr Demeter's book of which this is a complete revision, should have appeared in 1930. The ashes of the first World War were cold, the fires of the second were not yet being stoked, the Reichswehr played no overt role in the politics of the Republic; yet it was none the less evident that the German officer and his relationship to the rest of society presented problems of sufficient complexity and importance to justify a careful historical and sociological study of this scope. It is not to belittle Dr Demeter's industry and acumen to say that his task was made easier by the concern – almost the obsession – over these problems which had been so general in Germany for a hundred years past, from the days of Scharnhorst to those of Ludendorff. Information about the social origins of officers had already been carefully compiled, of a kind which only laborious research has subsequently accumulated for the French and United States armed forces and which for the British Army has not yet been collected at all. Ever since the dark days of Jena and the exhilarating, if controversial, experiences of the Wars of Liberation the German officer-corps had itself engaged in a continual self-examination, each generation re-defining its view of the nature and purpose of the German officer in society and seeking the best means of maintaining these in a changing world. For a British or an American equivalent of this soul-searching one will ransack military sources in vain. The nearest Britain has to offer is perhaps the Anglican Church in the days of John Henry Newman. But whereas the romantic antiquarianism of the Oxford Movement was an interesting, if influential, minority cult, the no less anachronistic views of Edwin von Manteuffel and his circle became and remained a political force of considerable and continuing power.

For like the Church of England, the German officer-corps found itself in the nineteenth century fighting a desperate rearguard action against the Spirit of the Age. The social pattern devised to meet eighteenth-century needs was becoming increasingly archaic. The Great Elector, Frederick William, had in the seventeenth century fashioned his corps of officers out of his nobility, particularly from the poorer families beyond the Elbe where the decline of a free peasantry into serfdom gave to landowners a habit of authority which might have proved troublesome to the dynasty had not poverty made them grateful for any offices, military or civil, that the dynasty could put in their way. The problem of the turbulent minor nobility which had plagued Europe in the sixteenth century was resolved by harnessing them to the royal service. But like all marriages, this arrangement involved obligations on both sides. If the Junkers settled down to become the King's men and to wear the royal coat, they demanded in return that the royal commission should wherever possible be reserved for them alone – a demand which the *noblesse* in France were to make with no less success. Frederick the Great made no difficulties about meeting it once the Seven Years' War was over and his army could be pruned of the excrescences which it had grown during the years of national peril. The middle classes were far too precious to him as money-spinners to be allowed to usurp the noble privilege of the sword. The closing decades of the eighteenth century saw the Prussian Army, like the pre-revolutionary French Army, become almost explicitly a system of outdoor relief for the upper classes; this at a time when the development of military science was beginning to demand of its practitioners a new kind of professionalism, and when changes in social and political awareness were calling into question the whole concept of the army as an extension of the royal household and an instrument of the dynastic will.

In the minds of the great Prussian military reformers – Scharnhorst, Boyen, Clausewitz – military, social, political and moral factors were firmly linked. For them the officer-corps was no longer to be a branch of the royal establishment holding office by virtue of hereditary claims, but the leaders of an embattled Fatherland who must show themselves worthy of their primacy through their professional attributes and a moral strength drawn from that deeper understanding of the world which education alone could give. Boyen in particular, when as Minister for War he had the opportunity of remoulding the

Prussian Army at the close of the Napoleonic Wars, hoped to refashion its officers as a *corps d'élite* nationally recruited and selected by examination, without privilege of birth; a demand we find again in the proposals of the Frankfurt Assembly of 1848. But the idea of introducing such examinations caused bitter offence to the conservatives. It would bring a lot of undesirable young men into the officer-corps: worse, it would keep a lot of desirable young men out. It would implant, in the words of Prince William of Prussia,[1] 'a wholly different character, a wholly different spirit, from those it has had hitherto.' That such a change might be politically dangerous as well as socially undesirable became clear in 1848, when the attitude of the officer-corps, literally *plus royaliste que le roi*, was a major factor in bringing about the failure of the revolution. In 1861 we find further protests against the introduction of high educational qualifications as being likely to cause 'a radical change in the character of the corps of officers'. This time the meaningful question was added, 'Would this new kind of officer-corps show the same behaviour as was shown in 1848[2]?'

Apart from these political overtones this debate, between those who wanted educated officers and those who wanted the qualities of 'character' supposedly brought out by good breeding, was not peculiar to nineteenth-century Germany. Anyone concerned with military education today will discover from Dr Demeter's analysis how hoary is the controversy which still rages over the best kind of training in cadet schools. 'We are not concerned with "science" at the War Schools, as if they were academies, but with the truly difficult task of initiating young men into the basic principles of war, and, so to speak, the tricks of the trade.'[3] So runs a memorandum from the Prussian Inspector-General of Military Training and Education in 1890; but comparable views have been expressed more recently, and nearer home, than that. There would still be considerable support in military quarters both in Britain and in the United States for the view, as expressed by Hilaire Belloc, that –

> The Thing Of Ultimate Effect
> Is Character – not Intellect.

But by the end of the nineteenth century the growing need for large numbers of officers to serve in von Schlieffen's *Millionenheer* was making it as impossible for the conservatives to pre-

serve the officer-corps as a social élite as it was for the reformers
to turn it into an intellectual élite. In 1890 we find the Chief
of the Military Cabinet, the official primarily responsible for
maintaining the quality of the officer-corps, admitting privately that the entrance examination should be treated as a
matter of form. 'The main thing was to "get 'em into uniform
quick"'.[4] His successor in 1909 considered it impossible anyhow to get enough properly qualified officers, but added 'I do
not regard this as a great calamity either, so long as the supply
of character keeps up'.[5] For much as the old Junkers may have
disliked rubbing shoulders with the sons of bankers, lawyers
and merchants, great as were their efforts to avoid them by
congregating in a few socially élite regiments (and this was no
purely Prussian phenomenon either), they could no longer
dismiss them as politically unreliable. The classes who had
during the first part of the century seemed the worst infected
with liberal and radical views, the men who had been admitted
only on sufferance to the army in the dark days of 1808–14 and
who had been purged from it very quickly afterwards, these
same classes after 1870 swung massively to the support of the
dynasty and the régime, humiliated themselves to get their sons
into fashionable regiments, and swaggered out in their Reservist uniforms on every possible occasion. When William II
formally opened the portals of the officer-corps to them by his
Imperial Order of 1890 there was little overt protest from the
Old Guard. The newcomers were quite happy to take the mould
of the old order, and indeed to outdo it in their maintenance of
all its rights and privileges.

For the status of the officer-corps as a kind of Samurai
class, the First Estate in the land, remained unchanged by this
dilution. The status was a complex one, and it is not easy to
disentangle the historical reality from the romantic myths
which were woven around it during the early part of the nineteenth century. The position of the eighteenth-century noble
officer, an autocrat on his estates but wearing the King's coat
and devoted to the King's service, seems comparatively
straightforward. By the 1830s and 1840s it was becoming
sophisticated by antiquarian lore. The officer was not only the
'King's man', standing to him in a direct feudal relationship
cemented in an oath sworn before God. He was also a member
of a self-governing, self-perpetuating Order, a guild remini-

scent of the *Landsknechte* of the sixteenth century with their elaborate professional code, or, better still, a quasi-religious order of chivalry such as the Teutonic Knights. In a world of rapid and disagreeable change such members of the officer-corps as were literate enough to do so cheered each other up with gobbets of such ill-digested historical nonsense – much as in England during the same years the apostles of the Oxford Movement bored and embarrassed their more staid colleagues by reminding them that the Church whose incumbencies they placidly enjoyed was the Visible Body of Christ on Earth. It may be doubted whether von Manteuffel found any more amiable reception for his ideas; there is certainly no sign of it in the writings of that master of common sense Prince Frederick Charles. Yet the concept of the officer's code of honour as something distinct from his duties of obedience, the sense of belonging to an autonomous, self-perpetuating corporation with which even the King interfered at his peril, set apart from the rest of the nation, resentful of its prying eyes and disdainful of its complaints, all this grew stronger as the century wore on. Loyalty to the person of the Ruler, of a totally anachronistic kind, became the more strongly emphasised with the growing danger that military affairs might become the concern of the Reichstag. The attempt to keep defence questions separate from and beyond the reach of the democratic process was again no purely Prussian phenomenon; but nowhere was the attempt made more consistently, or with greater success.

Yet the officer-corps could not be kept insulated from the general course of the nineteenth and twentieth centuries. The warning given to officers in 1911 not to attend afternoon tea parties in big Berlin hotels because of the very mixed company to be found there has a desperate Canute-like ring about it. An army stationed at home, in constant and unavoidable contact with the civilian population, marrying and educating its children, cannot remain an isolated garrison. Changes in the social structure or the political climate will sooner or later affect it for better or worse. So von Seeckt found when he tried to reconstruct the officer-corps after the first World War. For one brief decade – the decade during which most of this book was written – he seemed to have achieved all that his predecessors had desired. With the compulsory reduction of the Army to a tiny cadre he could insist that its officers should come up to the most exacting standards not only of birth but also of education and technical expertise. As in other countries the pressure of the nobility to get into the Army, almost the only *milieu* where their standards remained relevant and one could still live like a gentleman, assumed the proportions of an *émigration intérieure*. By 1932 over one third of all officers being commissioned derived from the nobility. At the same time Seeckt insisted that all cadets should have attained at least University admission standards; while as his nucleus in 1919 he selected so far as possible only the intellectual élite of the old army, the members of the General Staff, to preserve which, he wrote, 'is to preserve the Spirit of the Army.'[6]

To the professional success of Seeckt's measures the brilliant performance of the German armies in the second World War bears eloquent witness. In his political objectives he was not so successful. He wished to preserve the old detachment of the officer-corps from democratic politics, even though there was no longer a Crown to command its devotion. In place of loyalty to the Crown he attempted to set loyalty to the idea of the State. The Reichswehr, in his words, was to be 'the prime expression of the power of the State'.[7] So far as domestic politics were concerned, the officer was to set an example of undeviating neutrality. But this was asking too much. One might as well have asked for such neutrality from the French army during the early years of the French Revolution. If the nation was in ferment, nothing could prevent ideas, discussion, even conspiracy from penetrating the ranks of the army as well. Meetings were going on of considerably greater importance and influence than afternoon tea parties in Berlin hotels. National-Socialist ideas seeped easily even into the ranks of the old Reichswehr. When Hitler struck off its shackles and the intake of cadets increased from 120 to 2,000 a year all attempts at isolation broke down, and the older officers found themselves swept along on a massive and alien tide.

It is interesting to see how one of these old-school officers, General von Senger, echoed the complaints of Prince Frederick Charles seventy years earlier. Senger wrote that in the 'thirties the older officers did not 'relish the servility that was now the mode'.[8] Frederick Charles had complained in 1861 that 'bootlicking is not punished but rewarded by success, telling tales commands a hearing like the secret police ... now that we have to put up with the declining quality of the officer intake.'[9] The camaraderie of the club could not be transplanted into a great military bureaucracy. How can one expect behaviour worthy of an officer and a gentleman when officers need no longer be gentlemen? To study the same problem in a more familiar setting, the reader need only consult the military novels of Mr Evelyn Waugh.

The officer-corps had thus already been torn from its familiar moorings when the second World War broke out. Subsequent claims that the Wehrmacht did not participate in Nazi atrocities do not stand up to examination; but the Wehrmacht itself was a new mushroom growth over which the older officers had very little control; while the para-military formations which spawned round it belied Hitler's promise that the Wehrmacht should be the sole *Wäffenträger* of the Third Reich. Dr Demeter has extended his study to cover this final, tragic and discreditable chapter in the history of the German officer-corps; but by 1939 Hitler had destroyed its corporative independence so effectively that this is little more than a grisly epilogue to a story which properly ends in the 'thirties, when the corps found itself effectively *gleichgeschaltet* in the Third Reich. Thereafter some of its members behaved well, some horribly badly, most of them simply got by as best they could. Deprived of the protection of their caste, they reacted like any other ordinary men during a prolonged crisis, and no general conclusions can be drawn from their record. We can only hope that ordinary men, whatever their profession and whatever their nationality, will not be required to undergo such a crisis again.

MICHAEL HOWARD

PART ONE

SOCIAL ORIGINS

I

Prussia: Before Jena

When we speak of the social origins of a class or community like the German corps of officers, two questions are involved: first of all, the professional or social standing, at any given moment (in plainer language, the social class), of its members' parents; and secondly, the system of classification in itself. The latter may well go back to some earlier stage of social development, but it can still have important social significance at a later stage. In other words, what we are dealing with is ranks in society. We are dealing with questions of status or, if you prefer, the distinction between nobility and *bourgeoisie*.

With these points in mind, let us begin by looking at the social origins of the corps of officers in Prussia, since it was this which largely set the standard for German officers in general. Research into the beginnings of the new Prussian Army – starting, say, with the Great Elector* and continuing into the first decades of the nineteenth century – reveals gaps in our knowledge that we are never likely to be able to fill. Even before the second World War the archives were sadly defective. For the seventeenth and eighteenth centuries we know next to nothing about the professions to which the fathers of Prussian officers and officer-cadets belonged. There were no statistics in those days – or, if there were, they have been lost. Nevertheless the available documents and the historians who have drawn upon them do provide us with some clues as to the respective shares of the nobility and the *bourgeoisie* in the make-up of the corps of officers. Clues, however, are all they are, and they do not enable us to deduce accurate figures for the whole of this period.

Not only were the lists of officers very patchily kept in the

* Frederick William of Brandenburg (1640–88).

3

time of the Great Elector and his immediate successor,* but often the same person may appear in them sometimes with a nobiliary prefix (*Adelsprädikat*) such as 'von' before his name¹ and sometimes without. But when we find that noblemen serving as non-commissioned officers or as private soldiers appear in the lists of *officers* we are entitled to draw some important conclusions. It looks, indeed, as if in the Thirty Years' War (1618–48) the social line between nobleman and commoner was no longer drawn so strictly as it had been in the time of the *Landsknechte†*.² Three peasants' sons – Derfflinger, Lüdcke and Hennigs – were frequent guests at the Elector's table; but under his son, King Frederick I, the bulk of the commissions were held by noblemen;³ and indeed it was the nobility – especially the Brandenburgers and the Pomeranians – that provided the core around which other officers, foreign or bourgeois, gathered. Bourgeois officers, incidentally, were to be found even in the Guards; and by an Order of the 11th March 1704, the King expressly assured the bourgeois officers of his bodyguard that in matters of promotion they would be given the same treatment as the nobility. The nobility persistently looked down on the erudite, bourgeois corps of artillery-officers because a whiff of the workshop and the forge still hung about their cannon, but the King conferred on them a status equal to that of the Guards.

The shrinkage in the revenues drawn by the nobility from its estates was one of the reasons why that class bowed more and more to the wishes of the King not only in matters of State but also in sending their sons to serve as officers in the Army. But the more they did so, the more they predominated in its upper ranks – a process which continued under the second King of Prussia, Frederick William I.‡ *On purgea dans chaque régiment le corps des officiers de ces gens dont la conduite ou la naissance ne répondait point au métier de gens d'honneur qu'ils devait* [sic] *faire et depuis la délicatesse des officiers ne souffrit parmi leurs compagnons que des gens sans reproche.*§⁴ The numerical ratio of nobility to commoners

* Frederick II of Brandenburg (1688–1713) who became Frederick I of Prussia in 1701.

† The mercenary German infantry of the sixteenth-seventeenth centuries.

‡ 1713–40.

§ 'In every regiment, the officers were purged of people whose conduct or birth was not compatible with the profession they sought to exercise – that, of men of honour – and since that time the officers' own sense of propriety has suffered none but men without reproach to be their comrades.'

among Frederick William I's officers is shown by the *Rang- und Quartierliste* for May, 1739 – the penultimate year of his reign. It reveals that all 34 general-officers were noblemen and that of the 211 field-officers all but 11 were noblemen likewise. As for officers of the rank of captain and below, the lists unfortunately do not record titles of nobility at all (see above p. 4). The corps of engineers was not covered by this list but its numbers of noble and bourgeois field-officers were about equal. It should be remembered, however, that in the circumstances of the times it was not too difficult, at least for wealthy people, to obtain a 'nobiliary prefix'. Anyone, for example, who contributed to recruiting-funds or sent along an exceptionally tall recruit or, indeed, built a fine house in Berlin, was soon rewarded in this way.[5] On the other hand it was still possible for non-commissioned officers of long service to be commissioned as second-lieutenants.

The reign of Frederick William I also saw the introduction of a new kind of cavalry, the hussars, which present some interest in this context. Their social origins and standing, like those of the artillery, were very different indeed from what they later became; and a characteristically humorous light is thrown on the point by General von Pape.[6] In a paper dated at Berlin on the 2nd March 1887, he wrote: 'When Frederick William I felt the need to have some hussars, every kind of riff-raff was scraped together and formed into a squadron. In order to lick them into shape my great-grandfather, then a captain of dragoons, was appointed their commanding-officer. These hussars enjoyed the worst possible reputation not only in the Army but throughout the country but the appointment, of course, could not be refused. When, however, my great-grandfather put his hussar-uniform on, looked in the mirror and saw himself in that "harlequin get-up", as he called it, he fell dead of a stroke. But he was the first commanding-officer of the first hussars all the same.'

Frederick the Great,*[7] like his father before him, occasionally filled up gaps among his officers with bourgeois; but it was really only the heavy losses of the Seven Years' War that made him do so. In general, things ran the other way. His three predecessors had with difficulty brought the raw country gentry (*Junkers*) of their dominions to heel and gradually got them

* Frederick II, King of Prussia, 1740–86.

5

to serve in the Army; but Frederick II not only gave these
people preference but attached them to his person. The story
goes that every now and then when officer-cadets were paraded
before him, he would strike a bourgeois cadet out of the ranks
with his own crutch-stick, and he went so far as to refuse to allow
marriage with bourgeois ladies. For all his 'enlightenment' in
other matters there was a streak of feudal class-consciousness in
him which gradually gained the upper hand, especially in later
life. It may have been justified, of course, by the conditions
of the time and by the economic interests of the State. Nevertheless I do not think Prince Frederick Charles of Prussia
was right, a century later, to call it (*see* Appendix 1) 'one of the
many French ideas that great man blindly copied'. In France,
it is true, no less a military authority than Vauban held that
in order to have good officers 'one must recruit young noblemen
of good character, good health and sound intellectual capacity –
preferably younger sons of families whose fathers are not
well-off'.[8] In principle, therefore, Frederick the Great was
certainly not unique in thinking that honour resided, in the
main, among the nobility alone, while admitting that merit and
talents cropped up here and there, though rarely, among bourgeois.[9] Significant of the social standing of the officer-intake
during the reign of Frederick II is the state of affairs in the
Apenburg Dragoons. At the start of the Seven Years' War
that regiment still had not a single bourgeois officer. At the end
(1763) there were five among thirty-seven – a figure which,
however, had sunk by July 1784 to three. This is a process which
we shall often meet with in the nineteenth century and it is
only partially explained by the difference between the demands
made upon officers in peace and in war.

Thus it came about that in the year of Frederick II's death
at least nine-tenths of his officers bore noble names; and even
the bourgeois tenth was pretty well isolated from the rest –
partly in garrison-regiments, but mostly in the artillery. Indeed
a study of the higher ranks, from majors up to and including
general-officers, reveals a proportion of 689 to only 22. In conclusion it can safely be said that Frederick the Great gave full
practical effect to his well-known saying: *Die Rasse des alt-
preussischen Adels ist so gut, dass sie meritiret conserviret zu werden.**

---

* 'The breed of the Old Prussian nobility is so good that it deserves to be
preserved.'

These proportions remained essentially unchanged for twenty years after Frederick's death. Among the 7–8,000 officers of the Prussian Army in 1806[10] there were 695 bourgeois, 131 of whom were in the line regiments (83 of them in the musketeer garrison-battalions), 76 in the light infantry, 289 in the artillery, 84 in the cavalry (in the hussars, perhaps), 37 in various other corps, and 82 listed as sick (*Invalide*). The bourgeois field-officers numbered about thirty. It is true that Frederick William II,* and especially Frederick William III,† had strong instinctive feelings of sympathy for the *bourgeoisie*. Nonetheless, it required the great disaster that befell the Army and the State (at Jena in 1806) to bring the former's perhaps rather superficial sympathies to the point of decision and effective action. The 'brass-hats' of Prussia still lived mentally in the days of 'Old Fritz',‡ and it took a shock to make them realise that modern times could no longer be measured with impunity by the standards of former victories and bygone principles. That shock was administered with shattering effect upon the Prussian troops and their commanders by an upstart of genius named Napoleon.

* 1786–97.   † 1797–1840.   ‡ Frederick the Great.

2

Prussia: Reform and Reaction

There is certainly a case for saying – as historians often have – that the cause of the disaster that befell the Army and the State at Jena in 1806 was the social, and therefore the military, backwardness of the Prussian Army or, to be more exact, of its officers.[1] The most striking thing about the senior officers of that Army is that they were old. Here are the figures for 1806:

142 Generals: 4 over 80, 13 over 70, 62 over 60.

Field-Officers:
    540 in the infantry: 7 over 70, 110 over 60, 187 over 50.
    227 in the cavalry: 25 over 60, 129 over 50.
    39 in the artillery: 4 over 70, 22 over 60.
    14 in the engineers: one over 70, 2 over 60, 7 over 50.
    65 on the general list: 4 over 60, 5 over 50.

Captains of infantry and cavalry:
    945 in the infantry: 2 over 70, 18 over 60, 119 over 50.
    241 in the cavalry: 18 over 50.
    63 in the artillery: 6 over 60, 26 over 50.
    28 in the engineers, etc.: 3 over 50.
    29 non-regimental officers: one over 60, 2 over 50.
    261 artillery-lieutenants: 1 over 70, 5 over 60, 9 over 50,
                     7 over 40.

Even if everything else in the Army had been in first-class condition, one thing is perfectly plain: two-thirds of the general-officers were either nearing the biblical age or had long since passed it; a quarter of the regimental and battalion-commanders – the men who have to carry the main burden in battle – had passed the age of 60 at which the average man can no longer stand up to the physical strains of war; and company and squadron commanders were not much younger. From such officers, under the conditions then ruling, no great results could be expected in battle – and least of all against a numerically stronger army commanded by a young genius like Napoleon, with years of active service behind it, and inspired by the national ideal of a great civilising mission to the world.

But there must have been other grave defects within this Army. Even before 1806, public opinion on the subject of the Army and its commanders was divided although, on the whole, it seems to have been favourable. At any rate the sceptics did not dare really make themselves heard until the disaster at Jena put new heart into critics of the Army and its management and made such criticism a patriotic duty. Even before that, however, there had been independent, creative minds that held existing conditions to be out-of-date and thought reforms were needed. Of such men we may take Freiherr vom Stein as typical. Four years before Jena he had labelled as 'ridiculous prejudice' the nobility's privilege of filling the most important posts in the Army; and with that comment he went to the very foundation of the whole system. It is significant that our source for that comment is his *confidential* letter to Sack at Hildesheim.[2] After Jena, it is true, this point of view became almost a public axiom, or at any rate this appeared to be the case for, if the partisans of the old feudal régime had not found their convictions shaken by events, at least they kept quiet on the subject.

But once the Napoleonic war was over, the old guard, either from conviction or from sheer self-interest, took the field again. Their spokesman and, as such, the modern literary father of the conservative idea of the class-State, is to be found in a Brandenburg aristocrat named Friedrich August von der Marwitz. He was a highly intelligent man, with an acute and cultivated mind, of a warm and effervescent temperament, polished both in character and utterance – in brief, a man of the world such as the nobility of Brandenburg may never have produced before and has certainly never brought forth since.

It is well worth while to see how things looked thirty years after Jena, to a man like this who represented his class with rare distinction and integrity. Here is what he wrote in his memoirs:[3]

So much evidence of neglect of duty has been brought to light that one might suppose the Army had been nothing but a collection of cowards, traitors and idiots, whereas those who represented it as such were in fact merely ignorant, malicious, Frenchified scribblers.

It should not, however, be forgotten that:

(i) the main defect was at the top, and therefore all the acts of real bravery, devotion and self-sacrifice that took place at the lower levels had no effect upon the whole, while the bad was universally known and had terrible results;

(ii) the commanders who from 1813 onwards won glory for the name of Prussia, inflicting such defeats upon the enemy that they entered his capital twice as conquerors, had all of them been officers in the Prussian Army in the year 1806 and were in most cases already serving as its commanders. Among them were sixty commanders of army-corps, divisions and brigades, more than 100 regimental commanders every one of whom had been in service in 1806. The same was true of all but ten out of nearly three hundred battalion-commanders and of more than 1900 company and squadron-commanders out of 2000. If the same men could produce one result in 1806 and the opposite in 1813, the cause must be sought not in the officers themselves but in the decisions taken higher up – in the regulations, the equipment and the circumstances: but first and foremost in the grace of God.

That the main weakness was at the top is undoubtedly true. Nevertheless, a number of fortress-commanders were over-age and incompetent, and that fact is in no wise disposed of by the second point in Marwitz' argument. It may well be true on the one hand that, as established by later military historians, nearly 4,000 of the 7,000-odd officers in the Prussian Army in 1806 went through the subsequent War of Liberation and took part in its hard-won victories; but it is a fact, on the other hand, that the officers of 1813 were, to a large extent, a new generation. The question is not whether the 4,000 were still there, but what positions they held. An important reduction in the size of the Army had had to be made and it was therefore fairly easy to discharge elderly generals and field-officers who had not made good. Those who took their places were often very young; and men who had been subalterns in 1806 were commanding battalions and whole regiments in 1813 – a fact which indirectly proves that many officers in 1806 had indeed been over-age and that this is what had led to calamitous results.

We must, however, relate this particular phenomenon to the more general principle that underlies it, viz: that too much attention had been paid to forms and not enough to material requirements. More accurately put, there had been an un-thinking adherence to old forms that had been shaped by other circumstances and other needs but which were no longer suit-able. This is true not only of military tactics but also of the matter that concerns us here – the questions of officer-recruit-ment and promotion. In a struggle for life and death such as Napoleon's revolutionary armies forced upon Prussia, sinecures are fatal. But a system of sinecures was exactly what the rigid privilege of the nobility had brought about through the per-manent occupation of senior appointments. It may be that the King's authority, if wisely used, could have prevented such abuses in time; but they were rooted in the system itself, and the system was bound to collapse when the Army did so. Such an end was made all the more certain, too, by the fact that in Germany as elsewhere the old system had during the last few decades come more and more sharply into conflict with the new social, political, philosophical and educational movements of which Voltaire and Rousseau can be taken as the ideal repre-sentatives and the French Revolution as the practical expression.

In Germany as in France a main feature of the new *Zeitgeist* was the desire to restore a 'natural' simplicity to all aspects of public and private life; and this was coupled with hostility towards the old, feudal, social order since the latter was re-garded as the artificial creation of a selfish, privileged class. The nobility and its special preserve, the corps of officers, thus came under attack. It would not be possible to go any deeper here into the workings of this spirit from the points of view of historical sociology; but it is permissible to quote the judgment of a well-disposed military historian (and senior officer) of the late nineteenth century:[4] 'The composition of the corps of officers (in 1806) showed beyond question a bias that was no longer appropriate to the social conditions ruling in the edu-cated world or to the spirit of the times. It demanded isolation and ossification in the name of tradition and it caused the coun-try's strength to be dissipated. But the origin of these conditions lay much less in the corps of officers or in individual members of it than in higher authority, which alone could have brought about an improvement. From its isolation and from the pre-judice that this gave rise to within it and without, the corps of officers reaped nothing but harm.'

When disaster had struck, higher authority took action. On

the 25th July 1807, the King set up a Commission for the Re-organisation of the Army.[5] This most important Commission at first contained more die-hards than reformers; but the King himself drafted its terms of reference in his own hand. The document consisted of nineteen points. It was in Point 5 that he tackled the social composition of the corps of officers, and wrote: 'Should not some change be made as regards the admission of bourgeois, and more of them admitted?' This single sentence, this one thoughtful question, with its slight ring of reluctance, set in motion a massive process and, in fact, opened a new chapter in the history of the Prussian corps of officers – indeed, in the history of Germany.

The first draft report to be laid before the Commission was prepared by an opponent of reform, Lieutenant-Colonel von Lottum, and he dealt with Point 5 as follows. The experience of other German States, he said, showed that no advantage to the Army was to be expected from the admission of bourgeois officers. If it were nevertheless believed that this step would swing a large and influential body of citizens over to the Army's side (which indeed seemed likely), that would certainly be a ground for recommending it. But in that case (he added, *inter alia*), those who were admitted must be chosen from respectable and cultivated bourgeois families lest their connections prove incompatible with their future social status. A similar point of view was put forward by Lieutenant-Colonel von Borstell in a memorandum dated the 20th September 1807. That the need for granting commissions to bourgeois was widely accepted in the Prussian corps of officers is shown by the number and the tenor of the memoranda submitted to the Commission, as well as by the explicit testimony of Boyen. But Lottum's general view was also held by Borstell, and many another will have thought the same – that the commissioning of bourgeois must be kept within strict limits so as to safeguard the predominance of the numerous members of the poorer Prussian nobility. What Friedrich Meinecke* said of Borstell can be applied no less to Lottum and his school of thought: 'The solid trunk of his aristocratic and military convictions was now to be decked with liberal garlands.'

This truth will have escaped no one less than the friends of reform on the Commission itself which, through dismissal of the

* *See* Note 5.

die-hards and their replacement by reformers, was approaching unanimity in favour of change. Lottum's first draft, with its numerous safeguards, was totally discarded, and the report eventually submitted to the King breathes the unmistakable spirit of Scharnhorst and Gneisenau – neither of them Prussians and both of them keen adherents of the movement for reform. In the end their views (and to some extent their actual drafting, e.g. in the two basic introductory sentences) were reproduced in the Royal Ordinance (it took, however, nearly twelve months to appear) which was finally issued from Königsberg on the 6th August 1808 with the heading: 'Regulations for making Appointments to Vacancies among Ensigns and for the Selection of Officers for the Infantry, Cavalry and Artillery'. It began as follows: 'Applications for commissions will in future be considered only on grounds of attainments and education in time of peace, and on grounds of outstanding bravery and general outlook in time of war. It follows that any Prussian who possesses these qualifications can aspire to the highest military posts of honour. All advantages hitherto enjoyed by the [noble] Estate in the Army are hereby abolished and all men, regardless of their origins, shall have the same duties and rights ...'

In reality this Ordnance did no more than apply the tenor of the first Prussian Reform-Edict, dated the 9th October 1807, to the conditions obtaining in the corps of officers. That Edict, which had abolished all differences between classes (i.e. *Stände*, or Estates of the Realm), and in particular the institution of serfdom, had given bourgeois and peasants the right to acquire landed property from nobles and allowed noblemen to engage in bourgeois occupations. Other measures logically followed from all this, such as the abolition of corporal punishment (*Prügelstrafe*) in the Army and other things of the kind. As with every great reform one is bound to wonder whether this was really a reform and nothing more, or whether in fact it was not a revolution – a revolution from above. At all events the Ordinance of the 6th August 1808, taken together with all the other innovations, subjected the battered body of the Prussian State and Army to a very grave operation; and as such it had its full quota of critical *sequelae*. Proof that this was after all the right last-minute treatment lies in the victories of the War of Liberation and the ultimate restoration of the Prussian State, its

Army and its corps of officers. The obstruction had been cleared and the patient was breathing well again.

Yet the patient, once recovered, was by no means wholly grateful to the doctors who had cured him. It is recorded of Borstell (who soon afterwards had to leave the Commission) that many years later, and after Scharnhorst's death, his eyes still blazed with hatred and indignation when anything brought that great man back to his mind. And another old diehard, General von Yorck, cast bitter words in the teeth of Prince William when the Prince, in conversation with him, tried to defend the new dispensation: 'If', he said, 'Your Royal Highness robs me and my children of our rights, on what, pray, do your own rights rely?' Jacobinism, nothing less, was the charge the old generals and the down-graded nobility of Old Prussia cast at the authors of the new régime.

The King himself, once he felt firmer in the saddle again, had second thoughts about his own temerity and he showed it in the way he handled the problem of the cadets. In the cadets' schools,[6] as developed in Prussia since the days of the Great Elector (and also in other German States) men like Scharnhorst, Gneisenau and even Humboldt had seen a sort of conservatory for exclusive, out-of-date class-consciousness. They therefore wanted to see such institutions abolished. But in this matter Boyen, as Minister of War, showed the greater insight. With an eye to getting the essentials of what the King wanted, he aimed only at bringing the spirit of these schools into line with the spirit of the Army's new character, viz. with the principles of equality before the law and the stimulation of talent and energy. In particular he wanted to widen the range of families whose sons were now eligible for the Cadet Corps so as to include the whole class of civil servants. Accordingly he laid emphasis on the latter's dignity. But even this went too far for the King. He therefore brought the limits back again to officers' families – to families whose father had either been killed in action or to which he wished to give this particular mark of his approval. For a long time at least, this meant in practice the acceptance of hardly any cadets who were not of noble birth. Officers, after all, who at that time (1816) had sons of an age to enter the cadet schools must normally have been officers themselves before 1808; in consequence they could hardly have failed to be of noble birth. Bearing this in mind it is therefore obvious that to limit admission to sons of officers killed in battle could only mean (apart from exceptional cases of royal favour) limiting admission to sons of the nobility.

The King himself had thereby re-erected a defence against one possible result of his Ordinance of the 6th August 1808, namely an excessive influx of bourgeois into the corps of officers. After all, on the advice of Scharnhorst, many hundreds of 'volunteer riflemen' (*Jäger*) from bourgeois families had been commissioned into the territorials (*Landwehr*) in order to make good the losses incurred since May 1813; and by the end of 1815, indeed, almost a third of the whole corps of officers consisted of these Jäger.[7] When peace had been re-established, moreover, many of these men did not return to civil life: professional careers seemed unattractive perhaps or offered too small prospects, or there may have been other grounds. The best of the Jäger – perhaps 1,300 in all – were posted to line-regiments as 'supernumerary' officers (*aggregirte Offiziere*) and thereafter they gradually filled up vacancies on the regular establishment. Their social and intellectual level, however, was very varied: and among them there were certainly some pretty dubious characters[8] and what Prince Frederick Charles once described as 'strange creatures'. We can take it as certain that acquaintance with these new-comers very soon aroused strong opposition among the regular officers.

That opposition, however, could not have become effective unless it had been, so to speak, borne along on a rising wave of restoration and reaction which now began to drown the young seed of reform. Since suffering the effects of the general disaster of 1806, the Junker element in the Prussian corps of officers – which had played an honourable part in the War of Liberation and its victories – had regained a sense of its own worth. Naturally it tried to fight back against the humiliation inflicted on it by the Reform-Ordinance, and recover its former position. After the Liberation and reconstruction of the State, therefore, a determined struggle for mastery broke out, and it was nowhere more clearly to be seen than in the corps of officers. The Land-wehr, indeed, was already almost entirely officered by bourgeois; but for the rest, the lists[9] for 1817 show 4,138 noble and 3367 bourgeois names; in 1818 the figures were 3,605 to 3,053. Clearly, then, the Junkers only held a bare majority; and naturally they now began to use every means of warding off the

imminent danger of submersion. At the same time the ferment
of the age was so strongly at work among the Junkers themselves[10] that a general swing to the left was just as possible as
a swing to the right. But one is tempted to say that when
the pendulum had been swinging leftwards for a matter
of ten years, a swing to the right was dictated by the very laws
of nature.

Something more must be noted none the less. There was
another force that gave the rightward swing an additional
impulse – a force whose origin was neither military, political
nor social. This was the Romantic movement. It was not just
literary and artistic in nature, but embraced the whole range
of human feeling and outlook. Its genius was many-sided; art
and science, politics and sociology, religion itself, all felt its
impact in turn. But common to every aspect of the Romantic
movement in Germany was the exaltation of Christian-German
chivalry coupled with the patriarchal and corporative institutions of the German Middle Ages.[11]

If the Romantic aim was to portray the Germanic spirit
in all its purity, to revive in every walk of life the ideals of Faith,
Manners and Morals, one practical result – as people saw things
– was bound to be the re-establishment of the old class-insti-
tutions, the Estates, in constitutional and social life, to say
nothing of the old Empire, the Reich, into the bargain. It was
the Reich, no doubt, which made the greater appeal in western
and southern Germany (reinforced, as it was, by the Catholic
and catholicising trend of Romanticism) while the class-conception of society had the greater appeal in the East where the
tradition of the Reich was more recent, less deep-rooted and
more fragmentary in general. In the East, on the other hand,
in the heart-land of Prussia, the exaltation of the class-structure
could not help involving a denial of what had been achieved
by the absolutism by which the seventeenth-century state had
been formed. In other words, the objective was a loosening of
Prussia's constitutional unity in favour of special aristocratic
and corporative rights. Haller, the constitutional authority,
raised these ideas, indeed, to the status of a doctrine and he
found devoted and influential supporters for it in the Crown
Prince (afterwards Frederick William IV) and his friends,
later the 'Camarilla'. But when it came to translating such
romantic notions into practical measures, the trouble was that

16

they had too recently been realities, and opposition was still too strong.

The political solution was sought in loyal collaboration after 1819 with Metternich's Austria, and in the agrarian question the great landowners gained solid practical advantages for themselves. Likewise in the corps of officers the trend since Boyen's departure from the Ministry of War (1819) had been not merely towards the ejection of those dubious elements I have already mentioned but above all towards ensuring that the 'unsuitable', i.e. the bourgeois-liberal, elements[12] had no share of the all-too-scarce promotions. In his second tenure of the Ministry of War (1840–48) Boyen was as powerless as the revolution of 1848 itself to alter these trends. If the latter, indeed, left any trace at all upon the composition of the Prussian corps of officers the effect was to strengthen its determination to resist the whole world of liberal ideas and to render the community of interest between Crown and aristocracy stronger and more explicit than it had ever been.

Yet the strains within the corps of officers were undoubtedly made tenser and more severe by the activities of the two contending camps – if that term be not too military itself. Prince Frederick Charles of Prussia[13] relates, for example, in an essay (Appendix 1) that when the survivors of those 'volunteer riflemen' had at last, in the 'forties and later (i.e. around 1855), begun to reach the influential ranks of regimental-commander and upwards, they had behaved with irresponsible laxity over the acceptance of officer-candidates so that once again 'many a strange creature' was commissioned. The Prince then describes how it became ever harder for noblemen of the poorer kind, and for hard-up officers' sons to enter upon a military career; and how in the end (say 1845 to 1860) officers had to be recruited 'from wherever one could hope to find anything suitable: young bourgeois were commissioned in numbers hitherto undreamed of, and such aristocrats as were accepted were all too often the stupidest sons, the ones who had abandoned their studies – and such like. Around that time, too, our military academies all began to leave much to be desired – and they do so still. In the Berlin cadet-corps there was a good deal of stealing.'

And yet these things, as they emerged and took new forms, could look very different, even at the time, to people in senior

positions that required the taking of a wider view. One may
cite, for example, the comment of Field-Marshal Manteuffel,
a personal opponent of Prince Frederick Charles, which shows
that he was flatly opposed to the 'preference for incompetent
aristocrats' that prevailed from 1840 to 1857, i.e. in the reign
of Frederick William IV. Schmoller[14] reports Manteuffel
as frequently telling him how he had had to clean these people
out of the Army when he was Chief of the Military Cabinet*
between 1850 and 1857. 'That', he used to say, 'was my
greatest political achievement. If I had not cleaned things out
we should not have won in 1864, 1866 and 1870. The officers
were much worse in the early 'fifties than in 1806.'

A concurrent but less brutal judgment, one that was far more
detailed and perspicacious, was given by another historian – a
man who had close contact with the leading personalities and
whose scientific cast of mind enabled him likewise to see things
as they really were. This was Theodor von Bernhardi.[15] In
Berlin on the 18th May 1855, he noted: ' ... Major von Schweinitz to dinner. Much talk about politics and the Army. Schweinitz' behaviour is rather odd but he is a cultivated man. Like
other engineers, of course, he is rather liberal-minded but he
has learnt to talk like the *Kreuzzeitung*† too. The regimental
commanders are making difficulties about taking on bourgeois
as ensigns. They have their orders! The idea is to have only
aristocrats as officers as far as possible, just like in the good old
days. Schweinitz produced non-political arguments in favour.
He says it has been noticed that bourgeois officers are highly
irresponsible about getting into debt. Aristocrats, i.e. sons of
hard-up officers, are used to doing without things. Plans are
afoot to enlarge the Cadet-Corps so that officer-vacancies can
be filled entirely with Cadets – (the best way of estranging the
Army from the country – which is in fact the aim, although they
really ought to know it will make the Army's name stink like
it did before 1806 – yet these are the miserable, rotten conditions
that are supposed to strengthen the Crown's position). – The
bourgeois who want to be officers are crowding into the gunners
and sappers because they can't get in anywhere else. People
like Schweinitz are disgusted because gunners and sappers will
be looked down on as before and rated as inferior to the rest of

* ie of the military staff at the Palace.
† The leading Church newspaper of the time.

the Army. – Things have gone so far that when Prince Charles was appointed *Feldzeugmeister** the Queen and the Princesses teased him for sinking so low as to become a gunner!'

Coming from such a well-informed contemporary source, this is a most revealing piece of evidence, and its final point deserves some elaboration. The social origins of officers entering the engineers and, even more, the artillery contrasted as sharply as in the eighteenth century with those of the officers commissioned into the infantry and cavalry. In the latter group there was a strong preference for aristocrats; the former often contained 'the sons of postmen, tax-inspectors, ticket-collectors, superannuated students, post-office clerks, etc; the artillery was the God-sent dumping ground for everyone who could not get into any other branch of the Service.' Von Hahn, who was then Inspector-General of Artillery, deplored this situation[16] and felt obliged to try to raise the artillery's social standing. Accordingly, he sent a special order to his four subordinate Inspectors, enjoining them to stiffen the tests in the selection of officer-candidates – social background included.[17] This effort was successful and the artillery was among the most respected branches of the Army in the last decades before the first World War; it considered itself, indeed, much smarter than the infantry.

Outside observers were in general very struck with the old rivalry between the various branches of the Army – ranging from harmless mutual ragging to professional and social friction that sometimes took a serious turn. This, indeed, was very much the case as regards relations between the officers of line regiments and of the Landwehr. Normally they were cool. From the professional point of view this was quite understandable, for in the ordinary way the Landwehr man, both as a soldier and as an officer, was rarely the equal of the regular whose whole life was spent in the Army. But, apart from this, a factor of social contrast was strongly at work, for the Landwehr officer normally came from a bourgeois family and quite often from much more modest folk, and was therefore looked down upon by the regular officers with their mainly aristocratic background and way of life. From the very start these contrasts were a hindrance to Boyen's army-reforms and to some extent indeed they brought his labours to nothing.

* The senior General of Artillary, or 'Master Gunner'.

3

Prussia: Expansion and Dilution

The reorganisation of the Army in 1860, which the Prince of
Prussia* had already thought out during his time at Coblence,
put an end to the separate existence of the Landwehr and fused
it with the Regular Army. As a measure it was the final step
that resulted from conditions that had become intolerable. It
led on to a further development of Scharnhorst's idea of universal military service, by increasing the intake of recruits in
proportion to the growth of the population. Concurrently, moreover, the whole Army, officers and all, was nearly doubled.
This was the first great expansion since the Peace of Tilsit in
1807. The need for it had been shown already, however, by the
mobilisation of 1850 when two, instead of four, lieutenants were
all that could be found for regular and Landwehr companies
alike. It was this vast increase in the demand for officers,
much more than the internal reorganisation, that now transformed the class-composition of the Prussian corps of officers by
widening the social circles from which the future intake was to
come. A similar general effect was also produced by Manteuffel, when Chief of the Military Cabinet, through the reduction
of the age-limit for senior appointments, although the King,
who knew all his officers personally, scrutinised every case
with care and took all the final decisions himself.

If even a sizable proportion of the newly created posts were
to be filled it now became necessary in very truth to take officers
'from wherever one could hope to find anything suitable', and
to do this on a far greater scale than in the previous twenty

* William (1797–1888), 'Prince of Prussia' during the reign of his childless
brother Frederick William IV (1840–63) and Regent from 1860; King William
I of Prussia from 1863 and Emperor William I of Germany from 1870.

years (see above). One group was found from the senior classes of the Cadet Schools[1] but if the account given by Prince Frederick Charles in 1860 (see above) is any guide, this group was far from being up to standard. Another group was obtained by the transfer of *Landwehr* officers; but here again the opinion of Prince Frederick Charles may, in its very bias, be typical of what other general-officers were thinking. Moreover it is detailed. Though of course it only described the division that he himself commanded, some wider degree of relevance cannot be denied to it.

Delicate phrasing combines with factual content to lend much interest to the Prince's appreciation and it gives, I consider, a valuable insight into the sociological climate and tendencies of those who set the standards. It comes, moreover, from a man with a comparatively independent mind. 'If they do these things in a green tree', one is tempted to ask, 'what shall be done in the dry?' After this, there is no ground for surprise when General von Schack, commanding at Magdeburg (in a letter to his friend Manteuffel) is found lumping together 'doctors, minor officials, store-keepers, in other words, peasants who have made money – and especially clergymen' as belonging to those 'other classes ... which rarely provide useful material for the officer-class.'[2]

It was, of course, the wars of 1864* and 1866† which first really demanded the commissioning of officers from social classes that had been rarely represented thitherto in the infantry and cavalry. In consequence doubt soon began to be felt in the Military Cabinet and the Ministry of War whether the old foundation of 'chivalry' in the Prussian corps of officers was not in some degree of danger. To these misgivings we owe a statistical survey of the 'Officer-Cadets who passed through the Military Examination Commission, in the years 1862–63, 1863–64 and 1866–67, arranged according to the social standing of their fathers'. This survey was made in 1867[3] and is the first real modern statistic to be found in the archives. It is another sign that the times were now much more sober and realistic but also more concerned with facts and figures than in the days of Boyen.

This survey reveals that in the three chosen years the total numbers who took the ensigns' examination‡ were as follows:

* Against Denmark. † Against Austria. ‡ The *Portepéefähnrichsprüfung*.

Social Origins

I. Noblemen	1234, or 49%
Bourgeois	1282, or 51%
II. Sons of officers	835, or 33%
Sons of senior officials	657, or 26%
Sons of landowners	498, or 20%
Sons of clergy and teachers	179, or 7%
Sons of minor officials	151, or 6%
Sons of merchants and manufacturers	121, or 5%
Sons of rentiers	75, or 3%
	Total: 2516, or 100%

The first point about this table is the general one that the division into noblemen and bourgeois does not tally with the analysis of the 'social standing of their fathers'. It indicates that the processes of social shifting and classification that had taken place since the nobility's privileges were abolished had already reached a point where membership of the nobility or the *bourgeoisie* no longer sufficed by itself to determine the social level of an individual. Moreover we can take that statement as valid in both directions. The second part of the table, in consequence, is far more revealing than the first. The two sets of figures, incidentally, represent two deeply-intersecting circles. In all probability the bulk of the 1,234 noblemen's sons in the first part are distributed across the figures of the sons of officers, landowners and, to a lesser extent, of senior officials in the second part. These are the classes that henceforth are always meant when confidential military and official papers speak of 'good, Old-Prussian officer-material'. The only additions were the sons of clergymen, teachers with university degrees, lawyers and doctors – groups that had formerly been represented only here and there but which had entered in fairly large numbers since the 'sixties began. Their entry was not regarded as a disadvantage.

Great misgivings, however, were aroused by the sons of merchants and manufacturers who were now, for the first time, taking almost every opportunity to present themselves as candidates. It was assumed that 'they had been attracted by the more rapid rate of promotion in modern times, and reckoned they could do better for themselves in the Army than anywhere else'. Before the new Empire was founded and Germany's economic expansion had begun, this was typical of the way in

22

which people thought about the capitalist *bourgeoisie* that was soon to be so prominent in supplying the smartest regiments with officers and with heiresses for wives. Nobody paused to consider whether by 'merchants and manufacturers' he meant common shop-keepers or the superior type of large-scale trader and factory-owner. Commercial life was yet to be measured by the material standard of later times. It was reckoned as socially inferior and was not yet counted among the sources of 'good' officer-material. People of that kind had to be allowed in all the same, provided they were otherwise qualified, simply in order to keep pace with the rising demand for officers.

For in the course of the 'sixties the candidates of Old-Prussian stock fell away. The following table[4] shows the decline that took place, relatively and absolutely:

	1860	1864	1869
Total entries of officer-cadets	774	553	683
Cadets of Old-Prussian stock	690	462	532
Old-Prussian percentage of total	89%	83·5%	77·8%

The acceptance of cadets from other States of the Confederation and the addition of nine provinces to Prussia was bound, of course, to have a certain effect on the above proportions in the Prussian corps of officers, but the effect was only slight. In 1867, for example, the candidates included only 36 from Hanover, 14 from Hesse, 16 from Nassau, 10 from Schleswig-Holstein and 3 from Lauenburg, with 47 from other States of the North-German Confederation, and 5 foreigners. On the other hand the figures for sons of minor officials, merchants, manufacturers and rentiers rose betweeen 1863 and 1866 from 8 per cent to 18 per cent. While 690 officer-cadets of Old-Prussian stock came forward in 1860, the enlargement of the corps of officers would have called for about a thousand by 1869; but in fact only 532 appeared. In other words the Old-Prussian contingent had really fallen by about half in comparison with 1860.

Almost the same situation is visible if one compares the figures for officers of noble family in the two selected years. In 1860 there were 4,286 (in 1843 there had been 4,230) and as the officer-establishment had been almost doubled there should have been about 8,400 by 1869; but in fact there were only 5,455. Immediately after the Army's reorganisation and its expansion in 1860–61 regimental-commanders who were 'all too rigidly set in the old outlook on the choice of officer-cadets ... found it went against the grain to widen the field of choice to all the classes of society from which candidates for the status (*Stand*) of officer now came forward.' Units must simply do the best they could, was the opinion that von Weder, the general-officer commanding the 1st Army Corps, expressed to Manteuffel.[5] As the figures have shown, this is what units did – and to such effect that even William I, to whose initiative the whole reorganisation with its far-reaching repercussions was due, felt himself moved, early in 1870, to complain, in a social context, of 'the visibly deteriorating behaviour of the younger officers in several garrisons', and he thought it his duty to draw attention to the irreplaceable value of a good upbringing in the home, an inborn sense of decency and, where possible, the tradition of ancestors who had been officers. 'It is a grave offence against the Army, which made him what he is, for any regimental commander to help undermine the well-deserved reputation of officers as a class by accepting officer-cadets who are unsuitable'.[6]

Well-meant exhortations of this kind were, of course, mere waste of words. The demand outran the 'good Old-Prussian' supply and regimental-commanders had no option but to 'do the best they could' by tapping other sources than the traditional ones. In the war of 1870–71 even William I admitted that he could not require the higher commanders 'to produce officers where none existed'. As a result, all he could do was to lay upon higher commanders 'the responsibility for maintaining at all times and with all strictness the sense of honour among their officers'.[7] Prussia's concern at the time was indeed to produce 'at least some replacement for the many vacancies that had occurred' in the establishment of officers. Men on the retired list and Landwehr officers were used, but among them were many 'both whose past and the manner of whose leaving the Army made this unacceptable'.[8]

Such misgivings were certainly justified in individual cases; but it was none the less true in general that the victorious war of 1870–71 had shown that the new, no longer socially exclusive corps of officers was capable of fighting and of winning. By increasing the demand for officers still further the war had also had the effect in practice (and in principle, too, on the *argumentum ex eventu*) of further diluting the Prussian corps of officers with bourgeois. Yet the out-dated phrase 'the chivalrous fellowship of the corps of officers' continued in use – with what justification we shall later be enquiring – and likewise in the following decades there was frequent complaint about the persistent falling-off in the quality, both social and moral, of the younger officers.

Each of these requirements, however, – the need for 'chivalry' and the need to draw upon lower social classes – received a certain recognition from the Emperor William II. At the very beginning of his reign – whose character indeed was set by other well-known proclamations (*Erlässe*) in the field of social policy – he issued an Order, dated the 29th March 1890[9] in which he declared: 'The rise in the people's level of education makes it possible to widen the social circles from which recruitment to the corps of officers can be considered. It is no longer nobility of birth alone that can claim the privilege of furnishing the Army with its officers: nobility of character has at all times inspired the corps of officers and must be maintained there without diminution. But this will only be possible if officer-cadets are drawn from quarters in which nobility of character is the unquestioned ideal. As I see it, the future of My Army lies in the hands not only of the offspring of the country's noble families and of the sons of My worthy officers and civil servants, whom ancient tradition has made the chief pillars of the corps of officers, but also in the hands of sons in whom respectable bourgeois families have planted and cultivated a love for their King and Country, a warm feeling towards the profession of arms and a sense of Christian morality.'

In actual fact, the Emperor was naturally not announcing a new source for the recruitment of officers; that source had of necessity been tapped for thirty years already – indeed since the time of Frederick William III (1808). The significant thing was that this source should once again, and finally, be certified as pure. It was significant, too, that such democratic language should issue from a Hohenzollern monarch not at a moment (as in 1808) when the Throne had been shaken but at a time when it was at the very peak of its material success. To that extent William II did indeed announce a new departure, and his meaning was clearly understood by regimental-commanders and by officers in general throughout the length and breadth

of the land. Furthermore the military expansion and the formation of new units that followed in the next twenty years left no
other practical possibility of recruiting the necessary numbers
of officers save by recourse to the social classes that had now
received the Emperor's *placet*. There was another factor, too.
Very often the sons of the old military families, of the country
gentry and officials did not wish to continue the tradition of
service in the Army but preferred to seek their fortunes in commerce. In their place the sons of rich *parvenus*, actuated in the
main by snobbery, flocked into the corps of officers, while many
young gentlemen of the older type were diverted from the
Army to the Navy, where opportunities for promotion were for
the time being better.[10]

At a later stage, therefore, William II himself changed his
mind to some extent and more than once he urged with emphasis that officer-cadets should be carefully chosen. In 1902, for
example,[11] he found cause for disquiet in the fact that almost
half the ensigns already accepted 'belonged to professional
classes from which the corps of officers was but sparingly recruited in the past, while fewer and fewer sons of officers and
country-gentlemen were entering the infantry each year'.
Better a small and high-class corps of officers than a large one
with a high proportion of men whose family and upbringing
made them unsuitable: such was the ideal that showed once
more in every Order touching the *supply* of officers, and
it ran strangely counter to the *demand*, which the size of the
standing Army had once more raised to staggering dimen-
sions.[12]

The point is brought out clearly by the table in Appendix 2
which I have compiled from the unpublished annual reports
of the Inspectors of War Colleges (*Kriegsschulen*), in order to
show the social origins of the pupils during the last eleven years
before the first World War. I have added comparative figures
for the years 1888 and 1899 so as to give a general picture of
developments in this respect between the accession of William
II and the outbreak of the war.

This development can be described as follows. The only thing
that shows hardly any change is the intake drawn from tenant-
farmers and estate-managers. There is a fall in the number of
sons of officers and landowners. The figure for the sons of uni-
versity-men (Group 3) increased, on the other hand, especially

after 1911, and so did the figures for merchants and manufacturers' sons and for sons of minor officials *inter alios* (Group
7), as well as for those of private persons in general among whom
one must no doubt reckon traders, artisans and such like, who
had retired with a modest competence. Properly to appreciate
the large increase in the number of fathers with university
degrees would require the division of the whole group into
officials and non-officials. This was not done in the documents
on which these figures are based, and it is unfortunate that it
was not, for it might well have shown – if the statistics from the
'sixties are accepted – that the striking rise in the figures for
university men derives less from the higher officials than from
the 'free' professions of medicine and the law. Such professions,
after all, belong more to the world of free competition than the
civil service does; and, with the rise both in general prosperity
and in population after the Empire was founded, these professions, like the merchants and manufacturers, had also,
grown in numbers alone.

It was, at all events, not always or necessarily a matter of
free and unfettered choice on the part of the various professional
and social classes whether they should contribute more, or
fewer, of their sons to the corps of officers. In actual fact, as we
have seen, a powerful stimulus was the economic situation and
this is true, at any rate, for the nineteenth century once free
competition had broken loose from the old bonds of class-
restriction. Almost throughout the century, but especially in
the 'fifties and 'sixties and even as late as the 'eighties, the
margin of profit on large agricultural properties in Prussia
had steadily been rising,[13] only to be reduced again, despite
protective duties, by competition from overseas and Russia.
Trade and industry, too, had flourished more and more in the
course of the century; and so far from suffering a serious set-
back in its latter years it was not until the first years of the
twentieth century that they really reached their peak of prosperity. Drawn on a graph, these two lines of development run
strikingly parallel to that of the officer-intake as shown hitherto.
So far from being a coincidence it appears to be a case of cause
and effect. If the contrary influence of sundry factors is ignored,
the economic rise of some competitive profession will make the
profession of an officer – 'the first Estate in the land' – though
less lucrative, seem all the more honourable and worth entering,

whether the motive is ethical and patriotic, social and 'decorative', or simply traditional. Economic pressure will have weakened or extinguished such motives, according to its strength. On the graph of social origins of the corps of officers in Prussia especially – where the social and economic upheaval of the nineteenth century had gone exceptionally deep – this point of view throws a light that would be very different if the matter were regarded solely from some moral or political angle.

To these general economic factors must be added one that was peculiar to the hereditary nobility, viz. the factor of its relative powers of survival. Viewed over a matter of centuries what is revealed, on the average, is a gradual extinction, uncompensated numerically by the new creations of nobility in modern Germany.

Let us now apply this fact to the problem of the Prussian corps of officers. In doing so we must bear in mind, of course, the great increase in the population and the steeply rising standard of living produced, especially, by trade and industry. If we remember these things, and the fact that the demand for officers had grown immensely with the expansion of the Army since 1860, we shall not be surprised at the change that had come over the social composition of the Prussian corps of officers as a whole, nor even at the massive reversal in the proportion of nobility and *bourgeoisie* in the course of a few decades. Sixty-five per cent of all Prussian officers in 1860 were still noblemen and thirty-five per cent were bourgeois. By 1913 however these proportions had been overwhelmingly reversed, so that only thirty per cent were still noblemen while seventy per cent were bourgeois. This trend was very plain, even in the higher ranks, viz. generals and colonels:

1860	noblemen	86%	bourgeois	14%
1900	„	61%	„	39%
1913	„	52%	„	48%*

The junior ranks – captains, lieutenants and subalterns – in 1913 were only 27 per cent noble but 73 per cent bourgeois: while of the lieutenants alone, 25 per cent were noble and 75 per cent bourgeois. It will be seen, therefore, that the percentage of

* Those ennobled in the course of their service have been reckoned above as bourgeois. The figures for 1913 would otherwise have been 56 to 44.

bourgeois among the officers was highest in the lower ranks, and *vice versa*. Apart from the Guards Regiments, it was the infantry that showed the greatest fall in the nobility's participation. In 1873, for example, just after the Franco-Prussian war, more than 62 per cent of the lieutenants already were bourgeois and this figure rose in the next thirty-five years to 78 per cent. In absolute terms, the number of lieutenants of noble birth fell by 300, i.e. by almost one-third, while the figure for bourgeois rose by 1,000 or about one-half. It was the same story in other branches of the Army: both relatively and absolutely, more and more bourgeois entered as officer-cadets, and the nearer they came to being promoted the more the percentage rose and with it the *embourgeoisement** of the whole Prussian corps of officers.

Moreover its élite, the General Staff (*Grosser Generalstab*) itself, underwent a similar transformation. In 1906, for example, it contained 60 per cent of noble officers and 40 per cent of bourgeois (including temporary attachments, the railway section and commanders of line-units) but by 1913 the numbers were even. In the same period, on the other hand, a higher percentage, indeed a majority, of bourgeois was to be found among the officers in the Ministry of War. This was the real administrative centre of the Army and its head was the only soldier responsible for military affairs to the Reichstag, save for matters reserved to the Emperor himself.

The more the process of *embourgeoisement* proceeded and drove them from the centre of the stage, the more the nobility reacted against it. At an earlier period, around the middle of the nineteenth century, the nobility had had no great trouble in stemming the bourgeois flood. It made sure that preference should be given to 'good Old-Prussian officer-material'. But things were different now: the 'good' material was simply non-existent, or at any rate was not available. Once it had irretrievably lost its position of overt privilege and found itself out-numbered, the nobility acted in accordance with the sociological law of minorities, which enjoins on them stricter exclusiveness with closer internal cohesion. This tendency to seal oneself off from the outside world is universal wherever

---

* i.e. The progressive acquisition of a 'bourgeois' character by a person or institution whose character was previously different, usually 'noble' or 'aristocratic'.

there are minorities that have no hope of ever becoming the majority.

Conscious of its own peculiar identity and bent upon maintaining it, the nobility in the Prussian corps of officers acted accordingly. It sought to concentrate and fortify itself against bourgeois officers in a certain number of regiments – notably in the Guards and the cavalry; and in the latter, of course, the philological link between 'chivalry' and 'cavalry' had always exerted a certain social influence. Regiments stationed in the capital cities of other German royal families were favourites on account of their social relations with the local Court. These monarchs and princes were often colonels-in-chief and they used their influence to keep up the proportion of noblemen among the officers in their regiment. Other stations, too, had their noble partisans because of such attractions as the local society, the theatre or the surrounding country, and these stations tended to become the headquarters of a 'Provincial Guard', as the saying went.[14] Some officers, however, preferred the remote and lonely garrison-towns on the eastern frontier of the Reich – the reason being, no doubt, the agreeable company of the neighbouring landowners. In Lorraine, on the other hand, where the country-side was incomparably more beautiful, life in a frontier-regiment was wholly different; political factors drove the officers in upon themselves and as early as the 'eighties such regiments had continuous trouble in keeping up their officer-strength – especially with 'the right sort'. Lastly, of course, in many of the older regiments, tradition played its part – in eastern Germany for example where noble families were proud that their sons should serve in the regiments in which their ancestors had served and fought and died.

It was this factor of tradition (in itself quite unobjectionable) that was always emphasised by higher authority whenever any case of abuse or excess in this field received publicity – for example in the Reichstag or the press.[15] In many cases this explanation was true, but even so it was not enough to justify the corps of officers in question being made up exclusively of noblemen. As von Einem, the Minister of War, himself declared on one occasion, there were regiments that now contained none but noblemen as officers whereas in 1813–15, 1866 and 1870 some of the bourgeois officers then serving in them had been killed in action and had thereby helped to give the regiment its reputation. The excuse of tradition, therefore, could not be used in every case. Such a public condemnation of exclusiveness in the Guards and the 'Provincial Guards' had the immediate effect of making conservative people, senior Guards officers and other soldiers at Court try to set the Emperor himself against von Einem. William II, however, expressly assured the Minister that he fully agreed with everything he had said.[16] In the last years before the first World War the Prussian Ministry of War[17] privately listed by name, with percentages attached, seven cavalry and forty-nine infantry regiments at 'good' stations, in which bourgeois officers predominated; and nine cavalry regiments at 'less good' stations, in which the bulk of the officers were noblemen. Doubtless, however, there were good reasons for not applying the opposite test – that of comparing the numbers of predominantly noble regiments at 'good' stations with the predominantly bourgeois regiments in 'bad' or 'less good' stations. It could not be denied, and the Ministry of War itself admitted,[18] 'that public discussion in the Reichstag and the press have contributed to showing up abuses in this connexion that threatened to become permanent and which were certainly not calculated to benefit the Army as a whole'.

This effort on the part of the nobility to 'seal off' certain regiments in accordance with its sociological ideas goes back to the time of the Emperor William I, and was concentrated first and foremost on the Guards. Under William II it became ever more successful and striking in the provinces until, about 1908, the brakes were applied. No impious hand was laid upon that 200-year-old cornerstone of the Army's structure, the freedom of choice enjoyed by regimental-commanders and their officers as a body: but in the annual postings of officer-cadets on graduation, and to some extent in the transfers of officers, the Military Cabinet still possessed the means of directly intervening in the business, and from this time onwards it put them to good use. In the spring of 1910, for example,[19] a total of 42 noble and 88 bourgeois cadets passed into the Prussian Army and of these, five apiece went to the Guards while nine of the bourgeois were posted to infantry regiments that were either stationed at minor royal or princely capitals or were otherwise regarded as the smartest in their own Army Corps, and whose officers at the time were wholly or almost wholly of noble blood.

Social Origins

A few young noblemen, moreover, were posted to small remote garrisons which a few years earlier they would probably have managed to avoid.

By these means it proved possible to set in motion at least a gradual transformation even in the Guards (i.e. infantry, cavalry and field-artillery units together); for in 1908 they had four bourgeois officers, in 1911 twenty-six, in 1912 thirty-five and 1913 fifty-nine. There were many among these *Konzessionsschulzen** who soon managed to get themselves accepted by their aristocratic brother-officers, especially if they themselves were above the intellectual average and had their heart in the right place. Others, however, were distinguished by neither military nor intellectual virtues but by wealth alone; as such they were no ornament or asset to the Guards or to the Army as a whole, and those who allowed such postings or even procured them must have some odd ideas about bourgeois and noblemen alike.

* 'Board-school boys' might be a rough equivalent in old-fashioned English university-terms.

4

Saxony, Bavaria and Wurtemberg

If we discount all interference with the natural run of things, and see how matters developed historically, it is clear that the genuine aristocracy's special position in the corps of officers was typical of Prussia, of the old authentic Prussia east of the Elbe whose social history and structure were different from those in the west and south of the Empire. Saxony, however, was exceptional.[1] In the social origins of the officers there, we find conditions similar to those in Prussia. Saxon officers in the eighteenth and early nineteenth centuries were almost always noblemen.[2] The Cadet-Corps,[3] which for a long time provided nearly all the replacements, was then accessible to the sons of noblemen alone. It was only when the revolution of 1830 in France had spread to Saxony that the Cadets' Academy was shorn of its aristocratic character. The admission of bourgeois youths to the establishment of cadets preparing for officers' commissions was then decreed and put into effect. Thus in Saxony, in 1831, six bourgeois were accepted alongside twenty nobles. In the following year there were seventeen nobles and eleven bourgeois, in 1833 the figures were nineteen nobles to eight, and in 1834 twenty-two to four, apart from a number of so-called 'volunteers' who were of bourgeois family. The predominance of the noble element among Saxon officers in general was then rather slighter but still very marked and so it remained until late in the 'seventies. The printed lists of Saxon officers (the medical corps omitted) show the figures on the following page.

Starting from the partition of Saxony in 1815 by the Congress of Vienna the number of nobles in the corps of officers remained pretty constant for many decades. In the 'sixties alone, and

33

obviously due to the wars of those years, the bourgeois element outnumbered the nobles for a while; but in the 'eighties it achieved a permanent majority. In particular it was the bourgeois who provided far the larger number of officers to meet the great expansion of the Army, so that more than four-fifths of the Saxon officers from that time onwards were bourgeois.

Year	Nobles	Bourgeois
1808	863	347
1818	415	344
1888	450	576
1898	600	2497
1908	572	3284

In Bavaria, however, things were by no means the same. This was the second largest military State in the Federation; it retained a trace of independence after the foundation of the Empire, but its unified Army developed along the same general lines as Prussia's. We must therefore examine the social origins of the Bavarian officers rather more closely – and all the more so as they can be taken as typical for southern Germany in general.

If we start with the years that followed the Thirty Years' War – a war that was a turning-point in the military development not only of Prussia but of all Europe – the first thing we find is that the nobility was far less numerous among the officers in Bavaria than in Prussia. It was only the higher commands that were mostly filled by noblemen, and these men to a large extent were foreigners – mostly Italians and Frenchmen, whose names were still common in Bavarian officers' lists in the nineteenth and early twentieth centuries. The lieutenants, ensigns and cornets on the other hand were recruited not from the nobility alone but also from veteran non-commissioned officers such as pikemen and halberdiers. It was nothing unusual, of course, for young officers of noble birth to be given accelerated promotion or commissioned with higher seniority than others of longer service, and promotions in general were more a matter of favour than of merit – at least under the Elector Ferdinand Maria (1651–79). The obvious aim was to flatter the native Bavarian nobility, for they showed little taste for active service. Did not the Elector Max Emanuel himself complain at the beginning of the War of the Spanish Succession that the whole of the true Bavarian nobility was represented in his army by barely a dozen names?

Under these conditions the social origins of officer-cadets could hardly receive such scrutiny as in Prussia. It was cause for rejoicing if enough men with qualities of leadership could be found at all, and this is why there was more than one way of entering the corps of officers. Private soldiers and non-commissioned officers could work their way up, men could volunteer with the object of getting promotion, they could be directly commissioned as a mark of the Elector's favour, or they could transfer from other armies. Careful expert investigation[4] has revealed that next to the last-named method, the commonest by far was the commissioning of men who had worked their way up from trailing a pike in the ranks. Increases in voluntary engagement with an eye to promotion were only temporary, and those concerned were mostly sons of officers, officials or others of respectable family, whether noble or bourgeois in name; and those of noble name were once again mostly of foreign origin. Coming from an army with such a motley corps of officers, General von Meindres must have found cause for much wonderment in 1751 when the Elector Max III Joseph sent him to Berlin to report on the Prussian army and he was able to see the social uniformity of its officers.

The main result of this mission was the establishment of the Bavarian Cadet-Corps in Munich in 1756[5] on the model of the Prussian one. It took another half-century for this institution to become a reality – i.e. to develop its potential as a training-school for future Bavarian officers like those in Prussia and Saxony. For in 1778 the Elector Max III Joseph died; and his successor, Charles Theodore of the Palatinate, reunited the Bavarian lands which had been separated for centuries. The authentic Bavaria of the Danube cared little for this achievement, and the cadet-school in Munich suffered much neglect. In the words of General Gaza, the Inspector of Infantry, it was 'more like a poor-house' and in consequence the regiments had been 'disgraced by every kind of clown and lout' because even the sons of coachmen, pikemen, halberdiers, secretaries and town-councillors had to be accepted, on account of the great protection they enjoyed. Such a judgment shows both the hauteur of its aristocratic author – a Latin – and the high degree of *embourgeoisement* of the cadets, as well as the range of their social origins. None the less in 1791 there were 84 bourgeois cadets (the 'louts') but also 34 nobles; in 1797 (as, incidentally,

35

in 1802) there were 61 bourgeois and 55 nobles – in fact the proportions were almost equal.[6] At all events the social complexion of the *Herzoglich Marianische Landesakademie*, as it was now re-named had no further practical effect on the Bavarian corps of officers. In the last decades of the eighteenth century it had become a purely academic school, with no preparatory function for the Army.

The really important thing for the Army, however, was the fact that the Elector Charles Theodore, as soon as his reign extended to the whole of Bavaria, announced his intention of raising the social level of his officers, and on the 22nd July 1778, he issued a Rescript which laid it down that 'regiments were to accept no cadet who was not the son of an esquire (*Kavalier*) or officer, or of good family at any rate'. This short but pregnant sentence is doubly significant for the light it throws on past practice and for the decisive weight it attaches to social origins in general. Moreover it places the sons of noble families (*Kavaliers*) on a par with those of officers and others of the higher but not noble classes, and expresses the desire that officers should be recruited from these classes only.

Charles Theodore's nephew and successor, Max IV Joseph (later King Max I) maintained this policy of social discrimination although it conflicted, at least in principle, with the measures of reform adopted by his minister, Count Montgelas.[7] Several years earlier, before Stein and Hardenberg had been able to start their analogous work in Prussia, Count Montgelas had de-feudalised the structure of the Bavarian State, suppressed the privileges of the Estates, unified and improved the internal administration, nationalised the educational system and so forth. Parallel with all this went a reformation of the Army; but this the Elector undertook in person, and with the help of Colonel Freiherr von Werneck he re-founded the Bavarian Cadet-Corps in 1805 on a wholly new basis. Henceforth its sole function was, and remained, the training of young officers. To this main object the entire organisation and teaching was subservient, and apart from some wholly exceptional cases no one in future was to become an officer unless he had been trained and educated in this Cadet-Corps.

With a total of 900 officers the normal wastage every year was about thirty-one. To meet this need, the strength of the Corps was fixed at 210 cadets; and to achieve this figure

required using in the first place the institution's charitable re-
sources – donations and scholarships – supplemented by the
appeal of honour and distinction which parents derived from
the admission of their sons, since entry was limited to (i) sons of
registered Bavarian noblemen, (ii) sons of meritorious commissioned (*patentisierte*) officers in the Bavarian service, (iii)
sons of various types of councillor (*Kollegialrat*) and other civil
servants of equal rank.[8] These were obviously the same three
categories the Rescript of Charles Theodore had designated
twenty-seven years before – at a time, moreover, when in
Prussia, as we have seen, officers were still selected on a wholly
feudalistic basis. It does not, however, look as if these three
categories were able to provide the Bavarian Cadet-Corps with
recruits in the numbers desired, for in 1828, under King Lewis
I, they were extended to include 'also the sons of parents not
covered by (i,) (ii) or (iii) and even foreigners, if they fulfil the
other conditions for admission'. Simultaneously, however, the
number of the Corps was reduced to 150!

The social classes from which cadets, and later officers, could
be drawn had thus been expanded without theoretical limits;
and the revolutionaries of 1848 were really wasting their breath
when they denounced the Cadet-Corps for serving the special
interests of particular classes at the expense of the general
public. These attacks resulted in part from the general ideology
of the revolution as all-German popular democratic movement;
but they had some justification too, for in reality, the same three
social classes were overwhelmingly favoured as regards entrance
into the Cadet-Corps. Not only was the revolution of 1848
powerless to alter this state of affairs but within the three
privileged classes it was the sons of officers who filled by far the
largest number of vacancies. Not until 1901 did the sons of
higher civil servants enter in any numbers; the middle class of
officials, the teachers and so on was still but poorly represented,
while the sons of artisans and peasants were hardly to be found
at all.

We must return for a moment, however, to the events of 1848.
The increase in the Army which took place in that same year
automatically made it impossible for the Cadet-Corps to supply
the bulk of the officers required; and the Cadet-Corps therefore
was less and less in a position to determine the social level of the
Bavarian corps of officers. At the same time the 1848 revolution

itself did have its effects – part transitory, part long-term – upon the matter. The short-term effect was the appointment of a number of ordinary non-commissioned officers to be lieutenants.[9] Nevertheless the revolutionary tide receded: and on the advice of a commission that was specially created within the Ministry of War this breach in the former system was soon repaired. By 1859 it was only the officers of the 7th Bavarian Infantry who still held the advanced view 'that in the light of modern conditions it would doubtless be advantageous to accept non-commissioned officers of long service and proven merit as officers rather than students and other young civilians'. Nevertheless the argument put forward by these officers was disapproved all up the line. From the regimental commander (himself a bourgeois) to the Ministry of War, everyone insisted on strict observance of 'the Regulations and Rescripts applicable in time of peace and all other times'. Another direct result of the revolution appeared on the 8th May 1848, when 89 subalterns were appointed directly from civil life 'for the strict duration of the emergency'; and what is more, these men were told that 'their appointment implied the prospect of their assimilation in due course to the rest of the officers in the Army' – to which the King, on the repeated insistence of Lüder, the Minister of War, eventually agreed. (A parallel to these unusual, limited commissions in Bavaria is to be found in the subalterns who were promoted in 1866 'for the duration of hostilities' (*auf Kriegsdauer*).

Finally, there is one long-lasting result of 1848 that must be mentioned, since it has all the more symptomatic significance for its small numerical effect on the supply of officers. It concerned that Munich institution called the *Pagerie*, which was an educational establishment for sons of the older Bavarian nobility. Until 1848, those who graduated from this school, as well as the sons of formerly sovereign families, could enter the Army directly as subalterns without any kind of previous military training. This was a survival from feudal days and it was out of place in Bavaria since Montgelas' reforms; but King Lewis I himself had expressly ordered its continuance. Lüder, the Minister of War, thought in terms that were both more modern and more military, and in August 1849, when the annual postings of the 'Pages' was due, he made a vigorous – and successful – protest against a custom so antiquated and so out of line with the spirit and the military needs of the times, calling it frankly a great abuse. The main ground for his objections was that the times required officers of the most efficient, experienced and influential type 'so as to win and hold the confidence of the soldiers and thus to immunise them against the incitements to which they are always more or less exposed. Commissions in Your Majesty's Army', so his memorandum of the 10th August to King Max II continues, and with some asperity, 'can therefore no longer be regarded as mere pensions to be given as a matter of grace to young men who apply for them before having proved, by personal service in the Army, their merit or their talent for training and leading Your Majesty's troops. Many people eroneously think the training and leadership of soldiers is an easy matter, indeed a matter of no consequence; but this is not at all the case.' The term 'many people' plainly included the King himself.

Science and art indeed were closer to King Max's heart than his army[10] and this strong but justified criticism of his lack of interest in it applies just as well to his immediate predecessor and indeed to all who followed him on the throne of Bavaria. None the less it makes a good impression – reminiscent of relations between Bismarck and William I – that on this important point of principle Max II eventually gave way. He expressly withdrew his adverse decision and approved the proposal that young men of noble birth should be commissioned only as ensigns. This was intended to be done at once only in the case that had been at issue, but in fact it became the permanent practice. Incidentally, only just over half the 'Pages' on average entered the Army in the course of the whole nineteenth century; the rest (49 per cent) went into other professions.[11] All other young men, whether noble or bourgeois, and even the sons of distinguished generals, had to start their military careers (unless they came from the *Pagerie* or the Cadet-Corps) as private soldiers and so-called 'regimental cadets', and they were only promoted officer when they had undergone the necessary military training. 'This rule has had excellent results', wrote Prankh, the War Minister, to the King on the 28th June 1862; 'the sons of the greatest and most respected noble families have entered as privates and cadets; and Your Majesty has been pleased to set this rule aside only for the sons of Your Majesty's Postmaster-General, Prince Taxis, and of the Imperial Councillor, Prince Oettingen-Wallerstein and, very recently, for Count Erbach's eldest son, as heir to an entailed estate that confers the rank of a former sovereign.'

But after the reformation of the whole Bavarian army and its reconstitution on the Prussian model in 1868 – in effect, after the foundation of the Empire – even these rare exceptions ceased. The Prussian model influenced not only the organisation of the Army but more and more the spirit of its officers – still only in the strictly military field, however. The social composition of the Bavarian corps of officers, its social climate and outlook, remained unaffected; and the reason was that its bourgeois character had existed for too many years and was too strong, not in point of numbers alone but as being really rooted in the country and its people. In the Bavarian army, nobility and *bourgeoisie* were distributed as follows:[12]

Year	Noble officers	Bourgeois officers
1799	260	279
1811	902	1341
1883	959	5310
1893	1122	7390

Thus from the earliest period for which accurate figures can be got from documents, the bulk of Bavarian officers were bourgeois, and in a century or so their numbers grew from a bare majority to a ratio of six-and-a-half to one. An interesting point is that over the whole range of ranks the proportions did not seriously differ in Bavaria, as they did in Prussia, from the ratio in the most junior ones. For purposes of comparison the year 1883 may be taken – a year in which there were about five times as many bourgeois officers as noble. In 1883–4 there were in the Bavarian War College[13] eighty-six bourgeois and seventeen noble ensigns – which gives the same ratio, 5:1. Whether the figures tallied in other years as well is a point I have not been able to establish for lack of accessible statistics; but the figures for 1883 are none the less useful as a comparison with the corresponding figures for the same date in Prussia.

On the other hand, however, the more the bourgeois preponderated during the nineteenth century (and probably much earlier too), the more it seems to me that a closer analysis of the social origins of Bavarian officers is called for. As regards Bavaria, especially compared with Saxony and Prussia, the real question is not whether officers were noble or not; it is the social class of the officer-cadets that matters, and this is revealed by their fathers' profession and by the social standing that mainly depended on it. Fortunately we possess at least a certain number of regimental diaries and a quantity of *Offiziersgrundbücher*,*[14] some of them going back to the first half of the nineteenth century, from which accurate information can be got. Brief figures for particular regiments follow, for they are nowhere else to be found and they give us a clearer picture of the Bavarian officers' social origins.

I will take the Foot Guards (*Infanterie-Leibregiment*) at Munich first, for they more or less corresponded to the Guards in Prussia.[15] The number of recruits being known for every year since 1814, several periods in the regiment's social composition can be distinguished:

1st Period: 1814–46. Totals: 131 noble and 98 bourgeois officers. In detail, 77 sons of officers, 90 sons of higher officials, 7 of landowners, 6 of gentlemen-in-waiting, etc., 4 of lawyers, doctors, etc. Altogether, therefore, 193 from the upper classes against 35 from other classes ranging from teachers and apothecaries down to farmers and even servants.

2nd Period: 1847–80. It must be borne in mind that these years cover the revolution of 1848 and the wars of 1866 and 1870–71. During this period 141 nobles and 193 bourgeois joined the regiment, i.e. a majority of bourgeois. In detail, 103 sons of officers, 118 of higher officials, 16 of landowners, 3 of factory-owners (who were missing altogether from the first period, as might be expected) 6 of princes† and of chamberlains, 26 of doctors, lawyers and clergymen. Altogether, therefore, 272 from the upper classes, against 66 from others.

3rd Period: 1881–91 (the latter is the year in which printed lists were first published). Forty-eight nobles and only seven bourgeois joined, so that almost all in this period came from the upper classes, viz. 29 sons of officers, 20 of higher officials, and one son each of a prince, a landowner and a doctor. The two sons of men of independent means should perhaps be included.

* *Offiziersgrundbücher* is the nineteenth-century Bavarian name for the volume in which personal details of officers were recorded. Each regiment kept them: every new officer was entered in a regular form, and as officers left they were crossed off.

† In approximate English terms these would be members of ducal families.

My investigation of the social origins of the Bavarian corps of officers can be summed up as regards the nineteenth century (for which accurate information is available) as follows. Throughout the century and up to the first World War, much the larger part of the officers came from the families of officers and higher officials, and the latter were often, and indeed at a very early date, more numerous than the former. To these must be added a small number of sons of doctors, lawyers, clergymen, landowners, factory-owners and the like. The remainder amounting to a quarter or a third, was recruited from the lower levels of society. What is striking in comparison with Prussia and Saxony is that in Bavaria the sector of society from which the officers were drawn (leaving aside the nobility as such) remained pretty much the same throughout this whole period, whereas in Prussia – the nobility again excepted – it underwent a very significant change. It is noteworthy, too, that from the very beginning of the nineteenth century the share of the higher civil servants was much larger in Bavaria than in Prussia, while the share of the officers' families was about as large. Landowners, moreover (unlike those in Prussia and Saxony), make a poor showing; so do the factory-owners and big industrialists – the reason being that Bavaria still had relatively few big landowners, traders or industrialists.

For this reason one must beware of blindly attaching the label 'upper class' to the 'commercial men', 'rentiers' and so forth who make only rare appearances, even towards the end of the period, in the records of the fathers' status in the *Offiziersgrundbücher* and other similar compilations. This label, however, could be used with far less hesitation in Prussia. There are, moreover, many other professions listed whose upper and lower social limits are very hard to define with certainty; and the difficulty lies in the very nature of the social test itself, for its principles usually vary with time and place.[16] None the less the statistical basis I have used enables the great majority of cases to be classified with confidence. And so, despite some uncertainty here and there as regards the placing, there is no room for doubt that in comparison with Prussia the classes I have described as 'middle' and 'lower' filled a high proportion of the total number of officers in Bavaria throughout the eighteenth and nineteenth centuries.

Bavaria's peculiar difference from Prussia and Saxony as

regards the ratio of noblemen to bourgeois among her officers
and the way in which the ratio altered is a matter which, I
think, needs no further demonstration. Connected therewith
was the way in which the nobility 'dug in' in particular
regiments. This was very typical of things in Prussia and it is
perceptible also in Bavaria – but to a negligible degree compared with Prussia. In 1911 the only regiments that were in
any sense noble preserves were the Foot-Guards, the 1st
Heavy Cavalry (both stationed in Munich) and the 1st
Lancers stationed at Bamberg.

Classified according to noble officers in higher ranks and in
the various branches of the Army, the Bavarian figures for
the beinning of May, 1904 and 1911 were as follows:

	1904	*1911*
Higher ranks	50%	36%
Ministry of War	20%	19%
General Staff	50%	36%
War Academy	25%	15%
Senior Adjutants	28%	30%
Infantry and Rifle Bns.	12%	11%
Cavalry Regts.	48%	45%
Field Artillery Regts.	21%	19%
Foot Artillery Regts.	4%	3%
Pioneer Bns.	4%	4%
L. of C. troops	4%	—
Army Service Bns.	13%	8%

Here again it is evident how small a part the nobility – the
hereditary element especially – played in the Bavarian corps of
officers.

Conditions in Wurtemberg were much the same as in
Bavaria. But, of course, the whole of south Germany, though
inhabited by three different racial strains (Bavarians, Swabians
and Franks) and for centuries more split up politically than,
for example, the north-east, shows an unmistakable uniformity
in general civilisation and social structure; and striking evidence of this is to be found in the social composition of its
corps of officers. For lack of adequate earlier sources we are
admittedly less well informed for Wurtemberg than for Bavaria
about the professions of officers' fathers; but regimental
diaries can give us certain clues none the less.[17] For the last
decades before the first World War, at least, it can safely

be said that in Wurtemberg, as in Bavaria, the officers were recruited from the same social classes and likewise very largely from the middle and indeed the lower sectors of society. But in the second half of the eighteenth century and the beginning of the nineteenth century the nobility's share was higher than in Bavaria – a difference that may have been connected with the question of religion.

The 'Regulations for the Wurtemberg Infantry Regiments' dated the 1st January 1754 contains the following passage on recruitment of officers: 'When an officer leaves a regiment, the colonel or commanding officer shall respectfully recommend to His Highness the Prince for promotion whichever nobleman most deserves it; and the colonel or commanding officer shall be responsible therefor if such an under-officer shall not possess all the qualities which an officer ought to have. No under-officer shall be recommended to His Highness the Prince who has less than three years' service in a regiment. If any under-officer who is not a nobleman should be very meritorious and of exemplary behaviour, of good appearance and should have served at least twelve years, he should respectfully be recommended to His Highness for promotion to second lieutenant.'* Apart from this, there was no nursery of officers in Wurtemberg at that time; far from it. Officers rose with little education either from the ranks, as shown above, or from the *Kavalierkorps* which was normally attached to the *Garde du Corps*. The first attempt at a more technical training for the duties of an officer in Wurtemberg was made in the *Hohe Karlsschule* – made famous by Schiller – which the Emperor raised to the rank of a University in 1782.

In the nineteenth century, ordinary long-service under-officers were only promoted lieutenant in exceptional cases, in times when the need for officers suddenly increased – for example, in 1859 when there was a mobilisation on account of the Austrian war against France and parts of Italy. The same emergency, in which not enough under-officers could be spared, led to the premature appointment of cadets and, after a little hasty drilling, of students too. But the former under-officers had none the less to pass an examination in their military and general knowledge before they were promoted. Ten or twenty years after the Franco-Prussian war some of

* (Quoted by Pfister: *Das Infanterie-Regiment*, p. 120.)

these 'old sweats' from earlier days were still giving excellent service as drill-instructors in the Wurtemberg corps of officers. Nevertheless the aim of achieving a uniform social level and a more solid *esprit de corps* among the officers in the nineteenth century demanded that the general level of education required of candidates for promotion should be raised and standardised too. Success in establishing this principle seems to have been made easier by the revival of the flow of bourgeois into the corps of infantry officers and its ultimate preponderance there.

It is clear that the Wurtemberg infantry had a large contingent of bourgeois among its officers at the beginning of the eighteenth century. This is a fair deduction from conditions in the 3rd Wurtemberg Infantry Regiment, No. 121, which was one of the oldest, and which is also one of the few for which details of its officers' social background in the eighteenth century are available. At the start of the Turkish campaign of 1716, all its four staff-officers were noblemen; of the captains, eight were bourgeois and six noble; of the lieutenants, eleven were bourgeois and seven noble; and of the ensigns, four were bourgeois and eleven noble – which makes totals of 28 noblemen and 23 bourgeois. By and large these proportions held good throughout the following decades; but noblemen always held the higher ranks and it was only in the lowest that the bourgeois sometimes held a majority. In the seventeen-eighties, when the nobility provided almost all the officers in Prussia, there was a period in which this Wurtemberg regiment was entirely 'noble' also. But this was only a temporary state of affairs; and by 1794 ten officers, four of them captains, again bore bourgeois names.

The Napoleonic Wars at the beginning of the nineteenth century, and the period of military stagnation that followed them, brought no essential change. Few, apparently, were the bourgeois who rose above the rank of captain into those that carried more responsibility and higher pay. In the war of 1866, on the other hand, and even more in the Franco-Prussian War of 1870–71, there was already a considerable number of bourgeois captains in the regiment, and from then on the bourgeois officers easily outnumbered the nobles. So far as figures and names are available, the same trend can be seen in the 2nd Wurtemberg Infantry Regiment, No. 120, as well as in the infantry regiments raised in the nineteenth

century and in the Field Artillery. The one exception is the
1st Wurtemberg Grenadier Regiment, No. 119, which was a
sort of Bodyguard, and the oldest infantry regiment in
Wurtemberg. In the war of 1870, certainly, three-quarters
of its officers were bourgeois; but by the 'nineties only two-
fifths. Only in a few cavalry regiments, viz, the 26th Dragoons,
the 20th Lancers (*Ulanen*) and to a less extent in the 19th
Lancers (the 'Danube Cossacks') was this trend towards
domination by the nobility more visible. The plutocracy, on
the other hand – mostly of North-German, mainly Hamburg,
origin – concentrated in the 25th Dragoons, the 'Mounted
Shopkeepers'. All this, however, amounted to nothing like
the out-and-out situation that ruled in Prussia, even though a
number of Prussians joined Wurtemberg regiments from 1870
onwards. In Wurtemberg, at all events, where the general
atmosphere was quite different from that of Old Prussia, the
nobility exerted no particular formative influence upon the
Army.

Likewise among German naval officers, who possessed
after all a certain knowledge of the outside world, the nobility
was neither numerically nor psychologically dominant;
in the 'eighties indeed, as in 1914, noblemen were much less
prominent in the Navy than in the Army. No ship was entirely
or even mainly officered by nobles; and this is all the more
remarkable in that William II notoriously showed special
favour to the Navy whereas in the Army, as we have seen, he
tolerated, at any rate, a very different trend. In this one can
perhaps detect the influence of the men who advised the
Emperor almost every day – the chiefs of the Military and
Naval Cabinets; but what it illustrates most of all is the powerful social influence of tradition.

5

Germany: Collapse and Continuity

The social aspect of tradition was strong enough to survive in spirit even the fearful test of the first World War. Germany fought that war with reserve and Landwehr officers far and away more than with regulars, half of whom in turn were young officers commissioned during the war itself. At its outbreak on the 1st August 1914, the Prussian contingent[1] within the peace-time establishment contained 22,112 serving officers and 29,230 in reserve. By the 15th November 1915 the following numbers had been killed: regulars, 5,633; reservists 7,565. New commissionings amounted by the same date to 7,537 regulars and almost seven times as many reservists, viz. 52,181. Over the whole course of the war the German Army had 45,923 regular officers (including the 11,357 killed) and 226,130 reserve officers of whom 35,493 were killed. Compared with the figure at the outbreak of war, therefore, the number of regular officers was no more than about doubled in the course of four-and-a-half years, whereas the number of reserve officers increased about nine-fold. In other words, the regulars in 1914 amounted to only about one-twelfth of the total number in the first World War.

The imperative need to multiply the fighting formations and thus the number of officers, as well as replace the unending casualties meant, of course, that the social origins of the replacements could not be looked at as narrowly as in time of peace. Officers simply had to be sought 'wherever one could hope to find anything suitable'. And in any case the social standards prevailing before 1914 mostly crumbled away under the strain of life in the trenches and the 'war of attrition'. It was not so much, of course, that they lost some validity as that the troops and non-commissioned officers mostly thrust them down into the sub-conscious vis-à-vis their superior officers: and in November, 1918, wherever this had happened, things blew up.

In the face of numbers such as these and of the lowered standards of selection, the tradition of quality in the corps of officers could not fail to suffer. In time of peace the reserve-officers had in all essentials been trained and schooled in the group-ideals of the regulars – and with undeniable success. In time of war, with its ever-increasing variety of demands, there could naturally be no question of maintaining this kind of standard (as distinct from purely military training) either for reservists or for newly commissioned regulars. So far as the growing shortage of manpower and time allowed, it was nevertheless attempted; but one can hardly hope to arrive at a scientific assessment of what was achieved – an assessment unbiased by subjective impressions, feelings or prejudices. At the time of the revolution of 1918 and even later it was very often said that the regulars had done better as leaders of men than the 'reservist-fellows' had. But the opposite was just as often to be heard. The commonest complaint was that the young regular officers did not know how to treat the common soldiers.[2] A typical ray of light is thrown on personal relations in the lower commissioned ranks by a comment made by General Groener in a letter he wrote to his wife on the 29th October 1917. Describing one of the visits he paid to the divisional commander almost every day in order to keep in touch with morale at the front, he wrote: 'The lieutenants are thoroughly good fellows, almost all reservists; there are very few regulars left. The best of the lot, I was told, are the elementary school-teachers. There were a few ensigns too, hardly more than children.'[3]

In the latter part of the war the relatively few peace-time regular officers that were left were more and more withdrawn from the trenches and transferred to staff-duties, especially on the General Staff. The idea was that the knowledge they had acquired in War Colleges or the War Academy as well as their experience at the front should be used for tactical and strategic tasks, and more generally to try and preserve a nucleus of what can be called the old, properly trained type of officer. It deserved, as Frederick the Great said of his

Old-Prussian nobility, to be preserved. What could have been more obvious after the collapse of 1918 than to use this nucleus to create the new Reichswehr? These men were after all the true upholders of the old tradition of the German officer; and the men who were called upon to create and organise the Reichswehr – General Reinhardt, Gustav Noske, the People's Commissar,[4] and especially General von Seeckt – deliberately placed that tradition among the foundation-stones of the new military structure. First Reinhardt and then Seeckt, in full agreement with him, saw the best hope for the future in the promotion of those very officers from the General Staff of the first World War. There was resistance from the represent-atives of officers who had served only at the front; and there-fore Seeckt, as chief of the Army Staff, wrote on the 29th August 1919 to Reinhardt as Prussian Minister of War, emphasising 'that we must look first of all to experienced General Staff officers; that among intelligent people no part of the old Army had so high and justified a reputation as the General Staff; and that to preserve the General Staff is to preserve the spirit of the Army'. Antagonism between General Staff officers and front-line officers within the German Army, he said, could only be artificially maintained; and where it actually existed it was due to the pettiest motives. 'A General Staff officer *is* a front-line officer', he continued, 'and indeed has been selected from among the best of them. This is not just a theory; it has been the practice up till now, and will remain so.'[5] Seeckt's view of the matter was shared by Reinhardt and also, in all essentials, by General von Braun, then chief of the Personnel Office.

This rather heated discussion of principles had been caused by the insistence of the victorious Allied Powers on the dis-missal of about 20,000 officers, and this entailed choosing which ones to keep. At the same time, the situation at home and abroad required the officers of the new Reichswehr to be found in the main from among those commissioned before the end of the war. With an army of first 200,000 men and later of only 100,000, the corps of officers was therefore drawn from the following groups which then existed:[6] (i) senior and medium-senior commanding officers from the rank of regimental-commander upwards; (ii) younger regular officers serving on the General Staff and in staff-appointments; (iii) a not very large number of regular war-time lieutenants who, though sometimes very young, had commanded companies and batteries for two years and more or who, at the end of the war, were holding junior adjutant's appointments in the field. Immediately after the war, a fourth group was added, viz. the so-called 'Noske-Lieutenants', numbering about 1,000 middle-aged long-service, non-commissioned officers. These were men who had been made lieutenants shortly after the revolution in accordance either with a long-standing Socialist demand or with the Law of the 6th March 1919 on the creation of a provisional Reichswehr. That law had laid it down that all meritorious non-commissioned officers and men were to be eligible for commissions; it had been adopted by the National Assembly at Weimar with the support of all parties, including the German Nationalists (*Deutsch-Nationale*). In the Navy, so Noske told the Assembly, half the new commissions in 1919 had been reserved for non-commissioned officers. In actual fact the proportion of former warrant-officers and petty-officers in the total of naval officers in 1920 (after the Kapp-Putsch*) was ten per cent.[7] and this is partly due to the fact that technical skills are more essential in the Navy than in the Army. It soon turned out, however, that the promoted non-commissioned officers were running into difficulties on account of their age, their lack of education and other factors, with the result that many of them preferred to leave the Reichswehr before their time was up. In the French Army, of course, a large proportion of the officers had for many years been recruited from the non-commissioned officers, *les sortis du rang*.† After serving for several more years with their unit they trained at the Ecole de Saint-Maxient for their role as officers; the other officers, however, received two years of instruction in military science at the famous Ecole de Saint-Cyr or at the Ecole Polytechnique in Paris. But even in France, with its far older democratic structure, the co-existence of these two kinds of officers, the *écoliers*‡ and the *sortis du rang*, can still create problems today and lead to social tension among

* An unsuccessful attempt led by Kapp, a right-wing politician, and General Lütteritz, to overthrow the Republic. Its defeat was mainly due to General von Seeckt.
† Literally: 'emerged from the ranks'.
‡ i.e. graduates of the Ecole de Saint Cyr.

officers,[8] though it does not affect the Army's fighting qualities to any serious degree.

In Germany the Social Democrats constantly raised this question, and in 1929 at their Party Congress at Magdeburg they included it in their defence-policy (Point 5), as follows: 'Suppression of educational privileges in the corps of officers, and legislation to establish a minimum quota of officers to be recruited from the ranks.'[9] But even if any such legislation had been adopted it is unlikely to have had the desired political and social effect upon the corps of officers. For the former non-commissioned officers, true to their rise in status, took a robust view of this sort of thing and their long years in the Army had made them at any rate so familiar with the outlook of the officers that they now made it more or less their own – which is doubtless one of the reasons why they were socially accepted by their brother-officers. No doubt, also, they had been chosen for promotion partly on an assessment of their acceptability, as forming part of their personality and character; for with the Army as small as the Versailles Treaty left it a great deal depended not merely on the officers' military training but on their *esprit de corps* as representatives of its tradition and fighting qualities.

Once the errors and confusion of early days had been overcome this aim was largely achieved, and the credit goes to the fixity of purpose shown by Seeckt in co-operation with Dr Otto Gessler, the Minister responsible to the Reichstag.[10] On the very same day (18th April 1920) on which Gessler installed him in office as chief of the *Heeresleitung** – that is, at a critical moment after the Kapp-Putsch – General von Seeckt issued a statement of the principles on which he intended to found and shape the corps of officers. The whole position was summed up in its opening words: 'The Reichswehr's corps of officers is in a crucial situation. Its behaviour in the immediate future will decide whether or not it will retain its hold over the new-born Army. That decision will also show whether the Reichswehr can salvage what is of value from the past, and put it to work in the present for a brighter future.'[11] This was, of course, an implicit recognition of the ideals and principles of the old Army in so far as Seeckt thought them of value or

* ie in effect, Chief of the Army Staff, though the Staff as such had been proscribed.

applicable in the altered circumstances of the times. Another who entirely shared this attitude was Friedrich Ebert, the first Reichs-president, who indeed had firmly supported the Army authorities in the view that the Defence Forces of the Republic must be organically developed out of the remains of the old Army and that the good qualities of the old one must be carried over into the new.[12] On these plainly 'restorationist' lines which were defined in a series of Ordinances as well as in Seeckt's essay *Die Reichswehr* (Leipzig, 1933), the growth of the corps of officers proceeded, both in Seeckt's own time and, in all essentials, under his two successors. Considerations of status or even of class may have played some part in it; but the true foundation of the principles and decisions adopted was the genuine conviction of both Seeckt and Gessler that the composition and training of the pre-war corps of officers had stood the terrible test of the long war, notwithstanding the defeat with which the war had ended. By and large, therefore, these fundamentals could be regarded as correct, indeed as absolutely so, i.e. independently of the form of the State. Being still valid under the Republic they must therefore be maintained. Seeckt and Gessler, furthermore, were convinced that officers of this standard type were necessary if the new Army was to protect the country, for the Reich's existence was currently in danger from both left-wing and right-wing revolutionary forces, not to mention the dangers that threatened its frontiers both east and west. But deeper and solider even than these purely military and patriotic motives was another 'restorationist' aim that called for the settlement of the officer-question. It was this. In view of the socially destructive, levelling tendencies of the age of industrialised masses and of the German revolution, it appeared imperative to make the corps of officers an élite again, a member of the team that was to give the German people leadership.

Even before the war, as we have seen, the corps of officers had mainly been recruited from the sons of such leaders, military and civilian. That tradition was simply continued now. The war had left large sectors of the German people indifferent to all military matters. The champions of the revolutionary spirit of 1918 spread the Marxist doctrine of class-warfare more and more widely among their supporters old and new, and it engendered in them a hostility to the profession of arms that was partly a matter of basic principle, partly a matter of tactics. Patriotic feelings and intellectual comprehension of the altered needs of the country's forces – both elements weak indeed and hedged about with every kind of prejudice – were mainly to be found among the old governing classes, materially ruined though most of them were, viz. the former officers, higher civil servants and university teachers.

As things were, therefore, the men in charge of the Reichswehr had, for the first years at least, hardly any practical choice but to go on recruiting from these classes and, in view of the basic principles governing the selection of officers, this policy was adhered to. The numbers promoted from the ranks each year were too small to affect the matter. So many of the documentary sources have been totally destroyed, or are at present out of reach, that statistics showing the social origins of the new corps of officers are far less easy to come by than those for the years before 1914. For the Reichswehr, in consequence, we must make do with less comprehensive figures – sometimes indeed with mere samples – rather than abandon the attempt, for such statistics as there are can still give a reasonably clear picture of the way in which things developed.

For the years 1926 and 1927 we have some figures which obviously originated in the Reichswehr Ministry of the day. They were compiled in 1930 by a Reichswehr officer named Franz Woertz[13] who used indeed the same system of tabulation that I used myself in the first (1930) edition of this book, for the social origins of the cadets in the War Colleges between 1883 and 1913. These same categories were later used by Wolfgang Sauer in evaluating the personal registers of officers in the Cornelimünster Section of the *Bundesarchiv*.[14] For the purposes of comparison I put first my own estimates for 1912–13, and the table of percentages overleaf emerges, with the absolute figures in brackets.

Compared with the last years before 1914 the later figures show remarkable changes in more than one respect. The lower classes, which contributed very few young officers even before the war, have become rare to the very point of vanishing. The sons of merchants too, of factory-owners and land-owners, have dwindled to half or even less – symptomatically, no doubt, of the growing value attached to material well-being and the converse depreciation of un-lucrative service '*pour le roi de*

| | Demeter | | Woertz | | Sauer 1921– 1934 |
	1912	1913	1926	1927	
Regular and Reserve officers	24·56% (290)	23·74% (279)	44·34% (94)	49·24% (97)	34·93% (22)
Higher officials, clergy, civil and military doctors, professors	39·88% (471)	39·06% (459)	41·51% (88)	34·01% (67)	36·50% (23)
Landowners	7·87% (93)	9·12% (107)	4·73% (10)	4·57% (9)	4·76% (3)
Tenant farmers	1·69% (20)	2·38% (28)	0·94% (2)	1·52% (3)	1·59% (1)
Business men and factory owners	15·41% (182)	15·57% (183)	6·13% (13)	7·11% (14)	9·52% (6)
Minor officials and non-commissioned officers	4·74% (56)	4·17% (49)	1·41% (3)	0·51% (1)	7·94% (5)
Other private persons	5·85% (69)	5·96% (70)	0·94% (2)	3·04% (6)	4·76% (3)

Prusse'.* Group 2, on the other hand, the university men, shows little if any diminution in its share. The really striking thing is the large rise in the contingent of officers' sons. In the last years before the war their share had already been the largest; now, in the Reichswehr, it has almost doubled. Seen from the point of view of the Army Staff, this may perhaps have looked suspiciously like a deliberate piece of class 'in-breeding'; but any such judgment would really have been biassed, for the true causes of this trend certainly lay more in the very classes whose sons sought commissions in the new Army. The fact of the matter is that their basic outlook had not really changed; and their economic circumstances were such as to make their material ambitions relatively modest – a factor to which I drew attention earlier.

Taken with a grain of salt, the same was true of the nobility too. In the Prussian and German corps of officers the nobility

* 'For the King of Prussia': the phrase dates from the eighteenth century.

had always seen, and grasped, professional opportunities that served its old-fashioned conception of itself as an élite: but the expansion of the Army in the nineteenth century had forced it to yield in numbers to the *bourgeoisie*.

Now, with the corps of officers forcibly reduced to just 4,000 it could easily supply the necessary recruits by itself. The number of German males of noble birth and of all ages in 1936 was reckoned by the *Almanach de Gotha* at 45,219,[15] and among these the figure for adult Counts and Barons *(Freiherren)* alone – leaving out the far more numerous class whose names began simply with 'von' – amounted in 1932 to 9,477.[16] It was out of the question therefore to oppose the natural flow, and there was no desire to do so either. But it is remarkable none the less that well-known names appear in the Reichswehr at every level of seniority, and some of them three to six times each.[17]

In the very first years after the revolution of 1918 – which, of course, was abhorrent to it as a body – the nobility refused to let its sons serve as officers of the Republic. No later than 1922, however, a change began to set in, for the Reichswehr was being properly organised and the Treaty of Rapallo had brought the Reich itself back on to the international stage as an independent Power. A contributory factor may have been – though of course there is no proof that it was – a favourable article, signed with a noble name, that appeared in the *Deutsches Adelsblatt* towards the end of 1921. The writer maintained that young noblemen need not fear any competition from 'the crowd' and, he asserted, the fact that the corps of officers was still being re-cruited from the best in the land was of the greatest importance for the country's future.[18] Many a monarchist at heart, desirous of serving his Sovereign, had clearly yielded to the delusion that this was the best way. Of the 167 ensigns commissioned in the twelve months following the 1st April 1922, thirty-five were noblemen – in other words, 21·6 per cent. Though the succeeding years showed a falling off, the proportion from May, 1927 onwards never sank below 20 per cent. and in 1931–32 it was as high as 36 per cent.[19] A political fact that may have acted as a stimulant was that on the 31st January 1927 the detested Inter-Allied Military Commission ceased its activities in Germany. On the other hand it is striking that the steep rise in the number of noblemen among the officers dated from just after Seeckt had ceased to be chief of the Army Staff. Possibly too, the improvement of pay in 1927 had something to do with the matter. Nevertheless this increase in the number of noble officers did little to alter the general social complexion of the corps as a whole; but the figures greatly varied from branch to branch of the Army, just as they had before 1914. The cavalry came easily first; and then (if we leave out the Staff) the infantry – though a poor second – followed by the artillery and the motorised units, with a surprisingly high percentage in the medical corps. In this field of sociology no particular trend in the Reichswehr can be established. The number of noblemen among its officers in general remained constant at about one-fifth. As the table in Appendix 3 will show, there were slight fluctuations within the several branches of the Army but one cannot really speak of any general trend in either direction without doing violence to the figures.

If, however, an attempt is made[20] to compare the contingents from the various provinces (*Länder*) in this respect, certain difficulties appear. The Reichswehr contained various regiments and independent units that were recruited wholly from particular provinces: for example the 3rd (Prussian) Infantry Regiment and the 17th (Bavarian) Cavalry Regiment. Other regiments, however, were made up of contingents from several provinces – for example, the 15th Infantry Regiment was drawn from Prussia, Hesse and Thuringia. Figures for 1932 none the less enable a percentage of noble officers to be established for the Prussian units as a whole; and in that year it was, at 25·6 per cent, above the average for the Reich. Moreover it was spread through every branch of the Army with the sole exception of lines-of-communication troops. For Mecklemburg the figure was 26·9 per cent., for the Hansa Cities 25·8 per cent, for Thuringia 22·2 per cent, for Schaumburg 25 per cent. The lowest figure (6·7 per cent) came from Oldenburg where, however, there was no cavalry but only infantry, rising for Wurtemberg to 12·1 per cent, for Bavaria to 12·6 per cent and for Baden to 13·2 per cent – these last three constituting the chief contingents from south Germany.

6

The Third Reich

After 1933, when the National-Socialists came into power, a quite different current to that which flowed before began to appear – first percolating down from above, and then gradually upwards from below. National-Socialist doctrine, in principle, respected and appealed to tradition only in so far as it could be made to serve the Party's general thirst for power. Where this was not the case, tradition was attacked, root and branch. For such a purpose National-Socialism naturally borrowed its intellectual weapons in the main from the rich arsenal of ideas to be found in Nietzsche – the despiser of all previous thought, the passionate revolutionary critic of bourgeois morality and of the Christian basis of western civilisation, the grandiloquent prophet of the 'Will to Power', of the 'Conqueror's Code of Morals' (*Herrenmoral*) and of a future 'Superman'.

This is not the place to go any deeper into the ancestry of National-Socialism and its relationship to Nietzsche, the poet-philosopher. But when a senior officer of the second World War, himself a native of southern Baden,[1] who had watched developments since 1918 from the inside with an observant, critical eye, analyses the intellectual position after 1933 in the following terms, his analysis is worth attention. In consequence of a mis-interpretation of Nietzsche's philosophy (it runs), and of a bogus philosophy of race-selection that flattered the masses, the prestige formerly attaching to social origins was henceforth displaced by a mystical doctrine of racial origin which embraced all and sundry and made a Superman, a *Herrenmensch*, of every-one. The rapid introduction of universal military service made it possible for Hitler to base the corps of officers broadly upon all classes of society, so as to bring it into line with

57

National-Socialist ideas, first of all in the lower ranks but later, especially during the war, in the highest ranks as well.

With the object of rapidly quintupling the strength of the Army, new elements were brought in from outside and set to work on this enormous task under the command, or rather the guidance, of the existing regular officers. These importations consisted of:

(i) officer-cadets, whose number was increased to 2,000 (from an annual intake of 120–180):

(ii) about 300 legal officials (*Referendare der Justiz*) for whom the Ministry of Justice had no employment:

(iii) about 2,500 provincial police-officers (*Landespolizei*) among whom in fact a sizable number of former officers of the pre-1918 Army were re-commissioned into the Reichswehr:

(iv) about 1,500 regular non-commissioned officers:

(v) about 1,800 former regular and reserve officers of the pre-1918 Army:

(vi) in 1938, about 1,600 former Austrian officers.

Very few of these new officers were of noble birth: they came, in fact, from every level of society. It was *la carrière ouverte aux talents** with a vengeance – more still, it was *la recherche de la paternité interdite*† according to another authority, a man who witnessed every shift and change from before 1914 until 1941.[2] 'At the beginning of Hitler's régime', writes General von Senger too,[3] 'they certainly contrasted sharply with the senior officers, who had not been recruited on a democratic basis. The senior officers of the Army ... created by von Seeckt came from the old Prussian stock or were at any rate steeped in its traditions ... and they did not relish the servility that was now the mode.' This servility was something different from military obedience to higher authority. It was the typical attitude of low-class jacks-in-office – the very opposite of what we normally regard as the mentality and behaviour of gentlemen, of what, despite great individual variations, history and sociology alike attribute to 'the aristocracy'.

---

* 'The career open to talents' (Napoleon).
† 'Enquiry into paternity is forbidden' (Art. 340 of the French Civil Code).

7

Summary: The Two Mentalities

The private mystique of the corps of officers, and the way the National-Socialists regarded it, are matters it is difficult to grasp unless one investigates, however briefly, the origins and evolution of nobility itself and the functions it once fulfilled in society. The only aspects of nobility that have been studied and written about hitherto, are either the purely genealogical or the historical and literary side.[1] Looked at from the angle of sociology, however, nobility presents two different, or rather, two distinguishable aspects, both of them primary: the one is mainly professional and military, the other economic. Taken together they describe a sort of parallelogram around the subject. In the course of recorded history, German and European alike, the dominant factors have been first the military and then the economic one. But the economic factor never quite robbed the military of all share in determining the final product. Some account of the way in which these two factors shaped the territorial and the urban nobility of Germany will be found in Appendix 4. Here, for our immediate purpose, I give the bare essentials only. But they are fundamental to much of what follows in this book, and they will constantly recur in one form or another.

Until a late stage in its development, Old Prussia had little that resembled the life and culture of the great Imperial trading cities of the south and west. East of the Elbe, the feudal world died hard: large-scale farming and, eventually, soldiering in the Prussian army, were almost the only outlets for the Junkers' energies, and together they formed the basis of the old nobility of Prussia. From this situation there resulted a dominant mentality that was feudal, military, un-intellectual and, of course, conservative.

c* 59

Social Origins

In the south and west, on the other hand, the princes felt less need to give such prominence to their armies, and in consequence the social status of the officer was not so great that the nobility sought to keep the *bourgeoisie* out or disdained any other career. On the contrary, they felt free to enter the professions – notably the law and the administration of the State. At the same time, the presence of an urban patriciate – a thing almost unknown in Prussia – that was itself in process of acquiring the status of nobility brought the territorial nobles gradually into contact with the larger world of trade and commerce, money and ideas. In the course of time the two groups, rural and urban, merged with one another; and the ruling mentality that resulted had a commercial, intellectual and liberal complexion compared with that of Prussia. The officers were less exclusively noble, and the professional and commercial world less solidly bourgeois.

PART TWO

EDUCATION

8

The Two Principles:
Character and Intellect

The state, or level, of education of the German corps of officers does not seem to me to lend itself to description or analysis by any scientific method or by any method of historical sociology. The thing itself is simply too personal, too bound up with the individual. The corps of officers forms a whole in itself, a community that transcends the individual; and general remarks about its educational level could at best be either a series of statistics or a series of worthless platitudes. In this chapter, therefore, I merely propose to bring out the main principles (other than the strictly military and technical ones) on which the German officer's preparatory schooling and further professional education have been based and, in general, I shall try and trace the variations these principles underwent in the course of history, and how they originated from various typical states of opinion and various changes of purpose.

The whole problem of education and training for any given profession, i.e. for the performance of a given task, is part and parcel of the great process of the division of labour which governs all civilisation.[1] As population grows, the struggle for existence is intensified; capabilities and actual performance must be improved. This is achieved by the specialisation of labour, the division of the whole into intellectual and physical work – the latter being essential to the maintenance of human life. What takes place, in other words, is a rational sub-division of work into various distinct groups of tasks or professions, and in the course of further development these will go on splitting up, narrowing and specialising. The further this process of differentiation and specialisation goes, the more the practice of a given profession will require appropriate education and training. Under patriarchal conditions where the structure of economy and society alike is pastoral, this teaching will be done within the family-circle – be it the child's own family or another – and for higher or for menial tasks alike the family-unit holds an educational monopoly. Upbringing and education thus remain in the same hand – indeed they are one and the same thing themselves. The inheritance of a profession by virtue of being suitably familiar with it gives rise to an institution appropriate to it at this stage of social development – the heritability of status with exclusive rights. Monopoly leads to privilege: it arises from status, and the feudal form of constitution based on status is rooted in the pastoral-feudal form of society.

Its opposite is the urban-bourgeois world. There were, of course, towns in Germany in the early Middle Ages, most of them dating from Roman times. But it was only after they had grown and multiplied in the last centuries of the Middle Ages that they became a serious factor in general historical development. Their very origin, it appears, resulted from the division of labour, and thereafter they followed this formative principle (in terms of economic sociology) to a marked degree. A town, after all, exerts two types of influence. Close cohabitation, on the one hand, is a great stimulant to the sort of social sense that finds expression in 'practical reason' – in other words, in common sense; and the freeing of human labour from the soil, on the other hand, promotes the domination of 'pure reason' in all thought and action. Problems of space alone are enough to raise the town-dweller's mind from the horizontal lines of agriculture to the vertical that symbolizes intense cultivation of the intellect. As determinants of the mode of life and its motives, the world of the submerged, unconscious, instinctive, emotional and psychical thus gives way to the world of the conscious, reasoned and intellectual. In the crowded conditions of a town – mediaeval towns included – the family's sphere of action contracts, especially as regards education; the 'intellect' makes itself, so to speak, independent and creates the instrument it needs – the school. From that point onwards the family remains the effective agent of upbringing, but education is a matter for the school: the one forms the heart and the character, the other, above all, the intellect. This is, of course, only a matter of degree, never a matter of water-tight compartments, for the school itself has always claimed to be a place of character-training, not merely one of education. But a school aims at bringing up a child mainly, though solely, by means of thought and knowledge, by teaching it the right use of reason.

And as things develop, the urban world with its immanent rationalism begins to govern the general shape of civilisation and the economy is governed by urban crafts and trade, the urban money-economy dominates the exchange-economy of the country and the latter succumbs to the town in the economic, intellectual, social and, ultimately, political competition between the two. The more this comes about, the more do we see the world of status, with its family system of vocational training, being undermined; we see the school, the very essence of the urban mentality, extending its scope and encroaching on the family's monopoly of education and vocational training. This is not the place to go deeper into the general development of upbringing and professional training; but a glance at the principles involved has been necessary because it is only against the background that we can appreciate the historical and sociological aspects of the special group of problems presented by the education of officers.

That whole question turns, in the last analysis, elliptically round the antithesis of town and country, mind and character, intellect and instinct, the rational and the irrational. This tension could no doubt be stated in other terms as well; but those that have been suggested should suffice to show what the problem consists of, and the rest of this Part will, I hope, make the matter clearer still. All the same I should not like to let slip this opportunity of making one thing absolutely plain. This interplay of two primary polar forces – sometimes in harmony, sometimes opposition – was not typical merely of the development of Prussia (i.e. Old Prussia) where very large estates were owned by the nobility and where the country gentry played so large a part in the corps of officers. It serves no less to explain the unmistakable difference between the corps of officers in Prussia and, for example, in Bavaria where the nobility's share was far less prominent and where the nobility was much more identified with the patriciate. All this naturally had its effect upon the nature of officers' education.

9

Prussia: The First Military Schools

Let us see how things actually developed. The first point that strikes us is that this question of the education of officers, like everything to do with armies, was linked with progress in the techniques of war and tactics. The need for giving officer-candidates some higher technical schooling, and for relating theory to practice, was felt in the artillery first of all and for a long time nowhere else. This arm had assumed an ever-growing importance since the end of the Middle Ages, and its employment required a degree of mathematical ability that was far from common by the standards of the times, modest though they were. Its acquisition in school seemed most desirable – the level of urban culture being already what it was. Artillery-schools, therefore, are the oldest military academies we know of and they date from the start of the sixteenth century. Similar measures were not adopted for other arms of the service for another hundred years; and even then their original concern was less with the needs of war than with the idea of helping 'the chivalry of Europe' to maintain its tottering status as an élite. For a variety of reasons, feudal revenues were steadily diminishing, and noblemen could less and less afford to travel abroad for their education as they had done in former times. The practical purpose of the steps that were taken was therefore to devise a cheaper, quicker and more systematic way of providing the more necessitous nobility with a sort of 'nobles' secondary-school'. The idea was not only to give instruction in the manners of the court, in sport and in foreign languages, but also to give a political education based on history, and to teach the art of war both in theory and in practice.

This new type of educational establishment for young noble-

66

men – sometimes called a *Ritterakademie* – was debated up and down Europe. The pioneer of it all seems to have been the Huguenot leader, François de la Noue, with his *Discours politiques et militaires*, published in 1587. So far as is known, the first institution of this kind was founded at Sédan at some date subsequent to 1606 by the Duke of Bouillon, brother-in-law of Prince Maurice of Orange. The first German to follow suit was Count John VII of Nassau with his *Kriegs- und Ritterschule* at Siegen, founded in 1617;[1] one year later the Landgrave Maurice of Hesse started the college at Cassel which bears his name; and lastly came Wallenstein himself, with his *Friedländische Akademie* at Gitschin, founded probably in 1624. All these ambitious efforts were naturally brought to nothing by the Thirty Years' War and only after the end of it were they renewed – this time with lasting success – by the Great Elector of Brandenburg. It is true that one of his predecessors, Duke Albert, had, in his *Kriegsordnung* of 1556, already recommended that attention should be paid to science and had protected those who studied it from their detractors; but he never founded any institute especially for the purpose. This was only done with the foundation of the Prussian Cadet-Institute at Kolberg, as an extension of the pre-existing *Ritterakademie*,[2] at which not merely the usual range of schooling was given but also instruction in the elements of mathematics and fortification.

At that time and throughout the eighteenth century it was, generally speaking, mathematics which formed the link between science at large and the science of war and which was likewise the principal support of both. The art of war, in fact, was then regarded as forming a branch of mathematics (*Grössenlehre*, as it used to be called), viz. as its practical application; one was supposed to follow geometrical forms when manoeuvring in battle, and foretell the fall of a fortress by arithmetical calculations. Napoleon himself who, after all, was a highly original commander in war, is reported to have said: 'To be a good general, one must know mathematics. It offers dozens of opportunities of checking one's ideas. Very likely I owe my successes to my mathematical knowledge.' It was notions of this sort about the value of a certain theoretical schooling that led, after the Seven Years' War, to frequent attempts to develop the professional value of officers by means of basic knowledge

67

through the founding of military schools. General opinion, however, attached far more value to direct, practical experience of warfare than to scientific or to higher education in general. What decided the intellectual outlook of officers was the example of that sound but wholly uncomplicated king, Frederick William I, who despised all scholars and 'drivellers' (*Blackscheisser*), or that tough, uneducated expert, Prince Leopold of Anhalt-Dessau. 'Anything going beyond what a good noncommissioned officer needs to know was regarded as useless swotting'[3].

But even practical professional knowledge was scarce in the corps of officers before the Seven Years' War, especially in the cavalry. We have a competent judge for our authority, namely Frederick the Great.[4] Unlike his father, he was educated far above the average of his day and he used exceptionally rough language about the hostility that even his senior officers showed towards book-learning. 'If experience were all a great general needs', he once remarked, 'the greatest would be Prince Eugene's mules.'[5] When the war was over, therefore, he took a number of steps to improve his future officers' education and give them more theoretical instruction.[6] Cadet-Schools were founded at Stolp and Kulm for the sons of nobility of Further Pomerania and West Prussia respectively, as well as a sort of *Selekta*, or special class, of the Berlin Cadet-Corps under the name of *Académie des Nobles*. At the seat of the new Army-Inspectorates the King arranged for lectures to be given in the winter months on geography and the art of fortification, and they were to be attended by the more talented officers. In due course he took the twelve best pupils and attached them to his own suite where he gave them lectures himself in order to make them familiar with the art of real warfare. Even though such methods did result in the creation of an élite of general-staff officers, some of them real scholars, the great mass of 'front-line' officers were hardly affected, and the Cadet-Schools were too few in numbers to keep up the necessary supply. General education and training in the business of war remained what it always had been, a matter of chance. In most cases it was very modest and the prime reason was that adequate schooling was hardly to be had at all in the country-districts from which the bulk of the Prussian corps of officers was recruited.

In consequence, the general attitude of the Prussian officer to technical knowledge was very much what it had been among the Gothic princes of the dark ages. Procopius, for example, tells us in his *History of the Gothic Wars*[7] that when Theodoric's daughter, Amalasuntha, wanted her son given some education, her companions objected. Reading and writing, they said, were different from bravery; a boy who had learned to fear the schoolmaster's rod would never make a warrior; Theodoric had never sent Gothic boys to school yet he had won a great empire without knowing how to read or write. To the extent that this way of thinking adopts the irrational principle (*Voluntarismus*) as opposed to the rational (*Intellektualismus*) we shall find it very prominent as late as the second half of the nineteenth century. What we are dealing with here is a fundamental question of education, and the way in which it is solved will always be a matter of general outlook (*Weltanschauung*) and of *a priori* inclinations. For the education of officers, however, the matter is of very great importance and is fraught with serious long-term consequences.

Apart from the principles involved, there were reasons of circumstance – reasons of a social and political kind – that account for the fact that in the eighteenth century and indeed in part of the nineteenth, in the world in which noble officers lived any interest in books and science was usually considered rather disreputable. There is no reason to doubt von der Marwitz when he tells us[8] that scientific books, and especially works of popular knowledge and the school-texts that were beginning to appear like mushrooms, were written in a tone of rationalist enlightenment and were often, therefore, attacked and ridiculed by established authority such as Junkers, landowners and, in Roman Catholic areas, the priesthood. It would be natural for the 'establishment' – or its representatives, social, political and religious – to feel its leadership threatened and to offer resistance, as a matter of pure self-preservation, as if it were faced with a revolutionary force. The men who harboured these fears – generalised, over-simplified, hostile to schools and education – may very well have thought them largely justified by the great French Revolution, by the way it had been prepared and preached by the *littérateurs*. And yet, whether uprisings took place or not, the future, the coming century, belonged to the revolutionising spirit of rationalism,

and that spirit left its mark on the whole question of officers'
education too. It determined not merely the fact that education
was now to be systematically taken in hand, but its very nature
and in the course it was to follow.

10

Prussia: Scharnhorst; Examinations and Resistance

Epoch-making inventions added to the speed with which production, commerce and communications were expanding, and
the effect was to increase still further the cultural and economic
domination of the countryside by the city. At an early stage it
was clearly recognised that this economic expansion (apart
from the independent cultural upsurge) was founded, and could
only be continued, on a basis of technical skill and universal
education. Schooling and book-learning thereupon began to
rise in public estimation. Side by side, moreover, with general
political and economic development – part cause and part
effect – went an uninterrupted growth in the population. As
the old class-barriers were no longer an impediment to rises in
the social scale, the result was that almost every profession was
taken by storm; and as a logical consequence of the ever-rising
standard of education that was required for entry to each
profession, education itself became a measure of social standing.
Differences of education more and more replaced differences
of birth; and likewise the *bourgeoisie* of the cities more and more
took the place of the land-owning aristocracy in social and
public life. The whole nineteenth-century struggle for constitutions and for German unity, with its parallels in the field
of national economy, is after all a typically bourgeois affair,
and it could, indeed, be described as the form which was taken
by the struggle of the *bourgeoisie* for emancipation from the
forces of autocracy and feudalism. Even the composition of the
National Assembly at Frankfurt, the 'parliament of professors',
was a particularly striking example of that identity between
bourgeoisie and nationalism which was the trend of the times.
It would indeed have been a marvel if the *Zeitgeist* had left

71

the corps of officers untouched at a time when even in Prussia, as we have seen, officers were being recruited more and more from the *bourgeoisie*. The question of officers' social origins could not be more closely bound up with the question of their technical education and training. The first lies at the heart of the second.

The main lines on which these matters were reorganised were destined to endure until the first World War; and their great protagonist in Prussia was Scharnhorst.[1] Himself a product of one of those small military schools that had been haphazardly started, even outside Prussia, after the Seven Years' War, his heart and mind were rooted not in the Prussian Army but in eighteenth-century rationalism. He thus had a sharp eye for the weaknesses – the military disadvantages – of the principles that Prussia had pursued to their very limits: the principles of blue blood and contempt for education. When vacancies among the officers were to be filled, he observed that it was usually connections that mattered, not capacity or knowledge, that exceptional ability was not always the best passport to popularity, and that it was their stupidest sons whom many families sent into the Army. The last years (1795 to 1801) of his service in Hanover seemed, on the other hand, to have taught him that young officers who had excelled by ability and hard work in the Artillery School were also the best and most efficient in action, and how comparatively little the elderly generals were worth – the ones who looked down their noses at scholars in uniform. Scharnhorst himself it is who recorded these conclusions; and the result was to convince him that officers ought to receive a good and general education that included military science.

When he was made principally responsible for the reform of the Prussian Army, this conviction led him to require that every officer, whatever arm of the service he belonged to, should pass an educational test. This principle was given the force of law by the King's Regulation of the 6th August, 1808 on the appointment of ensigns, etc. At the same time the relevant passage of the Regulation is limited, or rather expounded, by the following words: 'The chief requirements of a good officer are not knowledge and technical ability alone but presence of mind, rapid perception, punctuality and accuracy, not to mention proper behaviour.' There is nothing to be objected to in this

72

important passage in itself; but in its context and in the shade of meaning it gives to the rest, it reveals how uncertain were the outlook and purpose of the leading minds of the time and how unsettled the value they attached to the elements of education and upbringing. It shows, in fact, that the struggle between education and upbringing was still in progress. Yet the very inconsistencies to be seen in this passage determined the educational programme of the Prussian officer for the next hundred years.

Now in the very nature of things the Wars of Liberation were no sort of time for a reform of officers' education or of any intellectual programme whatever. Action, practical action, in the direct sense of the word, was all that mattered in those grim years; and quill-drivers were an easy target for derision. Only in the long years of peace that followed could the ideal of education spread its wings again and Scharnhorst's War Schools gradually assume their place in the Army's scheme of things. Soon, however, it became clear that a great gulf still divided theory from practice. It was not that there was any lack of young officers and cadets ready to get themselves a better education of the kind prescribed; part of the trouble was the state of things in Prussia at the time. From the report of a Commission headed by Prince William that considered the matter in 1825 we learn that[2] young men then began a three-year course in divisional schools'* at eighteen or nineteen years of age; but, it goes on, experience showed they had had very little previous education and were, moreover, at a stage in their mental and physical development in which they had often ceased to be receptive to the first impact of technical ideas. Nor were they any longer guided by the moral standards which their welfare needed. This class in the divisional schools was apt, in consequence, to show a spirit of resistance to study and morality alike. Pupils made no more than slow and unsteady progress; and they were so well on in years, as a rule, before they were fit to pass the officers' examination that the handicap showed throughout the rest of their careers.

As a remedy for this state of affairs the Commission went on to recommend 'the reduction of the courses in the divisional schools from three years to one, and the proviso that before they entered the schools the pupils must themselves have

* In fact these were schools maintained for this purpose in each regiment.

acquired the knowledge they had hitherto been taught in them ... But in the case of necessitous officers' sons who cannot obtain such a degree of education at home it is proposed, as the next best thing, that a number of boys proportionate to the Army's needs should be given the requisite degree of education at an earlier stage, in the *Gymnasien*.* . . . . This is a degree they have hitherto been given, but too late and always insufficiently, in the lowest class of the divisional schools, where none but elementary general education can be had. Such an arrangement will afford the real advantage that well-to-do parents who wish their sons to follow a military career will be obliged to provide for their sons' upbringing and elementary education *themselves*. . . . By the same token the divisional schools would cease to give excessive encouragement to the competition of the wholly uneducated working-classes for higher promotion in the Army. To be sure, the road to the highest military goal should not be closed, or made difficult, for any man who contrives through talent and hard work to overcome the handicaps of his origins. Nevertheless, the true interest of the Army cannot be served if mediocre and uncultured men are merely brought, at the State's expense, to the point where they learn to claim higher rewards before they made themselves fit to give greater service. The following is therefore proposed: in the *Gymnasien* in every province several hundred places should be created where the sons of necessitous officers can be given a four-year course of instruction from their thirteenth to the end of their seventeenth year and in which, if their parents live elsewhere, they can be fed, lodged and clothed.'

Thus by 1825 opinion in the ruling classes had moved a very long way from the ideas that were current in the days of Scharnhorst and Boyen. What a sharp recoil that passage represents! What an abyss again divides one *Weltanschauung* from the other! There is hardly a line that does not breathe an ill-concealed distaste for the 'competition' of the 'uneducated working-classes' who want to enter the State-financed divisional schools: 'mediocrity and lack of culture' are to be curbed – yet only in respect of 'undesirable' officer-material. For the 'good' kind (which means the Old-Prussian, drawn from the families of noblemen and officers) red carpets are to be rolled

* The *Gymnasium* was then the main type of secondary school, and included classical studies as a principal subject.

out, although this kind admittedly, was often noted for its
'mediocrity' too. Here, the question of recruitment was intimately bound up with that of education. In fact, however, the
proposal for 'bursaries' broke down, as it did again some
decades later, in the face of opposition from the Ministry of
Public Worship and Education, as well as on the question of
cost.[3]

But the second class of the divisional schools came to an end
in 1828; and then the country gentry and the officers complained all the more loudly how difficult it was to educate
their sons. This was indeed a change of tune from the days when
Frederick William I had had to apply main force to get the
small country gentry's sons into the cadet-schools. These
people now got influential spokesmen, such as General von
Rüdel-Kleist, to back their demand that the State should
again make special arrangements to prepare their sons for the
ensigns' examination. At this period, 1835, Boyen had long
since ceased to be Minister of War, but the Crown Prince*
had a great respect for him and asked for his opinion. Like
other soldiers, Boyen firmly opposed the Junkers' demand.[4]
The State, he observed, maintained the Army out of taxes
paid by all the citizens and it obliged all classes of them to
serve in the Army's ranks: it could not therefore allow any
particular class (*Stand*) a special claim to officers' commissions,
but must take the most capable; and next to military attainments the thing an officer needed most, if he was not to forfeit
the respect of other classes (*Stände*), was that degree of knowledge of the world which matched the requirements of the times.

What Boyen meant by that final phrase (*die dem Zeitbedürfnis
angemessene weltbürgerliche Kenntnisse*) was the ideal of a so-called
'general education'; and in 1836, the very next year – apparently for the first time – this idea was incorporated into the
syllabus for the education of Prussian officers.†

In the end, the full, new and typically bourgeois ideal of
general education was clearly accepted and expressed in
Frederick William IV's Ordinance of the 4th February 1844
on (i) the recruitment of officers for the standing Army in time

* Later Frederick William IV.

† Instructions of the Ministry of War (17th Dec., 1836) on 'Requirements for
the entrance-examination for officers', the section on the general principles to be
applied.

of peace and (ii) the organisation of the Cadet-Corps. The preamble to the Ordinance (the essentials of which, incidentally, were merely reproduced in 1861) expressly states that 'The greater degree of professional knowledge and general education which are nowadays required and found in every walk of life demand that the standard of examination and of preparatory education be raised likewise for officers, so that they can maintain the respect they now enjoy, and not find it too hard to change their profession if they should wish to.' The whole drafting of this general statement of intention, of course, betrays the reluctance, the distaste, the sense almost of *force majeure*, that was felt when the world of military ideas, or at least the language of Army Ordinances, had to admit the educational ideal of bourgeois 'competitors'. What was said by one of the best authorities on the affairs of the time is true: 'The corps of officers turned the intellectual achievements of the day to account, but it did not take them into its heart; it adopted the practical lessons to be drawn from them rather than the ideal they represented.'[5]

This was an attitude of mind that prevailed for many a long year among officers of the Prussian Army; and a typical example is furnished by the Prince of Prussia, later the Emperor William I. Faced with 'the constantly rising standard of general education' he declared himself fully in accord with the principle of raising the technical standard for candidates for commissions. 'But how', he anxiously enquired,[6] 'are the sons of the needier nobility, of impecunious officers, to be given the education that is now required? Where are they to find the money for getting their sons as far as the *Prima*?* Families of this kind live in the country or in country-towns. There they used to be able to find as much primary education as their sons formerly needed for their entrance, after which, up to the age of seventeen, they received their further education and their military preparation gratis in divisional schools. But now all this is entirely changed. Bearing in mind the fact that this sort of family is intimately bound up with the Prussian Army and derives from it the spirit that has led to such great achievements in battle, I think we owe it to them not to put their livelihood and their whole future in jeopardy. If we do so we

---

* The first or highest class of a first-grade secondary school, corresponding to the Sixth Form in English schools.

shall risk giving the Army a wholly different character, a wholly different spirit, from those it has had hitherto....' The Prince accordingly proposed increasing the budgets of the Cadet-Schools and creating free places in the *Gymnasien*, as had previously been suggested. This last proposal was not adopted, as we know, and in the following years it was only the institutions for cadets that were continuously expanded – the main beneficiaries being the sons of the needier nobles and officers.

On many sides, including the Inspector of Military Education and Training, General von Luck, it was urged that the standard set for university-entrance should be required. This, however, was turned down, and the position remained that the would-be officer must either get a *Prima*-certificate at a *Gymnasium* or show his general technical knowledge in the ensigns' examination before joining the Army. Thereafter his further instruction was strictly professional and technical, and on that account the divisional schools were simultaneously transformed into preparatory courses for the *officers'* examination, i.e. they became in principle the sort of War College (*Kriegsschule*) that remained the norm until the first World War.

The survival of these last, like that of the cadet-institutions, was only momentarily threatened in 1848 when the National Assembly at Frankfort considered a bill on the subject of German defence-arrangements. Section 62 of the bill read: 'All specialized (*einseitig*) military educational establishments are to be closed'; and Section 66 read: 'For the purposes of higher military studies Chairs of Military Science will be created at several Universities. The conditions on which serving officers may be allowed to attend these Universities will be laid down in special regulations.' In this we have an expression of a line of thought similar to the one already noted in Book I in connection with the Prussian reform.

It was obvious that the ruling military and aristocratic class, personified by the Prince of Prussia, would dismiss these proposals out of hand; but the grounds which were adduced are interesting because they were so typical. In the published 'Observations' on the bill[7] we read; *inter alia*: 'The duties of officers are onerous. If they are to be properly and successfully discharged an officer must either have entered the Army with a sense of vocation or he must have been bred up to it from early youth. It is thus of the highest importance that there should be establishments from which candidates *can*[8] emerge who from their childhood onwards have been accustomed to strict discipline (*Zucht*), order, frugality and obedience, for these are requirements they must satisfy throughout their lives if they wish to set an example to their subordinates and give encouragement to their brother-officers of the territorials (*Landwehr*)'. . . . After stating these basic objections the document goes on to point out the particular difficulties of the proposal that chairs of Military Science should be created. The science of war, it asserted, could only be taught with success by those who had had experience of it; but even if officers were to serve as university lecturers they would not meet the needs of the situation, for they would have no means of measuring the effect of their lectures upon the officers who heard them. This last objection was unsound, of course. Even with ordinary students the success of academic lectures cannot be assessed at once; this can only be done after group-tutorial work (*Seminararbeiten*) and eventually by examinations – and allowance must be made for the general human liability to make mistakes. Weightier, however, were the objections based on matters of principle as cited above; but on these there was naturally no possibility of fundamental agreement. Questions of general attitude, or *Weltanschauung*, were at issue.

The defence-bill died with the Frankfort parliament, and in essence the old arrangements remained in force. But as far as examinations were concerned, the events of 1848 brought at least a temporary relief to officer-candidates. For the King deemed it[9] 'appropriate to present circumstances that ensigns who bore themselves well in the face of the enemy shall, without regard to their seniority as ensigns, and without being required to take a subsequent examination, but subject to vacancies occurring in particular units, be recommended for commissions as officers.' To what extent use was then actually made of this exemption from examinations – a thing that was later only possible in time of war – is a point I have not been able to establish: but an Ordinance that followed very shortly (on the 19th September 1848) laid down the general requirements for admission to the ensigns' and officers' examinations respectively, and this dispensation reappeared in it only as a reward for distinguished conduct in the face of the enemy. 'Present circumstances' received no further mention.

Despite the officers' examination, however, anyone remained theoretically free to decide whether to acquire the necessary knowledge in the War Schools or in some other way. Only in 1859 did a Royal Order make attendance at a War School compulsory and at the same time create new ones at Potsdam, Neisse and Erfurt. Nevertheless in the very next year this rational unification of officers' schooling had to be breached. The reorganisation of the Army had made the temporary demand for officers so great that numerous ensigns and Landwehr officers who had not passed the prescribed examinations had to be sent at once to reinforce the officers of the Line. Little can, on the other hand, have resulted in practice from the expectation voiced in the Prince Regent's Order of the 6th February 1860, viz that the officers concerned would themselves make good the gaps in their technical and professional training. In most cases it can only have remained a pious hope; and the transfer, in particular, of so many Landwehr officers to the Line caused the Prince Regent and his advisers to have grave misgivings on social and political grounds. 'Affection, aptitude and zeal for the chosen profession, a sense of the importance and honour of the status of an officer, a mind receptive to the spirit that has always marked the Prussian corps of officers and which should continue to do so in future' – such were the qualities Prince Frederick Charles required: but with these, it appears, the 'new men' from the Landwehr were not easily credited. This was the reason why, as and when the officer-strength of the Line seemed to make it possible, the emergency-orders of the 6th February 1860 were suspended in respect of these Landwehr-officers and of no others.

I I

Germany: Expansion;
the Die-Hards at Bay

The emergency regulations of the 6th February 1860, except in respect of Landwehr officers, remained in force however, for many years; and round them, that is to say, round the whole problem they raised, there developed a bitter struggle in which the lead on the one side was taken by the Military Cabinet headed by Manteuffel, and on the other by the Ministry of War headed by Roon. The Prince-Regent was inclined at first to take the side of Roon, to whose active help he chiefly owed the success of his great reorganisation. But Manteuffel skilfully drummed up a team of fighting generals who shared his differing view, and soon he largely succeeded in bringing the Prince-Regent round. A somewhat closer study of this affair is called for because the struggle (from the sociological point of view it opposed the liberal and the feudal worlds) involved a decision of principle on the structure of the Prussian corps of officers.

The obligation to attend a War School was important; but much more so was the simultaneous stiffening of the ensigns' examination. The object was to discourage young men with wholly inadequate education from presenting themselves; and an Order of the 31st October 1861 accordingly laid it down that candidates must produce a certificate of fitness (*Primareifezeugnis*) for the *Prima* class of a Prussian *Gymnasium* or of a Prussian *Realschule**of the first class. Moreover, any candidate would be failed if his German-language paper was marked 'insufficient', or not marked at all, in respect of grammar and spelling. This last requirement may make us smile today, but at the time it was a real innovation, a stiffening of

* A 'modern' secondary-school.

the hurdle to be cleared. Everyone knows that, a bare generation earlier, such famous Prussian generals as old Wrangel or Marshal Blücher and even the learned Scharnhorst himself, were not too sure how to use such things as the dative case and the accusative.[1] Much still remained to be desired, even in the second half of the century – at least among the older generation of soldiers. Hans Delbrück tells a pleasant story on this point.[2] In 1879 his pupil, a young prince, was due to join the Cadet Corps, and when Delbrück was discussing the subject with the Chief of Military Education the latter, a cavalry general, assured him that he attached much importance to grammar – but made a grammatical mistake in saying so. The Order of the 31st October 1861 may have come too late to affect his grammar, but he had the sense to be guided by it – at any rate in theory – in carrying out his duties.

The Order at once let loose a real storm of indignation among the luckless 'interested parties' as well as among those who were still determined to preserve the 'homogeneity' ('exclusiveness' is what they meant) of the Prussian corps of officers at any price, not excluding the correct employment of the German language. The political strife and social bitterness so typical of the mid-century exploded once again, and with an open venom that was never seen again. This time, it must be admitted, instinct did not betray the 'interested parties'. They felt an embittered concern for the historic privileges of their kind – a fear that with the higher educational standard 'the sons of bankers who have made fortunes' would fill the posts of officers in the *Garde du Corps* – the personal bodyguard of the King. They foresaw, in other words, the Prussian corps of officers becoming de-feudalised and bourgeois. In Manteuffel, the head of the Military Cabinet, the most determined and influential sympathiser with their outlook and their demands, these people saw their last, best hope; and to him they addressed an appeal (the signatures, alas, are lost) – six questions of lapidary brevity that ended almost with a threat (see Appendix 5).

Manteuffel's next move (we cannot tell if it was the result of this imperious questionnaire, for the latter bears no date) was to address a longish memorandum (see Appendix 6), dated the 25th November 1861 to the Minister of War. Drawing on his own experience he stated why he objected to the new

81

Order on principle – though on this occasion he did so more temperately, perhaps, than was his wont. But the whole document, to tell the truth, is merely a sorrowful, resigned farewell to the crumbling foundation, the Old-Prussian feudal basis, of the corps of officers. The earlier stiffening of tests for entry had already lost it a good part of the Mecklemburg nobility, and now the Old-Prussian aristocracy itself was to be turned away. This bourgeois worship of book-learning was a thing he could endure no longer. But it is plain that he had still not grasped that this was all implied by the very first steps that had been taken to improve the education of officers – steps taken as long ago as 1836, more still in 1844, when Frederick William IV, whose views he shared, had prescribed the same level of 'general education' for officers as for the bourgeois professions, so as to maintain the social standing of the officers. Lip-service was all this move had then demanded, and the foundations of the old Prussian corps of officers had seemed unassailably robust. But spirits had been summoned from the deep to serve the reformist slogans of 1808, and now they could no longer be dismissed.

Manteuffel's warnings did not fail of their effect upon the King. They 'gripped him by the sword-knot', as Bismarck once did to the Emperor. A fortnight later,[3] barely six weeks after the Order had appeared, the King had the attention of regimental-commanders expressly drawn to the passage in his father's Order of the 6th August, 1808 which laid it down that certain qualities of character, as well as knowledge and 'science', were needed to make a good officer. This, however, was not enough for Manteuffel. He now applied all his powers of personal persuasion to ensuring that the hated certificates should should not be required until the 1st January, 1863. On the 18th April 1862 he sent a memorandum (see Appendix 7) to the King, in which he sometimes used the plainest language, and even called it necessary 'that in addition to making candidates go through a War School before taking the officers' examination, no less weight should be attached to especial zeal for the service and to a sound military outlook than is attached already to an especially thorough technical education'.

We must bear in mind, of course, that we are dealing with a period prior to the Cabinet Order of the 8th March 1883: the chief of the Military Cabinet was not yet even formally independent of the Minister of War, let alone superior to him, but was his subordinate. This alone explains why Manteuffel in his covering letter, begged von Roon 'most earnestly ... not to read the memorandum with the preconceived impression which, alas, you have of me, i.e. that I am against War Schools and technical education, but to read the whole thing right through before you go to work with your blue pencil'. Again and again he gives the assurance that his aim is simply that 'for the next few years', in addition to the prescribed educational ladder, there should be exceptional access by another route: but he promptly contradicts himself by admitting that this would also offer an insurance 'for the future' against the triumph of the current tendency to use non-commissioned officers for filling vacancies. This last is no doubt an exaggerated piece of pessimism – put in, perhaps, on purpose with an eye to its psychological effect upon the King. It is true that in Bavaria, but only as a sequel to the revolutionary year of 1848, no fewer than 250 non-commissioned officers had been promoted to lieutenant; but Prussia had not followed this example, and such a thing did not in the least deserve the name of a 'current tendency' even if it had been recommended in particular cases here and there. And, of course, Manteuffel's phrase 'only for the next few years' was simply meant to soothe von Roon.

William I, at least, did not mistake Manteuffel's meaning and in substance every one of his proposals was accepted. The Order of the 23rd April 1862 first of all postponed to the 1st October 1865 the date from which admission to the ensigns' examination would definitely require production of a *Primareifezeugnis* and it then announced, without limitation of time, that especial zeal for the service and a recommendation from the appropriate corps of officers would fully compensate for deficiency in scientific education. The King had thereby yielded to a skilful show of determination, and he passed the prime responsibility for the admission of new officers back to the officer-corps' collective judgment. What he did not do was to put an end to the dualism that had dogged the question of their education since 1808 and, was to go on doing so, though gradually weakening, until the first World War and even after it. Compared with the Order of the previous year, the new Order represented a far-reaching concession, a greater retreat in the face of certain movements of opinion within the corps of officers.

This complex of feudal and rural emotions formed one sector of a very wide front on which the age-old 'revaluation of values' – for the current issue involved nothing less – was proceeding; and a deep insight into its condition at this time is afforded by the replies which three general-officers commanding made to Manteuffel's memorandum, copies of which had been sent to them for comment. On of them in particular (whose name cannot be established for lack of any signature or covering letter) admittedly shows no great breadth of mind; but he shows all the more depth of feeling and especially depths of passion against schools. This unknown critic – doubtless he was one of the most respected generals – is incensed above all by the assumption that candidates would henceforth have to show the level of their education *before* the ensigns' examination instead of *in* it as had previously been the case, i.e. that in order to be allowed to sit at all he had to bring the appropriate school-certificate. For, as he rightly pointed out, the decision whether or not to let him take the examination used to lie exclusively in the hands of the Military Examinations Commission which had been free to take other than purely academic considerations into account, whereas this decision was now to be taken by the school-directors alone. In them, generally speaking, he felt no confidence: more often than not they were hostile on principle to the better classes (he really meant, of course, the country gentry and perhaps the officers too); they were filled with the destructive spirit of the times and most of them were rationalists to boot.

With that he cleared the air. Bluntly and straight from the shoulder he was saying what the others also thought, or what at least they dimly felt, viz. 'to Hell with culture and all its works'. The ordinary domestic tutor's lessons, which was all the education the country gentry's sons would normally get until they were sixteen, was, he granted, a little biassed and did not provide knowledge on the same scale as the public schools; it was preferable none the less, because it included the physical and moral advantages of an upbringing in a 'decent' family. But resistance was hopeless; for there was no withstanding the trend of the times towards the influence of the city, of intellectualism and uniformity, upon the whole field of education, not to mention the influence of the *bourgeoisie* on public life. Faithful to the line set by the two previous Kings, William I paid the spirit of the times his tribute, but he never quite gave that spirit a free run all the same. Still, the rising demand for officers was so hard to meet from the socially 'desirable' classes (so far as their numbers made it possible) that the date on which the *Primareifezeugnis* became a condition for taking the ensigns' examination had to be postponed again – beyond, that is, the 1st October 1865.

Year after year, on the other hand, there was an increase in the numbers who came forward with inadequate preparation. The examination figures for two months in the year 1868 show that out of 111 examinees, 69 had not reached the *Prima* but only the *Sekunda* or the *Tertia*, or had not been to school at all. Of the 69, in consequence, only 22 passed the examination; and all who had only been privately tutored were marked as 'failed'. 'It will be borne in mind,' say the files on the matter,[4] 'that all the above-mentioned candidates who did not pass will present themselves again after a further period at the 'crammers' and it will then be normal to treat them with special indulgence. There is no denying, therefore, that the number of officers who have not had the usual formal education is bound to grow and will give ground for anxiety.' This situation was offset to some extent by the fact that an increasing number of young men with educational certificates were joining the Army at this period as unpaid volunteers. Nevertheless the competent section of the Ministry of War saw a growing problem in the fact 'that the educational level of the corps of officers is uneven'.

In consequence (so it was reported in 1870), individual commanders 'when accepting candidates for commissions, have attached more importance to an exceptionally thorough technical preparation than to the sort of family the candidates came from and the upbringing they received at home. The result has everywhere been the same: the quality of the corps of officers has fallen off, and other elements have had to be brought in so as to raise it and strengthen the corps.'[5] These of course, were the elements of which 'our good corps of officers used to be composed but which, alas, as a glance at the lists will show, are becoming ever rarer'. This being so, the Military Cabinet considered it to be 'part of its essential task to maintain the old position regarding Prussian officers in this respect as well'. Indeed, maintenance to the utmost is expressly described[6] as being much more important than ending the emergency admission–arrangements that were still in force.

The Ministry of War had, in fact, invited the Military Cabinet to support it in bringing these emergency measures to an end; and when the latter refused, the Ministry attempted none the less[7] to justify its proposal in detail by citing the Higher Military Examinations Commission's report for the year 1869. For this purpose the Ministry drew a distinction – of the kind familiar to us from Part I – between 'Old-Prussian' and 'other' officer-material; and the statistical tables it drew up on this basis contain very useful factual clues to the technical education of the corps of officers compared with nobility of birth. These tables were partially used in Part I. The essence of the whole controversy between the Military Cabinet and the Ministry was that the former attributed the bad and visibly worsening situation shown up by the ensigns' examination (which was supposed, after all, to certify that the basis for later specialised training existed) to the excessively high technical requirements in force since 1844, whereas the Ministry took exactly the opposite view and complained that the tests were being applied with too much laxity.

Nevertheless the Ministry's expert advice did not prevail against the Military Cabinet, whose judgment and preoccupations were mainly political in nature. A few days later, on the 28th March, the Ministry's advice was finally rejected, and that rejection substantially held the field as regards all later developments up to the first World War. It is true that the requirement of a *Primareifezeugnis* did eventually come into force, but it made little practical difference, for an appeal for dispensation could be directly addressed to the Emperor – as was frequently done for many years, and with success. In the school-year 1883–4, for example, dispensation was granted to 118 pupils in the Prussian War Schools,[8] and the grossly inadequate technical instruction they received from the 'crammers' drove the Inspector of War Schools to make a most emotional complaint to the Emperor, pointing out, among other things, that 'a deplorably high proportion of them bear names that have been traditional for generations in the Prussian corps of officers'. It is clear that the Military Cabinet, which was the competent office for such dispensations, still held and applied exactly the same principles as it had put on paper in 1869–70 and had contrived to get adopted.

It would be a mistake, none the less, to conclude from these differences of opinion about formal technical preparation that the Military Cabinet and the competent sections of the Ministry were at odds in general, or were in any doubt about the aims and purposes of officers' preparatory education. In the appeal mentioned above, the Inspector of War Colleges adopted an almost passionate tone when stating his conviction that candidates 'should not be admitted to the chivalrous company of officers ... until they have proved by their mentality and feelings that they are wholly and truly fit for it'. In this case the underlying principle was stated in emotional terms: but the Inspector-General of Military Training and Education under the Emperor William II, expressed the principle at length and in strictly systematic form in his circular of 23rd November 1890: 'Subject: Purpose and Conduct of shortened Courses at War Schools'.[9] Every word of the circular is directed towards ensuring that the turning-out of men who would make good brother-officers and military leaders should take precedence over their technical education. It is stated quite openly – not just with reference to these shortened courses but as a point of general application – that 'we are not concerned with "science" at the War Schools, as if they were academies, but with the truly difficult task of initiating young men into the basic principles of war and, so to speak, the tricks of the trade; and our object is to produce sound apprentices who will ripen with time and practice into masters'.

The principle of instinctive, non-rational action could not be more plainly expressed than in these words. It was taken still further, however, in the following formulation, which was much used in actual practice: 'An accidental lapse of memory or even a serious error of judgment or decision may be forgiven; but failure to use common sense is the gravest fault of all. Slackness and neglect are graver sins than blundering.' This last may in some cases be a rather serious overstatement of the principle; but leaving that aside, the thing that stands out is this; strong preference is given to the factors of will and up-bringing, combined with purely professional training. By comparison, a subordinate role is assigned to the cultivation of a technical mentality. Even then the latter is only tolerated on condition that it serves professional military needs or else is made desirable or acceptable (as the case may be) by the sheer need of keeping abreast of the current standard of general education in the higher civilian professions – or, to put it frankly, by the need to meet the rising demand for officers.

It was under these conditions that the recurrent question had to be faced in Prussia too, whether a would-be officer should be required to present a certificate not merely from the *Prima* class but a higher one, a certificate from a *Gymnasium*, a *Realgymnasium* or an *Oberrealschule*.* But we have seen that many exceptions were already being made in respect of the certificate from the *Prima*. How could a higher certificate possibly be asked for? The exceptions would simply have become the rule. Some regimental-commanders were so strict about the required level of technical education that they demanded a leaving-certificate from a secondary school before accepting even volunteers (*Avantageure*). The Emperor William II expressed disapproval of this practice in the Cabinet Order of the 29th March 1890 which was mentioned in Part I; but the number of would-be officers with leaving-certificates continued to rise, not least on account of the advantage this gained for them as regards eventual commissions. Between 1880 and 1912 their proportion rose from one-third to two-thirds.

The table opposite gives the figures[10] of ensigns entering the armies of Prussia, Saxony and Wurtemberg. Compared with the almost uninterrupted growth of the numbers holding school-leaving certificates, it is surprising to see how many, up to 1900, were still being excused from bringing even *Prima* certificates, for these young men had mostly to be prepared by 'crammers'. Under the old Emperor, of course, this tolerance of inadequate education was still intended first and foremost to benefit the Old Prussian nobility; but what emerges from the files in his grandson's time is much more the sheer need for officers. This last was the result of further expansion of the Army, and it is this which underlay his Order of the 13th November 1890. Examinations, it said, were to be conducted with indulgence and those who had the right personality could be recommended for the grant of a *Reifezeugnis* as a matter

---

* These are all types of secondary school, the prefix 'real-' indicating a greater or lesser degree of 'modern' elements in the curriculum.

of Royal Prerogative. Detailed instructions for granting dispensations from the *Primareifezeugnis* were never issued; but von Hahnke, the chief of the Military Cabinet, observed in a Minute that, while it could not be said out loud, the examination should be treated as a matter of form: the main thing was to 'get 'em into uniform quick!'

Year	Totals	Excused from Prima certificates	Excused from ensigns' examination	With school-leaving certificates (*1880: 33%*)
1890	745	134 (17·99%)	9 (1·21%)	35·00%
1895	806	113 (13·97%)	47 (5·80%)	[caret]
1900	968	43 (4·44%)	14 (1·45%)	44·00%
1903	982	66 (6·72%)	6 (0·61%)	46·00%
1904	963	77 (8·00%)	9 (0.93%)	47·00%
1905	949	83 (8·72%)	7 (0·73%)	48·00%
1906	991	83 (8·38%)	3 (0·30%)	51·66%
1907	991	77 (7·77%)	5 (0·50%)	54·49%
1908	1042	95 (9·12%)	3 (0·29%)	52·68%
1909	1177	89 (7·56%)	4 (0·34%)	57·86%
1910	1303	69 (5·31%)	2 (0·15%)	63·16%
1911	1361	72 (5·29%)	8 (0·59%)	61·87%
1912	1449	54 (3·70%)	4 (0·28%)	65·10%

By 1899 the shortage of officers was easing off. Only then did the Emperor pay attention to the examiners' complaints of 'the very superficial general education shown by candidates who come from preparatory establishments' (*sc.* the 'crammers'). In consequence he made it known[11] that 'from the spring of 1900 onwards he wanted to see a reduction in the numbers of young men being taken on as ensigns without having a *Primareifezeugnis*. The percentage of dispensations thereupon fell off considerably; but between 1901 and 1912 more than a thousand, even so, were admitted to the infantry ensigns' examinations without this certificate.[12] In the cavalry and artillery the matter was taken rather more seriously since the numbers who applied to join these arms of the service, despite the expenses they entailed, was pretty satisfactory. But in the case of the infantry the Military Cabinet judged[13] that some liberality in dispensing candidates from certificates (which anyway had little value as evidence of their level of general education) must be allowed in order to keep recruitment up. For the same reason nothing was done about the way in which the 'crammers' establishments were run; but many of them left much to be desired and the Military Cabinet itself admitted that those who ran them 'were often only concerned with keeping their large income up'.

From many points of view the Military Cabinet was not wholly wrong in refusing to let the crucial *Primareifezeugnis* be treated as the sole test of general technical education. There is no denying, of course, that if they had to satisfy at least this minimum requirement the young men would have made a good deal more effort to build up a certain foundation of general knowledge, widen their mental horizons and generally improve themselves; but as things were, they could live quite happily in the knowledge that at a pinch they could get on all right without any of it. Herein lay part of the blame for the fact that, compared with other countries, the general level of education in the Prussian-German corps of army-officers was often held in pretty low esteem both at home and abroad. For the corps of naval officers the Naval Cabinet aimed from 1909 onwards at making school-leaving certificates obligatory[14] and the same criterion was adopted at a later date by the Inspector-General of Military Training and Education itself (see Appendices 9 and 10).

And yet, if one is to be historically objective, this view of the matter, however, justified in particular cases, was rather biased. What it overlooked most of all was the fact that the educational calibre of the average Prussian officer could not just be gauged by how he had fared in school before he was commissioned. Both in the officers' clubs and outside, the intellectual level of the officers in a regiment depended very much indeed on the personality and the general culture of the commanding officer at the time, and even more on the general level ruling in the station or garrison. A real capital-city such as Berlin, or a university-town like Königsberg or Göttingen, could naturally always offer very different stimuli and possibilities to the type of officer – and they were common – who was intellectually alert and keen to improve his mind, than could be found in a small, sleepy country-town, even if it could also call itself some prince's capital. This was already so in the eighteenth and early nineteenth centuries as we know, in the case of Göttingen,

from Scharnhorst's early years in the Hanoverian service, and
from the lectures Kant delivered at Königsberg. Moltke, too,
has recorded how, when he was working in the Survey Service
in Berlin in 1828–9, he attended not only lectures on French
literature at the University and a course on modern history
but even a course on Goethe – and Goethe, moreover, was still
alive. Nor was Moltke by any means a freak: he was proud to
report in a letter that almost one-third of the audience were
soldiers, and that at an English course there were more officers
than students. He also learned a fifth foreign language –
Russian. And in the 'fifties, we are told, a large part of those
who followed Stahl's lectures on constitutional and parliamentary history were officers in uniform.[15] In Berlin, where his
really creative period began, Scharnhorst himself combined
with several young officers and two civilian professors to found
the 'Military Society' (*Militärische Gesellschaft*) and under his
direction it rapidly made a great name for itself.[16] The secret
of this success lay not in any talent of Scharnhorst's for electri-
fying his audience (in actual fact, as his pupil Clausewitz,
among others, has recorded, he was rather a monotonous
speaker and quite unemotional) but partly in the attractive,
undogmatic content of his lectures, and partly, no doubt, in
the impressionable minds of the keen young officers who
formed his audience.

Such qualities were not rare among officers throughout the
country. Goethe himself spent much time in the society of
officers who had served in the Wars of Liberation;[17] and there
were military journals, such as *Bellona*, *Neue Bellona* and Scharnhorst's *Neues Journal* which made real intellectual demands upon
their readers. In times of such military, political and social
agitation, the fact that they appeared with regularity shows
that they had a wide circulation, and their subscribers included
even serving officers.[18] This line of development led on to the
'Military Weekly' (*Militär-Wochenblatt*) and to the 'Tactical
Quarterly' (*Vierteljahrshefte für Truppenführung*) which continued to sow their seed right up to the first World War. But
apart from all this it is well known that even under the Empire
there were countless officers who could not get along without a
box of books, even when on manœuvres. Nor were they only
General-Staff officers – the kind who personified the 'educated
officer' from Moltke's day onwards. Such men themselves were

anyway the product not merely of application and hard work but of the whole intellectual climate of the General Staff in which almost every one of them was raised to a higher level of general culture.

In principle, of course, the Chief of the General Staff was allied with the Ministry of War against the Military Cabinet,[19] as the table on the opposite page makes clear.[20] That officer too thought it 'urgently necessary' to procure officer-candidates with better preparatory education and had often pointed out the danger of falling behind other armies. 'But,' he added in a memorandum of the 2nd November 1911,[21] 'I should not wish to stress intellectual education alone; it must be allied to the training of character and outlook.' His difference with the Military Cabinet is perfectly summed up in these few words. Two years earlier, its Chief had written (see Appendix 10): 'It is certainly *desirable* that officer-intake should be as well educated as possible; but conditions being what they are, we must accept the fact that higher qualifications cannot be demanded... I do not regard this as a great calamity either, provided the supply of character keeps up.' Briskly and plainly Freiherr von Lyncker thus came down against qualities of mind in the training of officers and in favour of qualities of character, of the element of instinct; qualities of mind, indeed, he regarded merely as stepping-stones towards the desired end, whereas the younger Moltke wanted to see mind and character developed together in balance. In Prussia the struggle between these two points of view had been pursued under different forms ever since 1808; and in the end the decision, by and large, went in favour of mind-and-character together.

In the first World War, of course, these points of principle began to look academic as the peace-time corps of officers was more and more overwhelmed by the war's insatiable demands. A chronic shortage of officers developed; and on top of it, the public and the rank-and-file began to insist that officers should be older and more experienced. It was with a view to meeting these two needs that prominent generals such as von Einem and von der Marwitz suggested the extension of the *Bildungsprivileg** in a downwards direction. Their idea was that the practical needs of the war would be better served if

* The privilege of accelerated promotion that went with a certain high level of education.

SUMMARY STATISTICS

on the preparatory education of officers serving in January 1905 in the General Staff and of officers attending the War Academy on the 1st October, 1904.

	I. CADETS			II. CERTIFICATES FROM CIVILIAN SCHOOLS			III. Officers educated up to the Prima in civilian schools, who joined after passing the ensigns' examination	Remarks
	Ordinary Certificate	Special Class	Passed Ensign's Examination	Gymnasien	Real-Gymnasien	Ober-Real-Gymnasien		
General Staff	17	48	16	101	4	4	21 = ±10% out of 211	Includes Wurtemberg General Staff-Officers
		81 = 39%			109 = 51% ±			
War Academy	32	59	36	240	24	0	57 = ±13% out of 448	
		127 = ±28%			264 = ±59%			

NOTES: By adding the officers with ordinary cadet-certificates to those in Para. II, and the other cadets in Para. III, the following picture emerges:

General Staff ±60% with certificates, ±40% passed ensigns' examination
War Academy ±66% with certificates, ±34% passed ensign's examination

the command of companies were given to maturer men than very junior officers, even if the former were not up to the normal peace-time social standard or did not hold the regulation school-certificates. In this context, moreover, they pointed to the reserve of executive ability and leadership (*Führerpotential*) that was to be found in the higher officials of social and industrial organisations. A vain decision in this sense was taken by the Ministry of War at the end of October, 1918; but, apart from that, the minimum certificate of education needed by a pre-war *Einjähriger** continued to be required for an officer's commission. Exceptions were only made for distinguished service in the face of the enemy – and even so, the number of exceptions made was negligible.[22] The fact that proposals for reforms came from conservative, not socialist, quarters, made no difference; in the Ministry of War they were ignored until the very last moment. And as for the Military Cabinet, it had never thought officers ought to have more education, and it now refused to contemplate their having any less.[23]

* One whose level of education entitled him to serve for a single year instead of the standard three.

12

Bavaria and Saxony

In Bavaria there was no Military Cabinet separate from the Ministry of War; and the nobility – especially the country element – was much less strongly represented in the Bavarian corps of officers than in the Prussian. Aside from local peculiarities, these were no doubt the main reasons why the question of Bavarian officers' education developed along different lines. From the end of the Thirty Years' War until well into the eighteenth century there was hardly any difference between Bavaria and Prussia. Each could show officers with a classical, humanist education and others who could not even read and write properly. In those days no particular technical knowledge was required of them, and such military attainments as they had were either the product of their own experience or had been learned from senior officers who had had some training in foreign armies. Educational level and social level were still very closely linked, for it was usually the second which determined how much, or how little, any given family devoted to the first. But even among the lesser nobility and the higher civil servants and *bourgeoisie* at the beginning of the eighteenth century not much was yet required in the way of education. In this respect, therefore, it did not greatly matter whether the corps of officers in the second half of the century consisted, as it did in Prussia, almost exclusively of noblemen or, as was the case in Bavaria to a large extent, of the sons of educated officials and bourgeois too, or indeed of the sons of artisans.

The Bavarian Cadet-Corps which was set up in 1756 on the Berlin model following General von Meindres' visit had not yet had any serious influence on the general level of officer-candidates and it was only in 1805 anyway that, as part of

Montgelas' overhaul of the Bavarian State, it was converted into an educational establishment solely for officers. The man who played the main part in this conversion was Colonel Freiherr von Werneck, and he formulated its basic principles as follows:[1] 'As early as possible the pupils must be trained in the things that belong to the status of officers but which in many respects run counter to natural tendencies to liberty, viz. military obedience, subordination, discipline, a sense of military honour, bravery, high-mindedness, endurance of hardship and the study of military sciences.' Do these words breathe the 'Prussian spirit'? Where does this ideal differ from it? Was it not, really, one aspect of the struggle to achieve a rational, specialised education for the profession of a modern officer – part of the general movement described at the beginning of this part? Werneck goes on to say that the whole curriculum must contribute 'to making the pupil into a military business-man'.

From being a teaching and training school, the Cadet-Corps was thus to be turned into a *Gesinnungsschule* – an orientation-school, one might say today, almost a leadership-school; and Werneck tried to secure for it a monopoly of all future Bavarian officers. Like Scharnhorst in Hanover, he blamed the existing inadequacy chiefly upon poverty, stupidity and bad upbringing.

Despite all reforms, however, the Cadets alone were not numerous enough to supply the need for officers – leaving wholly aside the nominations made necessary by the subsequent years of war. Some of the so-called 'regimental cadets' had to be accepted too, and given the opportunity of promotion. The technical knowledge that was, or could have been, required of them was very modest indeed and hardly went beyond what a fairly competent boy might acquire in a primary school. To provide them with further education, therefore, regimental schools with two classes were started[2] (just as in Prussia, where they were called War Schools or divisional schools); and on the 26th April 1827 King Lewis I decreed that the regimental cadets must pass a written examination twice a year (after 1840 only once a year) on the knowledge they had acquired. These *Junkerprüfungen*, or ensigns' examinations, were the first step in Bavaria towards an examination for officers. To be classed as 'middling' twice within two years was enough to remove a cadet's name from the promotion list. In respect of previous education and, even more, of up-bringing, age, former occupation and length of service, the pupils at these regimental schools were extremely varied, and such schools could not even aim at anything like an average level of education. None the less, these schools did at least assure a sort of minimum of general knowledge as well as military training. But they were a makeshift, all the same.

On the other hand, in these early years after the reform of the State, the higher military authorities in Bavaria too were well aware of the value and importance of technical education for officers; indeed a comparative study of the relevant Bavarian and Prussian archives almost gives the impression that the Bavarian outlook on these matters was more consistent – though perhaps at some cost to the strictly military aspect – than in Prussia. In the latter, despite the basis created by the Scharnhorst–Boyen reform of the army, the subject gave rise, though at a much later date, to violent, even bitter, controversies. In Bavaria this policy continued to develop without serious opposition or change. The one brief interruption was due to the revolution of 1848, which called forth a sizable increase in the standing army.[3] This sudden large demand for officers was more than could be met by those who were regularly qualified for promotion. In consequence a large number of university students were accepted, as well as several hundred non-commissioned officers of long service without being given any further technical training. This latter was the interruption mentioned above. To judge the importance of this step at the time it must be remembered that it was not taken at once but only in the autumn of the following year, 1849, when the National Assembly at Frankfort and with it the whole democratic movement had ended in abject failure. It was then described as being 'caused by the temporary circumstances of recent times, and thus exceptional in character'. At the same time the previous requirements as regards technical education were put into full force again. (On all these events in 1848–9, see Appendices 11 and 12).

Nevertheless if the view of education that was maintained caused one revolutionary advance to be rapidly corrected, it also led in fact to the re-introduction of another. This very duality of action, indeed, seems to me to prove that the new

King, Max II, approached the matter not in any politically reactionary frame of mind but with strict impartiality, and that the enlightened intellectualism which he plainly showed in matters affecting the University was perfectly serious. The chairman of the liquidation-commission (that was not its name, but that is what it was) for the affair of the non-commissioned officers and whose ideas prevailed therein, was Lieutenant-General Freiherr von Heideck; and the self-same man presided over the commission that was simultaneously appointed to overhaul the Bavarian Cadet-Corps, of which he was a graduate himself. The latter commission's report is entirely in favour of 'intelligence' as opposed to 'birth' and 'upbringing'. 'Intelligence is to be found in all ranks of society,' it states. 'The gift of leading troops is not the exclusive property of any caste (sic) nor is it hereditary.' In the programme of reforms that was now drawn up this kind of lapidary sentence was frequent.

As far as the Cadet-Corps was concerned, the wine had to suffer a good dose of water in the course of actual developments; but in general the demand for intelligence – though somewhat out of line with the social factor – remained basic to the questions of the supply and education of officers in Bavaria. It held things, so to speak, on a middle course between the two extremes – the total amalgamation (*Nivellierung*) of the corps of officers and non-commissioned officers, and the notion of an hereditary élite. On the higher plane of intellectual education the principles of democracy and aristocracy joined hands.

But the officers' actual level of technical education was still very uneven. In 1847 the Ministry of War[4] was driven to express the opinion that regimental cadets were 'as a rule merely boys who had run away from school, and there are very few in whom a real taste for soldiering and a dominant sense of honour can be looked for'. This was a view that von Werneck might have uttered at the beginning of the century, and the conditions that caused the Ministry to utter it now were still the same. In 1855, therefore, King Max II charged the Adjutant-General, Freiherr von der Tann, who was in his confidence, with drawing up a memorandum on educational arrangements in the Army. The result was a paper which described the theoretical and technical education of officers who had been through the regimental schools in very unflattering terms compared with the educational level of officers from the Cadet-Corps. The War

Minister, General von Manz, was then expected to make positive proposals for reforms; and to provide himself with a ground-work of incontrovertible facts, he instructed the Inspectors-General to report to him. They were, he told them, to send for the reports on the officers' morale and capabilities, and to pay the closest attention to their intellectual and technical attainments, taking account of all factors affecting their education, mental calibre, quality of service, moral standard of life, expenses, and social behaviour in relation to their status as officers. Note how the points to be reported on are once again arranged, with the intellectual points preceding the moral and social ones.

The result of this inquest was that the second class of the higher regimental schools was suppressed and that 'combined divisional schools' were created in 1858 for training officer-candidates in military science. The curriculum and the conditions for entry were modelled on the Prussian 'divisional schools' (the later 'War Schools') which, it was reported, had 'long since proved their value for the maximum diffusion of technical education among the officers in Prussia'. The Bavarian War Minister's high opinion of the Prussian system extended to the Prussian conditions for entry; and this suggests that he either under-estimated or was quite unaware of the strong opposition developing in Prussia at that very time against these conditions and, what is more, against 'the maximum diffusion of technical education'. In a very few years' time that opposition was to lead to open warfare. In Bavaria, however, the whole affair thereafter developed in peace and harmony.

Furthermore, the personal initiative of Max II greatly contributed to raising the intellectual level among his officers. In 1859, from Hohenschwangau, his castle in the mountains, he wrote these revealing words[6] to von Lüder, his Minister of War: 'You know already how earnestly I wish to see My Army provided with reliable, intelligent officers at every level and especially at the highest. The present war* has shown again and again how little an army is worth if courage is not allied to intelligence and superior education.' And the King went on to ask his Minister to give an opinion based on his 'experience of the matter, on what our officers mainly need

---

* The Franco-Austrian war of 1859 in Italy.

(apart from tactical ability) and what steps would serve the purpose of improving their education'. The King reposed great faith in Lüder's judgment on military matters and Lüder responded to this invitation with alacrity. As one 'excellent way of getting more intelligent officers', he recommended 'more strictness and discrimination in the choice of new appointments', while in the improvement and extension of the Army's existing educational system, for example, he also saw a means of 'bringing forward efficient, talented young men, with a large stock of knowledge, as candidates for commissions'.

It is vain to search the archives of the Ministry of War or the Military Cabinet in Prussia for any authoritative judgment that lays the same great stress upon 'intelligence' among officers as these Bavarian examples do. In Prussia it was 'upbringing in the home' that took first place in all the relevant stipulations. Nothing, I think, shows more strikingly the difference between the two systems as the relative emphasis they gave to these two factors in education, for they are fundamental. They extend far beyond their formal aspects and into the primal darkness of *a priori* mental attitudes, where they cannot further be pursued. In their essence all the same they have some unmistakable associations: the one is linked with the country gentry represented by the 'Junker' from east of the Elbe; and the other with the *bourgeoisie* of the towns. This is not to say, of course, that 'intelligence' was lacking in the country-bred nobility or that the educated city-dweller, whether ennobled or not, lacked 'upbringing at home': all I have in mind is the dominant scale of values in each case.

The fact remains that in Bavaria, whose officers in the nineteenth century were more freely recruited from the educated *bourgeoisie*, much greater weight was attached than in contemporary Prussia (where the tone was set much more by the needier country gentry) to the intellectual side of officers' education. In 1868, moreover, at a time when in Prussia the battle over the *Prima* certificate was still in progress, Bavaria stiffened her test by requiring a leaving-certificate (*Gymnasial-Absolutorium*) from a *Gymnasium* and thereby showed once again what her basic convictions on the subject were. The fact that Prussia took a different attitude seems to have been partly due to the individual character of the leading personalities and partly – perhaps mainly – to the very nature of Prussia herself, with which the whole system of her schools and their organisation was so intimately bound up. Finally, of course, there was the vast increase in the number of officers required.

Bavaria remained open-minded on the problem of officers' education even though the war of 1866 and, more still, the constitution of the new German Empire had made military institutions of Prussia the model which, on the whole, she accepted. The passage of years, nevertheless, did not leave Bavaria wholly unaffected by Prussian ideas about the officers' education. After stating in 1878 that a number of pupils in the War Schools were deficient in 'the upbringing appropriate to cultivated society' the Bavarian Ministry of War continued: 'The main task of a war school is to train officer-candidates in the military sciences; an appropriate level of social and military behaviour must also be aimed at'; but a really strict standard of 'all-round merit' seemed not yet 'opportune'. Twenty-five years later, on the other hand, section 1 of the War School Instructions, dated 1905, read as follows: 'In the War School, the education and practical training of ensigns for the profession of officer will be continued and the foundation will be laid for their education in military science preparatory to their passing-out examination.' To call this a shift of emphasis from education to upbringing would be too much; all the same, the tone has changed and it is the idea of upbringing that is underlined. From then onwards the same thing is perceptible in the relevant files, although it is mainly to be sought and found by reading between the lines.

Seen in relation to general developments, this 'change of key', as I would call it, is consistent with the change that came over Bavarian policy at that time. The liberal Max II was followed on the throne of the Wittelsbachs by Lewis II, a romantic with a mind in many ways like that of Frederick William IV of Prussia. Finally, under his successor, Leopold, the Prince Regent, the ship of state took a conservative course which, Catholic though it was, could sometimes look rather like the Protestant conservatism of Prussia. And so, given the attraction which Prussia and especially her victorious army exerted in Bismarck's German Empire, it is not surprising that as time went on her military example should have been copied to some extent in Bavaria, although the imitation was more one of outward form than of substance.

As for Saxony, the whole problem of officers' education was firmly and clearly stated in 1835 by Lieutenant-General von Cerrini, general-officer commanding the Saxon Army, two years before his Bavarian 'colleague', General von Baur, using language more circumspect and less precise, wrote down his own ideas. In that year, with a superb eye for essentials, for the needs of the times and also for the timeless elements in the profession of an officer, Cerrini sent the King of Saxony his views on 'The future Education of Officer-Candidates'.[8] What he had to say may be summarised as follows: 'The necessity of general education is undeniable: it must not, however, take precedence over purely military training, but must be subject to it. A middle course is easy to find. Generally speaking, the radical change in the nature of war has gradually made the purely military side of an officers' technical training very much more important. Under modern conditions of combat the most junior officer can affect the issue of a battle; his intelligence and knowledge are thus of high importance. The objection that education in military science will make officers conceited and averse from practical service deserves to be thoroughly refuted for it is sometimes accompanied by apparent proof. If any such result were common it would certainly not be a consequence of technical education but of the way in which that education had been given. Conceit is the faithful concomitant of superficial education (*Halbwisserey*), not of true understanding: the latter therefore should be cultivated and the former scotched. Knowledge alone is useless to the soldier in the field: so much must willingly be granted. What he needs, on the contrary, is skill (*das Können*). On the other hand, especially in time of peace, the shortest, if not the only, way to acquiring skill is knowledge.'

13

The Reichswehr
and the Third Reich

General Cerrini's views on the whole problem of officers' education anticipate almost word for word the view that General von Seeckt expressed nearly a century later when he set about laying down principles for the education of officers in the Reichswehr: the step from knowledge to skill might be very great but from ignorance it was even greater.[1] Seeckt was not so much the creator of the Reichswehr as its principal architect. Starting from this basic conviction, and in the teeth of attacks from every sort of direction, he succeeded in establishing strict and exceptionally stiff qualifications for acceptance as an officer. Thus he unrelentingly demanded proof of thorough intellectual preparation, namely a certificate acceptable for entrance to a university (*Reife für die Universität*). The objections that had formerly been made to this in Prussia had now completely disappeared. But in the first place the Versailles Treaty required an enormous number of officers to be discharged; and in the following years enough young men came forward to make a real selection possible. With the Reichswehr as small as it was, supply exceeded demand. As a matter of fact Seeckt would have preferred to simplify the entrance-examination in every way. He was a man who was usually accused of being unapproachable and imbued with the spirit of caste; but one intelligent and wholly modern additional requirement which he made as a matter of course was of a very different kind, viz: 'that every man who wishes to become an officer and has not belonged to the Cadet-Corps shall join a youth organisation or a sports-club approved by the School. He will thereby strengthen and harden his body, get to know the more modest levels of society and thus understand their manner of thought and feeling.'² The same line of thought underlay his brusque abolition of the long-standing right of 'one-year voluntary service'. This right used to be obtainable by six years of successful attendance at a secondary school or by schooling reckoned to be of equal value, and it had always played a great part in both the social and the military hierarchy of the Empire. This innovation was no doubt consistent with the young German democracy; but for Seeckt it was a logical outcome of his policy of uniformity (*Homogenität*), a policy which he sought to apply not only to the officers but also, in a modified form, to the other ranks and to the auxiliary 'Black Reichswehr' as well.

One step that was entirely in line with the spirit of the times, quite independently of the Versailles Treaty, was the dissolution of the Prussian Cadet-Corps – an institution that had been a stumbling-block to the early liberals of 1848 and was much more so to the world of thought and feeling inhabited by the more recent types of democrat and socialist. It was dissolved on the 10th March 1920 by decree of the then Prussian Minister of War, General Reinhardt. He himself was a Wurtemberger, a former Cadet, not devoid of sympathy with the south-German democratic outlook; but in his decree he paid tribute once again to what was good in that venerable Prussian institution: physical toughening, the inculcation of trust in God, fidelity to duty, comradeship, honour, obedience and abnegation.³ Fifteen years later this same institution was unexpectedly revived, *mutatis mutandis*, by the National-Socialists, in the so-called 'National-political Educational Institutions'. There were competent military judges among those who complained that these institutions suffered just as much as the former Cadet Schools from systematic bias and a lack of universally valid intellectual training.

In Seeckt's eyes this sort of thing anyway belonged to the past. On the contrary, he conducted an outspoken and successful campaign in favour of intellectualism, of a higher standard of culture not only in the general staff but throughout the corps of officers. On the 26th November 1919, even before he was Chief of the *Heeresleitung*, he caused his office to announce that an examination would be held in January 1920 with the object of getting 'a broad picture of the level of military science and general education' among the officers. His real object was to reintroduce the examination for the War Academy, which was of course forbidden, without attracting attention – least of all from the Inter-Allied Control Commission. But he also left no doubt that faced with the demands of modern war the fighting soldier could not afford to be unthinking. Character, will and personal powers of decision he took for granted. As early as 1920 guidance for the training of subordinate commanders was promulgated, and it once again required that attention should be given to matters of theory. In this context mention should also be made of the so-called 'Thursday lectures' which Seeckt also introduced during his time at the Reichswehr Ministry. They were especially meant for officers who had fought at the front but whose general education was all too often inadequate. Leading personalities discussed problems of politics and history at these lectures, as well as a wide range of current affairs.

Another device was the frequent secondment of officers for study at universities and especially at technical high schools; and in this it can be assumed that account was taken of what was so often being said in public, e.g. that the defeat of the Central Powers in 1918 was due among other things to the fact that their officers, being ignorant of industrial matters, were slower to adapt themselves to the technical requirements of war than was the case among the Western Powers. With the technical development of war, so the argument ran, technical skill would be decisive. Put in this simplified form the argument was unsound. Then, as now, Clausewitz' doctrine of 'moral qualities' (*moralische Grösse*) held good on both sides. East and West. But the Army leaders were well aware of the importance of economics and technology for national defence, and this awareness gradually spread. Seeckt himself, in an Order of the 11th October 1920, pointed in general terms to the 'need for knowledge and understanding of social and political life'. And his very first instructions on education, in December, 1919, had stipulated that 'officers must be trained to have an eye for broad issues'.

Though efforts in the right direction had been made shortly before the war, these were thoughts and measures that had been too much neglected in the old corps of officers. Seeckt's direction of the Reichswehr was otherwise marked by tradition and a 'restorationist' approach; but he was highly intelligent, his mind had been trained in the school of the General Staff, and travel in distant lands had widened his horizons, so that the conservative bent of his character never made him cling to the past for its own sake alone. Gessler, his Minister, had no very warm feeling for him; but even Gessler has recorded that Seeckt 'never wore ideological blinkers, so far as could be seen. It was more in his general disposition that his limitations lay, whereas his strength was an acute intelligence which went straight to the point of things and held fast to realities. He was the enemy of all heroics, all emotionalism and amateurishness in soldiering'.[6] Without being dogmatic, therefore, he was able to detect the earlier weaknesses in the intellectual field and in course of a few years he succeeded, by new and modern methods, in making possible and actually producing a general level of education, over and above the purely military kind, throughout the Reichswehr's corps of officers, that broadly speaking very few in earlier times had managed to achieve. It speaks much for the largeness of Gessler's mind that he, whose prime responsibility was to the Reichstag and public opinion, had no hesitation in approving and, where possible, promoting Seeckt's far-reaching, indeed epoch-making, policies. But it is, I make bold to say, a matter of historical fact that the chief credit is due to Seeckt and to his personal staff. The course he set, moreover, was followed in the main by his successors.

In Hermann Müller's second cabinet General Groener had to work with the Social-Democrats and, it is true, he lowered the standard of the entrance-examination for officers' courses to such an extent that candidates with only a primary-school education could pass them. This was in 1930; and in the same year he told the Reichstag that when it was a question of promoting non-commissioned officers more importance should be attached to character and personality than to education. These were the decisive factors. Such language (from the lips of a former Wurtemberg general too) sounds like an echo of the old Prussian Military Cabinet; nor was it at all inconsistent with Groener's disposition although in general, and even in Berlin, he remained a South German democrat. Marginal nuances of this kind make no real difference to the picture of the high educational level of the Reichswehr's officers that had been established.

Far away in East Prussia, beyond the Polish Corridor, it

was no easy matter to keep this level up, still less to raise it nearer to the ideal. General Wolf, commanding the 21st In- fantry Division at Elbing, expressed anxiety on the matter in a frank personal letter to Beck, then Chief of the General Staff. Writing from Marienburg on the 4th June 1935, he said:[7] ' ... The draft of new officers (they call them "buyers" here in East Prussia) and the bulk of the new arrivals need a great deal of "settling in", for all the good will they show. In addition we get many here who come from "small garri- sons". It rather worries me to think of next winter. How are we going to inspire these officers with an intelligent interest in their profession and keep them away from the local custom of sitting night after night in the café or the beer-hall – and without any outside stimulus at all to help us?' In other places nearer the centre of the Reich conditions were much more favourable. General Dietrich von Choltitz* who had spent most of his life in eastern Germany, has gone out of his way to stress[8] 'that at many stations, most of all perhaps at infantry- stations and at those which are far away from the big cities, intellectual life was extremely active. Outstanding men of science gave lectures in the Officers' Clubs (*Kasinos*), well- known musicians were invited, books and periodicals were available in abundance. For all this, however, the young lieutenant had to make large contributions from his truly miserable pay'. Whether this can be taken as typical is not to be established.

Hitherto, at least, we also lack evidence to show whether and, if so, to what extent the older and middle-aged generation of officers, who had preserved a certain style, a degree of culture and social polish from the 'twenties, still managed in the later 'thirties to impart these qualities to their juniors. Complaints were certainly made about 'personal shortcomings' (in the above-quoted letter to Beck) about 'dilution' of the corps of officers,[9] about the way in which solidarity of outlook was being lost through the ever-growing influx of young officers with National-Socialist ideas, behaviour and vocabulary – things that were often hard to reconcile with the old *esprit de corps* of the officers or with the ideals and the level of education built up by Seeckt. The principles involved in these developments will be examined later in the chapters on 'The State'. The type

* Military Governor of Paris in the second World War.

of thought on these matters that was ever more strongly preached from on high is well represented by some lapidary sentences from a Special Order issued by General Schörner, commanding the XIX Army Corps, on the 6th March 1942: 'There is no difference between military and intellectual leadership ... The soldier of today will achieve victory by his weapons and by his outlook (*Weltanschauung*).'[10] On the 1st February 1943, after the disaster at Stalingrad, Schörner repeated these ideas in a new and lengthy Special Order which the Supreme Command (OKW) soon afterwards distributed down to divisional level as an outstanding example of good military morale-building. But this was extravagant language, a bold – not to say, a foolhardy – challenge to History and Fate. It was an attack moreover, on the very roots both of education and of the concept of honour.

PART THREE

HONOUR

14

The Dual Nature of Honour

Honour can be either a condition or a reflex, subjective or objective: it can be purely personal or it can be collective. This is a fundamental division, and it has its parallel in the different meanings of the word 'honourable'. Personal honour is based on morality and it exists by reference to mankind at large – in other words, to human society. It does so, moreover, by virtue of the universal validity which is implicitly or explicitly claimed by the moral principles of civilised human beings. Collective honour, on the other hand, has only an indirect connection with the personal morals of the individual: it is based on the independent *ethos* of some group, and originates in the objective needs of that group or 'community'.

At bottom, it has been argued, all[1] honour is only group-honour or caste-honour, and the kind of honour we regard either as individual or as common to mankind is an abstract idea which only the blurring of class-limits has rendered possible. It is further alleged that the only realities are merely the specific concepts of honour held by particular groups – for example, the honour of a family, the honour of officers, commercial honour, or the code of honour observed by naughty little boys – and so forth. If an individual belongs to more than one group, so the argument runs, he has a share in several sorts of honour, each distinct from the rest. An individual may thus preserve intact his commercial honour as a business-man, or his scientific honour as a chemist, even though his family-honour be ruined – and vice versa. Burglars may observe the code of honour current among thieves but cast every other kind of honour to the winds. A woman may lose her sexual honour, yet remain in all other respects the most honourable person alive – and so on. Honour, we are told, derives its potency as a code for individual observance from the fact that the man who preserves his own preserves likewise the collective honour of his social group, which has placed a part of it in his hands.

This theory strikes me as trying to prove too much by its over-sophistication. Modern sociology treats human society as a whole – not merely as a concept but as a living organism endowed with its own laws of life and evolution. On this view there is no denying that human society is subject in its turn to the primal injunction of every sort of life – the law of self-preservation. Now where better should that law, that instinct, reveal itself than in the moral code we call common to all mankind – common, at least, to all the more highly developed countries – in a series of broad precepts such as the Ten Commandments? It is not for nothing that modern psychology, when distinguishing social from anti-social acts, ignores the individual's membership of a family, a caste, or of some other group. Yet, leaving this aside, there is, of course, a grain of truth in that other, hyper-sophisticated theory: it is that there are naturally some definite attitudes, patterns of behaviour and actions that specifically or principally belong to definite groups, each of which is plainly marked off from all others by some particular point of view. One such group is, in fact, the object of this study – the German corps of officers.

Psychic life can only concern a single human being and must have its existence within that human being alone. But man is a *politikon zoön,** and as such his soul contains two spheres of activity and impact: one personal and the other social. The social sphere, of course, is irradiated by his own personality but it is also coloured by his group. Moreover, the simpler, the more identifiable, the colour of the group, the greater its cohesive power. It does not matter, in this context, whether the group is psychic or physical in nature although the purely psychic groups, composed of those who profess the same faith, belong to the same order or hold the same doctrine, can show greater cohesion under some conditions than a physical group such as a family. It is the nature and the purpose of a social group that primarily determine its cohesive strength. The closer the collaboration, the more intimate the bonds between its members that are demanded by the ends it serves or aims at

* A 'political animal' (Aristotle, *Politics*).

serving, the more will the group as such (being to some extent an entity that transcends the individual) stimulate in each member the development of all the attitudes and other personal qualities that serve its end and thereby serve the *raison d'être* of the group itself.

From these general considerations, let us now turn our attention to the corps of officers. What was its ultimate purpose, its *raison d'être* and the key to its existence? The answer can lie only in a single word, one that is fraught with meaning, the word 'war'. Even in a genuinely defensive war – the only kind that civilised peoples and the organisations responsible to them will still accept – this fact still applies to the defenders, for such a war is still the *ultima ratio*. We can condemn war in principle, of course, on rational and non-rational grounds alike, and we can do everything possible to banish it from the face of the earth; but there is no denying or arguing away the fact that war is a primary phenomenon in the life of nations. This is a fact we must accept, irrespective of time if not of history. Only by accepting it can we reach solid, scientific, sociological ground from which to survey and understand – beyond all good and evil and in the light of its own objective purposes – the thing called the officers' 'unwritten code of honour'. To understand it, moreover, we must observe it in operation against the background of its history. We shall then see that if a code of honour held by a group of officers is to be adequate for its unchanging task, the essential character it bears must be that of a moral instrument for preparing and achieving victory in some hypothetical war – though the men concerned need hardly ever be aware of it.

When a soldier in action[2] sees his life in immediate danger – for example in hand-to-hand fighting, the most primitive form of combat – even the bravest will be seized by a moment of fear. Biologically speaking, fear is the natural reflex-sensation of the instinct of self-preservation which dwells within every man, heroes included. If victory is to be won, this elementary physical sensation must somehow be artificially suppressed – over-compensated by a contrary reflex of a psychic and moral kind, converted into action. The negative content of this counter-reflex is the feeling of shame. 'If', it says, 'you don't stand fast now but run away, the others will laugh at you and despise you.' I have analysed this whole process of thought and sensation at some length but in practice, of course, it is compressed into a mere fraction of a moment, and is so brief that the man concerned is hardly conscious of it or at any rate will hardly remember it. This will often be the case (and in a good unit regularly so) when things are going well and every man is borne along on a wave of general confidence. It can happen also when a man is carried away by the excitement of action, and the laws of life and death seem for the moment in suspense. But moments such as these are rare in the course of a war and they cannot be taken as setting the standard to be aimed at in making an individual soldier fit for battle. As a campaign drags on, with its ups and downs of fortune, the first enthusiasm drains away and the finest part of a man, his feeling for heroism, is bound to become dulled.

For war is mostly a weary, long drawn-out affair, and for that reason a soldier must be provided – unless Nature has done the job already – with a set of automatic inhibitions that will save him in the moment of danger (within him as well as outside him) from a collapse of his own morale. Discipline, of course, can hold him steady from without; but his one moral defence against internal weakness is the sense of honour.[3] To arouse this sense in the ordinary soldier, cultivate it and, above all, inspire it by his own example, is the officer's highest duty; and to fulfil that duty he must himself have a sense of honour that is well-developed, active and finely tuned. For this reason officers have always attached greater importance to the *point d'honneur** than any other class of men – often to the exclusion of almost everything else. But to give the officer's profession (*Stand*) the name of 'profession of honour'† (as was often done in Prussia in former days) was to use a phrase that was bound to be regarded, even in the nineteenth century, as an offensive piece of arrogance implying that less honour attached to other professions and to other men. That phrase, like the whole system of terminology derived from it, should really be taken as a grossly exaggerated way of stating a sociological fact – namely that officers, as a profession, laid emphasis on the special, systematic sense of honour they had worked out, with its focus in that specific experience called war. That sense made the individual continuously aware of his fellow, and it shifted his

---

* A 'point of honour' is any matter that may affect some person's honour.
† '*Der Stand der Ehre*'.

ideal centre of gravity from within him to his surroundings, from his private world to the world outside him. This re-casting of his personality is the essence of the soldier's sense of honour. It is essential to any other group's sense of honour, too, as we shall see. In the end it can also be perverted.

Now this absolute concept of military life and military honour made its first appearance on German soil in the form of chivalry, or *Rittertum* – as the embodiment of the heroic conception of life and of its value. Battle was its ethical ideal – the very opposite of the Christian doctrine of love, with its strict injunction against killing. Disgrace, to the knight, was worse than sin: loyalty he rated higher than love of his fellow men; and the aim of his endeavours was not heavenly grace but secular heroism. In other words his ethics were rooted in paganism far more than in Christianity. But we must not forget that western Europe's notions of the cosmos were dominated then by the augustinian ideal of the City of God – the ideal that inspired the mediaeval Empire no less than it inspired the Crusades and the practice of pilgrimage to Rome. So great was the influence of this ideal that even *Rittertum* discovered a place for itself under that world-wide banner. It put its powerful secular arm at the service of the Church, and its *ethos* of heroism joined in the battle for Christian doctrine. Siegfried became St George. This alliance between Christian faith and pagan heroics is the typical – but also the non-rational – element in European chivalry; and this was the essential feature (taken in its narrower application to status) of the deep mark that chivalry was to make in the course of succeeding centuries on the whole of western civilisation.

Duelling: Origins and Early Efforts at Suppression

The basic elements of the synthesis of military life and military honour were heterogeneous, however; and that fact must be kept in mind if we are to grasp the historical and sociological meaning of the struggle between the two that continues, though latent, even today. The classic example of it is the officer-corps of the old German Army, and for the special reason that as a corps it originated – or at any rate its dominant Prussian prototype did – in the *Rittertum*, the corporate body in which that symbiosis first assumed a form and in which that form may well have been more fully developed than anywhere else. The historical development of the duel and its child, the tribunal of honour, hence offers the clearest evidence of this dichotomy in ideals, which so often brought the parties concerned into a tragic state of conflict not only with one another but frequently within themselves.[1] This was a problem of great gravity for the corps of officers; and the lines along which, by and large, it developed from the beginning of the nineteenth century up to the first World War were that the elements of extroverted class-honour (*Standesehre*) were very gradually displaced – not without sharp setbacks – by the elements of introverted personal honour.

In itself, of course, duelling is a miniature war between two individuals. But it is not the external factor alone that creates a certain natural link between duelling and the profession of an officer. There is an internal factor too, and it is far more important. When an officer, be he guilty or innocent, is challenged to a duel, or if he feels his honour so impugned that the law can afford no satisfaction he can accept as adequate, his opponent faces him with the tacit question: 'Have you the physical courage to risk your life for your honour?' At this point the dilemma arises: what is honour? and what does my honour require? No problem could be more difficult. It involves a man's own life, and it involves the livelihood of his family. The attitude adopted towards it by the group as such, and by the individual, is seen to depend to a very high degree upon how far the development described in the previous paragraph had gone at that particular moment.

The commonest psychological origin of duelling in general is the desire for vengeance, the urge for ideal self-assertion – which is in fact one of man's profoundest instincts. History can therefore only concern itself with the question of what kinds of outlet this basic instinct has sought; and we in turn need only examine one modern form, the pure duel of honour. So far as research has shown hitherto,[2] this form appears to be specifically modern. Following the precedents of Spain and France, no doubt, it began to be a subject of discussion in Germany from the sixteenth century onwards; and then, with the mingling of peoples and cultures in the Thirty Years' War and the resulting confusion of minds and excitement of passions, the practice of duelling spread through almost every class of society. But as early as 1617 the Emperor Matthias issued an Edict against such 'wholly out-dated, unlawful, presumptuous, bloody, private justice and self-willed execution'; and to prevent it he decreed that in cases of insult the authorities should 'at once summon arbitrators and settle the matter or else try it *summarissimo processu** so that the injured party shall receive suitable satisfaction with all speed.'

But, of course, these affairs of honour were a kind of feud and as such they were a breach of the imperial and public peace. The Imperial Constitution of the time therefore bound the territorial princes to take measures against it, and thus from the seventeenth century onwards almost every German land had special anti-duelling laws which pronounced that duelling was contrary to the laws of God and man and contrary to reason too. To the legislator's way of thinking the duellist, of course, took the law into his own hands; and this was incompatible with concentrating all the State's authority and jurisdiction in the hands of the absolute monarch or of the lawful government, as the case might be. By Bismarck's day, however,

* 'By the most summary method'.

these three points, including the constitutional one, were less strongly held by the Government than by the parliament. We must therefore examine the duelling-laws in the new Empire and especially in Prussia in order to see what effect they had in practice. In particular we must see what attitude the corps of officers took towards this attempt of the sovereign authority to override their special corporate doctrine on the subject.

The first Prussian law against duelling is dated the 17th September 1652.[3] The particular complaint the Great Elector made in it was that 'there are not only many young men who have been discharged in consequence of the Peace* that was lately concluded by the Grace of God, but also numerous other lawless persons, who seek out occasion to brawl and fight wherever they go, so that in many places men can scarcely meet together without its leading to brawls and fisticuffs; or else such disorder, noise and tumult breaks out that many a feeble old man or respectable woman takes fright, the landlord of the house is interfered with and the whole company outraged and upset'. The Elector then forbade 'on pain of corporal and capital punishment ... all wilful assaults, all uproar, fighting, brawling, scuffling and all challenging, "duella", and sending of cards'† and he promises his protection to 'every man who shall seek his rights *ordinaria juris via.*'‡ The interesting thing about this Edict is not just the prohibition in itself but the fact that duelling is still classed with common brawling and is treated as such by the law. Likewise, in the Elector's 'Laws and Articles of War' (*Kriegsrecht und Artikulsbrieff*) the heading to Section IX lumps mutiny and duelling together.

For all the plainness of this Edict, duelling had already provoked a division of opinion among jurists. There were in fact 'sundry eminent (*fürnehme*) jurists who assert that this sort of duel (i.e. on matters of honour) may well be allowed, namely when a person of quality is grossly insulted and ... can find no judge, or else the other party cannot or will not come into court, he may reasonably provoke him to a duel; but if, on the other hand, the injured party can find a judge he is bound to plead his cause in the ordinary court. Other leading *Juris Consulti Practici*§ however ... assert that duels of every kind, no

---

* The Peace of Westphalia (1648), which ended the Thirty Years' War.
† A method of issuing a challenge subsequent to the quarrel.
‡ 'By ordinary process of law.'   § Practising jurisconsults.

matter what their origin, are forbidden. ...'.[4] In this summary by a seventeenth-century civilian commentator it is worth noting that the jurists who consider a duel involving a person of quality to be admissible (since they plainly concede him the *jus de non appellando**) are themselves described as *fürnehm*, i.e. they were probably persons of quality, in other words noblemen, themselves. This is an argument of such wide application that it doubtless lacked any foundation in law. Yet this makes it all the more significant as a purported extension to the whole nobility of a privilege attaching only to its very highest ranks.

Once begun, of course, that process went further and was extended to cover the social class that stood closest socially and professionally to the lesser nobility, namely the judiciary and the higher civil servants. We saw in Part I indeed how the sword of law and justice as well as the sword of war could lead to ennoblement, or at least to a status of privilege equal to that of the lesser nobility. It looks as though the idea was taking shape in this period of incipient absolutism that he who wears a sword – be he officer, official or, by later extension, a student – is free in matters of minor jurisdiction to be his own judge and executioner. Such an idea points to the germ of the later notion of 'capacity to give satisfaction' (*Satisfaktionsfähigkeit*) that was to form a powerful bond between all the strata of society concerned, and strengthen their sense of belonging to a single privileged class, the *Herrenstand*.† How great a part this sociological fact played, especially in Bavaria, in prescribing the social origins of the corps of officers, we saw in the First Part. Nevertheless from the point of view of the constitution and of general policy this particular expression of class-solidarity was anachronistic, a pretension quite incompatible with the structure of an absolute State. All existing institutions had been destroyed by the Thirty Years' War, and for the Elector of Brandenburg-Prussia it was a prime necessity to make the rule of law felt by his subjects in the loosely linked provinces that now belonged to him and to establish a monolithic State there. The whole aim of the Hohenzollerns' domestic policy at that time was to break the indiscipline of their vassals, construct a centralised State by riding roughshod over the selfish obstinacy

---

* Immunity from summons to Court.
† 'The nobility and gentry' together.

of their subjects and as far as possible make the centrifugal forces centripetal.

In the preface, therefore, to his exhaustive Edict of the 6th August 1688 on duelling, the Elector Frederick II (afterwards first King of Prussia) took pains – and a very deep breath – to point out that 'Almighty God (had) reserved to his Majesty alone the right of vengeance and (had) ordained that there should be princes and powers upon earth to use the sword aright,* punish wickedness and avenge injustice including the presumptuous practice of the "duella" which leads not only to contempt of the laws of God but to detraction from the authority of the courts established by the sovereign Prince of the land, and brings down the just wrath of God upon land and people alike ... puts in imminent danger the souls, so dearly bought by Christ, of duellers, bullies and men of violence, and moreover causes irreparable loss to good and honest folk, inasmuch as such excesses, challenges, duels and fighting have oftentimes wantonly destroyed and robbed Us of those who have given good and sound service and might do so in future again to Us, to the Holy Roman Empire and to Our lands, by their bravery, experience and virtues both in civil and military capacities and in others as well, including young men studying at academies in the finest flower of their youth, to the great prejudice of the common weal and to the sorrow of their parents and relatives ... ; so that wanton fighting now threatens to become an almost common thing in Our lands and notably at Our Court and in Our Army ...' And therefore, he goes on, he has resolved to amplify his predecessors' prohibition of duelling, and to 'promulgate this Edict against all suspicious and unlawful *rencontres* (*sic*), duels, fights and breaches of the peace and to establish a perpetual constitution and regulations that shall put an end to such irresponsible evils, entirely abolish the "duella", secure to every man his honourable name, his well-earned repute and peace of mind and assure the sternest punishment without exception for all criminals and other delinquents who wantonly act in breach of this Our perpetual and beneficial constitution.' The prohibition is then pronounced: and the penalties follow in sixteen long Articles of model clarity, with an exhaustive list of cases. The mere issuance and acceptance of a challenge is punishable with dismissal from the

---

* An echo of the mediaeval state-doctrine of the two swords.

service or, where inapplicable, with the confiscation of three years' income, as well as with imprisonment. If the duel actually takes place, then, even if no blood was shed, the participants are to be sentenced to death and the same penalty applies if the duel takes place beyond the frontier; seconds and bearers of cards are liable to the same penalties as the principals. 'Those who denounce them are, however, to be rewarded by Us out of the goods and chattels of the guilty criminals and contemners of this Edict.' It is a promise that rather grates upon our modern ears and may not show a very delicate psychological sense; but it testifies to its author's solid sense of the law and it can only be explained by assuming the legislator was in something like despair when faced with this obstinate practice of duelling.

In the light of developments in the nineteenth century, great importance attaches to the attempt which this Edict makes (over and above the Elector's general promise of protection – rather too general indeed to be of practical value) to lay down really effective rules for giving suitable satisfaction, without a duel, to the party aggrieved by word and deed. To this end Article 11 lays it down 'that all insults, whether consisting of looks and gestures, foul words or abuse, shall, *pro ratione delicti et circumstantiarum** be punished by (ordering an) oral or written withdrawal (in which case the offending party, according to circumstances, very often has to contradict himself *in pleno judicio*)† by suspension from office (*Entsetzung der Charge*), by a monetary fine, imprisonment or banishment or, in the case of a nobleman, by forfeiting the right to wear a sword (*Verbietung des Degens*) ...'. 'But in so far as acts and gross insults to the person, *in specie*,‡ such as blows or a box on the ears or throwing things at a person's head, and so forth, are concerned,' then three or four years in prison are prescribed: 'but previously, and before the guilty party is taken to prison, he must, in the presence of some persons of quality, declare himself ready to receive similar blows and insults from the party he has injured, and declare either orally or in writing that he acted brutally and without reflection, requesting the injured party to forgive him and to forget the affair.' It was further enjoined upon all pastors that once a year, at the end of their Sunday

---

* 'According to their degree of gravity and to the circumstances'.
† 'In full court'.   ‡ 'To show what is meant'.

sermon, they should remind their congregation of this Edict; and in the last Article it was even forbidden 'to all and sundry, of whatever Estate or dignity they be, that no man shall presume to submit to Us an intercession or petition in such matters, whatever opportunity may offer such as, for example, a happy delivery of Our queen, the birth or marriage of one of Our princes or princesses, or the like, upon pain of Our indignation and displeasure.'

This Edict of 1688 gives us an insight into aspects of social life that historians are rather apt to neglect but which are a real help towards understanding intellectual and social developments in the period after the Thirty Years' War, when the world of modern states was taking shape. The Edict also gives us a glimpse of the world of constitutional and ethical ideas in which the Elector of Prussia lived; and for our purposes it could hardly be more striking. The valuable thing for us is that we here encounter the first thoroughly worked-out scheme for the complete suppression of duelling. To some extent the scheme is logical. It first states a principle deeply rooted in ethics, constitutional theory and plain opportunism; it not only proceeds by threatening duelling with penalties, but goes further and makes definite regulations for providing the injured party, through the ordinary process of law, with a satisfaction designed to meet his legitimate desire, untainted by revenge, and to punish the insult as such.

The thoroughness with which the Elector tackled the subject and tried, at least, to provide for all eventualities, accounts for the fact that his Edict was largely reproduced in the one which his successor issued in 1713. All the same, Frederick William I reduced the scope of the death-penalty; for duels without fatal results he prescribed only imprisonment for eight to ten years, and where a death was caused he made the penalty depend on the 'lethality' of the wound.

Frederick the Great confirmed the Edict of 1713, but added nothing of his own to it. His personal views on the subject were set forth in the dissertation he wrote in 1749 on *Les raisons d'établir ou d'abroger les lois** after he had read the celebrated *Esprit des Lois* in which Montesquieu called honour the principle of monarchy. In his own discussion of duelling, Frederick applied the following forthright expressions to it: *préjugés;*

* 'The grounds on which laws should be made or repealed'.

122

fausses opinions; point d'honneur mal entendu; cette mode barbare; ce point d'honneur mal placé, qui a coûté la vie à tant d'honnêtes gens, de la part desquelles la patrie pouvait s'attendre aux plus grands services.*
For all his objection of principle, he still considered duelling could be forgiven in the case of a soldier who would otherwise be dismissed and would be unable to take service anywhere else in Europe. In other words, Frederick the Great himself had to give way in practice when faced with the class-mentality, class-customs and class-despotism of his corps of officers. He rightly saw that this was an awkward problem that could only be resolved by public opinion, and he considered the idea of calling a general congress of all the princes of Europe, who were to agree to ostracise any man who, in contempt of prohibitions, should engage in duelling and, indeed, to refuse all asylum to this class of murderer and punish his presumptuousness with all severity. This idea does at least show the good intentions that moved its enlightened author; but it also shows the immense difficulty that faced even an absolute monarch of Frederick's calibre when it came to a head-on collision with his officers' deep-rooted class-conviction and prejudice – devoted as they were to him in every other way.

* Preconceptions; wrong views; confused ideas about points of honour; this barbarous fashion; this mistaken point of honour that has cost the lives of so many good fellows whom their country might have expected to render it the greatest service.'

16

Prussia:
Tribunals of Honour Introduced

Towards the end of Frederick the Great's life a different approach to the problem was made – this time without the other Powers. In 1785 there was published the draft of a general Prussian civil code, drawn up by the Grand Chancellor von Carmer with the assistance of Suarez. It was contemplated in this draft that cases of alleged insult, and the punishment to be applied, should be judged by a tribunal of honour composed of the parties' social equals (*Standesgenossen*): and heavy penalties were to be inflicted on those who engaged in a duel in contempt of the tribunal's decision, or in circumvention of it. In the case of a death, for example, the survivor was to suffer the penalty for murder. It is significant that the idea of a tribunal of honour composed of the parties' social equals, (in other words a class-institution) should have made its first appearance in the draft of a general civil code for Prussia. But the real purpose of this legal reform, which Frederick II had long desired, was to bring back more elements of Germanic jurisprudence into the prevailing system of Roman Law.

In any case the Prussian corps of officers, being aristocratic and exclusive by tradition, already embodied to a high degree the typically Germanic concept of a fellowship, and since the days of the *Landsknechte* it had given this concept a new meaning. In the seventeenth century the colonel of a regiment stood only in a private contractual relationship to the territorial sovereign. In consequence a regiment had a high degree of corporate autonomy and had, in particular, its own tribunal. The corps of officers thus held itself entitled to expel any undesirable member; and from the end of the seventeenth century onwards, at latest, an officer was classed as undesirable if he refused to fight a duel. Even after the territorial sovereigns had abolished this autonomy in principle, subsuming it in their own, large sections of it were retained by the corps of officers in every regiment. None the less it was clearly the sovereign's idea to take over this particular structural element and fit it into the new system of law and order he had to create. Experience going back at least a century had shown, after all, that the private group-jurisdiction enjoyed by the officers could lead to head-on collisions with the public law of the land. In the main, no doubt, the motives underlying this policy were of a purely practical, empiric sort; but they did derive from a definite principle of jurisprudence as well. The first tentative result of this policy was the section on tribunals of honour in this draft of a general civil code for Prussia.

That section, however, remained a draft. Frederick the Great, who had certainly encouraged it, died in the following year and its opponents then gained the upper hand. It is hard to say whether their outlook should be called conservative or anarchistic, for Prussian conservatism, faced with the advance of the new and absolutist concept of the State, had assumed a markedly revolutionary tone. Cavan, the Auditor-General, was certainly voicing no more than the general view of officers when he officially observed 'that the proposed tribunal of honour would be hard to reconcile with the self-respect of an officer; and even though the said self-respect may rest to some extent on custom in moral matters, those customs have, as is well-known, had such a beneficial influence on His Majesty's army that their essential spirit and character are held in the very highest esteem.' These observations by the senior military jurist led the Army Council to oppose the draft recommended by the highest civil authority. The Cabinet Order of the 21st March 1791 accordingly stated that while the total suppression of duelling remained the goal, the introduction of tribunals of honour into the Army would be a most unfortunate step since it would lead to many undesirable effects upon the Army's morale (*Esprit*). It was therefore laid down that as regards duels between officers etc., present and future legislation applicable to the Army was to be observed. This meant that Section 77 of the preamble to the General Civil Code ('On the contrary, no man has the right to seek justice by his own might') applied equally to officers, and likewise Section 79: 'Disputes are to be decided, and penalties are to be determined, only by the courts to which the law subjects every inhabitant of the State.'

This may perhaps have looked like paying attention to the formal position of the law, or rather to the legal fiction; but it did nothing whatever to improve matters in practice – nothing to bridge the gulf that had now opened between the law of the land and the code of honour held by one group of its inhabitants. For the first time indeed[1] the King himself had now accepted this gulf as an unalterable fact, for he had indirectly given permission for officers to seek their own redress in matters of honour and at the same time he had frankly avowed that the newly codified civil law was inadequate. Such an avowal may be praised for its candour, but it is impossible to call it wise. At all events the legislator had spontaneously declared himself bankrupt and had thereby diminished the State's authority. How could a lawyer reconcile this with the Civil Code, Part II, Chapter 9, Section I? That Section reads: 'On the nobility, as the first Estate in the land, lies, by its own choice, the chief responsibility for defending the State and of upholding its outward dignity and internal constitution.'

Yet the idea of letting quarrels and other occasions for duelling among officers be settled by tribunals of honour lived on. If at first it found no favour in public debate, it was very far from dead. Indeed, it determined the lines on which the matter developed over the following hundred years, and the influence of each successive Hohenzollern gave it a different nuance and a different practical effect – sometimes emphasising the corporative aspect, sometimes the authoritarian. The reform, if one can call it such, began in Prussia in the very same month and year as the 'liberalisation' of the recruitment of officers which we examined in Part I. The link between these two innovations and the catastrophic battle of Jena is plain enough; but their appearance in the very same month makes it plainer still.

It was, in fact, on the 3rd August 1808 that Frederick William III issued an important Order on the punishment of officers. He laid it down therein that an officer who led a loose life or was insubordinate or otherwise showed baseness of mind, was to be declared unfit for promotion. It was a majority of his brother-officers who were to decide the matter. Every officer was entitled to have recourse to this 'tribunal of honour' and, if he felt he had been wrongly accused, he had the right to appeal for an enquiry by another regiment. The words that follow constitute a sort of manifesto: 'If the officers of a given regiment keep a careful watch on one another, if the senior officers warn their juniors in good time that the scrupulous execution of an order must be made a point of honour, if the good name of the whole corps of officers is made the responsibility of each one of them and if each is zealous, as he should be, to see that nothing shall detract from it, the commanding officer will rarely be faced with the unpleasant necessity of disciplining officers whose birth and education should ensure that they need no such incentive to do their duty.' Matters involving insult are still not assigned to tribunals of honour; but this was done (it will be observed) in respect of all other shortcomings in matters of duty and private behaviour that could detract from the essential dignity and good name of the officers as a group, or of any one of them as a member of it. If, moreover, appeal was made to the influence that brother-officers can have on one another (though it was frankly described as 'keeping watch') there was only a short step left to making 'affairs of honour' in the stricter sense subject to the same procedure and, ultimately, entrusting them to tribunals of honour to decide. It was twenty years, none the less, before that step was taken.[2]

Frederick William II's declaration of the 21st March 1791 had been too candid; and the calamitous results it produced are shown by the decision of a court-martial in 1809, which uttered the even franker opinion that in matters of duelling it was not the law of the land but 'honour' alone that applied. To this Frederick William III reacted sharply. As regards the law on duelling, he said he must retain the right to judge whether, and if so to what extent, to take account of 'prejudice' and let his clemency override the law. Social conditions within the corps of officers in the years that followed the Napoleonic wars were such that they gave rise to duels between officers almost every month,[3] and it is obvious that the officers were counting firmly on the fact that not all duels would become known, but also on the sovereign's clemency. In 1820 that clemency was actually extended to a case in which the corps of officers had not expected it, namely when the King, contrary to a court-martial's finding, retained in service a lieutenant who, without giving any offence, had been seriously manhandled, but had not challenged his man to a duel. The general-officer commanding at Königsberg, where the incident had taken place, and who now had to execute the King's command, was von Borstell. So far from sending in his resignation, he sent in a memorandum in which he made a number of proposals for the avoidance of duelling by means of tribunals of honour (see Appendix 13). Borstell was an upright and most efficient officer, impulsive and always ready with ideas and opinions that were often excellent[4] and the King, as we know, had already shown sympathy with the ideas in question.

Borstell's proposals, therefore, fell on fruitful ground, and they led to the promulgation of the Cabinet Order of the 19th September 1821. The question of tribunals of honour for officers was thereby taken to a stage which, if not its final one, was a turning point; for it introduced a principle that was essentially new. Tribunals of honour were now to be entrusted with cases in which an officer's behaviour not merely disgraced the officer himself but also reflected upon the honour of his whole class (*Stand*). Henceforth, therefore, the tribunal of honour was to be the competent organ by which the corps of officers as such, i.e. as a community of social equals (*Standesgenossen*), could of its own motion intervene in order to bring about a peaceful, judicial settlement of affairs of honour among its members. It could not yet choose to do nothing (that came later): it was obliged to act. Subject to royal approval it could even prescribe discharge from the service and loss of officer's status (*Stand*).[5] By the grant of these far-reaching powers it was intended to convert the class-spirit and class-interest of the corps of officers into a prime and active agent for the suppression of duelling.

Leaving aside their natural emphasis on the legal supremacy of the State or the sovereign, the old anti-duelling Edicts issued by the Great Elector, by Frederick III and Frederick William I had relied only on the postulates of personal Christian morality. In the present Order, however, Frederick William III tried another approach. For the first time he recognised in principle the existence of the officers' class-consciousness (*Standesgeist*) and their collective idea of honour; and he did so in the hope of reinforcing these with elements of personal morality and a sense of personal honour. In 1823, for example, in connection with a duel between a certain Count von Blücher and an actor named Stich, he bluntly declared: 'I will not tolerate officers seeking to maintain the dignity of their Estate by shedding blood in reprisal for insults they have themselves provoked. On the contrary I expect them to rely for this purpose upon decent, proper behaviour and to avoid acts that are condemned by the laws of morality and honour alike.'

These same notes of 'morality' and 'true sense of honour', and the same appeal (dating back indeed to 1808) for mutual surveillance and correction, ring out once again in the Cabinet Order of the 13th June 1828 (see Appendix 14). There, indeed, the Order of the 15th February 1821 is directly cited on the question of subjecting duelling matters to the procedure of tribunals of honour; and in that context the new Order adds: 'A corps of officers which puts an end to duelling by the appropriate handling of these affairs of honour will acquire a claim to My favour and will prove that the true spirit of honour dwells in it.' As a matter of fact this fresh expression of the royal Will merely consolidated the earlier Orders of 1808, 1821 and 1823; but it did proclaim more clearly than before that the tribunals of honour were competent in duelling-questions too, 'in order to counteract a pernicious habit'.

The Order also contained the following passage: 'Any man who, by deliberate offence against decent manners or by wanton insult, gives provocation to a duel shall be treated without consideration'; and no more than nine months were to pass before a miscarriage of justice in a court-martial led the King to expand his views – spurred on, too, by the aged Zieten's memorandum on duelling (see Appendix 15). 'If', said the King in the Cabinet Order of the 29th March, 1829, 'there are insults that by current standards are so injurious to personal honour that they can only be wiped out by blood, it follows that he who is capable of recklessly uttering insults of such baseness has thereby made himself unfit to belong any further to an Estate of whose sacred character he has lost all sense. For the man he has gratuitously offended, his forfeiture of this Estate also constitutes the fullest satisfaction, and I wish to see it universally recognised as such.' By this decision officers called upon to judge future cases of the kind were to be guided.[6]

Compared with the previous year, it will be seen, much clearer and sharper language was used this time to expound the view that it is less the offended party than the offender who is unfit for further membership of the officer-class. In other words an attempt was now being made to shift the centre of gravity of honour from without to within, and replace the collective concept of honour by the criteria of personal honour and personal morality. But the next two Kings abandoned this principle by degrees, and the ideas held by Frederick William III, as outlined above, only came back into favour under the Emperor William II.

In 1837, the Royal Commission[7] for Revising Military Law produced draft regulations on tribunals of honour and on the penalties to be imposed on officers in connection with challenges and duels. Once again the Commission judged that one of its main tasks was to do all it could to help expose the strange inconsistency of the views commonly held on the honour of officers – for example, that while an attack upon one's honour was a calamity incompatible with life, the gravity and recklessness of bringing this calamity upon a social equal was not by any means outrageous. Such was, at bottom, undoubtedly the King's own view: yet the Commission promptly departed from the underlying principle in the very preamble to its draft, for it is there asserted that the man whose honour had been impugned did not care in the least whether the offender was punished by the civil law: what he cared about – and cared more than life itself – was to give his slanderer and the world at large (sc., especially his social equals) a better account of himself. From this consideration, the Commission said, the custom of duelling derived its 'astonishing power and vitality'. A sense of honour, it pointed out, must by its very nature be impervious to the influence of authority, if not opposed to it. Faced, therefore, by the undiminished power of the old class-spirit, the Commission thereby capitulated once again. It had made a feeble gesture in the direction of reforming the tribunals' functions and of turning officers' ideas of honour a point or two towards personal morality, but it had quickly reverted to the old idea of honour – of honour as a thing directed outwards, i.e. to the opinion of others. Compared with the King's unambiguous convictions on the subject of personal honour, and with his own wishes, it was thoroughly retrograde.

From this Commission, therefore, no real reform was to be looked for. Its draft was recast in the light of the views expressed by the Ministries of War and Justice, but the redraft found no favour with Frederick William IV who had succeeded in the meantime to the throne. What he objected to is now unknown.[8] Nor is it known what the new King's attitude was to the questions of honour and of duelling themselves. We can deduce it none the less from the papers left by his new Minister of War, the elderly Boyen, who had his full confidence at the time. Frederick William IV, after all, would surely not have sent for Boyen and given him his ideas about the reform of the tribunals of honour had they not seen eye to eye on the matter. In any case it was no small omen that Boyen in his younger days – in 1815, to be exact – had once challenged Wilhelm von Humboldt to a pistol-duel, which happily ended without bloodshed, on account of some misunderstanding. Early in the 'thirties, too, he had written that duels seemed unavoidable in any State whose laws aimed at giving every citizen the maximum freedom that could possibly be reconciled with the ends for which the State existed; moreover, he had written, the idea that honour should be rated higher than life itself contributed to developing the national character and was indispensable to the State. This, however, was merely the old refrain of *laisser faire, laisser aller*,* sung in another key and with different sets and costumes.

In Boyen himself this liberal cast of mind was strangely mingled with romantic, conservative notions of a class-based society. To the Commission of 1841[9] he put the view that the honour of officers was not the only matter at issue: it was also a question of sowing the seeds of new and comprehensive legislation on class- (*Standes-*) and bourgeois honour, for a crying need of the times would be met if this could be worked out. His hope was that the tribunals of honour for officers would soon be matched in every district by others for owners of feudal estates and their compeers, others for senior officials of provincial governments, and ultimately others for every other class and organisation that might apply and could prove its need. Indeed he went further and (although he does not seem to have raised the matter officially before the Commissions of 1841 and 1842) he wanted tribunals of honour even for noncommissioned officers and for private soldiers.[10] Grandiose ideas of this sort based on general notions of class were undoubtedly very close to those held by the romantic who occupied the throne; but the only part of this general blue-print for the State and society that was ever carried out was the part relating

* 'Leave things to take their course'.

to the corps of officers. This was the sector of society which, as we have seen already, was busy cultivating the spirit of fellowship on psychological and sociological grounds; in Prussia, moreover, it was keen to assume the mantle of *Rittertum* or mediaeval chivalry. 'Thus', so Boyen's biographer has summed the matter up, 'the whole of his labour only served to strengthen a single bastion of the military and aristocratic spirit of class'; thereby, however, served to consolidate and legalise the peculiar situation of the corps of officers within the growing body of the constitutional State, where it made itself manifest in so many different ways.

17

Prussia: Further Efforts,
Councils of Honour and Reaction

Boyen set to work, basing himself on the directive given him by Frederick William IV. Single-handed and in manuscript he drafted an entire new set of regulations on tribunals of honour (54 clauses long) as well as a set of 36 clauses 'on the treatment of affairs of honour, on the maximum prevention of duels among officers of the Prussian Army, and on the penalties to be attached thereto.' Broadly speaking, both of Boyen's drafts received the hearty approval of the general-officers commanding.[1] The only one who could not approve the proposal in the first draft, section 1, viz. that the tribunals of honour should be made the guardians of the honour of officers, was Prince William – he who was afterwards Regent, King and Emperor. The Prince thereby rejected the basic thesis of the whole draft itself[2] without succeeding, however, in killing it in its final form. On points of detail the final draft took constant account of the comments received; but in substance it was the work of Boyen alone. Formally it was divided into two separate parts: 'Regulations for Tribunals of Honour' and 'Regulations for the Procedure of Tribunals of Honour when investigating Disputes and Insults occurring between Officers, and for the Punishment of Duelling among Officers'. Both sets of Regulations were issued on the 20th July 1843.

In the very first Section of the first Regulation its divergence of principle from the views expressed by Frederick William III makes a typical appearance. In the past, the key phrase had been 'baseness of mind (*niedere Denkungsart*)', but this had now become behaviour 'incompatible with a proper sense of honour or with conditions governing the status (*Stand*) of an officer'. In the past, that is to say, the chief criterion had clearly been one of personal ethics, but now it was one of purely collective ethics and consequently a-moral; in the past the standard had been pure morality, but now it was mere custom.³ The second Regulation seemed, at least generally, to adhere to the position taken in the Orders of the 13th June and 29th March 1829, but it was still not calculated to put a stop to serious duels arising from causes of real gravity.

On the other hand the tribunals of honour were given exclusive jurisdiction over all quarrels and alleged affronts occurring among officers save for those that might directly arise from acts committed in the course of duty. It also made it compulsory to appeal to a council of honour (*Ehrenrat*)* in any case that could lead to a duel. If the council of honour was satisfied that a case did not lend itself to peaceful settlement or if the parties refused to be reconciled, a tribunal of honour was to draw up a formal acknowledgment that a conflict existed, and no further concession (*Genugtuung*) was to be required of the parties to it. One feature, however, robbed these provisions of much of their effect: for the parties could bring the proceedings of the tribunal of honour to a standstill by declaring their belief that they could not hold themselves bound by the tribunal's verdict 'owing to the peculiar conditions that govern the status of officers' (*wegen der eigentümlichen Verhältnisse des Offizierstandes*). An additional feature was a procedure for disciplinary action in the case of duels that had taken place – though not if pistols had been used – and for utilising the council of honour as an umpire (*Kampfgericht*), the latter being a device that in effect placed a criminal act under the direct supervision of the State and thereby to some extent made it legal.

This went too far even for the Prince of Prussia, much as he wanted favour shown to the corporate spirit of the officers as a body. He was opposed, of course, to the basic principle of this whole reform on account of the role assigned to these tribunals of honour, for it was still partly moralistic in character. That being so, he was all the quicker to notice the contradictory, not to say grotesque, idea of making them umpires. In vain he had tried to get this item removed from the draft; and with a scepti-

* Henceforth the reader should bear in mind that there were two distinct bodies, viz. the *tribunals* of honour, with executive functions, and the *council* of honour, with mediatory functions only.

cism akin to Frederick William III's – compounded of determination and despair – he had urged that the penalties should first be brought into line with current opinion and then most rigidly enforced. This would at any rate have replaced a major half-measure by a minor one.

But a measure that suffered from such inconsistencies could not possibly make the impact that was needed if old, traditional prejudice or, rather, deep-rooted instincts, were to be overcome. A large proportion of the officers regarded the very appeal to a council of honour as a disguised way of refusing a challenge – i.e. as being dishonourable in itself; and the idea enjoyed little favour in consequence. On the 16th May 1844, therefore, barely a year after issuing these Regulations, the King found himself driven to reinforce the penalties for duelling in deliberate circumvention of a council of honour by adding that of dismissal. Whether this punishment was ever applied there is no means of telling. At all events, even this still seemed 'much too mild'[4] to the King, who was evidently not content with his own work – most of which, of course, was Boyen's; and that work suffered indeed from its own irreconcilable inconsistencies, let alone its conflict with the civil law.

This being the case, it was really no wonder that the Defence Committee of the National Assembly at Frankfort should have proposed that the tribunals of honour should be totally suppressed. They were held in contempt not only by a large part of the corps of officers, as mentioned above, but by political opinion as well. 'For it is not the cases which fall within the competence of the tribunals of honour that have done them such harm in the eyes of the public, but the political trials, the tribunals' investigation of political opinions and tendencies, of conversations held in public places, and of gossip.'[5] It is not known what reception this proposal had, or what it might have had if the National Assembly had been able to complete its work. Nevertheless it is worth noting in this context that on the 8 March 1849 a declaration was submitted to the Assembly in which 119 deputies said they did not wish to take part in the by-elections of the Defence Committee 'because all the members of this Committee already represent the views of one side only (sc. the right) of the House, and that the candidates proposed are all of this same political colour'. The malcontents could not therefore 'persuade themselves that a Committee which is really supposed to create something new should consist almost entirely of technicians of the orthodox school'.[6] This piece of sarcasm throws much light not only on the situation at Frankfort but on the situation that obtained for several decades afterwards.

One of the high priests of military orthodoxy was Edwin von Manteuffel; and in a letter[7] he wrote in 1871 to Ranke, the historian, he expressed its creed in the following terms: 'In the Army I was brought up in, it simply was not done to ask a judge to get you satisfaction. You got it for yourself. You drew your pistol, and if the other man refused to fight, you had him soundly beaten by your own fellows.' Refreshing as it is to read such a robust account of the matter, one thing shows very plainly. The narrow path towards a new conception of honour so laboriously cleared by Frederick William III was quickly overgrown under his eldest son;* and under his second son† the trail entirely disappeared from sight.

Prince William, as we have seen, entirely disapproved his elder brother's Regulations on tribunals of honour. It was obvious, therefore, that he would want to set them aside once he succeeded to the throne. Ten triumphal years intervened, in which he reformed the Army, overcame domestic troubles and vanquished France; but then he tackled the matter. In 1872 he set up a large Commission[8] of general-officers commanding. But they reported that 'by and large, the Regulations as amended', had proved their worth, that the councils of honour ought to be retained, even in their role as umpires. Again and again they insisted that if its work was not to be in vain, a council of honour must complete its mediation very quickly – within twenty-four hours or so. Circumvention should be punished with severity and the penalty should extend to dismissal. Only four generals were against the obligation of recourse to a tribunal of honour[9] on the ground that this would make personal decisions harder, and so forth; the tribunal, they contended, should not be called on to settle the dispute but only to establish the extent to which a quarrel had harmed the honour of the profession, or was capable of doing so. There was some support for this point of view; but of course it meant treating the ground for the quarrel and its settlement as minor matters while making 'correct' behaviour the major issue.

* Frederick William IV.   † William, Regent, King and Emperor.

Of this school it was Lieutenant-General von Pape who took the most extreme position – which was also the most logical. His main contention was that the best judge and guardian of his own honour was the officer himself: every officer therefore must be able to justify his own behaviour without any interference by third parties. Tribunals of honour should take no action at all before a duel, and all penalties for duelling should be abolished save for duels arising out of the discharge of a military duty. In other words, duelling was to be a lawful activity for officers but not for anyone else. Broadly speaking, this was the position the Royal Commission finally adopted. It recommended total withdrawal of the second Regulation of the 20th July 1843, and this was approved by the King. The one remaining obligation was that in the case of a private quarrel involving honour the council of honour was to be seized, at the latest, when a challenge to a duel had been issued or received; and the council's task was limited to making a report at once and if possible (*n.b.* not compulsorily) before the duel took place and then, if agreeable to the general custom of officers (*Standessitte*), it was to attempt a reconciliation; and in the last resort it was to try to see that the terms upon which the duel was to be fought were not inappropriate to the gravity of the case. Finally, if a duel actually took place, the president or a member of the council was to be present as a witness and see that customary form (*Standessitte*) was observed. As for tribunals of honour, their action in connection with duelling was limited to cases in which one party to the quarrel had offended against the honour of the profession (*Standesehre*) either in the manner of its provocation or in the subsequent stages. Simultaneously a secret Order made disciplinary action in the case of particular duels (except of pistol-duels) a matter of discretion again.

The Regulation of the 2nd May 1874 (see Appendix 16) thus leaves it to the discretion of the council of honour to declare whether or not custom among officers permits a reconciliation (i.e. a peaceful settlement of the quarrel) to be sought. As a result, duels were actually brought about in many cases in which the parties might have thought it reasonable and better to be reconciled. And there is another passage to be noted, viz. 'An officer who is capable of wantonly impugning the honour of a brother-officer is no more to be tolerated in the Army than one who is incapable of defending his own.' In other words:

if you force a brother-officer to fight a duel by insulting him, you will be dismissed; and he will be dismissed himself if he fails to challenge you.

The Regulation is prefaced, of course, by some admirably terse and elevating words on the concept of honour – the 'finest jewel' of the 'fellowship' of officers – on doing one's duty to the last letter, on true comradeship and *esprit de corps*, on respect for other classes (*Stände*) and professions, on the 'well-tried tradition of chivalry in the corps of officers' and on the latter's 'higher obligations'. These are noble exhortations and sound theoretical points; but they cannot disguise the fact that in the body of the Regulations, at the very points where the text should have spelled out their practical application to disputes, the lack of serious guidance is obvious. Taking their stand on higher considerations that were not only military but statesmanlike as well, Frederick William IV and Boyen had tried to build up a new and more personal concept of honour among officers. It was to be nobler and purer than the collective extrovert concept formerly held, and they sought to give it an ethical standard of a more refined, introverted and subjective sort. Now, however, the spirit of class was raised to the status of an absolute, sovereign principle of conduct. Under the Regulation of 1843 the role of the councils of honour, though impracticable in many details, had been wisely conceived; but now, instead of being adapted and extended, their role was reduced to zero and the former system was scrapped. Its inconsistencies were, of course, removed; but in their place a far more serious conflict was created – between the new constitution of the tribunals of honour and the civil law of the modern legal and constitutional State.

18

Germany: The Gradual Victory of Personal over Collective Honour

At the beginning of this Part an attempt was made to give an historical analysis and a sociological account of two radically different concepts of justice, two divergent general outlooks on life (*Weltanschauungen*), two distinct conceptions of it. These two now stood face to face, each of them legally sanctioned. In the year of grace 1874, a pure 'class' system, appropriate to a feudal concept of the State and of justice, was totally out-of-date; and the fact that on the contrary it was given open, unvarnished legal sanction is chiefly, no doubt, to be explained by the great preponderance which the military element in the State derived from the impressive triumphs of Prussian-German arms in the three wars of the previous decade.

But the dazzling prestige of the sword was destined gradually to fade with the memories of those heady years of victory; little by little the forces at work on public life shifted and formed a new pattern of relationships – one of greater sobriety and balance. The struggle of ideas, of viewpoints and of parties seeking power and influence could not ignore the special position the corps of officers occupied in the State – a position whose most striking feature was the jurisdiction of its tribunals of honour. To what extent the struggle of ideas was taking place within the corps of officers itself is a matter which probably can never be accurately determined now. There is no doubt, however, that the ferment there was real. Evidence can be found in the many complaints from officers themselves that reached the parliamentary deputies, especially those of the Left, and which thus became topics of widespread political discussion. The whole question was kept alive, too, by the publicity which the press gave to the more serious kind of duel.

The subject first appeared in the Reichstag in 1885, on a petition from a Berlin tailor named Röhr, who demanded, on grounds of history and reason, that duelling should be abolished or curtailed by applying the severest penalties to those who broke the law, and by punishing the members of tribunals of honour. The matter was first raised on the floor of the House by a deputy of the Centre (Catholic) Party named Reichensperger. At first, on the 26th November 1886, he did so in general terms; but later, from about 1900, with particular reference to military personnel. In the thirty years that remained before the first World War, the arguments used in Parliament, both for and against duelling, especially duelling between officers, never varied. Conservatives and National-Liberals defended duelling because it called for courage; Progressives and Social-Democrats opposed it on constitutional and social grounds, while the Centre Party denounced it as unchristian. Even Count Westarp, a Conservative, once declared[1] 'that he and his friends were firmly convinced that duelling was an offence against the laws of God and man alike' – but he went on at once to warn the House against attacking the tenets of the officer-corps.

The right wing and the Government itself argued more on traditional and emotional lines, and held fast to the ideas that inspired the regulation of 1874; but their speeches were too often made with an astonishing lack of psychological insight, and in consequence they made little impact upon a public that largely disagreed. All the stronger, therefore, was the permanent pressure which the majority-parties were able to exert on the military chiefs in this connection. The reports of the relevant proceedings in the Reichstag during these years are very revealing; and the first impression they make on anyone who reads them is that the two sides were mostly talking at cross-purposes (since they started from different premises and consequently used the same words to mean very different things); but the constant revelations of what went on in the Army and the ceaseless clamour of the majority-parties were probably the reasons why governing circles themselves were keen to limit duelling as far as they possibly could and – which is more important – were trying to transform the concept of honour too.[2]

In particular, there occurred a whole series of sensational duels, some of which consisted of no more than the process known as 'shooting yourself well again'* but involved some rather dubious personalities. These affairs caused the Emperor William II to take the matter up. He reverted to the Report of the Commission of 1837 and the Regulations on tribunals of honour issued by Frederick William III and thus to the fundamental principles of the Prussian anti-duelling Edict of 1688. People generally came round again to the conviction that the essential questions were whether, and if so to what extent, the act that had given offence still left its author *satisfaktionsfähig* – in other words whether a man found guilty of acts grave enough to be classified as criminal, acts that showed no sense of honour, could still be of a quality to give any kind of satisfaction to another man of the same social class. It was agreed that this quality could survive if the man's own moral integrity was intact, and that collective honour and custom were conditioned by factors of individual morality. This basic proposition then led the Emperor back, of course, to the question how the councils of honour, in dealing with these matters, could be given a more decisive role than they had performed during the past fifty years and especially since the Regulation of 1874. The solution, he considered, must be sought along the lines of proposing a compromise by means of a formula binding upon both parties, provided the facts of the case admitted such a thing. By this device, duelling itself would be repressed and, moreover, the councils of honour would incur the obligation – and this was a new thought – of standing up for the honour of one who had been guiltlessly insulted, while forcing the offending party either to withdraw or, if he refused, to go before a tribunal of honour. It was a personal direction given in this sense by William II which underlay the publication, on the 1st January 1897, of 'Rules Supplementary to the Introductory Order to the Regulation of the 2nd May 1874 on Officers' Tribunals of Honour in the Prussian Army'.

The thing that was entirely new and psychologically important in these 'Supplementary Rules' was that the council of honour was to 'intervene' on behalf of the officer who had been insulted without provocation. This could really only mean that, subject to circumstance, it could also influence the opinion of his brother-officers in the direction of holding the offended man in undiminished honour and respect, and that the council of

* *'Sich-gesund-schiessen.'*

honour should throw the authority derived from its impartiality into his scale. In actual practice of course, this was a psychological experiment, the success of which largely depended on the temper of the corps of officers at the moment but indirectly also on the commanding officer's qualities of leadership. On the other hand it carried the risk that in fact the council of honour's role would only turn out to be advisory, with the decision in all serious cases being taken by higher authority, and in the last instance by the Emperor himself – as indeed the text of the 'Supplementary Rules' envisaged. That, indeed, is how things actually developed up to the first World War;[3] and to all appearance it was precisely this factor of authority in the officers' outlook on duelling that duly steered the purely collective 'feudal' spirit, little by little, into the path of personal 'bourgeois' morality. There is little doubt that the majority of officers welcomed it; they were glad to see reason getting the upper hand in this delicate business so as to free them from this pagan worship of honour – from what Theodor Fontane once called this 'idolatry'[4].

Influence and education in the direction of reform were now sought by yet another method. It is surely no coincidence that the catechism published in the 'nineties by Dr Richter, the Prussian chaplain to the forces, which was used by candidates for confirmation in all Prussian cadet-schools and military establishments, branded duelling as immoral, as a wrongful defence of a man's own honour – a defence of something that nothing can take from him but his own sin and shame. Courage, it says, can never be proved by transgressing the Law of God but by obeying it despite the power of prejudice. One may well believe religious teaching in terms as novel as these was not without effect upon its hearers in their subsequent careers.

This, indeed, partially accounts for the fact that von Heeringen, the Prussian Minister of War (who on other occasions had stoutly defended the principle of duelling) told the Reichstag in 1913 that[5] 'all who have been in the Army for a certain length of time will bear me out when I say that the views of the corps of officers on the need for duelling have gradually undergone a considerable change since 1897. Many affairs of honour are nowadays settled peacefully; but before 1897 it was unthinkable to settle them except by fighting.' In the previous year, too, von Heeringen had already pointed out that in seventy-one proposals for reconciliations that had come before the Emperor since 1897 (i.e. almost five cases a year) it had been ruled that the proposal must be upheld.

Lieutenant-Colonel Fischer, the War Ministry's liaison-officer with the Duel-Committee of the Reichstag, was therefore right when, in a memorandum written for his chief a few months before the first World War, he said: 'Such convictions (e.g. on the need for duels) do not last for ever. They change with the times and they have now entirely vanished. Even the German attitude to duelling has undergone a change.' In the last few years before 1914 the officers' tribunals of honour were more and more taking the view that an officer who, maybe when drunk, uttered an insult or seduced another man's wife, was no longer *satisfaktionsfähig*. He must simply disappear from the corps of officers and no duel was therefore necessary. Here indeed is personal morality at work as a ferment in the ethos of the class! Or was it 'the spirit of true chivalry and true Christian morality' as Falkenhayn, when Minister of War, told the Reichstag on the 13th March 1914, speaking of the efforts the Army had been making 'for a long time past' to put an end to duelling? What the phrase 'for a long time past' really meant in this connection is what I have tried to show in the present Part.

But for all their gaps the statistics of duels between officers in the nineteenth century are interesting and valuable enough to justify my giving them here. Figures were drawn up in Prussia for the first time in 1842, when Boyen was drafting his bill on tribunals of honour. They show[6] that in the years 1817 to 1829 (i.e. in the last thirteen years before Frederick William III's crucial Regulations) a total of thirty-nine serious cases, an average of three a year, led to punishment: twenty-four of these duels had only ended in wounds, fifteen in deaths.[7] But whether the prison-sentence was one or twenty years, pardon followed in a few months – in eighteen months at most. One man, who had been sentenced to severe corporal punishment (*Strafe des Beils*) was pardoned after six months; a 'lifer' after a year, another 'lifer' after six years. Four cases of detention were accompanied by dismissal but it is likely – though not clear from the files – that the latter was revoked by a pardon after four to twelve months.

Between 1832 and 1842, when the strict Regulations of 1829

were in force, the Auditor-General's annual Reports on Military Justice show that twenty-nine cases of duelling an average of 2·6 per annum, attracted punishment – slightly fewer than before. Of these, five had led to deaths.

The first fourteen years' working of the Regulation of 1843 (i.e. 1843 to 1856) brought the yearly average up to 4·6 and that average can hardly have altered much in the years 1856 to 1861 (no figures are available), for the percentage remained pretty constant for the last twelve years (1862 to 1873) of this Regulation's existence. In absolute figures it rose to eight; but we must remember that the great reorganisation of 1860–61 had almost doubled the standing Army's strength.

On the other hand, between 1874, the year of William I's Regulation, and 1885 (the only period for which adequate figures are available) the annual percentage of serving officers punished for duelling rose from eight to twelve.

Once William II's Order of 1897 had helped re-establish the basic principle held by Frederick William III, the annual figure for serving officers dropped at once to about four, and from the turn of the century until the first World War it sank even lower.

The figure for officers of the Reserve, however, remained pretty constant. Though it had notably risen after 1876 it was almost always a good deal lower than the figure for serving officers. The Order of 1897 hardly reduced it and the effect was that from then onwards it appeared larger by comparison with the figure for serving officers. This fact gave rise to frequent debate in the Reichstag, and it was also noticed and discussed in the Ministry of War and the Military Cabinet. The likeliest explanation of it is that officers of the Reserve did not spend their lives, as the Regulars did, in a closed circle of brother-officers and social equals; they therefore lacked the security that such a life would naturally afford; but here and there, one may suspect, there was a certain readiness to take offence – a reservist's tendency vis-à-vis a Regular to think that in courage, at least, he must prove himself the Regular's equal.

These statistics, I must repeat, only cover the more serious cases of duelling; but even so, taken as a whole, they go to show that in the last hundred years before the first World War the Regulations on duelling and tribunals of honour issued by the sovereigns of Prussia succeeded in exerting a greater influence on officers' notions of honour than William I, for one, thought possible.

On the question of duelling among officers in other German armies, as well as in Austria, France and England, up to about the middle of the nineteenth century, the Bavarian Ministry of War produced a memorandum in 1858 (see Appendix 17). There is no need, however, to discuss the matter in detail, since Article 61 of the German Imperial Constitution of 1871 applied Prussian rules and regulations (including those on duelling and tribunals of honour) to the non-Prussian contingents in the German Army – including the Bavarian.

There was nevertheless one point on which further developments, peculiar to Bavaria, diverged considerably from those in Prussia and elsewhere in Germany: for on the 1st January 1870 the proceedings of all military tribunals in Bavaria were made accessible to the public.[8] In later years it was often asserted in the Reichstag and the press that a reduction in duelling among officers had been brought about in the Bavarian, compared with other contingents, by holding these proceedings in public. The *Kölnische Volkszeitung* was a newspaper that took a special interest in the subject; and an article it published on the 18th August 1901 caused the Prussian Ministry of War to ask its Bavarian counterpart for statistics on duelling for the previous four years (1897–1900). On the basis of the Bavarians' reply, the Prussians then calculated the respective numbers of serving officers in the two armies in order to arrive at the correct ratio for the year 1900, viz. 7:1. In respect of duelling among Regular officers, however, the proportion was 18:1, and it was 10:1 even if the figures for officers of the Reserve were included.[9]

If, before we leave the point, we compare these Bavarian figures with earlier ones, say from the 'forties and 'fifties when the duelling rate was much higher among Bavarian officers than among Prussian, we are justified in deducing that the almost total disappearance of duelling in Bavaria (the reports for 1897 to 1900 show only one case a year for Regulars and reserve-officers together) was indeed due to the military tribunals being accessible to the public. One is tempted, indeed, to recall Kant's dictum that all measures which require publicity must for that very reason serve the happiness of the people, since that is the supreme end of all policy. At all events this

Bavarian 'publicity' seems to furnish one more argument for
the view that the ethical code of the corps of officers was not so
impervious to influence when faced with the personal will of a
leader – though for 'not' one should perhaps have put 'no
longer'.

19

The Reichswehr: The Third Reich

Independent, arbitrary, self-regulating – the collective ethical code on duelling was losing its force; and one of the visible signs was a gradual but decisive change in the views that officers commonly held on the necessity of a personal duel and on what an officer's honour required of him in general. The change led in the direction of admitting the factor of personal morals to a greater degree and also, in most cases, of shifting the responsibility for decisions from the individual to the Emperor. It seemed at the time to be an epoch-making success for the cause of order, a victory for the Christian spirit over tyranny. For an historical analogy one must go far back into the Middle Ages, to the triumph of the chivalrous St George of legend over the pagan ideal of Siegfried. And yet – who, at the dawn of the twentieth century, could have foreseen what came to pass less than fifty years later? But in 1935 Hitler decided to give a Field-Marshal's bâton to an elderly German general named Erich Ludendorff; and when the Führer's secret adversary, General Beck, then Chief of the General Staff, sought to deliver the bâton, Ludendorff justified his refusal with the bitter words: 'Tyranny can remove the landmarks called honour and freedom' – words that were to be all too abundantly fulfilled.[1]

This was the Ludendorff who had served at Hindenburg's side in the first World War from 1916 until he himself proposed an armistice – almost, that is, to its bitter end. That war with its almost unendurable sacrifices, with its desperate assertion of national will in the face of the enemy's often superior strength – that war itself was partly to blame for the fact that absolute obedience was now more important than absolute honour. Yet the first symptoms of that change in the inmost nature of the corps of officers must have taken place at least half a century earlier. In 1860, the year in which Prince Frederick Charles wrote his essay (Appendix 1), the great expansion of the Prussian army had caused its corps of officers to spread far beyond its ancient social limits and to take in many unfamiliar elements. It was not without reason, then, that the Prince, using almost the language of entreaty, set the concept of an officer's honour even higher than that of obedience. Frederick the Great, however, with the experience of a long war to guide him, would certainly not have tolerated such a notion; and likewise in the first World War the basic law of self-preservation engaged the whole military machine, and the struggle for life and death raised the principle of absolute obedience at every level of command, even the highest, to the power of a supreme and absolute value. This was an existential experience of war: it was nourished and intensified by the opposite experience of the 1918 revolution; and it was on these two experiences that the Reichswehr officers from the old Army based the whole of their thought and feeling as soldiers. There was never any question but that first Reinhardt, then Seeckt and after him Groener, would lose no single opportunity of asserting this principle of absolute obedience. In a circular of the 4th November 1923, to all commanding officers, Seeckt indeed went so far as to say: 'A soldier's honour does not lie in knowing better or having better ideas, but in obeying.' His choice of words owed something, of course, to the political situation at the time, and we shall be discussing that in the next Book, for the main subject there will be the theoretical relationship between obedience and the nature of the State, with special reference to National-Socialism.

At all events it was of fundamental importance that Seeckt's circular plainly declared obedience to be an integral part of a soldier's honour, and of an officer's most of all. General Reinhardt, predecessor of Seeckt as Chief of the *Heeresleitung*, was well qualified to judge where Seeckt's main achievements in that office lay; and he was not far wrong when, in after years, he wrote, of Seeckt's 'success in restoring discipline in the Army'.[2] Not the least of the items that stood to Seeckt's credit was his persistent effort to establish an adequate substitute for the existence and jursidiction of the tribunals of honour, which the Republic had abolished as symbols of class-privilege. At the end of January 1924 he issued his first 'Rules for the Maintenance of honourable Conduct (*Ehrenhaftigkeit*) in the Army' and they frankly re-stated 'the principles that were in force in the old Army'. In the old days, indeed, there had been a special Adjutant-General for this subject. His appointment clothed him with exceptional authority that enabled him (if he was no servile courtier but a man of independent, upright character) to see that the standard of honour in the Army was maintained. Within the Reichswehr Ministry the new Personnel Sections of the military and naval staffs enjoyed a much less independent status; in consequence they had far less power and could also make their authority far less felt. The same applied to the Ministerial Office (*Ministeramt*) that was later created under the Reichswehr Minister and which, when Schleicher was its chief, was much more concerned with the political side of things.[3]

Many of Seeckt's decisions too were taken, of course, with politics in mind; Dr Otto Gessler, indeed, whose judgment was anything but suspect, credited him with political sense and even with political ambition. To that political sense we can perhaps ascribe his scheme for introducing appropriate regulations for the defence of the honour of non-commissioned officers, though he had not time enough while in office to work out his idea in detail. On the other hand there was one point on which he made a political miscalculation – on the question of duelling, which admittedly had become a very delicate one under the Weimar Republic. For years Seeckt had very skilfully managed to keep it from becoming a matter of public discussion. In early October, 1926, just before he had to lay down his office (on account of the irregular acceptance of a Hohenzollern prince as a short-term volunteer in the Reichswehr), he had drafted a new regulation on tribunals of honour. The main thing about it was that it would have allowed duelling again. Dr Gessler, however, as the Minister responsible to the Reichstag, had to point out that the section on duelling was politically impossible. When Seeckt resisted, Gessler overrode him. No counter-signature was needed, and he struck the section out.[4]

It was not until much later, when National-Socialism had deeply penetrated the corps of officers and gained more and more adherents even in the highest ranks, that a decision of the Supreme Army Command, dated the 22nd February 1937, made duelling fully legal again. Entitled 'Challenges to Duels, and the subsequent Procedure', it called duelling the ultimate means of defending the honour of officers, both individual and collective. A year later, on the 1st March 1938, it was repeated in a circular by the Commander-in-Chief, von Brauchitsch, entitled 'Defence of Honour'. That circular extends to forty-seven printed pages, and an extract is given in Appendix 18. Every officer was to have a copy and its main purpose was to lay down 'the manner in which the concept of honour is to be maintained in the corps of officers'. Point 2 of the first and general part goes so far as to state the following as a fundamental: 'The right and duty of a superior officer to watch over the honour of the corps of officers and of its members does not relieve the individual of the right and duty to watch over his own. . . . By every available means he must defend, or restore, the purity of his own and his family's honour; and the married officer is therefore responsible for any action or negligence of his wife that raises a question of honour.' This last was an absolute novelty which seems almost to foreshadow the 'breeding' argument that was later to be such a popular – and barbarous – feature of the National-Socialist 'order'. The whole tone of the document, with its mixture of new and old, is marked throughout by the National-Socialist mentality and language. But there is still an echo of older thoughts and notions to be heard – for example when the 'Estate' of officers and other ranks is mentioned – and this despite the fact that otherwise any reference to class was usually countered with the notion of 'community' (*Volksgemeinschaft*) and that Hitler himself derided his generals as 'old-fashioned knights with fly-blown ideas of honour'.[5]

This document is important as a piece of evidence for the history both of the armed forces and of the times; but the preamble contains one sentence that deserves special mention, for it is taken straight from the older world of ideas, from the old order of things. Even in the official text it has a paragraph to itself. It reads as follows: 'True honour is unthinkable without respect for the honour of others!' Thus it was written, and signed at a ceremonial announcement, by the Commander-in-Chief of the Army. He was the highest officer in the service of a Führer and a State in whose name large numbers of German citizens, and even officers who wore its uniform – the names of Schleicher and Fritsch will be reminders enough – had seen their honour vilely dragged in the mud. Coming from a man like Brauchitsch, who was Schleicher's immediate successor, such chivalrous words, pillaged from an earlier age, should have rung in every ear like blasphemy. But even Schleicher's murder had not aroused the corps of officers to action or to protest, and every subsequent outrage upon decency and honour, though secretly deplored perhaps, had been accepted. As a body, the officers had no use for Theodor Fontane's wise and subtle words: 'Times change; there are times for waiting and obeying, and there are times when action is the first of duties'. . . . 'It is contemptible to tell a people its highest virtue is dumb obedience. The highest things we know are freedom and love.'[6] The act of General Yorck at Tauroggen,* the outcome of long waiting and a hard struggle with himself, in which the issue was decided by the higher interest of his country and his King[7] – that act was now a myth and had no relevance. And a man of Hubertusburg-Marwitz' stamp 'who chose disgrace where obedience brought no honour' (as his gravestone records) – he, too, had long since been forgotten. 'Times change' indeed, and now the corps of officers laid its better self to sleep, with every twinge of conscience disregarded, repeating to itself that minor things like these are bound to happen in any revolution, that underlings were anyway to blame for most of them, and that after all the Führer had achieved incredible things at home and abroad, and had done so much for the Wehrmacht in particular that this sort of irregularity should really be put to his credit. Lastly there was the fact that, for an officer, physical resistance would have been branded as 'mutiny'; and what is more, for officers of the old school and officers who had served in the World War, it would have been a downright crime – a crime that had literally meant 'a red rag' to them ever since November, 1918.

Nowadays, it is true, senior officers of that time have uttered the harsh verdict that the Army forfeited its honour when it failed to react against the crime of Schleicher's murder.[8] But

* In December, 1811, when Prussia was France's unwilling ally against Russia, Yorck disregarded the Convention of Tauroggen which had 'neutralised' his Corps, declared war on France and thereby forced Prussia over to the allied side.

we should not forget, nor should we wish to, that in respect of the *point d'honneur* the German corps of officers had lived for many a year, if not from time immemorial, under the immanent law of tragedy – of tragedy in the classic sense of Euripides and Sophocles and, in their inheritance, of Schiller. It was a disastrous stroke of fate that the concept of honour held by the Prussian corps of officers, and almost all others in Germany, was so intimately linked with the sovereigns and their service. In that exclusive form it had been cherished for century after century. Then all the monarchies collapsed, and suddenly this traditional faith showed another, wholly unexpected side – a terrifying one. Robbed of its royal pole-star, the officers' code of honour lost its fixed and ancient bearings and drifted into a dangerous state, an alarming state of instability. Then, little by little, it seemed to be finding a new fixed star, a new focal point in *authority*: first in the authority of Seeckt and then, as regards the Navy, in Behncke's and finally, once he was President, in Hindenburg's.

But then came further, shattering blows. The man whom Hindenburg had lately derided as a 'Bohemian corporal' he himself appointed Chancellor. Soon afterwards, Hindenburg died; Hitler succeeded him as head of the Reich and of its Armed Forces; and, worse still, Blomberg's *coup de théâtre* obliged the entire corps of officers to take an immediate oath of loyalty to the Führer's person. The cumulative effect of all this was to make it not merely possible but absolutely certain that, given the monarchical tradition still alive in the corps of officers, a treacherous image, the myth of a bogus monarchy, would arise there.

The new, dynamic personality at the head of the people, the Reich and the Wehrmacht had very little trouble in obtaining absolute obedience to anything he wanted. In the past the oath of loyalty had been sworn to the monarch: now it had been sworn to the person of the Führer, and very soon it was made to override everything else – including, by implication, the concept of honour, individual and collective alike. There is no other possible explanation of the fact that General Jodl (whom I only name as being typical of countless senior officers and generals) could, on the 13th May 1945, say such a thing as this: 'As a soldier I obeyed and I believed my honour required me to maintain the obedience I had sworn. . . . I have spent these five years working in silence although I often entirely disagreed and thought the orders I got were absurd and impossible. I have known since the spring of 1942 that we could not win the war. . . .'[9] The code of honour had been a useful tool for training officers in their duties – permanent and transient alike – under the old, authentic monarchy; but under that bogus monarchy, the dictatorship, it was condemned to a sort of bogus existence. Therein lay, in this particular connection, the tragedy of the senior officers. The tragedy was rooted in the same soil as themselves; but it had only been laid bare by a concatenation of exceptionally adverse circumstances – the war, its aftermath, and two revolutions as well.

Every revolution is to some extent a break in continuity. Despite the Civil War, a land like the United States has hitherto been spared such a break and so it has been possible for West Point, its admirable Military College, to remain true to a tradition of loyalty that goes back to its foundation in 1802 – a tradition which itself is founded on a scheme drawn up in 1783 by General Friedrich Wilhelm von Steuben, once an officer under Frederick the Great and later an American citizen. The German visitor cannot fail to be struck at every turn by the almost Prussian character of West Point's conception of honour as expressed in the College's motto: 'Duty, Honour, Country'. At the other pole, and in very different conditions than in Germany, is the break with tradition which the Bolshevik Revolution of 1917 inflicted on the army of the Czar. We know too little about the way in which the Red Army dealt with the consequent problem.

As for our neighbour France, whose history has had so many 'points of contact' with our own, we may recall that in 1959 her oldest and most respected general, Maxime Weygand, delivered a lecture before the officers of the Ecole Supérieure de Guerre in which, drawing on his long practical and technical experience, he gave an insight into the thought and feeling of French officers.[10] On the matter that concerns us here, the following extract appears significant and typical: *C'est qu'il importe de bien distinguer de l'honneur ce qui peut n'être qu'un 'point d'honneur', dans lequel se glisse toujours quelque chose de personnel, tel que l'attachement à un homme, une réputation à soutenir. . . . C'est pourquoi il me paraît capital qu'un officier se conserve libre de tout serment prêté à une personnalité . . . Car il peut en naître un 'point d'honneur' qui entrerait en lutte avec l'honneur tout court, obscurcirait le sentiment du devoir absolu, et troublerait la conscience.* That is precisely the tragic situation, the tragic temptation, to which the National-Socialist leaders and the German corps of officers alike succumbed. Yet that predicament involved still deeper principles of State, as the following Part will show.

* 'The question here is to distinguish clearly between honour and what may be no more than a *point d'honneur*, for in the latter there is always some personal element at work, such as attachment to a man, or a reputation to be maintained.... For this reason it seems to me of prime importance for officers to avoid taking any oath that binds them to a person.... For a *point d'honneur* can arise from it that may involve conflict with honour itself, dull the sense of absolute duty and torment the conscience.'

PART IV

THE STATE

20

Relationship with the Sovereign: '*Liberalism*'

Two remarkable military studies appeared in the eighteen-thirties. One was Clausewitz' posthumous book *Vom Kriege* and the other was a work in which the forty-year-old historian Leopold Ranke, approaching the subject from an angle of his own, adopted a new interpretation of military history derived from France, viz. that military institutions must by their very nature reflect the state of civil society.[1] To us this may seem a glimpse of the obvious; but in its day a long scientific review of history was needed to detect it amid the welter of events, develop it and make sure that it was solidly based. The rightness of Ranke's programme of historical research has been amply shown in the preceding pages of this book; and nowhere does it emerge more plainly than in connection with the officers' code of honour – above all, in the business of duelling that seemed so important once upon a time. Yet the terms in which that problem was conceived up to the first World War seemed to involve it in irreconcilable conflict with the legal and constitutional ideas of the State – a State that was becoming ever more democratic and one which ultimately rested, in theory at least, upon Christian values and on the dignity of the individual. To that extent, therefore, the moral conflict involving the individual was matched by a conflict involving the moral character of the State. The one worked itself out in the other, but from time to time the whole complex underwent a change of aspect.

In this process there are three stages of development, three successive climates of ideas, to be distinguished, viz. the feudal, the absolutist and the constitutional. Feudalism characterised the mediaeval State, based on the pure notion of status (*Stand*).

For practical purposes its typical features were on the one hand a sort of republic of territorial lords and on the other, the government of towns by guilds. It was in constant danger of falling into political anarchy or into an inorganic conglomeration of political entities, tiny and consequently powerless. What preserved it was the creation of the mediaeval Empire which in theory, if not in fact, was universal. The direction in which the Holy Roman Empire of the German Nation evolved – only the briefest indication is needed here – was that its constituent territories, and especially the eight Electorates, became more and more independent. Finally, with the Peace of Westphalia in 1648, they obtained full international sovereignty, while the Empire as such declined into a miserable shadow of its former power and prestige and finally ceased altogether to exist.

At first the territorial sovereigns left intact the feudal organisation of society, i.e. the feudal sub-structure of their States. In Germany, meanwhile, and especially in Prussia, as in France, they contrived to erect upon it another structure that was wholly new – the rational State whose *raison d'être* was power. Unlike the authentic feudal State, this was not composed of horizontal strata, but was vertically conceived. All power was gathered and personified in the sovereign, and he in turn sought to make himself the sole source of all law; he aimed, moreover, at detaching the law (where necessary still) from inanimate things and attaching it to personal things alone, to the individual man. The abolition of Estates in consequence of the social revolutionary movement let loose by the French brought this process to a formal end. That end was anything but voluntary; it lay none the less in the logic of developments.

The old Estates had, after all, had some value as a form of popular representation and as a means of control over the government; but they were gradually replaced during the nineteenth century in almost all the German States by modern parliaments, which govern by majority-vote, and are based on the new idea of the national State in which all citizens are equal before the law. Thus the absolute power of the sovereigns was gradually diminished – more in some places than in others – and the power of parliaments increased. The product of this gradually perfected equilibrium of forces is the constitutional State; and from this process it is clear that each of the three systems – feudal, absolutist and constitutional – merged into the next one following.

This fact is of very great importance as regards the organs of the State, more especially the Army and its organs of command. Their broad lines show unmistakable traces of their three-fold origins.[2] From the feudal era the German corps of officers derived its communal, corporate spirit, its dominant traits going back to mediaeval chivalry yet showing traces of the guild-system inherited from the days of the Landsknechts; and the whole was combined with the no less mediaeval, chivalric concept of loyalty, the loyalty owed by vassals. In the age of absolutism, which gave the corps of officers its basic modern form, nobility was wholly transformed from an Estate into a mere rank, and the sovereign reserved for himself the right of appointing not only generals and colonels but officers of every grade.[3] The officer thus became both servant and representative of the power of the absolute State, and of its monarch as a person. The rule, therefore, was absolute obedience to the monarch and absolute autocracy vis-à-vis the people. Lastly, from the legal, constitutional, nineteenth-century State the corps of officers absorbed the idea of nationalism which was its historical concomitant and essence. Nevertheless, after a period of uncertainty and of compromise with reforms, the final attitude the corps of officers assumed toward the principle of the liberal constitution was one of aloofness, if not of outright rejection.

On the administrative side, matters developed logically as the absolutist conception of the State and its service gave way to the constitutional. But this was not the road the German corps of officers took, for until 1918 its essential relationship to the State was a matter of personal relations with the monarch. Undoubtedly in Prussia, and to some extent also in the post-1870 Reich, the officer corps was strengthened and stiffened in this attitude by the fact that there were certain structural elements in the State itself which pointed in the same direction, i.e. towards the past and in some respects indeed towards the feudal past. Examples enough will be found in the class-based franchise for the Prussian House of Deputies, in the class-based nature of the Upper House (*Herrenhaus*)[4] and in the fact that the Reichstag had no financial control over the measures the Emperor took as Supreme Commander (*oberster*

Kriegsherr*). It was natural therefore that the typical nineteenth-century German officer regarded Parliament's concern with military matters as being, by and large, no more than a presumptuous interference with his own peculiar province – with his own private affairs, as it were.

His sense of the bond between him and the monarch and the monarchy thus grew all the stronger: so did the bond itself. The military oath (*Fahneneid*) is a most important illustration. Unlike the oath the civil servants took, the military oath was an oath of loyalty not to the Constitution but directly to the person of the King – and thus it continued to be sworn even in the modern constitutional State. It was a marked advance that, in the context of the general reform of the Prussian Army, Stein was able to get the text of the military oath changed from *Kriegsherr* to 'King and Fatherland'. He did this on the theory that *Kriegsherr* was suitable for mercenaries but that military service was now to be regarded as a function of the relationship between the citizen and the State; the King thus came into it as Head of the State, not as *Kriegsherr*, and the soldier should therefore swear loyalty to him in that character – and also to his Fatherland.[5] Those two little words 'and also' are important. They throw a revealing light on the scheme of reform that Stein was pursuing, although even he was prevented from carrying it beyond its initial stages. His innate practical thoroughness was so great that if he had been able to carry his scheme right through, Army and People would have become identified and in the resultant 'military democracy' (*militärischer Volks-staat*) the officer's place would have been the same *mutatis mutandis* as the civil servant's.

But movement in that direction suffered such serious setbacks that it was not until December, 1848 that the King of Prussia – and even then for a short time only – promised the Army should take an oath to the Constitution; but when the Constitution was debated on the 10th October 1849 this idea was expressly rejected. That was the end of the matter. The corps of officers itself, of course, would not hear of any oath to the Constitution. The thing must have seemed quite incompatible with its own strong monarchist ideas, with its loyalty to the King. It was a shocking lapse in the direction of liberalism, of 'the destructive tendencies of the times', of a 'democratic

* Literally 'Supreme War Lord'.

swindle' – to use some of the phrases current in those days.

In Saxony the officers took a different attitude at first than in Prussia. On the 22nd March 1848, the new 'free-thinking' Saxon Ministry began work by causing the Army to take an oath to the Constitution. Most of the officers thought this oath a needless formality; some die-hards resisted it: but there were very few who thought it offered a way out of the conflicts between the Army and the people that were so real at the time.[6] The day before a Saxon Guards Regiment and a rifle battalion were due to take the oath at Wurzen, each officer went to great trouble to get hold of a copy of the Constitution in order to read it once at least himself and go through it with his men, so that they could all see what they were swearing to. But neither the local squire nor the mayor, nor the parson, nor even the school-teacher, had a copy; so that when the moment came and the Auditor read the formula out in a voice so feeble that the wind carried it away, not a man really knew what he was pledging his loyalty to.[7]

In March, 1848 the Wurtemberg corps of officers dutifully swore the oath to a Constitution that was abolished three years later. In Bavaria, on the other hand, the question had come up a quarter of a century before, and the officers' general attitude was one of misgivings and refusal. Even in Franconia, which had only been united with Bavaria a short time earlier, the few who favoured the swearing of an oath to the Constitution melted away very soon – less perhaps from loss of conviction than from a fear of losing promotion. On the latter point, of course, they were given no comfort from above. In the Würzburg garrison, for example, there was even a meeting of the junior officers (lieutenants and captains) at which the swearing of an oath to the Constitution was debated. 'Nearly all the officers', we are told, 'judged that although the Constitution was a voluntary gift that testified to His Majesty's benevolence, it (viz. the swearing of an oath to it) might not meet with His Majesty's approval, for so the word had been passed down from higher up, and because evil tongues could falsely interpret the request (viz. to be allowed to swear such an oath)'. When the incident was investigated a witness declared upon his honour[8] 'that all the officers showed the greatest possible affection for His Majesty the King and that although the proposed request was generally held to be innocent and harmless, the issue was decided by the sense of propriety (*die Deligatesse:* sic) born of the evident affection that all the officers felt for the sacred person of the King'.

Even more instructive than these proceedings are the causes that had given rise to such a movement and to so much unrest, both at Würzburg and in the Rhenish Palatinate. On this point too we have a hearsay report from the same witness – the only one who could be found by the general-officer charged with the investigation, Count Becker, from headquarters at Nuremberg. First of all there was dissatisfaction with the most junior officers' pay; but there was also a desire for security from the personal whims of unfriendly superiors as well as from military justice that was unfair and unduly severe. But all these were professional complaints – things that were naturally commoner among the junior than the senior officers. The same witness (he was in any case the only one who could be found) claimed that the root of the constitutional trouble was that at a legal debating-society in the far-off year of 1821 the question had been debated (among others) 'whether an officer who had not sworn allegiance to the Constitution of the country[9] was in the service of the State or not, and whether any satisfaction was owed to him for an insult received in the course of his duty'. It appears to have been decided 'that the officer was to be regarded merely as a mercenary, not as a servant of the State, for he depended only on the pleasure of the King and could thus be dismissed whenever the monarch should so decide; and that the mercenary (who only served for money) had no right to claim satisfaction from either the citizens or the servants of the State.'

This view of the constitutional position of officers as professional soldiers will probably interest the philologist more than the lawyer. At the same time, such a view – or rather the formulation of the question that evoked it – is in itself symptomatic of the confusion, the ambiguity, the neither-one-thing-nor-the-other-ness that beset the constitutional position of officers – and not in Bavaria alone – once the old structure of the absolute State, being plainly unfit to withstand the rough winds of change, began its constitutional overhaul. If the files of the Prussian and Bavarian Ministries of War for the twenty or thirty years after 1848 are compared, one thing emerges clearly. In Bavaria, thanks to the absence of a special Military Cabinet distinct from the Ministry of War, there was a greater readiness than in Prussia to equate the position of the officer vis-à-vis the State with that of the civil servant. But even in Bavaria no such equation took place: it was prevented perhaps by the Constitution of the new Empire which determined the general lines on which the two armies were amalgamated. For the life of the State, for the people, and above all for the corps of officers, that fact was not without its consequences.

Its effect on the individual officer could be either favourable or the reverse. It depended on the extent to which his political views supported an absolute monarchy free of liberal and constitutional trammels, or on the extent to which he was expected (though tacitly) to hold such views by his superiors. This became very clear during the years in which constitutional ideas began to be put into practice. Their novelty engendered powerful emotions and their downright revolutionary ring still caused alarm to monarchs and supporters of the old régime. Typical examples of the way the military chiefs regarded liberal-minded officers in Bavaria for some years after the constitution was introduced in 1848 will be found in the documents printed as Appendices 19 to 22. The criteria by which such officers were judged are remarkable and so is the sharpness of the language (unusual in official papers and thus all the more revealing); but these documents seem to me to be of particular interest in that they do not come from Prussia but from Bavaria, where a degree of constitutional government had existed for a good many years.

Officers suspected of liberalism in those years of crisis were not so rare in the Bavarian Army as the documents suggest. A royal letter (*Signat*) of the 23rd July 1831[10] shows it was unhappily evident 'that, reliable as the senior officers are, there are younger ones with no experience of active service who have been infected by the deplorable principles now current.' But in 1848–9, when the liberal movement reached a momentary peak – over-reached it, indeed – these fears proved groundless. Things flared up here and there in the Bavarian Army, it is true, and notably at Kempten, a place which then acquired the reputation of a 'focus of republicanism'. But the officers hardly anywhere lost control of their men and they themselves remained wholly loyal to the King[11] for all the slight fits of liberalism they suffered here and there. And when the whole movement had – for the time being – petered out, officers of this kind were only regarded as a minor blemish: and the whole corps of officers was given a certificate of 'reliable' in the monarchist sense (see the War Minister's assessment of the 5th November 1858). Even a man like Captain Count Bothmer, who in his day had been suspected of liberal views, was later made chief of the Bavarian General Staff.[12]

On feeling in the Prussian corps of officers the movement of 1848 left no trace at all, unless it were that it left the noblemen among them feeling yet more strongly and more consciously – if either were still possible – attached to the Crown and to the person of its wearer. The social reaction – if it deserves the name – which the events of 1848 produced was thus, at the most, a negative one. And anyway, as the well-informed Theodor von Bernhardi has recorded, the younger officers had no political convictions whatever.[13] Nevertheless the 'Junker' party gradually managed to convert the whole Army to its own way of thinking. And by the time Bismarck's statesmanship allied to Moltke's strategy had made Prussia the leader of the new German Empire Bismarck had become the idol of the corps of officers. In their eyes he could do no wrong. We have this from the temperate Bernhardi's passionate son, the General,[14] whom we can well believe, however, when he writes: 'We officers never had any real idea what the *Kulturkampf** was about. We only saw that the Government had failed and it was not so much the dazzled German people we blamed as the political and religious agitators – and the Reichstag.' Here we have almost unimpeachable evidence of the officer-corps' dislike for the Parliament – that is, their dislike for the way in which it curtailed the rights of the sovereign.

Ludwig Freiherr von Gebsattel, who was Bavarian Military Plenipotentiary in Berlin, described this state of opinion as 'real Old Prussian irritation with the people's representatives'.[15] But such a man as General Groener, who thought like the Swabian democrat he was, admitted that during his time at the Berlin War Academy in the 'nineties the many newspapers he read made him 'furious at the perpetual bickerings in the Reichstag'. Furthermore, in his memoirs,[16] he describes (we can take him as un-biassed) the conservative political temper

---

* This term covers the general conflict between old and modern ideas, and in particular the religious conflict in Germany that followed the first Vatican Council.

of the Academy: 'Politics', he writes, 'played no more part in the Academy than they did in the Regiment, and my fellow-cadets from North Germany were no more politically-minded than I was. On religious matters we had differences now and then, for a few, very few, of the cadets were strong adherents of Chaplain Stöcker[17] – but the majority had no use for him at all.... Bismarck's dismissal, and especially the Chancellor Caprivi's disingenuous letter of the 9th June 1892, seemed to us all to put a certain strain on our monarchist consciences. In the differences between the Emperor and the former Chancellor most of us were on Bismarck's side.... Even the senior officers had no political sense – and not just the ones who had been through the Cadet-Corps either.... In the Navy it was different. Foreign travel had left the naval officers better equipped to judge political events. In the Army the only people who took an interest in politics were the military attachés.'[18] And, he might have added, the Military Plenipotentiaries whom the larger States of the Reich maintained in Berlin.

2 I

Military Journalism:
The Press, Politics, Civil Liberty

The black sheep who followed Chaplain Stöcker were mainly
concerned with domestic politics, of course; but they had their
counterparts in those who held passionate views about foreign
affairs. A typical specimen of this sort was the above-mentioned
General von Bernhardi, who aired his views not merely among
his friends but even in public.[1] The officer who 'played politics',
the political writer in uniform, was a rare phenomenon all the
same; and those who earned that label during the last twenty or
thirty years before 1914 did not, of course, all think and write
in terms of Pan-German nationalism as Bernhardi did. But if
there was hardly any upper limit to those who went in for
this kind of thing, there was a lower limit all the same. For
regular officers it was sometimes a rather delicate, border-line
matter; but as a rule the disciplinary side of it was more
theoretical than real for them. Not so, however, for officers on
the half-pay or retired lists. The multiplication of officers
consequent on the expansion of the Army in 1860 was bound to
lead in due course to an increase in the numbers retiring.
Most of these had only reached the rank of major and were in
full possession of their physical and intellectual powers; but
their pensions, as a rule, were small. If they had no private
means they were often driven, or at any rate they were tempted,
to try and earn something more in civilian life. They ran State
lottery offices, or became hospital-secretaries or such like.
Many, however, tried their hand at writing – just as many had
done in the seventeenth century when the end of the Thirty
Years' War left them to earn their daily bread as best they
could. It was then that a poet at Cleves wrote this satirical
doggerel:

166

Military Journalism: The Press, Politics, Civil Liberty

Sonst war der blanke Degen
der Feder überlegen,
nun wendet sich das Blatt:
Der Degen steckt im Leder,
man sucht hervor die Feder,
dieweil man Frieden hat.*

Newpapers, periodicals and printed matter in general sprang
up everywhere towards the end of the nineteenth century
naturally and gave the retired officer more and more opportunity to try his hand at scribbling. Moreover the intensive
drive for better education in the corps of officers had removed
some of the sting (though far from all of it), from the old
antagonism between 'quill-drivers' and 'cocked-hats'.† Two
further factors had increased the general public's interest in
matters affecting the Army: on the one hand, the rise of Germany to the rank of a world-power, and on the other the growth
of pacifism. But the evolution of politics brought yet another
factor into play, for it emerged that there was a section of the
public which took a keen pleasure in reading the occasional
articles in which officers more or less sharply criticised the Army
or military policy in general. Perhaps it was just the law of
supply and demand at work; perhaps such officers sought to
do their ideals or their country a service by airing the disappointment and bitterness which (rightly or wrongly) they
felt and by exposing the Army's shortcomings; the fact remains
that many an officer, when dealing with these matters, found
himself writing things that suited the views of left-wing newspapers and parties.

But, consciously or not, such writers thereby came into conflict with the officers' code – with those parts that were still
unwritten until events in 1876 and afterwards caused them to be
made the subject of Regulations. General Constantin von
Alvensleben, a well-known figure of the war of 1870, put the

* Doggerel for doggerel, this might be rendered:
Lately we knew a season when
The sword was mightier than the pen.
Now all is turned about.
The soldier puts his blade away,
His pen he sharpens for the fray:
For peace has broken out.

† The antithesis goes better in German: '*Federfuchser*' vs. '*Federbüsche*'.

problem in a nutshell when he wrote: 'A Prussian general dies, but leaves no memoirs behind';[2] and he added that the Prussian tradition forbade an officer to address the public. This was austerity indeed; and if it applied to the simple narrative of past campaigns, it must apply with far more strength to the political journalism practised by the younger generation – by men like General Bernhardi, not to mention those who held the opposite views. The foundation of the new Empire had led – not without some critical passages – to the creation of new economic and social conditions; but it was barely five years old[3] before the Emperor had his first occasion to intervene. He then caused 'retired officers of every rank to be reminded that as regards public discussions they must observe the regulations that apply to regular officers, and that any lapse would be dealt with by the appropriate authorities'.

Again and again thereafter the point was made 'that it is an intolerable state of affairs for officers publicly to express opinions that conflict with those which His Majesty has approved'.[4] Frequent Orders and Regulations drew attention to the fact that in their political activities retired officers, too, were morally bound to observe the code of their profession (*die Standespflichten*) 'which enjoins on them a becoming reticence in speech and writing, and assumes they will only give their support to parties whose loyalty and patriotic sentiments are beyond all question'.[5] The limit of what the Emperor and his responsible advisers were prepared to tolerate was shown, for example, in the case of Prince Schönaich-Carolath. In 1885 this man was a Liberal-National member of the Reichstag and also an aide-de-camp to William II; but once, on a question that mattered to the Emperor, he voted with the Progressive Party. He thereby caused a tremendous scandal and lost his right to wear uniform.[6]

In 1892 William II wanted to go still further and expressly forbid officers to have any contact with the daily press; but in view of the Press Law of the 7th May 1874 and of Article 27 of the Prussian Constitution he had to refrain. Two years later, however,[7] he ruled that officers accused of publishing objectionable matter were to be brought before courts martial or tribunals of honour. This was a far-reaching threat, and one that touched officers on a very sensitive spot. It also had the undesired effect of producing a sharp and striking reduction in the number of regular officers who contributed to military journals of any kind, even the purely technical ones. In the end the Ministry of War and the General Staff had to agree that some latitude must be allowed in respect of certain military journals – the *Militär-Wochenblatt*, for example.[8] The military efficiency of the Prussian-German Army depended, after all, to a large extent on an active and flourishing specialist press in German. The Prussian Government as a whole, and not merely the Ministry of War, had always held the view that the general rights of the subject – and nothing less was at stake in these limitations of personal liberty vis-à-vis the press – could be overridden in respect of officers and civil servants alike, since it must be subordinate to the special obligations arising from their service. The only question was how to define these special obligations correctly, i.e. in such a way as to preserve to the maximum degree the general rights of the subject and to curtail them no more than urgent necessity required. In individual cases, of course, this curtailment led to endless dispute, both as regards civil servants and, even more, as regards officers. The reason – quite apart even from the sociological problem referred to above – was that the officers' service was much more conditioned than was the officials' by that vast complex of status and responsibility that goes by the simple name of discipline – though that name is applied to it more by instinct than by reason. On one occasion even the Ministry of Justice took this view[9] though it drew attention to the 'special loyalty' which the officer and the civil servant owed to the State.

But this very notion of loyalty was still charged with very potent meaning for the officer-corps, the Emperor and the military authorities. It was a meaning which in the sociological sense went deeper than the mere loyalty required of civil servants, for in the officers' case it was more deeply dyed with the hierarchical tradition of earlier times. An officer, therefore, who published something that offended against the decencies of his station committed a far graver offence *mutatis mutandis* than the civil servant: and in the eyes of the Emperor and his military staff an officer who did such a thing was branded not just professionally but downright morally too. This is the tenor of all the Regulations already mentioned, but it is clearest of all in the Cabinet Order of the 1st January 1904. On that occasion the Emperor, using highly personal language, made a bitter complaint about the gross lack of taste shown in the writings published even by senior officers of the regular Army; he observed, moreover, that the administrative method of assessing officers paid too much attention to the purely military attainments and too little to their character; the training of officers in the Old Prussian spirit had been defective on this point, he said, whereas the corps of officers 'was often assailed on social grounds'; 'now that it had begun to be recruited from classes other than the usual ones', additional importance attached to the cultivation of a real sense of chivalry and integrity of mind, especially in relation to subordinates.

In sociological terms, of course, the real subject of this military and moral elegy was the modernisation, de-feudalisation and *embourgeoisement* of the corps of officers. In spite of repeated urgent exhortations, threats and disciplinings, the corps of officers had in fact begun – sporadically at first, but with some persistence – to undergo a change that affected even its relationship to the State. The eighteenth century had denied the 'subject' political freedom of action and had denied him even the right to demand it. The nineteenth century had then secured that freedom to every 'citizen'; and now the spearhead of the same demand was beginning to penetrate the corps of officers. The threat now was that it would go on to penetrate the internal hierarchy of the Army, menace the traditions of the officer-class and thereby endanger one of the main pillars of the Emperor's personal power. The same demand had even made itself heard in Parliament. There was no stemming this advance towards the achievement of full freedom and independence for every citizen; and in the course of it some officer now and then overstepped the limit (or rather, the limit in force at the moment) of what a State servant's duty allowed. From the academic point of view, however, this was merely a phenomenon that normally accompanies developments in the intellectual sphere. Such developments always proceed by way of advance and retreat, and the constant line of their advance only becomes apparent when the process can be looked at as a whole. In the 'seventies, the line this advance was taking became ever plainer until at last the Emperor himself became aware of it. Not that the corps of regular officers as a whole had become politically minded. Franz Oppenheim, the sociologist, was right when he said the corps of officers was conservative, but un-politically so. The exceptions only prove the rule.

This was not quite so true, however, in respect of officers of the reserve. As a body they had inherited a very different tradition, a liberal one, from the first half-century of the Landwehr's existence, even though the Landwehr, once incorporated into the standing Army, had done its best to adopt the latter's style and outlook. But for lack of continuous 'training' of the individual and of continuous contact with the regular element a single 'type', imbued with the same 'conservatism' as the regular corps of officers, was not so easily produced. And so concessions had to be made to the spirit of the times – concessions which in spite of many things the corps of regular officers still regarded as preposterous. The Cabinet Regulation of 1876 (see above), enjoining reticence on retired officers with regard to public discussion, remained the basis of all subsequent Orders and itself was never revoked. But when in 1907 some subordinate official sought to interpret this passage as preventing a retired officer from signing 'an otherwise harmless electoral appeal', higher authority overruled him. Four years later, indeed, it had become the accepted thing[10] that officers on the reserve-list (*des Beurlaubtenstandes*) could even engage in political activity on behalf of the Social-Democrat Party without attracting attention from a tribunal of honour. What a short span of time and yet how great a distance divides such tolerance from Bismarck's laws on socialism! In his day every German citizen was forbidden all activity on behalf of social-democracy and it would have been unthinkable that one duly authorised to wear the King's uniform, a temporary member of the 'chivalrous company' of the German corps of officers, should so much as lift a finger to help the party of revolution.

It was only in the 'other ranks' that deliberate – and known – supporters of the social-democratic movement were to be found at that time; and even before Bismarck's laws on socialism appeared some of these men were kept under observation by the widespread political and military intelligence system. Even so, it was noticeable, as Colonel General von Kluck, among others, relates, that they usually carried out their duties well and 'made good soldiers'.[11] But the laws on socialism were eventually repealed, and in accordance with the trend towards social reform which more and more inspired the Government in its dealings with the working-class, there was no lack of effort in the Army to win back the sympathies of the men, largely social-democratic as they were, for the existing order in State and society. Lectures were given by the officers; and in the 18th Army Corps at Frankfort-on-the-Main in particular, thanks to the personal initiative of the general-officer commanding, von Eichhorn, such efforts were well under way by the turn of the century (see Appendix 23). In the War Ministry, however, which heard of them only by chance, these efforts aroused serious misgivings and were only partially approved.[12] The main cause of anxiety was the fact that in their lectures to the men the officers dealt with social and political matters. The Ministry contended – not without reason – that the officers could not really know enough about such things; the men would go on discussing them after the lectures, and the social-democratic leaders among them would then have the best possible opportunity for agitation. The Ministry therefore asked the Emperor to issue a prohibition against the discussion of social and political questions in officers' lectures. This was duly done in the Cabinet Order of the 3rd January 1907.

Afterwards, however, the Ministry had second thoughts about the effects this Order might have, and tried to tone it down by way of interpretation.[13] They let it be known that the Order of the 3rd January 1907 did not forbid officers' lectures to give instruction and enlightenment about social-democratic attacks on the Monarch, the State and religion; but they advised officers to avoid discussing agitation over pay and other conditions of work, relations between labour and capital, and the role of public assistance in economic conflicts. It was the younger officers who bore the main burden of the work; and as if it were not ticklish enough already, they now were faced with an insoluble task – that of squaring the Emperor's *Verbot* with the commentary by his Ministry of War.

The same objective, but with a much more obvious political intention, led the Supreme Command (*Oberste Heeresleitung – OHL*) to institute 'Patriotic Schooling' in the summer of 1917 – at a time when the course of the first World War was heading straight for disaster. This was supposed to 'establish uniformity among the divergent tendencies of education'. To this end a wide network of 'Education Officers' was created in the Army; and by maintaining a strictly uniform approach, especially when dealing with political and economic problems, they were expected to revive the Army's flagging faith in victory and drive home the consequences of defeat.[14] As General Groener wrote (from his greater political experience), 'it was sheer madness to try and overcome social-democratic sympathies with Pan-German leaflets and lectures. Thoughtful, sensible senior officers told me they had confiscated some of the material they were supposed to distribute to the men since it would have had the opposite effect to what was intended. Nobody believed in the theories and demands it contained. If stuff of that kind had been circulated, they said, it would simply have destroyed the men's confidence in their officers.'[15]

Nevertheless, to win and keep that confidence even in peacetime, let alone in time of global war for life or death, was a major example of what Clausewitz meant by 'moral qualities' (*moralische Grösse*). Admittedly this bright idea on the part of the Supreme Command was matched on the home front by the 'Patriotic Party' inspired by Tirpitz; but the Landwehr mostly consisted of men of a certain age, men who had problems of their own – perhaps family-problems – to cope with. In terms of method and psychology it was wholly misconceived to tackle such men with 'patriotic education'. Such a thing was simply 'not a starter'. As we shall see later on, even the 'National-Socialist Leadership Officers' (*N-S Führungsoffiziere*) at the end of the second World War were a failure; and yet the 'Education Officers' of 1917 had no sort of training for their job and, besides, they had the whole tradition of the Imperial Army against them. But the front-line officers whom Groener quotes were fundamentally right: at the heart of the matter – especially in twentieth-century Germany – lay the vital psychological question of confidence – of the officer's confidence in his men, and the men's in him.

22

Leadership, Discipline
and the Humanitarian Spirit

This brings us to the question of military leadership as such.[1]
The place it occupies in the whole of this study is so important
that it might well deserve a chapter to itself, but it will be better
dealt with now, for historically and sociologically it is inseparable from the wider question of the position of the officer-corps
vis-à-vis the State and the people. That is the only angle from
which the matter will be considered here. Various studies of it,
some of them very useful, were made both before and after
the first World War; and the primary point to make is this.
Ever since the time of Scharnhorst, Clausewitz and Marmont
(for whom Prince Frederick Charles of Prussia had a great
admiration) all treatises on military psychology written in the
nineteenth and twentieth centuries[2] are agreed that the prime
requirement of all is mutual confidence between officers and
men. The officer must understand the psychology of his men
and gain their sympathy for himself; he must look after their
physical and moral health, and the men must respond with
willing discipline.

Nevertheless it was rightly noted a few years before the war
of 1914 that the concept of discipline had changed along with
the conduct of warfare (*Kriegführung*). As van den Bergh wrote
in 1906: 'What the officers will order into action nowadays are
not clockwork Guards from Potsdam. The human material that
will be called up in some future war is not the same as it was.
We have no more use for soldiers who obey their officers
blindly and automatically; what we need is wide-awake
soldiers – men who will contribute their whole mind and personality to the common cause, each as far as in him lies.'
But, of course, the change in the conduct of warfare was not the

main factor that was beginning to alter the concept of discipline. Methods of waging war are subject to the spirit of those who wage it – the peoples and their governments: in brief, the States. Furthermore the change in the concept of discipline implies a similar change in the forms taken by leadership, both in war and in training for war. In other words, the relationship of the officer to his men was itself subject to this change, in both its form and its content; and to all appearance it was governed by the relationship of the officer to the State or (according to circumstances) by the real relationship between those who rule and represent the State and those they govern.

This brings us right back to the series of stages in the evolution of States and constitutions that was outlined at the beginning of this Part. In the time of the Landsknechts,[3] which was really part of the feudal age, a troop raised and commanded by a captain was a kind of brotherhood of warriors, a sort of guild, and the relationship of the captain to his troopers was simply that of master to apprentices, based on a limited contract of service – usually three months. Discipline, like justice, was handled partly on guild-fellowship lines, and partly on patriarchal lines derived from ancient German popular law (*Volksrecht*). But the soldier's trade was still the most casual of occupations, for troops and regiments were always dispersed after a few years or months. Nevertheless the increase of population, together with the disappearance of ossification of guilds and companies, did not decrease the supply of soldiers, but increased it. The apprentice who could not become a master, or was out of work, was easy game for the recruiting-sergeant. And so the rough business of war brought together more and more men who were only 'bad characters, tramps and such riff-raff, who had only their lives to lose'. These were the types who brought the *Landsknechte* into such bad odour at the end of the sixteenth and the beginning of the seventeenth centuries. If such a rabble of ruffians was to be reduced to any kind of order and made any sort of use for war, discipline and especially punishments had to be greatly stiffened and brutalised; and this in turn made the command of such ruffians less and less attractive to decent, educated men – or else made it simply a matter of making money. It was the Thirty Years' War that brought these disgraceful, indeed shocking, conditions to their tragic climax.[4]

But even in the earlier years of decline, when the soldiers were no longer the 'God-fearing' *Landsknechte* of Reformation days, a change had come over the relationship of the officer to his men. We can see this from the fact that Wallhausen, one of the most respected military writers of his day, had pleaded, even before the Thirty Years' War, for the office of the *Ambosat* to be abolished – the man, that is, whom the *Landsknechte* used to elect as their 'regular spokesman, father and guardian' to defend their interests against the officers. The reason, we are told, was that he did the troop more harm than good, stirring up trouble and parleying for the men in every mutiny. The problem of discipline was involved no doubt, but the problem of confidence too; and to that extent one is reminded of many a misguided debate in the Bundestag at Bonn today on the question of creating the post of 'soldiers' commissioners' (*Wehrbeauftragte*). But in those days the important thing was that instead of the patriarchal system of enrolling of soldiers into a kind of guild the men were forced into absolute subjection to their captain, colonel and general; fellowship was replaced by authority, and fear of a thrashing took the place of spontaneous discipline. The theory began to grow that soldiers must fear their officers more than the enemy. How could a war have been carried on for thirty years with troops so morally debased and leaders who were not much better even by their own standards – how could this have been done unless the troops' 'morale' had been maintained, as it somehow had to be, by savage punishments? 'War feeds war'* – such was a famous summing-up of the fearful results that flowed from German disunity; but it was figurative no less true of conditions within the military units of the time.

Delbrück[5] called this new and effective system of military discipline 'rule by strengthening superior authorities'.† It was not only maintained when the war was over, but stiffened and extended. The typical forms of drill employed were marching in step, weapon-drill, marching past, saluting-drill and so forth;[6] and by these methods the soldier was broken in to the will of his officers. Wallhausen – to quote him again – records that if a soldier had been told a couple of times how to stand, and still did not do what he had been told to, 'the next thing

* '*Der Krieg ernährt den Krieg*'. (Schiller: *Die Piccolomini*).
† *Herrschaft des Aufbaus der Übergeordneten.*

was a good whack: for a man who will not take orders without a cudgelling must take the cudgelling too.' Again and again the princely commanders-in-chief issued warnings against using the cudgel too brutally; but the only thing that really restrained the subordinate commanders from going too far was fear of desertions and the expense of recruiting substitutes. On the other hand a man who had once taken up – or been pressed into – the soldier's disreputable trade (especially once the Estates* had authorised 'standing' armies for several years ahead) could hardly hope to get better treatment by deserting to another general: and besides, after leading a rough nomad life in war it was no easy matter for him to resume the regular ways of the bourgeois. Both these factors therefore combined to rivet on the armies a system of maintaining discipline by violence; and in the German armies, unlike the French of the day, it grew into a tradition whose roots went deep – all too deep, indeed.

And yet, the very deepest roots of all drew their sustenance from the intellectual soil of early rationalism, for that was what underlay the psychic and physical treatment by drilling and marching as well as the whole movement towards absolute government, with its mercantilist economic and social policies. The more it was recognised[7] that better discipline meant better troops, the more did the soldiers' own well-being, their right to retain their own personality, become subordinate to the law of war. The demand for submission to the will of authority, moreover, not merely broke the defiance of the old-type *Landsknecht*; it called into being a machine whose harshness formed the strongest possible contrast with that other product of the age – the humanitarian spirit. Yet as the 'enlightenment' of the eighteenth century advanced, its rays began to warm the murky world to which the treatment of soldiers belonged. Five whole years before the French Revolution a man such as Boyen could write[8] that those dreadful scenes in which the wretched recruit was kicked and beaten into moving his arms and legs correctly belonged already to the past. 'The present generation of commanders', he wrote, 'almost all detest it and the accepted principle today is that recruits are to be taught their business without being beaten.' Such a generalisation may well strike us as too optimistic altogether. But Boyen was not a biased

* The 'parliament' of the time.

witness and we can take his word for it that if discipline itself was no less strict, the punishments were less severe than they had been in the robuster days of the Great Elector. By the time young Boyen wrote his account, a greater power, in the shape of death, had removed the dreaded crutch-stick from the hand of Frederick the Great as well. His later plans for military reforms in Prussia seemed, in one important respect, to have been realised already.

It would be wrong, of course, to attribute this improvement to 'enlightenment' alone. A good deal was due to universal military service (the so-called *Kantonpflicht*). It had been reintroduced about the beginning of the eighteenth century – with the usual, not to say notorious, *Exemtionen* (sic), of course – and with no change in the recruiting methods. But universal service did give the new intake a different and rather more 'popular' character, as well as a higher intellectual and moral tone, and these factors gradually began to make their mark on the officers' treatment of their men. But even if one can say that this was the general tendency as early as the eighteenth century, it received its real stimulus only when Prussia lost the larger part of her non-German provinces and introduced universal military service in earnest. The army now became 'the people in arms'; corporal punishment had to disappear as a result (*vide* the Order on Military Punishment, dated the 3rd August 1808) and efforts were made to establish a more personal, less purely mechanical, relationship between officers and men. Once again the Order on Appointments of Ensigns provides an illustration: 'Officers are to take an interest in their subordinates. It is not enough to get to know the more efficient men; they must be made more efficient still by gaining their confidence.' It was this same Order which, as we saw in Part I, sought to put an end to the régime of class-privilege in the Army.

The fact is that the idealist reformers of the Prussian State had a new conception of the private soldier and his dignity, and their aim was to stamp it indelibly upon their whole reorganisation of the Army. Nowhere, perhaps, does this ideal emerge in more radical, indeed more revolutionary form, than in these moving words from the 'Soldier's Catechism' which Arndt wrote with such patriotic, democratic fervour in November, 1812: 'German military honour is this: the soldier must feel he was a man and a German ere ever he heard of German kings and princes. He must feel this land was German ere ever kings or princes were; and with all his inmost soul he must desire that the land and its folk be deathless and everlasting, but that lords and princes with their honours and their shames may pass away.' And to the soldier he uttered the cry: 'Thou art a man: thou puttest the King's coat on; put not thy manhood off!'[19] Here is the firm melodic line, the line that ran, with many a variation, right through the nineteenth century and swelled in a great crescendo as that century neared its end – but ever and always with that other line, the idea of an absolute State, running with it in majestic counterpoint.

In the course of the nineteenth century, it is true, the democratic principle of government that derived from France and England swung the balance of sovereignty and power more and more towards the people. But in Germany the older principle of absolute authority had a vitality that kept it very much alive: and in the close connection between the officer corps and the person of the sovereign this principle attained its maximum potential. Short of disturbing that situation, the Army leaders did attempt, none the less, to adapt the officers – the future leaders of the Army – to the new conditions obtaining in the State and in the people. Even so, it was clear that the absolutist structure of the building and its stylish modern façade were not entirely congruous.

These conflicting tendencies had come out clearly at the start of Boyen's army-reorganisation, when he aimed at imparting the same spirit to the Landwehr and the Line-regiments alike. He required[10] that on manoeuvres with the Landwehr the Line should take account of the age, the bourgeois outlook and the intellectual level of many Landwehr men. This drew a tart enquiry from the Prince of Prussia. 'Why', asked Prince William, 'should the bourgeois outlook, the intellectual level and the riper age of fathers of families, foremen, factory-owners, etc., justify their performing their military duties any less well than raw recruits?' This exchange, of course, really applied to much more than the Landwehr. It raised the whole question of the spirit of the new Army; and implicit in it were the same antithesis, the same incomprehension that marked the Army's further evolution in the nineteenth century and right into the first World War. The dynamic principle was ranged against the static – the former represented first by Boyen and then by democracy, the latter by William I and conservatism.

It was a clash of principles, true enough; but the spirit of the times had a considerable effect even in the regiments of the Line – above all in the field of discipline, theoretical and practical. In 1818 there appeared a commentary, specially printed for officers, on the revised Articles of War of the 3rd August 1808.[11] There is no mistaking, it says, 'the advantages that distinguish this new attitude towards the men from that of former times, nor the humaner treatment of them which has flowed from the assumption that they possess moral instincts and habits. All regulations now presuppose a higher standard of honour among the men; the severe, and public, corporal punishments that were previously applied have been abolished: the birch entirely so. Beating is retained only for those who cannot be kept in order and corrected by more lenient methods, and even so it is never used in public now but only in the presence of other soldiers. Other punishments, more suited to the dignity of the officer's profession (*Stand*) and to the men's sense of honour, have been introduced.' The central aim of all the later regulations on discipline was to arouse and maintain a sense of honour even in the private soldier, and this aim was expressed in terms of human dignity. By 1844 already we find a threat of punishment for non-commissioned officers who abused their authority; and lastly there was the Prussian Military Penal Code (finally published on the 3rd April 1845 after thirty years' preparatory work) which appealed in the same way to the private soldier's sense of honour, while recommending he be treated with greater justice and kindliness.

This was a bold and vigorous return to the reformist ideals of 1808, and the measures taken all point to the same conclusion: that not only in the treatment of the men by their officers but in many other matters the forces of reaction had been at work since Boyen's first tenure of the Ministry of War. It was not against the non-commissioned officers alone that the King was forced to act. Officers too were involved, and the King felt obliged to issue an Order to the effect that any officer who maltreated his men contrary to the King's command would be punished.[12] There were objections, of course. Prince Frederick Charles, for example (then a captain in the Guards Hussars, and no stickler for forms), insisted[13] that the officer *must* always be right; he was not alone, either, in holding that the King's uniform was a coat of honour and that a recruit's best friend was his officer. But the Order was necessary all the same.

Among those who shared this Prussian prince's views – or rather theories – was the Bavarian Quarter-Master General's Staff (as the General Staff was then called). In 1868, when genuinely universal military service was introduced, the Staff laid down[14] 'that in the sum of his capacities the commanding officer must be better than those he commanded: that an officer's influence and authority did not reside in his sword and épaulettes alone, and that true authority, of the kind that would be proof against calamities in war and in peace, rested solely upon moral and intellectual superiority'. The crisis of 1848 brought out very clearly the fact that true authority and discipline – in the nineteenth century at least – could not just be imposed: they also required a relationship between officers and men that should not be professional only, but personal as well. Higher authority, moreover, was consciously working in this direction. The revolutionary movement of 1848 did indeed penetrate the Bavarian Army a good deal more deeply than the Prussian; but in the periodical reports[15] on the temper of the men that were called for by the Ministry of War the emphasis almost everywhere was repeatedly laid on the officers' serene behaviour towards their men and on the men's unshaken confidence in them.

It was in that year of revolution, too, that corporal punishment, in particular, was declared 'out of use' by a royal *Handbillet* of the 11th October, after the special Commission on the subject had recommended this step in view of what had been done on the matter elsewhere in Germany (see Appendix 24). As prescribed by the regulations, very little use had in fact been made of this punishment since 1819, while the birch and the bâton had been abolished as far back as 1821 and 1826 respectively. These were plainly concessions to humanitarian principles; but in 1848 reaction was still at work in higher military circles – in Bavaria even more than in Prussia – and in Bavaria the total abolition of corporal punishment, among other things, was still resisted. But humaner ideas soon gained the upper hand, and the credit was largely due to General von Lesuire (see Appendix 25) who was shortly afterwards appointed Minister of War.

Generally speaking, discipline in the formal sense evolved rather unevenly in the different constituent armies after the foundation of the Reich in 1871; but in essence they all moved in the same direction and with the same end in view. There was a new spirit in the air, a new conception of the people and the State; and, as Arndt once put it,[16] there was a new basic idea of the monarch as ruling *through* the law, not *above* it. These were the factors that exerted the strongest influence on developments – stronger, at any rate, than the reactionaries' fear that looser discipline or lighter punishments would end in loss of authority and leadership. But the rightness of the policy now being generally followed was proved by the fact that the Army, and even the men, had hardly been infected at all by the revolution of 1848 and that the united German armies had gone on to win resounding victories over France.

Yet unless precautions were taken these very factors of success were liable to give a powerful impetus to the eighteenth-century outlook on drill and on parades – and with it to a more absolutist, authoritarian conception of leadership. This risk was increased, in particular, by the reactionaries' exasperation at the speed with which revolutionary socialist ideas spread among the young recruits. These widely varying trends and states of mind soon came into collision and gave rise to incidents that furnished the press and the Reichstag with material for copious discussion. The very nature of press and parliament, let alone the real power they wielded, made them, after all, the typical products and vanguard of the modern, individualistic outlook on society and of the popular, social State. From the 'seventies onwards the ugly subject of the maltreatment of soldiers became part of the stock-in-trade of debates in the Reichstag and of a section of the press.

23

Maltreatment of Subordinates

The statistics of punishments for maltreatment of subordinates are a pointer to the fact that even in the last quarter of the nineteenth century and the first years of the twentieth the German corps of officers had still not entirely shed the old authoritarian, coldly professional approach to the officer's rôle and his function as a leader. Here and there we still run across traces of the tradition that dated from the time when the *Landsknecht* days were ended by the rise of absolutism. In modern times it was quite out of tune with social-insurance and workmen's compensation Acts – all of them designed to reconcile the working class with the State, the 'property-owning classes' and the capitalist order of society. There is no denying all the same, that the social policy introduced by Bismarck did contain some features that smacked of patriarchal feudalism.[1]

One product of this feudal spirit, dating from much rougher times when there was no such thing as a nation in our sense of the word, was, of course, the way in which soldiers were maltreated. In those earlier times little value was placed on a man's life, least of all one from the lower classes; and such kindliness as the upper classes showed to the lower was more a matter of grace than of duty. But from the 1870's onwards until 1914, maltreatment of soldiers was a matter of frequent and justified concern. Some acts were perhaps committed, or overlooked, by young officers in the course of training recruits; and in others, no doubt, non-commissioned officers misused their power in this way behind the officers' backs. The latter type of case indeed was ten times as frequent as cases of maltreatment by officers themselves – that is, cases where officers were punished for this offence. In an officer, of course, it was much graver than in a non-commissioned officer; the former had more education, he was expected to have a higher sense of responsibility, and in other contexts he was never slow to show how lively and delicate his sense of honour was. The moral is obvious: but the degree to which such cases reflected on the officer-corps as a whole and harmed its general repute is still not easy to assess.

The surprising thing is that an offender's brother-officers themselves did not react more strongly against such social slurs, for a combination of solidarity with the *point d'honneur* might well have been in the best way of excluding these 'unsuitable' elements in the long run. But the collective, professional instinct for moral self-preservation was evidently not strong enough; and this in turn hung upon that class-solidarity which, as we saw in Part III, made it so hard to adapt the officers' concept of honour to the basic injunctions of personal, Christian morality. The same sociological basis accounts for the very light sentences that were imposed on officers who committed this sort of offence. A few days' or weeks' confinement to barracks was normal. It was only on the eve of the first World War that General Falkenhayn, then Prussian Minister of War, expressed sharp disapproval of this leniency (see Appendix 26). And yet it was well-known that for lack of any right of complaint (a matter we need not go into here) only a small proportion of such cases ever came to the notice of higher authority. In addition there were cases in which an officer, though supposed to exercise supervision, was so indifferent or inexperienced that he more or less made himself an accomplice in some act of maltreatment by a non-commissioned officer. In this sort of case the circumstances were often obscure, of course, and the responsibilities impossible to establish. Such cases, therefore, seldom reached the stage where the officer could be punished. Even in this connection, however, abuses came to light; and they caused the Emperor William II to issue a serious warning at the very outset of his reign (see Appendix 27).

By way of excuse for all these disagreeable events it was pointed out *inter alia* that a high percentage of the recruits had usually been convicted already of civil crimes such as theft, causing bodily injury, and so forth. But if the higher aims of the command and the training of recruits are borne in mind, such facts can at most serve as grounds for leniency, not for acquittal. It was a sore point, however, and no doubt it played a part – though not in every unit. There were very many regiments, whole Army-Corps indeed, in which, despite the 'rough but hearty' manners of the barracks, such things were virtually unknown. By and large, too, it can be said with justice that the bulk of officers in charge of recruits – young and mostly inexperienced officers, charged with the very first training of young men of their own age – remained innocent of any such excess.

24

The Weimar Republic: The 'non-political' Reichswehr

The *fons et origo* of the whole question of the officer's role as a leader and trainer of men was (I must insist) the basic attitude of the officer-corps in the time of the monarchy to the very idea of the State as such. This was partly due to the nature of an officer's profession, partly to the historical tradition of his class (*Stand*). The fact of being responsible not to the people, nor really to the State, but in the last analysis to the Crown alone, carried with it the risk that, in the exercise of their authority, the less balanced characters (such as exist in any large community) would be governed too little by personal respect for their fellow-men and too much by the impersonal standards of their class, of the institution, of 'authority'.

It is, of course, only when we see it from a distance that the picture I have drawn reveals its grand design. If we approach it closer and study the details we notice some discordant features here and there. They appeared soon after the foundation of the new Empire and attention has already been drawn to them in these pages. But no one could then have suspected that the mightier seed of a tragic conflict lay concealed beneath them. That conflict first emerged and began to develop after 1918, though the social and political eruption of those days was really due to quite other causes. A contributory factor, none the less, was the state of social exasperation that reigned among the senior military officers – not that it was quite as intense as it had been. Speaking of Catiline's conspiracy, the Roman historian Sallust observed that the same means by which power is won are easily employed to maintain it.[1] In a negative sense this axiom applies no less to a close-knit organisation such as the corps of officers. The corps was formed round the person of the

King and remained bound to it by the most intimate links. Then, in November 1918, the personal, intellectual and ideological core of its being suddenly disappeared. The fall of the monarchy, the tame abdication of the Emperor and all the other Kings and princes – these were calamities that left large sections of the people stunned. None were more so than the officers. They were flung into confusion like a leaderless swarm of bees.

As early as the 29th October 1918, from the General Head-quarters to which he was attached as liaison-officer of the Foreign Ministry, von Hintze wrote the following words to his State-Secretary, Dr Solf: ' ... rumours are going round in the Army that Field-Marshal Hindenburg and the Emperor will be got rid of. These rumours are playing havoc. Officers are beginning to take sides. The junior officers are against them both, the more senior ones are firmly *for* them both. There is talk of civil war already.... After the frightful peace that awaits us, any Government is going to need the Army – at least the solid nucleus that can be got from it. People ought to be working out how the Army can be saved. Surrender and revolution are going to wreck it. There are officers whose judgment I respect, and this is what they are thinking ...'.[2] These few pro-phetic words forecast the whole predicament that faced the corps of officers for the next fifteen years in its relationship to the State: its attitude towards the State's new form, its gradual penetration by politics, the gulf between the generations, and the preservation of the Army's essential character in the teeth of military defeat and the disappearance of the monarch....

A few days later the whole edifice collapsed – State, monarch and all. But the foundation, on which something new could be built, remained to a large extent intact; and the credit was mainly due to the *ad hoc* alliance, made as early as the 10th November between the Army Staff, i.e. Hindenburg and Groener, and the Social-Democrats' leader, Friedrich Ebert. It saved the life of both parties. In Berlin great public meetings of officers were held. At one of these the new Prussian Minister of War (himself a Wurtemberger), General Reinhardt, was present and was the object of attack by junior captains, while at others the theoretical justification of Bolshevism was already being discussed. Then came the 19th January 1919 – the day for elections to the German National Assembly; and with the backing of the Hindenburg-Groener-Ebert pact it was possible for the *Army Gazette*, which was still appearing, to publish an appeal by Reinhardt,[3] containing these simple but epoch-making words: 'In response to their leaders' call, the officers and non-commissioned officers have placed their services at the disposal of the new régime. The great breach has been avoided.'

At the same time, Reinhardt laid down two elementary conditions to govern the creation of a new Wehrmacht for the Republic: firstly, there must be a clear structure of command in the Army, and secondly, a start must be made with removing practical power from the soldiers' councils in their then revolutionary form. In later days he rightly described this decision as 'a sort of mutual peace-pact for the benefit of the defence-forces'. And on the 6th March 1919, barely six weeks later, after a few days' debate in the National Assembly, Reinhardt was able to publish the Law on the Formation of a provisional Reichswehr* which he had largely drafted himself. Nothing more was said about soldiers' councils, and moreover the Regulation that accompanied the law contained the elements of the Reichswehr's later structure. Reinhardt's great historic service, so his first Chief of Staff[4] considered, was that by straight dealing he prevented the people's deputies and the first President of the Reich from taking a radical course. 'Thus on the one hand the birth of the Reichswehr was closely connected with the re-formation of the Reich while on the other hand its roots lay deep in the rich soil of the old Army.'[5] In this, the first post-war year, the Reich and its social foundations were assailed by the utmost dangers; but the skeleton of the new Army's structure was erected, and its strongest buttresses were the magnanimity of Noske and the calm sense of military and political purpose displayed by Reinhardt and his staff.

Among the latter was Seeckt. He held the post of Chief of Personnel while Reinhardt was Chief of the *Heeresleitung*, and in March 1920, he took Reinhardt's place. Under Seeckt the second stage began – the period in which the Reichswehr was built up and given its distinctive image in the public's eye. It was only at that stage, when the worst appeared to be over and firm ground could be felt under foot, that the latent tensions began to appear both within the corps of officers and in its relations with the world that had brought the new State

* R. Ges. Bl. 1919, p. 295ff.

into being. Soon they were visibly acute. The strain appeared, for example, in the problem of the *Freikorps** whose officers were now trooping into the Reichswehr. They had got no further than mounting a local *Putsch* here and there; but the plain fact was that for the first time in Prusso-German history since 'Lützow's wild, foolhardy ride' in 1813† officers had tried to influence politics. What is more they often behaved like *Landsknechte*, and the Reichswehr was quick to see that they could be a menace to the structure it was planning. They were got rid of. But there were other officers, so it is reported, young men who had served in the trenches and who thought it was their role to put Machiavelli into practice by playing the devious politician.[6] Such ambitions brought them, however, into head-on conflict with the standards of the older officers in command who had been brought up in the Imperial Army.

But the latter had their political problems too. Up to the outbreak of war there had been much animosity, understandable on both sides, between the corps of officers and the Social-Democrats. When the latter voted the necessary sums for war at the crucial session of the 4th August 1914, the hatchets were buried. In the trenches and under the shattering artillery-barrages both parties had other worries, and a degree of reconciliation was born of their common service and self-sacrifice. What is more, a certain number of Social-Democrats received commissions – a thing that would have been inconceivable before 1914.[7] These reconciling factors bore further fruit in and after the revolution, when the Army Command found it possible to co-operate with the people's representatives. In the turbulent times of civil war, the two groups were able to rely on one another in maintaining the integrity of the Reich and in warding off Bolshevism. In the November revolution the officers had been denounced as 'members and representatives of the capitalist class' among other things; but now the two worked hand in glove. Still, the abuse hurled at the officers had left a sting; and this was partly the reason why, below the surface, the bulk of the officers – they all came from the old Army, of course –

* The 'Free Corps' were spontaneously formed by demobilised and unemployed officers in order to fight against anything that smacked of 'bolshevism' and separatism; but they had no legality and few principles. Among their exploits was the 'Kapp-Putsch'.

† *'Lützows wilde verwegene Jagd'* (Theoder Körner) was an episode in the Wars of Liberation against Napoleon.

now seethed again with 'genuine Old-Prussian touchiness' against parliament, democracy and all their works. In general too, of course, defeat, revolution and civil war were all of them calculated to nourish and intensify the officers' traditional dislikes. They searched for some means of compensating for the humiliations heaped upon them since 1918, and eventually their self-esteem pitched upon the myth of the *Dolchstoss* – the 'stab in the back'. The main responsibility for their defeat was thereby thrust upon the left-wing politicians, the very men whose hands now held the reins of power.

The same mentality was likewise turned against the Germans who had signed the Treaty of Versailles for its severe disarmament-clauses touched the officers on the raw.[8] These were the conflicting emotions at work on both sides in the 'Kapp-Putsch' and in the counter-measures that followed.[9] The other aspects and sequels of that affair need not be examined here. All that need be mentioned is Seeckt's unambiguous declaration that 'the Reichswehr will not fire upon the Reichswehr'. This was not wholly fair to the legally constituted Government, but it was not revolutionary either. What it expressed was a deliberate policy of 'wait-and-see'; and this was destined to become the typical attitude of the Reichswehr's generals, and no doubt also of most of its officers, towards the Weimar Republic and later towards the Third Reich too. This does not mean that what the Reichswehr and the corps of officers were perpetually 'waiting to see' was a chance for a *coup d'état*. On the contrary, the experience of the idiotic 'Kapp-Putsch', together with memories of the calamitous revolution of 1918, had undoubtedly caused them to reject all thought of armed revolt. Discipline alone – that highest of the virtues which Seeckt was always preaching to his officers – discipline alone forbade any sort of 'mutiny'. Thus it was only logical for him to ban all party politics from the Reichswehr at a time when disruptive forces were loose and the corps of officers was being wooed as much by the Left as by the Right. Even Noske, the Social-Democrat, when Reichswehr Minister in the summer of 1919, had banned all political propaganda from the barracks. The liberal Reinhardt's view was the same: and to the eye of Seeckt in existing circumstances, it was nothing less than a matter of life and death for the Reichswehr, and for those who were in charge of it most of all, to keep every sort of 'politics' out.

Under the monarchy, of course, these senior officers had been inhibited from politics anyway. And now, in place of the monarchy, there was implanted the idea of the country, the 'Fatherland' – in reality, the State – which the officer was bound to obey. The idea of being 'above party' was then incorporated in the Reichswehr Law of the 31st March 1921, which naturally had to conform to the Versailles Treaty. In actual fact the very first draft had been written in the last weeks of 1919, ie before the 'Kapp-Putsch'.[10] That Law of 1921 remained in force for exactly fourteen years, viz. until the 31st March 1935. Many basic matters of internal organisation naturally could not be covered in the text of the Law. Chief among these were the 'Principles of Training in the Army', officers included. Right at the beginning of the year 1921, therefore, Seeckt had cast these principles in the form of a fundamental Order which remains of lasting value both as a military document and as a piece of contemporary history (the text is given in Appendix 28). A year later, on the 6th April 1922, the old army's 'Articles of War' were revised and re-issued as 'The professional Duties of the German Soldier'; and the two documents together show plainly what the policy was – to base the new army firmly on tradition.

None the less this policy and the success that attended it were twice defied by groups of junior officers even during the life-time of the Weimar Republic. The first assault was made in connection with the 'Hitler-Putsch' of the 8th November 1923 in Munich, the so-called 'capital of the Movement', the 'headquarters of order in the Reich'.[11] The political atmosphere there was dominated by the extreme right-wing, and Munich was where National-Socialism had its first successes – notably in the Munich garrison, where it was obviously helped by Bavarian animus against the Prussian tradition that coloured the Army Command in Berlin. The appeal for help which a lieutenant wrote on the 22nd October 1923 (see Appendix 29) gives a good idea of the political atmosphere that reigned in Munich at the time. This document suggests – though there is more than one opinion on the matter – that the Munich Infantry School, to which young officers were posted from all over the country, had been seriously infected too. It seems to be a fact, at any rate, that practically the whole personnel of the School took part in the 'Hitler-Putsch' – though it did so on a false pretext put forward by a former 'Free Corps' officer, Lieutenant Rossbach. He claimed that the School had been summoned to action by General Ludendorff, who was then still a highly respected person. Seeckt called the participants 'mutineers' at their next encounter (though he did not act on that judgment) and, apart from that, all that happened was that the School was removed from the infection-ridden climate of Munich and transferred to Dresden. The 'Hitler-Putsch' itself was a failure – the main reason being probably that the garrison-commander, von Lossow, and the other chief holders of military and civil power refused to be stampeded and just managed to maintain discipline. The affair none the less blew the first undeniable breach in the advertised claim of the officer-corps to be 'above party'. For the moment, however, the affair was overlaid by other events.

The Putsch, though a failure, produced a far greater effect on the public and on politics than it had on the Reichswehr. One consequence of it was that the Chief of the Army Staff (HL) was entrusted with supreme executive power (*die vollziehende Gewalt*) in the Reich. The fiction that the Reichswehr was the trustee of the State and the Reich thus became a legal reality.[12] Seeckt, however, to the disappointment of the extreme right-wing, did not cross the Rubicon, but loyally surrendered his trust to the Government when it expired on March 1st of the following year. In official circles, of course, this added greatly to the Reichswehr's standing and strengthened confidence in its loyalty to the Constitution. Its star rose higher still in the spring of 1925 when Field-Marshal von Hindenburg was elected President of the Reich. For the corps of officers it was almost as if the good old days had returned. One of their own kind was head of the Reich again; he had their fullest confidence and under his protection they felt safe. As a result, the departure of Seeckt in the following year was not such a wrench as it might have been. On the one hand the senior officers grew accustomed under Hindenburg's wing to the republican form of the State. On the other hand, however, the over-growth of parliamentary life had a weakening effect on the whole body politic; and when Dr Gessler left the Reichswehr Ministry, his successor, General Groener (though likewise a monarchist at heart), determined to bind the Reichswehr and its corps of officers more closely to the democratic forces in the State. Such a move had been made all the more necessary by the dangerous pressure of the growing National-Socialist movement upon the very foundations of the Constitution. As was mentioned above, the officers' ancient tradition of serving a strictly monarchical State contained the seeds of tragedy; and once the monarchy, the authentic monarchy, fell, the tragedy began to unfold. When the Reichswehr Ministry, for tactical reasons, altered course some points to the left, the threat of tragedy began to cause serious disquiet.

Once again, as at Munich in 1923, it was the most junior officers, boys who hardly felt the pull of tradition, who were the first to succumb to the mounting wave of the 'national' movement. In 1929 and 1930 they were impelled to action again. Two lieutenants, named Scheringer and Ludin, in Artillery Regiment No. 5 stationed at Ulm under the command of Beck (later Chief of the General Staff), and a retired lieutenant named Wendt,[13] held discussions at the Brown House at Munich with a former Captain who was senior officer of Storm Troopers. Later, they went around visiting military units, recruiting for the Hitler movement and setting up Nazi cells in the Army. They were then arrested for conspiring to commit high treason; and on the 4th October 1930 they were convicted by the High Court of the Reich at Leipzig. Underlying these events was the fact that many young officers – and not only those convicted – had lost confidence in the Army's leaders. The gravity which General Groener attached to the matter is shown by the Order he addressed two days later to all officers of the Reichswehr, and by his Special Order to general-officers and regimental-commanders (see Appendices 30 and 31). He told the commanders they had 'insufficient self-confidence' and called them 'lacking the courage of their convictions', while he denounced the young officers for 'great presumption' and 'extreme sensitivity'; but he saluted the young officers' passionate sense of honour, their high average intelligence and the exalted ideals that moved them. The climate of opinion and the unreliable attitude of many senior officers towards the State as it then was are thrown into sharp relief by these criticisms, and indeed by the contents of these Orders as a whole.

These homilies, however, took no account of the social background that obviously made so many officers, especially the younger ones, an easy target for even the socialistic points in Hitler's programme, to say nothing of the 'patriotic' or nationalist ones. For the officer in Imperial Germany, the enviable prominence of his social position was a kind of compensation for his poverty compared with prosperous civilians. The 'revaluation of values' caused by war, revolution and inflation put an end to all that. Most of the young officers now came from families that had shared the same fate, and they themselves had never had the feeling of belonging to 'the first Estate in the land'. As a result they were all too liable to feel socially inferior and lend a willing ear to doctrines that may not have been Marxist but at any rate preached a social revolution.[14] Many of the younger officers had this sort of social outlook, while an anti-democratic 'non-political' attitude was common among the older ones. These two factors, taken together, were probably the real reason why Groener's pair of Orders do not, on the whole, seem to have produced the effect he had hoped for. The 'orientation-lectures' that General Schleicher afterwards made his staff deliver to units out in the country (questions, of course, were ruled out by military custom) are said to have been heard sometimes in icy silence. The audience may not have been Nazi-minded already; but few among them felt that the Reichswehr's interests were being properly looked after 'at the top'.[15] The general aversion from everything to do with parliament may well have played a decisive part in all of this and, so to speak, set the tone.

25

The Impact of National Socialism

Quite independently of attitudes to parties and their policies
something else was also at work in the last years of the Weimar
Republic. A change was coming over the whole military world
and in particular over the officers' attitude towards the State.
In 1931, six months after the affair of the officers at Ulm, the
situation was very clearly analysed by Dr Julius Leber, the
Social-Democrat Party's parliamentary specialist on the Wehrmacht,* in the following terms: 'I fear the Reichswehr has been
built up on a colossal mistake of von Seeckt's. He believed that
discipline was enough, and obedience to the commanders' will
was a sufficient guarantee, for the proper functioning of the
Army. But no unit in these times will place itself unreservedly
in the hands of its commander. The links between the soldiers
and the public are far too intimate for that, and all sections of
the public are far too closely concerned with social and political
trends of every sort. It is not enough to give a soldier orders.
He must have a mental image of what his task consists of.... He
needs not only discipline but other kinds of incentive.... It is
axiomatic nowdays that rulers and ruled, their ideas and their
aims, form a single whole with a common purpose and must be
sustained by common ideals.... If these ideals and symbols
are withheld from young men in the Army they will run after
other ideals and find themselves other symbols – substitutes
such as the recollection of imperial glories, and patriotic
language. Why has the National-Socialist movement been able
to find support in the Army? Because it has been intelligent

* He was later one of the leading members of the resistance-group formed by
Dr Gördeler, the Lord Mayor of Leipzig, and was executed on the 5th January
1945.

enough to offer the young men substitutes for the things the Republic has not been able to offer....'[1]

Over and above the need for a coincidence of ideals between the Wehrmacht and the State, it will be seen that Dr Leber also recognised that youth and young officers at that time had a right to idealism, imagination, and some degree of romance – though Goebbels' idea of 'romance with steel' still lay in the future. And in any case, very young officers were not the only ones in the early 'thirties to whom the swastika-flag was the symbol of their dreams and their desires. Far from it: there were stations where every officer in the place was infected with National-Socialism – and one of them, strangely enough, was the garrison at Potsdam, the very heir to the traditions of the Prussian Guards. At the Berlin War-Academy (whose commanding-officer was a Nazi sympathiser) the officers doing the course were highly intelligent and not so very young; but even there, three groups could be distinguished – those who were passionate Nazis, those – a good deal fewer in number – who rejected National-Socialism, and the third group – the majority – who were indifferent or sympathetic. The first group was largely composed of Bavarian officers, some of whom had been close friends of Röhm since his Munich days.[2] But among the older generation too, many felt attracted to the new movement – some of them instinctively, others only by degrees. Evidence on the point was given by Major-General Hans Oster, the former chief of the Central Section of the Counter-Espionage Department at Supreme Headquarters, when interrogated after the attempt on Hitler's life on the 20th July 1944. His statement contains such important and enlightening evidence on the intellectual attitude taken up by officers who had served in the imperial Army that it is reprinted in full as Appendix 32.[3]

Feeling in the corps of officers for and against the ideas and activities of the National-Socialists can only be described as highly complex. Even of groups and of individual officers this is just as true. Opinions, in many cases, changed from time to time, oscillating between sympathy and hostility. For present purposes, therefore, it may be best to make a broad comparison of the relevant arguments and factors. Some, of course, were calculated to attract, and did so. There were others again which, *a priori* and as matters of principle, or else objectively, or *ex officio*, were more or less certain to drive an officer in the opposite direction. Either way, moreover, these factors were of several kinds according to whether they bore upon home, or foreign or military affairs; and to some extent all three were interwoven, especially the military factors and those that concerned the outlook at home, for and against the second World War. One thing, of course, must be realised and accepted if any sort of catalogue of arguments is made. Some set of facts, some state of feeling, some movement of opinion, is bound, for the sake of the broad picture, to be presented in words that do less than justice to the finer shadings which historical exactitude requires. But when the scientific method is used there is frankly no other way of keeping the variegated world of phenomena under control and of fitting it into the framework of this study – least of all a world so bright and iridescent as the world over which the swastika waved. Let me therefore try and summarise it as follows.

In favour of Hitler and National-Socialism, the factors that appealed to the higher ranks in the Army were the following. First of all, preceding Hitler's *Machtergreifung* or seizure of power, there was the fundamental declaration on legality which he made on the 25th September 1930 in the context of the Supreme Court's trial of the officers from Ulm. In itself that statement was unambiguous; and coming from the leader of what was after all a revolutionary movement it was a promise that could not fail to impress all open-minded people. For example, as late as the summer of 1932, Schleicher, the Chief of the *Heeresleitung* told Hitler: 'If you come into power legally, that will be all right with me: if not, I shall shoot.' Simultaneously, he gave identical warnings to Göring and to Röhm. From the formal point of view, of course Hitler did in fact come into power 'legally', for Hindenburg summoned him and appointed him Chancellor. The leaders of the Reichswehr had imagined they could legally accept the new movement as a factor making for national renovation and 'take it into camp', i.e. they thought their rôle was to bring it to a sense of responsibility.[4]

A deep impression was then made by Hitler's emergency measures to stimulate the economy, He started by building 'Autobahns' which his propaganda-machine played up as a great work of peace, and he managed to put a fairly rapid end to unemployment which had grown to fantastic proportions as a result of the world economic depression of 1929–30. What he did was clean contrary to all accepted economic theory, and could only be done by anticipating the future output of the economy: but most people were unaware of that. At all events there was no denying the fact that Hitler practically ruled out the risk that the German working-class might be 'bolshevised'. Nor should one forget the skill with which the National-Socialists worked on the masses and gave them 'patriotic' leadership.

Before we leave the subject of domestic politics, there was another point that favoured Hitler. It was a hope – or rather an illusion – that there were prominent men in the Nazi Party among those who felt concern at the way in which Hitler's breaches of the Versailles settlement were gradually increasing tension in the world, and that such men's hopes were turning more and more to the Army. This reading of the situation was shared by many people. Major-General von Stülpnagel, for example, writing to Beck on the 30th December 1936, said: 'No doubt we can keep the world in an uproar for quite a while yet: but one day the world will have had enough, and will call us to order. That is how it looks to me, anyway. What is very interesting in this connection is this. If one approaches the matter with caution when talking to leaders of the Party, it begins to dawn even on them that things are not going too well, and of late they have even been heard to say so. They are making up to us more and more....'[5] The man who wrote these words was a member of Beck's resistance-group and forfeited his life after the attempt to assassinate Hitler in 1944. The fact that this last great plot failed like all the earlier ones was not, of course, calculated to increase the Führer's popularity in the corps of officers; it did contribute, however, to the myth that Hitler really was protected by the 'Providence' he so often appealed to. Much criticism of him was thereby silenced or greatly weakened.

We now come to the military points that told in Hitler's favour; and the greatest of them by far was the *Tag* at Potsdam in March, 1933. There, in the Garrison Church and in the presence of all the leaders in civil and military life, Hitler, the Head of the Party, the new Chancellor of the Reich, the leader of the new 'patriotic revolution', bowed low before the aged President of the Reich, Field-Marshal von Hindenburg, in sign of his profound attachment – it may then still have been

genuine – to the old Prussian tradition. It was a handsome
gesture; and it implied, of course, attachment to the Reichswehr too.

Hitler was relieved at first that the Reichswehr had not
interfered with his assumption of power. He left the Reichswehr
to its own devices and handled it with velvet gloves. But the
personal interest he showed in technical military matters
aroused the liveliest hopes in the breast of many an officer of
Guderian's type. It was the same interest that accounted for the
expansion of the Luftwaffe. The young pilots were beside themselves with pleasure at being allowed to fly again. Everything
else was forgotten, and politics merely seemed to them like a
comic kind of noise in the background.

At first the Army may have come off rather less well; but
the new wind still looked to it capable of filling its own sails
too. The Wehrmacht, after all, was always being apostrophised
by Hitler himself as well as by Blomberg as the 'sole sword-
bearer of the nation'. Finally, universal military service was reintroduced on the 16th March 1935 (it was characteristically
done without previous discussion with the Army) and thereafter
the Wehrmacht was modernised and massively re-armed.
Such things could not fail to make every officer's heart beat
faster at first. They meant above all a fundamental change in
the Reich's defence-policy and a deliberate return to traditional
German military principles. This vast expansion, moreover,
opened a not unwelcome field to officers hungry for promotion.
The very limited prospects of the Weimar period had led their
ambitions in directions that sometimes seemed to conflict
with honour or even with common decency towards their
brother-officers. And even without gay uniforms the old romance
of soldiering seemed to be coming to life again.

The modernisation of the Wehrmacht had been preceded
by a number of sensational actions on Hitler's part, most of
them concerned with foreign affairs. Only the most important
need be named. There was the break with the Geneva Dis-
armament Conference and with the League of Nations on the
14th October 1933 – the League being regarded by most
officers and other 'patriotic' circles as a mere policeman for
the Versailles Treaty. To those concerned for the preservation
of peace, the German-Polish treaty of friendship and non-
aggression (26th January 1934) looked like a success, and even

more so, the Anglo-German naval agreement of the 18th June, 1935. The first of Hitler's real political triumphs followed on the 12th March 1938 when he marched into Austria without opposition and, by adding it next day to Germany, formed the 'Greater German Reich'. By these two acts he gave effect to something that a large part of the German-speaking peoples on both sides of the Austrian frontier had genuinely longed for ever since the Napoleonic Wars, the Students' Associations (*Burschenschaftsbewegung*) of 1815 onwards and the failure at Frankfort in 1848–49. Then came the Munich agreement of the 29th September 1938; two days later the bloodless invasion of the Sudeten-German areas of Czechoslovakia, followed by the occupation of the rest, and the creation of German protectorates over Bohemia and Moravia on the 15th and 16th March 1939. Lastly, there was the German-Soviet non-aggression pact on the 25th August 1939. This was a dazzling series of political and military triumphs, and the last of them was followed at once by victorious campaigns, first in Poland and then in France.

The French campaign, in particular, was the subject of some reflections put down by Field-Marshal Keitel, while in prison at Nuremberg, shortly before he was hanged. Reviewing his record as chief of Supreme Headquarters (OKW) he wrote – with some remorse – of 'the imagination and persuasiveness that were shown by the Führer and Supreme Commander' which, he says, 'impressed (us) so deeply that we – or I, at any rate – believed in his genius, and we followed him even in cases where objective study and the use of our *own* experience of war would have required us to resist'. By the word 'we' Keitel meant, of course, the inner circle of senior generals, the very highest commanders. What he says on the matter is confirmed not only by General Jodl (see Part III) but also, among others, by Field-Marshal von Kluge. In a farewell letter he wrote to Hitler before committing suicide, Kluge also spoke of the Führer's 'genius'. P. E. Schramm, the historian, is one of those who deduce that though the senior officers' training in the General Staff made them unsympathetic to Hitler's mentality, they gave way to him 'not simply out of obedience to the Supreme Commander and Head of the State but because they respected Hitler as a man who, for all his mistakes and shortcomings, had greater talents than themselves'.[6]

We ought, therefore, to assume, no doubt, that Keitel's generalisation (which must anyhow also have been meant to justify his own behaviour) should be applied only with a grain of salt to the most senior commanders as a group. How far it applied to the general mass of officers – the distinction must always be borne in mind – is a matter on which it is even harder to make an objective estimate, if only because so little evidence has become available so far. On the other hand Keitel's statement does give a pointer and enables us to gauge to some extent the degree to which that series of Hitler's successes (for all the bad things that went with them) did produce a profound impression on the officer-corps in common with all other Germans, and immensely raised the Führer's prestige. The fact that the Great Powers recognised him, feared him maybe, but anyway respected him, is likewise undeniable, and it was one more factor that gained for that political phenomenon named Hitler the support of the corps of officers.

So much for the things in his favour. On the other side of the ledger, of course, there were just as many and just as weighty ones. Many of these factors by themselves cancelled out the favourable ones. Others again raised only uncertainties and doubts. How far this or that factor weighed with individuals or with groups, and how far a wave of emotion may have determined their fundamental attitude – these again are questions on which, apart from a few cases, very little can be said with certainty. Moreover, it is even harder to disentangle and identify the unfavourable factors, because they can rarely be isolated from the more or less complex set of attitudes or circumstances in which they are embedded. There is much material here for detailed investigation.

A good example is the bid for power which the Storm Troops (SA) made in 1933. From their own point of view they had a right to it. Article 22 of the Party Programme had after all promised the dissolution of the 'mercenary army' and its replacement by a 'people's army'. Hitler himself, too, had insisted in *Mein Kampf* that the Storm Troops must be the nucleus of the future Army. In a letter written to his father in the summer of 1932 Keitel had already mentioned 'the Storm Troops' pretensions vis-à-vis the Wehrmacht' and that they were giving him a lot of work in the Reichswehr Ministry.[7] Fritsch's notes for the 1st February, 1938[8] give details on the matter. 'The Storm Troops', he recorded, 'aimed at taking the Reichswehr's place.... in 1933 a start was made with the Luftwaffe, but nothing was done for the Army. On the contrary years of hard work on the frontier-defences was wasted by the Storm Troops' behaviour. Such troops as were available were largely used to give them accelerated training, and the troops' own training suffered. Every thoughtful soldier, I suppose, shared my belief that the Storm Troops were meant to take the Army's place – though Blomberg and Reichenau denied it again and again. Yet I myself should have thought it perfectly natural if this had been the Führer's intention. All the same, it was frightening to think of the consequences – the total destruction of the Army's foundations: military, moral and ethical. It would have been many a year, ten or twenty perhaps, before a new Army worth the name could have emerged from the chaos. That period ended on the 30th June 1934.'*

This description of the strains of 1933–34 may remind us that the Army had been brought to a similar critical state by the Socialist manoeuvres which Noske and Reinhardt had defeated just after the collapse in 1918. The future that now lay open to the Storm Troops was so obvious that a certain number of Reichswehr officers decided to join them – even some very intelligent ones, such as the then Lieutenant Mertz von Quirnheim, a friend of Stauffenberg† whose fate he shared in 1944.[9] Another who did the same was Friedrich Count von Schulenburg,[10] a former chief of staff of the 'Crown Prince' Army Group and Beck's superior during the final year of the war. To Beck, however, 1st August 1934, he wrote: 'My resignation from the active service of the Storm Troops has been accepted.... I have escaped from a nightmare, from a strait-jacket in which (to say nothing of my personal position, which had become indecent and impossible) I was expected to behave like an automaton – a demand that neither the Army nor the Civil Service ever made. ... I am afraid those people still imagine they can work with the Wehrmacht again. ...'

Schulenburg's disillusionment was only with the Storm Troops; but by the time at which he was writing they had in practice been trumped by the Black Guards (SS) and were

---

* The date of the 'blood-bath' in which Schleicher, Bredow, Röhm and many others were assassinated.

† The organiser of the attempted assassination of Hitler on the 20th July 1944.

fading from the larger field of politics. General Halder, then chief of staff of the VI Division, was another high officer of the Wehrmacht who still believed in Hitler's good intentions. Nevertheless, on the 6th August 1934 – a few days after Schulenburg – he also wrote in the following terms to Beck: 'The Chancellor's intentions are pure and inspired by idealism; but they are being abused and sometimes actually reversed in practice by the swarm of utterly incompetent – often downright useless – Party-Organisations.... Where there ought to be collaboration there is a growing antagonism between the two groups. One group wants, like the Führer, to build on existing values, but the only aim the other has revealed so far is to destroy all existing values in the name of a lot of muddled, fly-blown slogans. The actual materials the two groups use are really the same as they were in the days of the Communist danger; but the group that represents the Communist danger nowadays shelters behind the Führer's authority. It has no right to do so of course, but in practice the shelter is effective. In many cases the people concerned are the local Storm Troop bosses and NSBO leaders.* If you knew the details of the local terror maintained by the Storm Troops, the way Stahlhelm men† are maltreated, the bare-faced intimidation of business-leaders – you would admire the patience the victims have shown in avoiding violence up to now. How much longer it can be avoided is another question. I feel quite sure, anyway, that the Röhm revolt was only one of the many abscesses on Germany's sick body, and maybe not the most serious one.'[11] The recipient of this letter had grounds for letting Fritsch see it, too, for in Fritsch (as Beck recorded later) the Party saw 'not only the man who blocked the Storm Troops' bid for power but the man who was trying to keep the Party's slogans out of the Army'. And Beck, (writing in 1938, and circumspectly) then continues: 'Quite apart from the fact that the Army's basis today is National-Socialist, as it must be, the Party's influence must not be allowed to penetrate the Army, for it could only have a destructive, disintegrating effect.' It is practically certain that most of the corps of officers, like the

---

* *National-Sozialistische Beamten-Organisation* (National-Socialist Civil Servants' Organisation.

† The 'Stahlhelm' was the 'patriotic' organisation of the non-Nazi conservatives led by an industrialist named Hugenberg.

bulk of the population, held the same views as Schulenburg, Halder and Fritsch on the terrorist acts by which the Storm Troops and other Party organisations exceeded the Führer's intentions; nor can it be doubted that officers and people alike disapproved of the Party's interference in purely military matters.

The murders which Hitler ordered in connection with the Röhm affair of the 30th June 1934, and in particular the deliberate shooting of Generals von Schleicher and von Bredow, were certainly enough to give a violent shock to all these malcontents and disapprovers. But nothing of the sort occurred – at all events, no overt action followed. It must, of course, be borne in mind that the totalitarian take-over of the press, like all other outlets for public opinion, was already far advanced. The *Frankfurter Zeitung* alone was able to hold out for a few years – carefully watching its step, of course – because Neurath, the Foreign Minister, believed it was the only newspaper still read and taken seriously abroad. The officer-corps, however, had always looked on it as the leading Jewish paper and it enjoyed little popularity among them in consequence. But even the *Frankfurter Zeitung* could not print the truth, and by now there was no other source that could give the bulk of the officers, or the civilians for that matter – even those very near the top, too – the background information they needed if they were to see through the dense fog in which the Party-manipulators had enveloped public opinion. In Seeckt's time the officer-corps could still pride itself on the completeness of its 'non-political' attitude; but Hitler's 'patriotic' movement asserted that its aim was to reverse the revolution of 1918, and in the space of a few years the officers' 'non-political' solidarity was undermined to the point where the officer-corps, when faced with the murders of Schleicher and Bredow, was incapable of action.

One reason for this was certainly the sheer lack of information referred to above. And yet – seeing what their Supreme Commander did, how could the corps of officers have acted in common? The aged President Hindenburg lay dying at his home at Neudeck, far away in East Prussia. Too senile to distinguish cause from effect, and kept in ignorance of what had really happened, he sent his Chancellor a message of thanks and congratulations on having crushed the Röhm-Putsch – in which he saw an attack on the Reichswehr. This was the official interpretation, and it reappeared in Blomberg's message to the Reichswehr itself, in which he announced that 'with soldierly resolution and admirable courage the Führer himself attacked and annihilated the traitors and mutineers'.[12]

26

The Oath to Hitler's Person and its Consequences

It is hardly a matter for wonder if the corps of officers obeyed without resistance (though with occasional misgivings) when Blomberg, on the 2nd August, 1934 – the very day after Hindenburg's death – boldly made the whole Wehrmacht swear allegiance to the person of the new President and Supreme Commander, Adolf Hitler. Beck regarded Blomberg's order as designed to take the officers by surprise (*eine Überrumpelung*) and his own first instinct was to resign; yet for all his moral integrity and high intelligence he had second thoughts. 'He appears', so his brother Wilhelm later wrote,[1] 'to have let Fritsch talk him into believing that, as things were, such a step was impossible and that the Reichswehr would not have understood it. A large number of senior generals had already thrown in their lot with Hitler and they, at any rate, must have known what an oath to Hitler's person could bring in its wake. In Beck's own case it led to the gravest searchings of conscience at a later stage.' With the greatest respect for Beck's personal integrity and for what he did in 1938 and especially in 1944, there is no escaping the fact that Lieutenant Scheringer of Ulm was right – if a little fore-handed – about the events of 1934 in general when he wrote: 'The struggle between the fighting soldier and the bureaucrat began.' On this occasion, bureaucratic reflection and timidity got the better of the soldier's eagerness to fight and win. In any army there must be obedience; but in Germany every officer – senior officers included – had been taught for at least half a century (partly under the pressure of the first World War) that obedience must be placed far and away above all other military virtues and treated as an absolute value, as a sacred taboo. For officers who had been schooled like this in the continuous tradition of the monarchy and, by derivation, under Seeckt's and Hindenburg's authority as well, there was really no room at all for questions or responsibility or conscience, or for querying the legal or moral justification of an order received from the very summit. The senior officers' failure to act in 1934 is not pleasant to recall; but if a charge is to be made out, the historian, who must always write *sub specie aeternitatis*, is bound to look not at the moment of decision alone but at the historical factors that made it what it was. Guilt and fate pose an insoluble dilemma.

The oath that was sworn – and sworn still 'before God' – bound every man of the Reichswehr to give absolute obedience to Adolf Hitler as Führer and Supreme Commander, and be ready at any time to give his life for him. This was an oath without precedent. Its text, which Reichenau drafted, was indecent in itself, and Blomberg had no legal right to impose it at all; he did so, indeed, in obvious contravention of the law.* But the oath was sworn. Neither officers nor men could have known it at the time, but that oath was a turning-point in the relations between the officer-corps and the National-Socialist State. From that day onwards, every innovation, moral or immoral, with which the corps of officers was reproached, went back to that oath of allegiance, sworn 'before God'. One example is the violent *deminutio capitis*† which the Reichswehr suffered in the winter of 1938–9. In the German Army, chiefs of staff from corps-level upwards who disagreed with an important policy-decision taken by their General – as distinct from its practical execution – were entitled to put their views on record. This system meant that a chief of staff shared responsibility for his General's decisions and actions. On Hitler's instructions it was abolished and no exception was made even for the Chief of Staff of the Reichswehr.³ The dictatorial character of the régime had been immensely strengthened already on the 4th February 1938 when Hitler assumed direct personal command of the whole of the Wehrmacht (Army, Navy and Air Force), Blomberg having had to leave on account of his marriage – with Hitler and Göring as witnesses – to a 'lady' whose police-record was not of the cleanest. The blow this struck at the reputation of the officer-corps was second only to what Keitel

---

* The Defence Law of the 1st December, 1933.
† 'Loss of (civil) rights'.

described after 1945[4] as 'the monstrous intrigue' against Fritsch.

The fact that Himmler's Black Guards (SS) had a hand in the affair, as well as the Party at large, is plain enough from the reliable record made by Fritsch himself which was quoted above. The methods used by the SS had filled the regular officers with the deepest forebodings from the very first days – at a time when Himmler's notorious 'Procreation Order' (*Fortpflanzungs-Erlass*) of the 28th October 1939 still lay far in the future, though its basic aims had begun to show. Many regular officers none the less transferred to the SS in the last year or two before Hitler seized power. They were mostly juniors, of course, who saw little future for themselves in an army of only 100,000 men.[5] Yet the machinations the SS started in the autumn of 1934 were not aimed at Fritsch alone but at the Army in general, within which their own Emergency Units – later called the Waffen-SS – had been created. The mere fact of these units' existence was bound to cause friction with the Army and its chiefs. Abuse was heaped upon the Army, its chiefs were spied upon, and it was rare indeed for an army officer to be saluted by an SS man. 'Incidents between the Wehrmacht and the SS', in fact, were the subject of frequent proceedings in open court; but this was naturally undesirable for 'they harm the standing of both parties and undermine the public's confidence in the unity of the Reich'. A general agreement was therefore made between the Wehrmacht and the SS and published on the 25th January 1938.[6] Its aim was 'to settle all incidents out of court'. For its part, the Wehrmacht attached 'particular importance to establishing a spirit of deliberate comradeship with the SS as well as with the other sections of the Movement'. The text of this remarkable Order must surely have been drafted by Blomberg when he was still Minister of War.

Such was the situation of the Army. In respect of the other branches of the Wehrmacht the situation was, of course, quite different. The Reichswehr was scattered over large areas and was therefore much more exposed to local friction, quarrels and trouble with all sorts of 'little Hitlers'. The Navy, by comparison, was in a much easier and simpler situation, being concentrated in a few large depots where it outnumbered all the others. 'The Navy', says Admiral Raeder, 'was given rather a wide berth, and in the Party it was not altogether the "done" thing to try conclusions with the sailors.'[7] This was not only because Raeder 'took care that all sections of the Navy should behave correctly towards the Party': there were deeper political grounds for it. Ever since the days of Tirpitz and the *Flottenverein** before 1914, Pan-German views had been common among naval officers; and the naval mutiny at Kiel in November 1918 had made the Navy especially bitter against Marxism and democracy – between which no difference was seen. Two naval Free Corps that had taken part in the 'Kapp-Putsch' were afterwards accepted into the Navy and used as cadres for its re-creation. They naturally turned into *foci* of National-Socialist infection. In consequence even Hitler's seizure of power was more warmly welcomed – not to say celebrated – in the Navy than it was in the Army, where the tradition was much older, and more aristocratic too.[8] As for the third branch of the Wehrmacht, the Luftwaffe, it was, of course, the National-Socialist government that had raised it to the status of an independent arm. Almost automatically, therefore, its members had a warm feeling for National-Socialism; and in any case its head was Hermann Göring, the second man in Germany after Hitler, who longed to get 'his Luftwaffe' the top position of all. Hitler once, in a fit of pique, is said to have caricatured these differences with the words: 'I have a Prussian Army, an Imperial Navy and a National-Socialist Air Force.'[9]

All the more reason, then, for his design (the *Tag* at Potsdam notwithstanding) to pervert this 'Prussian' army, and force it into the National-Socialist mould. Willing tools, moreover, were not difficult to find. Already the Nazi vocabulary had seeped into the Army's language, as can be seen in 'The Duties of the German Soldier' (Appendix 33) which was issued on the 25th May 1934 over the signatures of Hindenburg and Blomberg. That was the beginnning of the process: 'sword-bearer of the German people (*nb*: not 'State')' – 'the people, united in National-Socialism, and its living-space (*Lebensraum*)' – 'strength rooted in German soil and German toil' – etc., etc. all jumbled up, however, with clichés current in older times, but now of very dubious value and sometimes almost farcical: 'confidence, on which discipline rests' – 'upright and loyal, God-fearing and truthful' etc. These virtues were to make the

* The 'Navy League'.

soldier a pattern to others. A secret Order issued the following year (22nd July 1935) contained a homily on 'The Attitude of Reserve Officers to the State' and included the following instructions: 'As regards the State, it goes without saying that the Wehrmacht accepts the National-Socialist view. It therefore becomes necessary to convert officers of the Reserve to the same way of thinking. In consequence no one is to be trained for or commissioned in the Reserve of Officers unless he sincerely accepts the National-Socialist State and stands up for it in public instead of adopting an attitude of indifference or even hostility towards it.'[10] It was not very sensible to demand 'sincere' acceptance, however, and lying was unwittingly encouraged as a result. Mistrust, on the Party's side, grew ever greater and along with it, fanaticism, the enemy of reason and of all human relationships.

The strain increased from year to year. Following the Fritsch crisis in the spring of 1938, Hitler required the new Commander-in-Chief of the Reichswehr 'to bring the Army into closer union with the State and its philosophy (*Gedankengut*)'. One may well ask how this purpose was supposed to be served when on the 17th August 1938, three months after Fritsch's fall, the Waffen-SS was formally declared an independent 'sword-bearer', equal in status with the Army. This sort of challenge from the Party could do nothing but deepen the Army's latent mistrust of the régime. Reasons of self-preservation alone were enough to account for it. The war brought no improvement. Hitler's 'Euthanasia Order' of the 1st September 1939 was not widely known at first. But it was a different matter when, on the 28th October 1939, Himmler observed that war was 'a letting of the finest blood' and enjoined the SS to 'procreate children'. Some sections of the Army showed the utmost indignation,[11] and after a time Himmler actually had to issue a tortuous explanation by way of apology. The war had other shocking consequences too. The Army's attitude to the SS and the police after the conquest of Poland varied between hatred and disgust. Every soldier was revolted and horrified by the crimes that were being committed there by fellow-Germans – men who wielded their country's power; and the troops were shocked to think that things like that could happen under the protection of the Army – and go unpunished too.[12]

But it was the invasion of the Soviet Union, beginning on

the 22nd June 1941, that made the ideological aim of Hitler's war overwhelmingly plain. There is much to be said for the view that in Hitler's mind this attack was a further round in the street-fights he had once successfully led against the Communists in Germany. The struggle of ideas was simply being continued now in the area between the Vistula and the Volga.[13] As such, it was waged – and under orders – with a brutality that increased as time went on. On the 6th June, shortly before the attack, the guidance that was issued 'on the treatment to be given to Political Commissars' set international law and military tradition both at nought: 'in principle', it said, they were to be executed immediately if found in action or resisting'. Significantly enough, this order was to be distributed only to Army-Commanders (*Oberbefehlshaber der Armeen*) and Air Marshals (*Luftflottenchefs*); below that level it was to be disseminated orally.[14] After 1942, it was silently ignored.

The ideological note was sounded again on the 10th October 1941 in a very outspoken Secret Order which read: 'There is still much confusion about the attitude to be adopted by troops towards the Bolshevist system. The main object of the campaign against the Jewish-Bolshevist régime is the total destruction of its military power and the extirpation of its Asiatic influence from European civilisation. On the troops this objective lays tasks that transcend the ordinary functions of soldiers. The man on the eastern front is not just a soldier fighting according to the rules of war; he also bears aloft the inexorable faith of a people (*eine unerbittliche völkische Idee*)'....[15] In this respect the disaster of Stalingrad had no effect on the outlook of those in command. Evidence will be found in an Order by General Schörner which Supreme Headquarters rated highly enough to give it wide circulation. It was issued on the 1st February 1943 and it contains this sentence: 'A struggle between two *Weltanschauungen* is being fought out here, between two conceptions of life, two ways of living'.[16] But a struggle was going on behind the scenes as well – a struggle to 'revolutionise' the Army and the officer-corps. The campaign waged by Party Headquarters culminated on the 22nd December 1943 in an Order from Hitler which created a 'National-Socialist Leadership Staff' at Supreme Headquarters (OKW) and the posts of 'National-Socialist Leadership Officers' (NSFO). The document outlining their unenviable task is reproduced as Appendix 34. They were not to be some kind of chaplain; they were to be 'militants': and their work was just as important as tactical leadership and training.

The theory hitherto, as we know from other documents, had been that the State rested on twin pillars: the political one was the National-Socialist Party and the military one was the Wehrmacht. This theory was now replaced by another: the Wehrmacht was to be the 'sword-arm' of the Party – an obvious analogy with the mediaeval theory of the State as the secular arm of the Church. But the 'missionary' activities of the NSFO rested on an illusion that was already in bad shape, and they were stultified by 'very widespread lack of understanding' and, of course, by 'Old-Prussian military tradition'.[17] The Navy and the Luftwaffe, incidentally, were omitted from this exercise for they, of course, were reckoned to be sound. Hitler, however, was undeterred. The bleaker the outlook, the more fiercely he clung to the belief that his *Weltanschauung* could miraculously overcome weapons. It is hardly credible, but it is true, that as late as the 13th March 1945* he issued an order from his headquarters in which he said: 'The growing severity and scope of the war require the last ounce of effort if victory is to be assured. In such a struggle as this, the most powerful weapons we have are a National-Socialist *Weltanschauung* and political faith.... I therefore issue the following order: The prime task of commanding officers is to make their troops political fanatics, and commanding-officers will be responsible to me for the National-Socialist convictions of their men' etc.[18] With Hitler subject to such hallucinations, it is no surprise to find that in the very last things he wrote, the 'testaments' designed to commend him to posterity, he could still devote the whole of a page to denouncing the treachery of the Army's officers and the General Staff.[19]

Hitler's total and incurable treason-complex had been growing for many years. It was the product of a whole mass of subconscious elements of distrust – factors that were psychical and sociological, perhaps also physical, but certainly also military. On the 20th July 1944 that complex received the *stigmata* of absolute certainty.

There was, however, one officer at headquarters whose judgment of the situation must command respect. That officer's

* On the 30th April he committed suicide in Berlin.

duty was to compile the war-diary of the Wehrmacht; and in the final year of the war this placed him in a position to take an exceptionally wide view of what was going on. Being himself a trained historian, moreover, he was able to assess events with a practised eye. The conclusion he afterwards recorded[20] was this: '... at no time and in no theatre of war was the course of events at the front affected by treason. This is true, in particular, of the period just before the 20th July 1944 and of the situation that resulted. Admittedly the conspirators included Army Commanders (*Oberbefehlshaber*), as well as generals and staff-officers in key-positions; but on the eastern and western fronts alike they kept up military resistance to the enemy just as vigorously as others who were not involved. The behaviour of Field Marshal Rommel is a clear case in point.' After a brief outline of their strategic and political ideas he goes on: 'The conspirators thus had the same interest, exactly the same, as Hitler had in keeping the fronts ... intact. The theory of treason no more explains the outcome of the war than the theory of "sabotage". On the contrary, the course of the war was so logical in itself that its outcome needs no other explanation.'

It is well known, none the less, that in the blood-bath of revenge that followed the attempt on Hitler's life more than fifty General Staff-officers met their death, while hundreds of less important officers were quietly transferred. Many of them, like Stauffenberg himself and Mertz, had once been National-Socialists, and had soldiers' blood in their veins. Something quite exceptional must have happened to open the eyes of these men and others of their kind. The political and military factors at work have been examined in the present chapter. But in most cases there may have been other and even more powerful factors – religious ones – in operation. This is not the place to discuss such problems. Historians of the period have delved deep into them already.[21] The plotters' motives were drawn from many things, both at home and outside Germany: they were patriotic in nature, ethical and metaphysical – and no doubt much else besides. The plot itself produced effects at home and abroad and, of course, in the military field; and none of this varied material can be studied sifted or evaluated without a good deal of *a priori* assumption going into the process. For that reason alone it is unlikely that opinion about the affair of the 20th July 1944 will ever reach a single, accepted judgment. On one point, however, there must already be agreement among men of good will: the tragedy, great as it was, that overtook the victims of that day is eclipsed by the shining example they set, by their witness to the faith they had in their country and in humanity.

As for the man at whom their deed was aimed, the words apply to him with absolute justice which Theodor Fontane wrote[22] of another who sought to make himself dictator of all Europe: 'It is a vile ambition to bind the weal and woe of millions to the whim, and maybe to the madness, of a single man: and to invoke the name of the Almighty in such a puppet-show is nothing less than blasphemy.'

PART FIVE

SOCIETY

27

Introduction:
'Community' and 'Society'

The change that came over the relationship between the State and the corps of officers after the first World War began as a process of disintegration and then turned into one of partial adaptation.

'Adaptation' is rightly accepted as one essential mark of a modern industrial mass-society, and sociologists, since 1930 or so, have made it the corner-stone of their theories.[1] As a formal principle it derives of course, from Darwin's theory of the adaptability of species; but as a means of interpreting the phenomena of history and sociology it has too often proved inadequate. Another and more promising principle has come to take its place for these purposes – one that was first propounded by Ferdinand Tönnies: the polarity of 'community' and 'society'. Now in the German corps of officers these two poles, or categories, were in a state of mutual reflex – so much so, that it is often well-nigh impossible to tell which was primary and which was secondary. At the same time there is little room for doubt that in every context we have scrutinised thus far the dominant factor, the one that really counted, was the 'community' that was formed by the profession of arms. The purpose of this Part, therefore, is to investigate at least the main lines of tension between the two. They are concerned with the officers' life off-duty, the life they led not in the barracks but outside, a life that was only vaguely and indirectly related to military life as such. None the less, some of these non-military aspects of the military career contributed powerfully to the image of this community which was, and is still, accepted in Germany and abroad. Other aspects of it, moreover, helped create a type of social leadership that had nothing to do with national or class-considerations.

28

The Churches,
the Sects, the Freemasons

It will be best if we start our enquiry at the highest level with religion, the highest of all the factors that influence the social life of civilised peoples, past and present. Rather than 'religion' however, we had better say 'the church'. In the Middle Ages it was still the supra-national concept of Christendom and the Divine order upon earth that ruled relations between peoples; and the role of the sword (private feuds apart) was to serve that hierarchical idea. How far the individual knight pursued this religious ideal in his private life is a matter we need not go into here. There followed the great schism; then came a secularisation of life and with it a great weakening of the idea of the catholic universal Empire. Even if chivalry as such had not died out, this evolution must have caused a definite break in the traditional link between the sword and the imperial crown. When Luther decided to join forces with the separatism of the ruling princes who sympathised with his religious movement, he took a fateful decision; and one result was bound to be that the military powers (i.e. the leading military forces of the time) acquired a new political and religious character.

At first this breach with the old tradition of chivalry as the servant of the Empire was to some extent masked by the existence of the *Landsknechte* and by the contractual, or commercial, system of raising armies and waging war that went with them; but for that very reason the *Landsknecht*-system was wholly out of place once territorial princes became sovereign and absolute. This was especially the case in the Protestant lands, for the prince was now supreme head of the national church as well and was engaged, too, in converting his corps of officers into an outright instrument and symbol of his absolute power. In a Protestant country, therefore, the relationship between the officer-corps and its sovereign moved on to a quite different religious footing.[1] In a country that was still Catholic the monarch had no personal, organic link with the government of the church but continued, like his subjects, to accept the Pope as its supreme authority. Politically, too, the Emperor retained a greater hold upon the Catholic princes than on the Protestant ones, as personifying the ideal of universal Christendom.

In this, maybe, lies an additional reason why in Bavaria (which, until its union with Franconia, Swabia and the Rhenish Palatinate, was a purely Catholic country) the local nobility, the successors of mediaeval chivalry, provided a far smaller part of the officer-corps than in contemporary Protestant Prussia where the lesser nobility supplied nearly all the officers (see Part I). In nineteenth-century Bavaria, at all events, thanks to the attitude of most of her Kings, the question of religion played no such part as it was playing in Prussia at the time.

In Prussia, after the death of Frederick the Great, many of the most influential paladins of the Prussian spirit maintained a long resistance to any suggestion of equal rights for both religions. They wanted to see Prussia the leading Protestant power on the Continent.[2] Part of this widespread anti-Catholic attitude was certainly due to the fact that in the dominant East Prussian half of the country the Catholics were mostly Poles by race – doubtfully loyal, regarded as socially and culturally inferior, and rated pretty low in general. In the early eighteen-eighties, indeed, Count von Schlippenbach, the Inspector of Prussian War Colleges, went so far as to assert 'that candidates educated in the Old-Prussian *Gymnasien* and especially in Protestant ones were definitely of superior quality to those from Catholic or South German schools'. None the less, from 1885 onwards, such opinions and the general attitude they expressed are no longer to be found in reports from the Inspectorate. Probably the old Emperor had little patience with them. Ten years earlier, after all, when the 'Kulturkampf' was at its height, he had confidentially impressed it on all general-officers commanding 'that every effort must be made to ensure that matters connected with the unhappy religious strife of the present time are not brought before tribunals of honour'.[3] This is not to say, however, that the intolerant spirit of the 'Kulturkampf' was not alive among the senior Prussian officers here and there, even as late as 1914, and later.

Other religious bodies or sects were taboo in Prussia. For example, there was a case in which the son of a retired general of noble family wanted a commission. His father was intensely religious but had moved further and further away from his local Evangelical church until in the end he formed a religious community of his own. The son had not been confirmed and did not belong to either the Evangelical or the Roman Catholic church. When an uncle, who was also a retired general and a nobleman, enquired what the young man's prospects were, the reply was that His Majesty was unlikely to approve.[4]

This incident shows, indeed, that William II was faithful to his own religion; but otherwise he was generally tolerant in religious matters and, unlike a number of his ancestors, his benevolence extended to Catholicism too.[5] The officer-corps as a whole kept matters of church and religion on the plane of outward formalities – things that were part of the general conventions of society. Private soul-searchings were the individual's affair and, as a body, the officers paid little attention. Yet in those days religion, as 'church', served an important end in the Army and Navy alike, inasmuch as 'throne and altar' were treated and accepted as essentially linked to one another. Divine and military service were fused together, regardless of the individual's private convictions; and their fusion symbolised the State's foundation in Christianity.

The Weimar Republic declared religion to be a private matter, and in the Reichswehr religious activity was therefore voluntary. Seeckt, all the same, maintained the institution of military chaplaincies along with the old regulations that governed them. Even after 1933 no change was made at first. The mass of the people, after all, was still unconverted to National-Socialism; and it was in order not to alarm the public that the Party had adopted Article 24 of its programme, expressing adherence to a 'positive Christianity'. For the same reason the official Government statement of the 23rd March 1933 contained a passage asserting that the Government 'regarded Christianity as the unshakable foundation of public morality and ethics'. There were many other statements of the sort.[6] Even the campaign to unite the Evangelical churches

seemed at first to be honestly meant. But it was not long before
the *Deutsche Glaubensbewegung*, or 'German Religious Movement', began to wear a different look. Stirred up by Himmler
and Goebbels bitter strife broke out between the Catholic and
Protestant churches. In this so-called 'struggle between the
churches' the Wehrmacht not only tried to maintain religious
neutrality but also refused to tolerate denominational propaganda or allow individuals to change their religious affiliation.
Moreover, there is evidence to show that up to 1936 only
members of the two great denominations were accepted into
the Wehrmacht.[7] Fritsch and Brauchitsch in the Army,
Raeder and Dönitz in the Navy – all four of them, with Hitler's
concurrence and the support of a good many senior officers,
did their best to keep anti-religious influences out, and they
succeeded at least in maintaining the chaplaincies in both
services. In the Luftwaffe, of course, there were never any
chaplains at all.[8]

Chaplaincies were a traditional religious institution; but
quite apart from that, the period up to 1939 furnishes ample
evidence for the conclusion 'that at any rate in the Army
there was a solid core of officers firmly attached to traditional
ties and values'.[9] Hostile influence, and even directives, from
above were either ignored or deliberately misinterpreted.
For example, there are reports of cases in which the duties of
'National-Socialist Leadership Officers' were given to theo-
logians – which caused the Party's central office to take great
care that more of these jobs should be given to their own brand
of Christians, or *Gottgläubige*.[10] On the other hand the effort
these men made to spread the virus of the new totalitarian
Weltanschauung had the effect of calling forth increased resistance
from the infected body; and even those who had not been very
'Christian-minded' until then began to feel they must close
their ranks. A heightened sense of a common Christian faith
began to transcend all denominational bounds – a thing that,
broadly speaking, had been almost imperceptible until then,
but which now made religious tolerance a living force among
the German corps of officers once more.

This sort of tolerance, rooted in ethics and human feelings,
was, of course, the natural anti-pole to totalitarianism. Now,
however, it also became the symbol of a *Weltanschauung*, of an
attitude of mind of which the officer-corps had once, for more

than a hundred years, been among the chief exponents. In Frederick the Great's Prussia, after all, 'each man was free to go his own way to Heaven'*. As Crown Prince Frederick had joined the Freemasons[11] and as King he publicly installed Freemasonry, gave it his recognition and fostered it. Among its members were countless generals and other senior officers in the eighteenth and nineteenth centuries (especially in the Napoleonic Wars), in addition to many intellectual leaders and numerous reigning German princes. The Emperors William I and Frederick III even gave their formal patronage to the three so-called 'Old-Prussian Grand Lodges of Christian Faith' (*Christlicher Prägung*). In William II's time Freemasonry lost much of its interest for the officer-corps and the nobility, and the reason for this decline lay probably in the growing trend towards class-consciousness, towards a certain secularisation of life, along with professional specialisation and a narrowing of interests. For Catholic officers, of course, the Vatican's ever-growing hostility to Masonry must have been an additional deterrent. There is nothing, however, to show that any part of the officer-corps up to 1914 held Freemasonry in abhorrence or even rejected it on principle.

One result of the defeat with which the first World War ended was to send Ludendorff right off the rails; and from being a general he ended up as a 'world-revolutionary and harbinger of German tribal creativeness (*Volksschöpfung*)'.[12] The tribal (*völkisch*) and highly anti-Christian theories he developed and vigorously spread were an unconscious anticipation of the National-Socialist *Weltanschauung* peddled by Hitler and Rosenberg; and in the process he lumped Judaism, Christianity and Freemasonry together under the opprobrious heading of 'supra-national powers'. Save for a few ex-officers of junior rank, his extremist leanings and untenable assertions aroused no particular response from his former associates, young or old, although he never ceased to be regarded with the highest respect, indeed with veneration, as a soldier. In the Reichswehr, to the best of my knowledge, no officer was ever asked whether he was, or had been, a Freemason. It was only under the Third Reich that all officers, like all civil servants, were forbidden to belong to a Lodge or to anything else of the sort – even to such founts of innocent merriment as the

* '*Jeder nach seiner Fasson konnte selig werden*'.

'Schlaraffia-Bund'; but then, even membership previous to 1933 could do perceptible harm to an officer's career. If he happened to serve under a man who disliked him and was currying favour with the Party, it could lead to his dismissal. Moreover, this risk applied not only to regimental officers but to others, such as medical officers, too.[13] But even the degree of infamy conferred by this Regulation stopped short of satisfying Ludendorff. In April, 1935, shortly before he refused Hitler's offer of the rank of Field-Marshal, he sent written and oral messages to General Beck through one of the few ex-officers who still took his part, expressing his 'concern', together with urgent warnings against these 'supra-national' powers. What he wanted was that the men at the head of the Wehrmacht should give 'clear and vigorous guidance on problems that were arising from the racial awakening and whose solution called for the measures dictated by nature itself'. Neither Fritsch nor Beck, however, saw his way to acting on such suggestions.[14]

29

The Jews

It is time to face the question, however, what the attitude of the officer-corps to racial matters really was, and especially to the Jews. In the nineteenth century – leaving aside the small group who followed Stöcker and similar nonentities – these things had not been questions of principle, let alone of *Weltanschauung,* either for the public at large or for the corps of officers in particular. It was only around the turn of the century that the racial problem as such began to be publicised and gradually focussed on the Jews. The background of this development was, on the one hand, the growing popular acquaintance with the theory of evolution and, on the other hand, a falling-off in the general prosperity of the recent past. It must however, be admitted that the Jewish question had already possessed a certain practical importance for the officer-corps, especially in Prussia, back in the nineteenth century, for it arose whenever the point came up whether a Jew could be an officer.

Even in respect of faith alone there was no actual regulation that excluded Jews on principle from receiving commissions. Statistics of their commissioning in Prussia are only available for the last few years before 1914. But it can be taken as a fact that Jews, i.e. adherents of the Mosaic faith, were not commissioned into the regular Prussian Army.[1] The usual explanation given was that in respect of diet, observance of the Sabbath and so forth, Jews were bound by religious law; and indeed a formal opinion given at Fulda in 1913 by Dr Cahn, the Chief Rabbi of the province, showed that no dispensation could be given. In Bavaria, all the same, Jews were commissioned not only into the Reserve but into the regular Army – a thing that Prussians noted with severe and widespread disapproval.

As regards officers on the reserve-list the position in Prussia had previously been the same as in Bavaria, and up to the year 1885 Jews were frequently commissioned in the Reserve. After that year, however, this practice ceased both in Prussia and in the states, including Saxony, whose armies were run entirely on the Prussian model. A circular issued by the Prussian Minister of War on the 10th June 1908 contained, indeed, a reminder that it was not in order (*unstatthaft*) to exclude one-year volunteers and candidates for the Reserve of Officers from special training and promotion 'solely' on the ground of their belonging to any particular religious denomination. Arising out of this circular the Minister of War, von Einem, stated in the Reichstag on the 19th March 1909 that it was not in order for the corps of reserve-officers to refuse a young man who was otherwise qualified simply because he was a Jew. His successor, von Heeringen, however, speaking in the same place on the 10th February of the following year, frankly admitted that 'here and there perhaps, in isolated cases, there might be unwillingness – quite unjustified, of course,' to pro-mote a Jewish one-year volunteer into the Reserve of Officers. The reason he said was, that uneducated people sometimes imagined a Jew would not command the respect due to a superior. Such notions could not be disregarded. A year later, on the other hand, the Union of German Jews[2] was admittedly able to quote twenty-six cases (I have not been able to check their authenticity) in which the baptised sons of Jewish parents had become reserve-officers in the Prussian Army. In the last resort a baptismal certificate was treated as sufficient, though it was very flimsy evidence of racial origin.

Race-consciousness really played no part even among Prussian officers, and the fact is shown by the following incident which occurred in 1913. The Belgian Legation enquired whether a half-caste, a man of mixed white and Indian blood, whose father or mother was a German subject, could become a Prussian officer. The Prussian Ministry of War could not find that the question had ever been considered, and concurred with the Foreign Minister's view that it all depended on the candidate's personality (education, etc.) and on the social origins and position of his parents, and that his religion might also be relevant; but that there was no regulation that would exclude a half-caste as such from receiving a commission. The

War Ministry observed *en passant* that 'the law admits of no exception based on mixed blood. We have accepted Egyptians, Chinese, Japanese, Americans, Brazilians, etc., and some of them have become officers; but one may doubt whether the question of mixed blood was examined and resolved in every case!' This incident also makes it clear that there was no objection to other races; there was simply an aversion from Jews. All the same, there was no objection to marriage with baptised Jewish females, provided they were rich enough.

The range and confusion of opinion that existed as regards the Jewish question is shown up still more by the fact that while Jews could be officers of the Reserve, some Christian 'dissenters' could not. What is more, 'dissenters' were rejected not on any ground of principle but simply because Jewish free-thinkers, atheists and such like had also taken to using this description of themselves. It was therefore possible 'that with a view to qualifying for commissions certain individuals might classify themselves as dissenters in order to conceal their membership of some religious denomination which would normally preclude them from selection for the Reserve of Officers'.[3] Local military authorities were therefore confidentially instructed to investigate the term 'dissenter' in each individual case and to act likewise in respect of members of free-church denominations. A case then occurred in which a lieutenant of the Landwehr who was a magistrate in civilian life had left his local Evangelical church but refused to give the military authorities his reasons for doing so. As a result, the whole principle involved in the question of admitting 'dissenters' to the Prussian corps of officers was gone into, and was decided very much on the lines indicated above. 'Classification as a dissenter', so the Minister of War informed the Reichstag late in 1907, 'does not automatically disqualify a man from being selected for a commission, nor does it entail his resignation either. Membership of a religious denomination recognised by the State is, however,* so desirable in an officer as to make it necessary, when an individual leaves his church, to investigate the grounds for his action. . . . In any case this procedure furnishes a safeguard against individuals seeking to get commissions

---

* It is significant that in the first draft[4] of this statement the word 'however' was followed by the words 'even today'—an important qualification that pointed to the future. But they were afterwards struck out.

by calling themselves dissenters when their aptitude for commanding and training troops is rendered dubious by their attitude towards Church and State.' At the time, as it happened, only two officers and seven medical reserve-officers in the whole Prussian Army described themselves as dissenters.

Thus the way in which the problem of dissenters was handled also goes to show that in reality the Jewish question itself – which was really the one at issue – was judged officially and in principle less from the racial angle than from the religious. Anti-semitism as a matter of principle arose in the ancient and mediaeval worlds out of economic and religious conflicts. In modern times it spread – partly overtly and partly covertly – throughout Europe and America; but in Germany, while there was a certain amount of disdain and cold-shouldering, there were large sectors of the population where it had hardly taken any root before 1914. Only in the intelligentsia, and then only among those who read Wagner, Nietzsche and Houston Stewart Chamberlain, did it find some adherents. Otherwise, generally speaking – in the *Hochschulen*, for example, in spite of Adolf Bartels and a few other cranks – the doctrine of anti-semitism remained something rather odd, something that did not quite make sense. It was much the same in the corps of officers. 'The Army was not pro-Jewish, but it was not anti-semitic either.'[5] If a Jew in the first World War behaved with distinction, showed bravery in the field or was an outstandingly efficient soldier, he was recognised and honoured like anyone else. Two thousand 'German subjects of Jewish faith' (as the phrase then went) were commissioned in that war, as well as 1,200 medical officers and military officials, and among them were many who earned high decorations – even the *Pour le Mérite*.*[6] On the other hand people were apt to think there were too many Jews in 'cushy' jobs behind the lines and at home, and especially in the War Economic Organisations (which were anyway unpopular); and this caused so much bad feeling at the front that from the winter of 1916–17 onwards the authorities ordered a certain amount of 'combing out'.

Walther Reinhardt, the Wurtemberg General who was made Prussian Minister of War (for the future Republic) in November 1918, was generally in favour of full equality of rights for Jews

* The highest German decoration for gallantry. Dating from 1667, it was re-founded by Frederick the Great in 1740.

– including the right to be commissioned. At the same time he was well aware that this was 'not the attitude, perhaps, that was expected of him'.[7] Reinhardt was a man with the habit of thinking for himself, and his career in the Army had made him exceptionally well qualified to know the mind and temper of the officer-corps, from top to bottom. The cautious utterance I have quoted strikes me therefore, as evidence that a great variety of attitudes was to be found among the officers. But things were on the move. The winter of 1918–19 saw revolutionary upheavals, and the leading parts that were played in them by Jews must have done some damage to Jewry in general. Countless officers already felt the earth rocking underfoot; and the effect of these events upon such men, who were anyway not pro-Jewish, was, of course, to arouse antipathy. The Reichswehr's policy, however, remained unaltered by waves of emotion of this kind. It was deliberately 'restorationist' in character; and from the vast numbers of officers available the number of Jews selected was not impressive. It followed that in later years very few officers were forced out of the Wehrmacht by the so-called 'Nuremberg Laws'.[8] According to Admiral Raeder[9] only two in the whole Navy were obliged to leave, and care was taken to see that they got good and suitable jobs in civilian life. When war broke out they were taken back. Senior officers, moreover, stood up with success for any junior who was in danger on account of his 'not purely Aryan descent', and only a few of them even knew which officers were affected. There is no reason to doubt that, by and large, things were managed like this in the Army too, and that the same *esprit de corps* was shown there. The thing that really mattered was the decency of the commanding officer. In the Luftwaffe, of course, the question who was a Jew and who was not was decided by Göring himself.

With the second World War, and especially with the Russian campaign, the Jewish problem took on a fundamentally different aspect for the whole of the Wehrmacht. In Russia it was quite different even from what it had been in the Polish campaign. There, for the first time, the thing called the *Weltanschauung*, in its most brutal form, was brought into action as a weapon of war; nor had Stalingrad yet opened the final act of the gruesome tragedy. It was not merely that every Army newspaper – most of them edited by Party members – on every front from the 'Atlantic Wall' far into the steppes of Russia, from the African desert to the Arctic Circle, waged a campaign of systematic hatred against the Jews. Words, on the Russian front, were followed by deeds – in fact, by mass-murder. Many generals did their best to counteract the widespread horror that such things aroused in the rank and file. On the Russian front the generals seem to a large extent to have succeeded at least in keeping the Wehrmacht clear of this butchery itself and of formal responsibility for it. On the 24th September 1941, for example, the Headquarters of the Southern Army Group (von Rundstedt) sent the following circular to all units: 'In occupied territory the task of investigating and countering hostile activities and elements (Communists, Jews, etc.) that are not incorporated in the enemy's armed forces belongs exclusively to the Special Commandos of the Security Police and the Security Service, and they will take the necessary measures on their own responsibility. Individual members of the Wehrmacht are forbidden to act on their own, and members of the Wehrmacht are forbidden to join the Ukrainian population in excesses against the Jews: nor are they to be present or take photographs when the Special Commandos' measures are being carried out.'[10]

Orders of this sort are seldom issued unless acts of the general kind they prohibit have already taken place. There is evidence, moreover, that even after this order had been issued the Wehrmacht sometimes helped the Special Commandos in their monstrous work. There is, for example, a report by the Security Service on 55,432 executions carried out in the second half of October, 1941 in the Ukraine alone and by a single Special Commando; and it is stated there that the victims were 'primarily Jews and, once again, largely Jewish prisoners-of-war handed over by the Wehrmacht'. Again, a detailed report on Borispol, where 1,109 Jewish prisoners-of-war were shot in two days, makes a point of recording 'that the smoothness with which the operation at Borispol was carried out was due, not least, to the efficient support given by the local units of the Wehrmacht'.[11] Things being what they were at the time, this sort of 'success-story' was apt, no doubt, to contain a good dose of exaggeration or colouring-matter for the benefit of headquarters in Berlin; but, faced with a definite report of co-operation by particular local units of the Wehrmacht (matters which higher authority, after all, could easily order to be checked) it is hard to believe one is reading a pure invention. The Security Service was engaged in fanatical orgies of extermination, and Lieutenant-General Heusinger, then Chief of Operations at Army General Headquarters, can scarcely have been alone in the opinion (which he later stated upon oath) 'that he had always regarded these brutal methods as a military imbecility that needlessly added to the Army's difficulties in fighting the enemy'.[12]

In the words of General von Senger und Etterlin[13] the use of such organised cruelty and brutality against defenceless racial minorities was an insult to every sort of military honour. There was indeed an unbridgable gulf between the Party and the soldiers. The Party pretended this hellish handiwork was a necessary consequence of its false religious 'faith' – and invoked the name of Providence and an allegedly historic cultural 'mission'; while the Army upheld the idea of 'chivalry' that had gone unchallenged in every civilised country and in every age, the code under which the German officer had been nurtured from his earliest beginnings right up to 1933.

30

Morals, 'Materialism',
'Militarism', Manners

These nightmares of organised cruelty and brutality were born of the darkest side of human life. Compared with them, the ethical problems that beset the officer-corps right up to the end of the nineteenth century wore a bourgeois, decent, almost child-like air. People were troubled for example, to know how an officer ought to behave when a brother-officer committed suicide, and the problem worried everyone, right up to the Emperor himself. In 1879 William I still took the strict religious view:[1] he disapproved the fact that 'the corps of officers itself should often have announced in the newspapers the death of officers who had recently committed suicide'. Suicides of this kind might well arouse deep sorrow, he admitted: but they did not justify 'the corps of officers expressing public sympathy for one who had departed this life in disregard of his duty towards God and his fellow men'. William II, however, took a rather more indulgent line: he agreed[2] 'that an officer who has departed this life by way of suicide may, in exceptional cases, be buried with military honours and the officer-corps may announce his death in the newspapers'.

The moral behaviour of officers when off duty need not greatly concern us here. It is anyway unlikely to have been either better or worse than that of contemporaries with the same degree of education. All that matters to us is their attitude, or at any rate the attitude of those who set the tone, as regards individuals who committed the grosser breaches of the moral code. Here, in fact, the same evolution of thought is to be seen as in the question of duelling. In the days of Frederick William IV of Prussia and Lewis I of Bavaria it was still the ethical standard that prevailed. The King of Bavaria took no particular pleasure in hearing sermons himself; but when it came to keeping mistresses he took a serious view. He called it a 'state of affairs that went against both the dignity of an officer's profession (*Stand*) and against morality'. He gave the inspecting generals the strictest instructions on the matter and made it clear that he expected senior officers to set a good example; for the most effective remedy to his mind, was 'the appeal to the sense of honour and, failing that, transfer'.[3] His father before him had not been much inclined, either, 'to give promotion to those of his subjects who do not trouble to uphold their honourable status (*Stand*) by conducting themselves in a manner that is steady, moral and deserving of respect'.[4]

In 1841 a scandal at a masked ball in the Berlin opera-house also moved Frederick William IV to make it known, in his own emotional way, that 'this honourable calling (*Stand der Ehre*) will not suffer if it loses one whose conduct shows that the true concept of honour has acquired no meaning for him'. This occurred, of course, at the moment when the draft Regulation on Tribunals of Honour was before the Prussian cabinet. In the preamble to that Order[5] the King used the following language: 'This nobility of mind, which is the only real nobility and without which there can be no public decency, is what I expect from the higher ranks of society in general, and especially from the officers of My Army; by that standard I shall measure an individual's worth and assign him the appropriate place both in relation to higher things and in the social order.'

There is no means of telling whether in practice this exalted notion of private morality was applied in full to the judgment and punishment of each individual case – or only in principle. If the question of duelling is any guide there is room for legitimate doubt. In royal Orders of that day the same ideals were expressed as in those of earlier times; but in practice the traditional moral code of the officer-corps prevailed. On general questions of morality, as on duelling, it looks as though things evolved in the direction of a non-moral official attitude that was solely concerned with protecting the impersonal, collective interest of the officer's profession. It was not strictly moral values that were looked at so much as the question whether 'the conduct of a brother-officer threatened to do harm to the reputation or standing of the whole fraternity' (*Genossenschaft*).[6] The question, therefore, was rather one of custom than of morals, of etiquette than ethics. The real test was the conduct of a 'decent man'.

To the extent that a 'decent man' behaves as those who set the standards expect him to and avoids what will incur their disapproval, he is referring his acts and omissions to an *external* standard.[7] This transfer of a man's moral centre from within him to the collective moral centre of his group is typical of any close-knit human community, as we have seen already in the Part on 'Honour'. The dominant thing – to borrow a phrase from Friedrich von Wieser – is *die Psychologie des 'Man'*, the psychology of anonymity, which is based on what 'people' think. If a community-spirit is deeply rooted in the group's collective moral code, and if *esprit de corps* is a vital 'biological' need for the group in question – the more these things are so, the more plainly the group will tend to have this faceless psychology. In the corps of officers this was the case to the very highest degree; and the specific experience of war was bound to make it so. The fear of imminent death, as we saw in Part III is automatically counteracted by honour and courage; and these in turn are partly actuated by the thought of what the others will say 'if you funk it'. By its very nature the heroic instinct is contemptuous of death; but unless that instinct is strong and active the factor that really makes a man face physical combat is this awareness of 'the others', of his fellow-officers and, directly or indirectly, of the men under his command.[8]

Herein lies the idea that explains why comradeship plays a major part in the whole of an officer's life, and why it has always been methodically fostered by higher authority. The officer's first duty, he was told, was to cultivate the true spirit of comradeship; 'it is the senior subalterns' business to train the junior. This is a responsible task; they must always keep it in mind and foster the closest relations between brother-officers.' This is the note most commonly struck by regulations and admonitions on the officers' private life. In Prussia the higher command was especially active in pursuit of these ideals; and the reason for this lies, no doubt, in the fact that the size of the Prussian Army made it difficult for senior officers to know what was going on. In Bavaria, Saxony and Wurtemberg the corps of officers were much smaller. Personal contact and supervision were all the easier in consequence. Evidence of a capacity for good fellowship was one of the factors even when junior officers and officer-candidates were under consideration: what degree of respect they enjoyed, whether they were inclined to keep to themselves, whether they were popular with their fellows, and so forth.

One great means of cementing relations between officers began to emerge, or was established, in the latter part of the nineteenth century – the officers' common dining-club which the Army called the '*Kasino*' and the Navy the 'mess'. Any society or club derives the greatest benefit from possessing its own permanent meeting-place; be it a whole house or only a room, it is just as effective as an uniform or any other kind of distinguishing mark.[9] Human beings, after all, need some outward sign of the invisible. These clubs were originally meant to make life cheaper and more convenient for the younger, unmarried officers; but as time went on they became 'the best and most suitable meeting-places', as was said. It was there, first and foremost, and not in public places, that the young officer was to be trained and earnestly advised to look for company – so all regimental-commanders were enjoined by the Emperor's Order of the 1st January 1897. We have seen a sociological parallel to this in the Prussian nobility's tendency – which also belongs to William II's time – to concentrate in certain Guards regiments and Provincial Guards, and make them private preserves.

Now as soon as this sort of thing achieves success it begins to show certain sources of weakness too – namely fear, fear of the outside world, fear of its rivalry, its alien, seductive, divisive strength. The community then begins to lose confidence in its own powers of cohesion. There is a sign of this in the above-mentioned Order of the 1st January 1897, where the Emperor shows anxiety lest young officers, by frequenting public places, 'come in contact with a state of affairs that may bring them into conflict with their duty as officers and may, moreover, have the gravest consequences for them'. The same note was sounded in 1911, when officers were warned against attending 'afternoon teas' in the great Berlin hotels on account of the 'very mixed' company to be found there. This was an almost panic closing of the ranks, and it involved, at any rate in Prussia, the danger that the ranks, once closed, would fall victim to a sort of intellectual inbreeding, the self-isolation of a caste in the face of ideas that were transforming the rest of the world.

234

Graver still was the risk that the isolated caste would start adopting the mere externals of modern capitalist society – its material standard of living. The officer-corps, in fact, was too much infected already by a hankering for luxury to be held in check by the sort of means the Emperor recommended.

This urge to maintain a higher, often extravagant, standard of living was typical; but the deeper reason for it – one that covertly worked upon the instinct – was certainly never realised either by the individual officer nor by the corps of officers as a whole. A further factor was the economic revolution that was taking place, but it was probably not the major one. The real reason lay elsewhere – in the transformation being undergone by society itself. The Prussian corps of officers (which is all that concerns us here) was 'the first Estate in the land', and as such it had spent the last two hundred years or so in possession of an undisputed right of leadership. Of its superior merit compared with other Estates and classes in Prussia it had no doubt. But the French Revolution had opened an enormous chasm in the private and public structure of all European States; and from that time onwards the younger generation of the Prussian *bourgeoisie* – the older generation too, by degrees – was always pressing the State to admit new types of leader and new rights of leadership. The aim was to bring about a renovation of the old, incompetent Reich in the form of a new and stronger Reich that should really dominate its component parts. More than anything, they wanted the people's natural rights to be codified in a Constitution. The *bourgeoisie* was on the march; and though it exerted pressure both upwards and forwards the forces of 'reaction' seemed too strong for it at first. But in the Army, none the less, the higher ranks had been made to feel that the old social superiority had been fatally challenged, and this suspicion gradually spread. The more their real social domination was exposed to the incalculable assaults of the times, the more the sheer instinct of self-preservation made the officers cling to the outward trappings of 'authority', of 'respect', to the value of fiction, to what is nowadays called 'prestige'. The concept of prestige, admittedly, is one to which modern students of mass-society attach too much importance; but, as historians know, it has always been a very real factor, and in other social systems too. This clinging to status, this attachment to externals which everyone knew no longer fitted the realities of social and political life – this yearning for prestige is what really drove officers into 'luxury and debts', as the military histories call it.

In the context of the present study one might well go further and ask whether luxury is really the mark of the bourgeois and not of the aristocrat. In principle, of course, it is obvious that if expenditure is proportionate to income or at any rate keeps within it, no tension results, no psychological strain. It is merely a question of behaviour. Now the lesser nobility were far more imbued with the social standards of their superiors than was, or could be, the case with the *bourgeoisie*, and moreover they took their superiors' mode of life and scale of living as their model. The tone was thus set for the whole of the nobility (and indirectly for the *bourgeoisie* as well) by the *grand seigneur* who disdained money and money-values (since he himself was amply provided) and had no taste for the orderly management of his affairs – a thing he left to his employees. Again, class-solidarity bound all ranks of the nobility together; and this had two further results. The lesser nobility first of all preserved their privileges and then, having lost them in the nineteenth century, kept their leading position in society, even though they could not afford to lead the life of a *grand seigneur* and lived indeed much more in the style of the penny-pinching *bourgeoisie*. Their social position being secure, they had no need to try and seem more than they were by spending more than they had. The advantage due to noble birth still always gave them the edge over the bourgeois, however rich he might be.

The *parvenu*, in consequence, tried all the harder to disguise the handicap he suffered at birth by aping the outwardly visible and attainable manners and customs of the old aristocracy. He might think them in reality over-rated, but it was luxury and outward show that seemed to command respect. It was now the turn of the lesser nobility to feel unsettled, threatened, sometimes even humiliated, by this process of compensation – real or apparent – for the advantages brought them by their birth; and in their turn they were easily tempted to live on a larger scale. Thus they hoped to keep up with the newly-rich bourgeois whose social competition they felt, and whom they envied. The process drove them then to live beyond their means – and left them more impecunious than ever.

It was only natural that the officer-corps should also feel

this urge to compete in show with the wealthy *bourgeoisie*, and above all in Prussia where, as I have said, they had gone unchallenged for centuries as 'the first Estate in the land'. It was the rulers of Prussia themselves who were really responsible. First of all they bestowed a high social status on their officers and took pains to keep it up; and then, by pursuing a highly mercantilist economic policy, they helped create and enrich the capitalist *bourgeoisie* whose materialism was now a menace, real or imagined, to the social standing of this 'first Estate'. In addition, the officer-corps possessed, as I have shown, its own peculiar outlook on the world around it, a sort of spiritual extroversion that naturally made it uniquely receptive to the outward, material charms of life.[10]

It was no wonder, then, that this attraction grew stronger as the other strata of society began to improve their standard of living. This upward trend was not due to the increase in prosperity alone; another cause of it was the fact that mass-manufacture brought about a real, or apparent, fall in the cost of many articles. This in turn resulted from freedom of employment; and as early as the eighteen-thirties its effects were becoming plain – a rise in the average standard of living and a simultaneous rise in the general level of prices.

For one particular section of the Prussian officer-corps these factors were reinforced by another that began to operate during these same years. Prussian officers who came from areas of large-scale farming were already acquainted with the world that lived on speculative credits. Large landowners of this kind were the Prussian Army's normal source of officer-material and, from about the middle of the nineteenth century, various conditions (which need not be discussed here) combined to make them familiar with speculative deficit-financing as a means of maintaining or enlarging a property or leased estate, or of keeping up the old social position. There are detailed statistics on the subject.[11] A home-life spent in this sort of 'capitalistic' atmosphere was all too liable to colour the life of a son in the Army, and it sometimes rapidly led to insolvency.

We have Manteuffel's word for it that in Prussia 'being sued for debt was fully compatible with all law and custom on the status of an officer', and Manteuffel's wide experience of the Army lends his evidence authority. It was only at a later period, he says, that exalted notions, based on a false idea of the officer's peculiar situation, began to circulate. It was in fact from the angle of commercial ethics – if the phrase be allowed – that the progressive de-feudalisation and *embourgeoisement* of the Prussian officer-corps really became visible. The truth, as Sombart's researches showed, is that, the strict fulfilment of contracts is a typically bourgeois trait, whereas the wealthiest nobleman, the *grand seigneur*, adopts an attitude of elegant unconcern towards his financial obligations, and treats them with *grandezza*.

From what we know of Frederick William III's views about duelling it might well be supposed that so essentially bourgeois-minded a man would have taken rigorous action against this sort of loose behaviour. But nothing of the sort is on record, and the surviving archives are silent on the matter. Probably the reason is that this sort of thing was still too rare to obtrude upon the public mind and call for regulations to be issued by the King himself. Poverty was still so general after the Napoleonic wars and the standard of living was still so modest that officers can hardly have found much occasion to be ashamed of their own poverty, or to try and seem more than they were by living up to a high standard of comfort.

Things underwent a great change in the next thirty years, and they offered the new King an ample field for reform in the direction of religion and morality. Within a year of his accession[12] Frederick William IV felt himself obliged 'to dispense with the services of officers who are unable to refrain from dissipating their means to a degree which reflects on their professional utility'. Commanding officers were to keep an eye on the financial situation of their juniors, issuing warnings and admonitions in the event of irregularity. As for extravagant expenditure on horses (a matter that caused frequent appeals to the King's private generosity), his desire was that cavalry officers should, of course, keep good and well-schooled horses; but he could 'not approve expenditure thereon which exceeded an officer's means and was incurred simply for the purpose of appearing smart'. After this, he continued, came the need 'to avoid all expenditure in officers' dining-clubs that was inappropriate to the purposes for which they existed'; and all general headquarters were strictly enjoined 'to keep expenditure in these dining-clubs down to a level that would not bear hardly upon those of slender means'. What Manteuffel wrote ten years later to Bismarck, viz. that the Prussian officer was quite used to starving with dignity[13] had evidently ceased by then to be true. Nor, as regards this period, can one wholly credit the tale of the poor Prussian lieutenant who, in order to make both ends meet, gave himself indigestion once a week at the pastry-cook's so as not to have to spend the rest of the week suffering from a hunger he could not afford to satisfy.

Frederick William IV followed the Order of 1841 with a whole series of proclamations, appeals and warnings in similar vein – with the difference, however, that from 1843 onwards they brought in the question of honour. In 1845 the King went so far[14] as to make it the duty of all regimental-commanders 'to maintain regular contact for this purpose with the local police and thus to obtain the necessary reports'. It was probably on account of this final passage, which amounted to putting the private financial affairs of most officers under police supervision, that the Order was, contrary to normal practice, held up for two weeks before being circulated to general headquarters. A personal commentary was then added by Boyen, the Minister of War; and on this final passage he explained that 'what His Majesty had chiefly in mind was borrowing money at exorbitant rates of interest, pledging of officers' word of honour, playing for high stakes in public places, private gambling parties as well as so-called 'private' parties of unmarried persons in public places at which those taking part often indulge in luxury far beyond their means'.

All this did very little good. The reason is to be found in a Minute that was written at the time in the Ministry of War.[15] Commanding officers, it observes, 'have always been cautious about expressing their real opinion in confidential personal appreciations for fear of provoking transfers. Unqualified praise is probably inescapable. For years past, any man who ruthlessly cleans out his regiment, corps, etc., has run the risk of getting replacements who are little, if any, better than those he felt absolutely right to get rid of.' Whoever wrote these words put his finger on a weakness that was common to the corps of officers in every part of the Army. It was no use for Frederick William IV to order that, in principle at any rate, the frivolous contraction of debts should be brought before tribunals of honour. The reason why an officer who was always in debt gradually came to be regarded as a bad officer was that he lacked the moral strength to keep his expenditure within his income by suiting it to his general circumstances, and that an individual who defaulted on his debts brought all the officers of his unit into disrepute.

If the efforts which Frederick William IV made on this subject are looked at as a whole, it is clear that he was trying, in a formal way, to deal with the symptoms more than with the disease. William I, his successor, was nearer the mark in that he concentrated on extravagance – which is what leads to debts and all their undesirable concomitants. Even so, he was unable to check it. As early as the 2nd August 1860, when he was still Prince-Regent, he spoke his mind on the matter in a way that gave as much weight to the principles involved as to the details: 'I also firmly disapprove', he said, in a Cabinet Order countersigned by von Roon,[16] 'the taste for luxury displayed by various units. It is most unsoldierly and very much at variance with the simplicity which is so desirable in military life. I also disapprove the practice of giving banquets and exchanging expensive presents on every possible occasion. It is professional efficiency, essential worth, that secures a man's standing in the eyes of his brother-officers and leaves a good name behind him when he goes; it is not an outward show of affluence or the recognition of brother-officers as expressed in farewell-dinners, expensive souvenirs, presents and so forth.'

Soon afterwards, however, came the wars of 1864, 1866 and 1870–71, and they can hardly have added to this sort of cause for complaint. In the war of 1870, none the less, the Bavarians were struck by the costliness and luxury of the Prussian officers' field-equipment: the latter's outfit included table-services, whereas the Bavarians had hardly gone so far as to equip themselves with a pocket knife and fork. During the armistice and the occupation of France, moreover, many officers drew large allowances and got into the habit of living in great comfort.[17] It was also true, of course, that the hot-house climate of the *Gründerjahre* had caused the weeds of Mammon to flourish in astonishing profusion at home.[18] In the context of the general run of things in Germany the corps of officers succumbed still more to the trend towards extravagance and status-symbols, and the point was one that continued to give cause for much concern to the Emperor and the Minister of War. Early in 1876, the latter, von Kameke, wrote a memorandum on luxury in the Army and its attendant dangers. Though von Albedyll, the chief of the Military Cabinet denied it, the Minister frankly admitted that materialism was gaining ground in the Army, that the officers were becoming very bourgeois in the worst sense of the word and that the old, traditional simplicity was no longer the sure foundation of the officer-corps that it used to be. He ended, it is true, on a faint note of hope; but the memorandum as a whole breathes a spirit of melancholy resignation to the power of circumstance, the overwhelming materialism so typical of the times. This assessment may be partly due to the fact that Kameke was a man given to deep and anxious thought – 'unlike the usual type of Prussian officer', as a Saxon general who was his friend once said of him.[19]

Kameke was not the only one whose anxieties were brought – perhaps by his own contrivance – to the ears of the Military Cabinet.[20] But Albedyll thought the young officers of the day had fewer debts than in the past, and he put this to the credit of the officers' clubs. Others, however, and they were the majority, thought the clubs gave occasion for much expenditure on luxuries that went beyond most officers' means. Albedyll freely admitted that 'good officer-material' was getting scarcer, but he ascribed the fact less to the expenses of an officer's life than 'to the dying-out and impoverishment of the lesser nobility and the decay of officers' and higher civil servants' families'. The conclusion he drew was a simple one: the nobility should be put back on its feet and officers' families be preserved from poverty. Just how this was to be done, alas, he did not say.

It will be seen that the views of William I's military advisers were untainted by social or economic factors, and in consequence nothing effective was done about this urgent problem. Even the War Minister's memorandum seems to have spent three years in Albedyll's tray, after which he had it filed away. Nor did his views undergo any change in the meantime. Only a single circular to regimental-commanders seemed called for: they were not to require that officer-candidates should have more than modest private means. Yet in view of the multitude of extra expenses that a young officer could hardly avoid, private means were just what he needed if he was to make both ends meet. Thus one thing led to another; and the Army's leaders missed the essential point. Whether it would have made any difference if they had not, is, of course, another question.

The Emperor himself, at all events, never failed to set his officers a good example by leading a private life of the utmost simplicity.

The same is true of his grandson, William II, whose private life followed the tradition of his family, as that of most of the German dynasties also did. At the same time he had a lively personal sense of a modern German Emperor's rights and duties when it came to his public appearances. The resultant expenditure had its influence on the officer-corps' idea of what was proper for the first Estate in the land. Whatever the intentions, all this could hardly fail in actual practice to stimulate the long-standing drift towards greater spending. The commitments that resulted were the officers' private affair, of course; but to a large extent they impinged upon their official lives as well and were therefore unavoidable. In consequence many an officer groaned under the burden of them (especially if he had married young), and would have been content, and probably happier too, with a far more modest life. There was a good deal of truth in the phrase about the 'splendid misery' (*glänzendes Elend*) in which the officers lived. But it was usually the richer officers who set the social pace; and their numbers were growing not merely in the 'aristocratic' regiments but in many others too.

William II in his turn had frequent occasion to complain of excessive luxury and to take steps to curb it. On the 5th July 1888 he issued an Order to the corps of officers (not in the Army Gazette (*Armeeverordnungsblatt*) but in a circular) and revealed all the views and wishes that he was later to express in individual cases. Among other things he made a particular point of reproving officers who wore uniforms of ultra-fashionable cut, and he announced that if the regulations on uniforms needed additions or amendment he reserved the right to see that this was done. At a later stage, as everyone knows, he spent so much time altering the uniforms of the various arms of the Service that he often put the officers (all but the Bavarians, who were not affected) to serious additional expense for which there was no real need at all.

All the same, it was not just for amusement that the last of the Emperors took such an interest in uniforms. His interest was a by-product, social and psychological in nature, of his great concern that his officer-corps should be united vis-à-vis the outside world by the closest bond of comradeship – a point he strongly emphasised in his Order of the 5th July 1888. Obviously the Emperor expected that this would lead to a reduction in the officers' standard of living; but the isolation it led to was too splendid altogether, for the officers merely spent more in their 'Kasinos'. Moreover, there are indications in the archives that cases of alleged extravagance in the smarter regiments were treated with much more indulgence, not to say encouragement, by the Military Cabinet than the more strait-laced Ministry of War thought proper.

One form of luxury that was naturally a favourite was horse-racing, and the betting that went with it was not very different from plain gambling. Despite the Emperor's disapproval, these two additions continued to spread not only among the Prussian officers but among the Saxons as well. William I had set up a Commission in 1886 with the task of considering whether officers should be forbidden to engage in public horse-racing altogether. The Commission reported an unanimous negative. The Emperor expressed his satisfaction; and approved only some minor limitations,[21] such as that officers should not compete against jockeys and should only ride horses owned by the officers' social equals, etc. This was the sort of attitude that William II also adopted, both in general and in particular cases.

One increasing source of danger that had already worried Frederick William IV received a great deal of publicity from certain sensational lawsuits around the turn of the century. It lay in the very mixed company to be found at race-meetings, which in turn led officers into closer acquaintanceship with people 'who, in spite of their dubious origins (*Qualität*), are treated as the social equals of officers'. An official in the Ministry of War wrote that 'even the standard of true patriotism seems to go by the board in the world of international sport'.

Among Bavarian officers, who can be taken as typical of those in South Germany, gambling and racing were really only known at second hand. One reason may have been the absence of great modern cities, for at that time the term 'big city' could hardly have been applied to Munich. But the main reason, I think, lay in the social and economic structure of Bavaria and especially in the social composition of the corps of officers. Here and there in Bavaria as elsewhere in southern Germany a certain amount of heavy industry and large-scale commerce

I

had grown up in the course of the nineteenth century; but the real centres of large-scale German capitalism lay north of the river Main. Moreover, from the eighteenth century onwards and especially in the nineteenth, the Bavarian officer-corps, as has been shown, was much more bourgeois in character than the Prussian. On the other hand, if we exclude the tin-selled *demi-monde*, it was in the *grand monde* that gambling and the allied sport of racing had always found their greatest patrons and supporters. At all events the last place where extravagance in any form is to be looked for is in bourgeois society.

These addictions, therefore, were not only un-bourgeois: they were by-products of super-capitalism, and that is enough to explain why they held few attractions for the corps of officers in Bavaria. The latter's social standing, after all, had always been quite different from what it would have been in Prussia. This does not mean that Bavarian officers, too, were not expected to keep a certain social distance between themselves and the common people. In the mid-eighteenth century the Elector Max Joseph still showed a thorough-going feudal spirit when he announced[22] that he had too high an opinion of his officers to believe 'that any of them would so far demean himself as to have dealings with a bourgeois or with any other sort inappropriate to his status; even if he should consider that such a person had insulted him, a Bavarian officer should deem it beneath his dignity to seek satisfaction. He should reflect that no such person is capable of abusing or insulting him; on the contrary, it is open to him to seek redress for any such impertinence from the authorities.' Bavarian officers mixed freely with the common people all the same, when the mood was on them. Otherwise the Elector would hardly have been impelled to mention in the same decree his confidence 'that officers would not go so far as to dance with waitresses or other common serving-maids in wine-shops or beer-halls; should such a thing happen, the officer concerned is to receive exemplary punishment for the baseness of his conduct'.

The same decree allowed married officers to entertain other officers, but not civilians. 'Should an officer, however,' it goes on, 'allow his wife to go shopping in the market or at the butcher's, with her basket on her arm, it is permissible for a private soldier to relieve her politely of her purchases and carry them for her.' Furthermore, 'should an officer demean himself so far as to seek in marriage the hand of a person who, however well-endowed, is not his social equal, he should not only be refused permission but should be punished and treated as an officer without ambition.' Elsewhere, regimental-commanders are enjoined to prevent their officers from staying in country-houses. 'His Electoral Highness gives his officers enough pay for them to have no need to make this kind of economy.' All these regulations or rather prohibitions had, it is clear, the object of standardising and raising the social status of the Bavarian corps of officers. Both this and the creation of the Bavarian Cadet-Corps (see Part I) seem to have resulted from sending General von Meindres to Berlin to learn about the state of affairs in the Prussian Army so that whatever seemed useful could be introduced in Bavaria too.[24]

But these Electoral attempts to raise the social prestige of Bavarian officers did not have much success. Another generation and they were out of date, for the general policy of constitutional and cultural reforms that Bavaria pursued during the nineteenth century would have left no room for a corps of officers in the Prussian style, sealed off from the civil population and exalted far above it. If in Prussia the civilians complained of military excesses, there were times and places in Bavaria where the opposite occurred. A 'case of honour' at Würzburg in 1827 led Headquarters to observe 'that civilians who have dared grossly to impugn the honour of the King's officers have still not been condignly punished'.[24]

All the same, relations between military and civilians in Bavaria were generally good and harmonious. Bavarian officers were not placed, even in theory, a step above civilians, nor did tradition lead them to feel superior save in so far as might be warranted by superior education. After 1870 there was a change. Bavaria did not remain immune from the influence of the Prussian (especially the Old-Prussian) outlook on the relationship between officers and 'the rest' – though there was admittedly a parallel improvement in Bavarian military efficiency. In both countries, however, certain marks of social exclusiveness were never quite effaced. Here and there, indeed, right up to the fall of the monarchies, they preserved the importance of elemental distinctions, deep-rooted in Nature and in history.

In Bavaria none the less, and especially from the eighteen-thirties onwards, we run across the same complaints about the officers' luxury and its harmful effects on their private finances. There, as in Prussia at the time, the Ministry of War deemed it urgent to 'take energetic measures against a state of affairs that blunts the officer's sense of honour, detracts from the honour of their status (*Stand*), reduces their professional value and lays unjustified burdens on the assistance-fund'. Even so, the private life of Bavarian officers in the last few years before 1914 was a good deal more modest than was the case with the average Prussian officer. This is accounted for in part by the same economic and social factors that told against horse-racing and betting, but also no doubt by the very simple bourgeois life the Bavarian monarchy and court were leading at that time.

On the other hand there was a connection – it was not so much causal as organic – between the almost *petit bourgeois* mentality of the last two Bavarian rulers and their rather lukewarm interest in their Army and its officers. In this respect the Bavarian corps of officers often looked with envy at the Prussian, for the latter had no less obviously enjoyed favour of its Hohenzollern masters for centuries. In Prussia the nobility and the officer-corps together constituted 'the first Estate in the land', and this held good for all practical purposes long after the State had shed its class-character and the nobility their privileges, and even when the officer-corps was being recruited more and more from the *bourgeoisie*. Accordingly its sense of being socially different from the common herd grew all the more conscious and emphatic; while the latter, once its sense of having equal rights had been aroused at the beginning of the nineteenth century, uttered frequent, bitter complaints about inconsiderate, high-handed treatment by the military.

Later on, however, towards the end of the century, in the reign of William II, when all classes in Germany had been gradually debauched and perverted to a vulgar adoration of power and prestige, this civilian distaste for the military was very largely transformed – and not in right-wing circles alone – into its very opposite: and the plain silver shoulder-boards of a beardless subaltern commanded a deplorable degree of adulation.[25]

All this was an expression, a symbol, of what is generally

called 'militarism' nowadays: a problem widely studied, much debated and of great complexity. This is certainly not the place to attempt even the most summary account of it – the more so as studies made in Germany and elsewhere, and even purely historical research, have not yet led to any fully satisfactory explanation.[26] In my own opinion, the real historical importance of its political aspect, as well as its duration in point of time, has probably been much overrated, especially in some of the denunciations made by British and American writers. Far weightier and tougher was the sociological factor that was at work in the internal evolution of Prussian militarism. Those who were rising in the social scale and who sought to enjoy social prestige in the reign of William II found more and more that they must conform to the image of the corps of officers, for it was widely accepted and much admired. This in its turn meant that the officer-corps imparted a military tone to other social classes – a tone which is hard to define and which is scarcely to be found at all in democratic countries. The notion of 'the Army as a formative power in the State' *alias* 'the militarisation of society', was another that contributed its quota to lending this state of imitation and dependence a certain glamour, and to strengthening its emotional impact even upon the intelligentsia.[27] The sort of thing that could happen, even in academic circles, is shown by the following anecdote, dating from Imperial days in Berlin.[28] It was proposed that the Emperor should confer some honour on a certain professor in order to mark the latter's seventy-fifth birthday; and the learned man was asked what form of honour would give him the greatest pleasure. It had been supposed that he would like to be made a *Wirklicher Geheimer Rat,* or Privy Councillor, which carried the title of *Exzellenz* and was the highest civil distinction at that time. Far from it: what the learned greybeard wanted was promotion from First Lieutenant to Captain in the Reserve. In 1927 a former staff-officer named Franz Carl Endres coined the amusing definition: 'Militarism is the state of mind of the civilian'.[29] One is tempted to agree.

31

The Reichswehr: National Socialism

A tendency to deference on the part of reserve-officers and large sectors of the civil population was not, however, the only thing that resulted from the officer-corps' prestige. On the social manners and customs of educated people it had an undoubted influence too; and that influence assumed additional importance after the first World War, when there was an unmistakable decline in the manners of almost every class. The Reichswehr then found itself exerting a notable 'restorative' influence in that field too. In time of war, said Seeckt,[1] every man had to fetch his food from the field-kitchen in his own bowl; but he could not see why people in an Army which laid such stress on leadership should not also get used to eating with a perceptible degree of manners. A man who could eat peas off a knife was not bound to be a hero, nor did it follow that a man who liked to wipe his mouth with a napkin was a fool.

General von Choltitz, too, has described[2] 'the astonishing social influence' exerted by the officers of the Reichswehr, though they numbered only four thousand. Units were mostly stationed in the smaller towns: they had substantial buildings for their 'Kasinos' and the officers often represented the only social group with the means (which included their own band) of giving parties and receptions on any scale. The 'Kasino' in consequence was a place where boys and girls could meet one another in a well-mannered atmosphere. In much the same way, relations were gradually built up with the local leaders of commerce and with the universities. There was much sporting activity too. The infantry reached a high standard in athletics, the cavalry and artillery likewise in riding; and public sporting events brought them into close and agreeable contact with the civil population.

Interference with the pleasantly civilised life of the officers' 'Kasinos' came only when the National-Socialists took power. The corps of officers of the Wehrmacht was, of course, expected to retain 'the leading place' in social life wherever it was stationed; but henceforth, it was ruled, social life off-duty was to be governed '. . . by the bond of blood and fate that binds all Germans together'. Tradition and progress were to join hands. 'The old practice of seeking company within a particular social class', it was plainly stated in a secret circular addressed to all officers on the 25th May 1934, 'is no longer any part of the duty of the corps of officers.' There was a threatening note, too, in the assertion that 'anyone who has still not fully adapted his thinking to the concept of the people as a community (*Volksgemeinschaft*) has ruled himself out. The Wehrmacht has no reason to take any further notice of him.' But the circular, had to admit, of course, that it was premature to try and 'define exactly what sort of personalities it was desirable to win over or to lay down a pattern for social occasions'; commanding-officers were simply expected to 'find the right way' for themselves.* This Order was issued only a few weeks before the Röhm affair, and its tenor leaves no room whatever for doubt about the nature of the social revolution that was implied by the views and intentions held by the National-Socialists at the head of the Wehrmacht. There is no means of knowing with any certainty how far commanding-officers succeeded in finding (if indeed they tried to) whatever was meant by 'the right way'. What is certain is that the sociological process of 'adapting' even the Army's corps of officers to the 'mass-society' (*alias* the *Volksgemeinshaft*) spread from the top downwards and from the bottom upwards. In the field of manners, as in every other, tradition was progressively abolished. As such it may have seemed unimportant: but it was, and always had been, an essential element in the officers' whole pattern of behaviour, the officer-corps' whole character as an élite.

* The full text of this Order, taken from the 1938 edition of the secret 'Political Handbook', is printed in Appendix 35.

32

German and Other Ideals of Conduct

Thus one more integrated model of education and upbringing was doomed to gradual distortion, if not to ultimate destruction. The fact is that there is one central feature to be found in the private social conduct of the whole German officer-corps in modern times – a feature that forms, as it were, a common denominator, basically valid in some degree for every separate phenomenon this book has described. This feature is the social ideal of the *chevalier*, of the 'gentleman'[1] Primarily it is an ideal pattern of conduct, the very essence of formal European civilisation, the essential part of social behaviour, of manners. In the seventeenth and eighteenth centuries the model was furnished principally by the French. In modern times, despite some variants, it has been developed chiefly by the British. In the latter's hands it shed its original class-character and was converted into a pattern for all, from the aristocracy down to the factory-hand.

Plain as it is to the eye and to experience, this ideal eludes precise analysis because its formative power is present in every department of life. It combines the chivalrous side of the Middle Ages with humanistic elements derived from antiquity; but the formal elements are always in the lead. *Erlaubt ist, was sich ziemt,** says Goethe through the mouth of the Princess in *Tasso*; a pithy and, sociologically most significant utterance. In other words, conduct in the *grand monde* is ruled by social convention

---

* 'Whatever is proper is allowed'. (*Tasso:* II.1.) It is relevant that a few lines later the Princess adds:

> *Willst du genau erfahren was sich ziemt,*
> *So frage nur bei edlen Frauen an.*
> (If what is proper thou would'st truly learn
> Ask none but noble ladies for advice.)

based on mind and spirit. What convention may prescribe in detail, what rules it may enforce, are matters that lie outside the realm of logic. They are only to be conceived and understood as the fruits of a process of organic growth, and a whole book would be required if we were to enter into detail.

More by instinct than by any process of thought the German corps of officers always felt called on to aspire to this ideal of the *chevalier*, or 'gentleman'; and even in States where contact with the nobility was slight, the officers' business with the Court did at least put them indirectly in touch with a world of elegance and etiquette, for it was there, at the courts of princes and of prelates, that such accomplishments were normally to be found and learned. This Part has brought out various aspects of the way in which the old corps of officers looked at such matters as religion, morals, race, luxury and prestige. In reality, however, they were mostly aspects of the cult of 'good manners', the cult of convention. What is more, that particular professional community called the corps of officers dealt with even the problems presented by education, honour and the State, realised them and lived through them, in a manner that owed something to the universally valid conventions of social life.

Closer study, however, will bring to light the fact that this social ideal had yet another variant in Germany. This is not, of course, to say that the formative influence of the other two upon this third variety was anything but real or powerful, but it was the third that made the deepest penetration of the German mind. This local variant was the concept of the *Herr* – the master, or the lord. To the other two, whose nature was more static, this concept added a dash of dynamism; and the reason why it was so typical of the corps of officers is that in Prussia, of course, the officers (for familiar reasons) formed an élite not only of leaders but of rulers too. Yet everything dynamic has its dangers; and the danger in this case was that the element of 'mastery' would grow. Now the National-Socialists, once they were in power, seized on an ignorant distortion of Nietzsche's concept of the intellectual *Herren-mensch*, the 'super-man', and proceeded to combine it with their own belief in a nordic Aryan *Herrenrasse*, or 'master-race'. Automatically it followed that the *Herr* must now be violently distorted into something he was never meant to be – something wholly alien to his very nature. He was now turned into a caricature of the 'gentleman' who had once formed part of the *Herr*-ideal – who had formed the part, moreover, that had been common to the whole of Europe, a thread that had bound her peoples and their varied civilisations together.

An élite was still desired, of course; but its chief constituent was now removed, seized for every purpose, for himself alone, by Hitler. That constituent was the very one the old corps of officers had prized and tended most of all, the one that, more than anything, marks the human race off from the beasts – the one, indeed, that really makes it human. The name of it is 'responsibility'.

33

Conclusion

With the eye of history and sociology we have now scrutinised five different aspects of the German corps of officers. The lines that divide them may waver, but the divisions are clear enough. Yet all these aspects are but different sides, or functions, of a single whole, a single organic reality, a single living community. For, on duty or off duty, that is what the corps of officers actually was.

And yet again – if anyone in the old days imagined the German corps of officers, or even the Prussian, was a *rocher de bronze*,* upon which time and tempest could work no harm, he was wrong. Primaeval rock it was, true enough, and so it towered with many a pinnacle and jagged point above the levelling plain of modern society. But when put to the test, primaeval rock itself proved less resistant than it seemed. Against the corrosive power of time it held firm for a while, but it could not last for all eternity. What is eternity, anyway? The one eternal thing in history is change.

And change enough the German officer-corps has shown us in the short span of time over which we have been able to examine it. Sometimes these changes were brought about by forces working from outside or from above, sometimes it was self-generated forces that produced them; sometimes both sets of causes were at work, inextricably mingled. But it possessed a solid core, compounded of conviction and tradition, and even that ordeal by fire, the first World War, appeared to have left

---

* The phrase is from Frederick William I's dictum of 1716: *Ich ruiniere die Junkers ihre* autorité *und stabilisiere die* souveraineté *wie einen* rocher *von* bronze. (I shall destroy the Junkers' authority and establish my sovereignty like a rock of bronze).

the core intact. 'The breach was avoided' – or so it seemed. Yet the tempest of the nineteen-thirties, the hurricane that devastated society and State alike, proved more than it could endure. Year by year it was worn away and undermined until at last it began to flake and crumble, and in the end it broke up.

Assaulted from without and from above, tradition in countless forms had been overthrown and trampled in the mire. Its place was to be occupied by something wholly new, something the world had never yet beheld; and this Thing, which was an outrage on the laws set up by God and man for the governance of men and nations in their life together – this Thing was supposed to last a thousand years. What *hubris*, what measureless presumption! No wonder Nemesis was close upon its heels. The blows of Fate lie heavy on us yet; our path is darkened by a shadow that will not lift for many a day to come. Yet we should be wrong to let our vision be obscured. It is we, not others, who must overcome our past.

To that great end the writer hopes this book may make a modest contribution, albeit his immediate aim was simply the dispassionate laying bare of facts. The history and sociology contained in these pages may, perhaps, help rediscover the authentic tradition of the corps of officers and sift the timeless elements in it from the rest. It is, however, the task of those who would follow in their place to search the rubble of the recent past, pick out and try the stones that can be used again, and judge where they can best be inserted in the new structure of today. But the useful stones should not be made to serve only the new edifice of Germany's defence. That structure cannot stand save as part of an ordered plan for the State and for the wider association of which the State is part. If this be done, then time will not be slow to reveal that the value and the living strength of the German tradition of arms are rooted in the universal principles of human decency, and can serve no other end than the peace and freedom of the human race.

APPENDICES

APPENDIX I

Essay by Prince Frederick Charles of Prussia on 'the Origins and Development of the Spirit of the Prussian Officer, its Manifestations and its Effect'

STETTIN, 3RD JANUARY 1860

I consider the true founder and teacher of our Army was Frederick William I. It was also he who really made its officers a corps, the true upholders of the Army's spirit and service, and stamped his personality upon them.

The needs of the times, and the views of subsequent commanders are among the factors that have greatly modified the tactics of those days, the methods of drill applied by the great 'drill-sergeant' (to give him his nickname), and the spirit of the officers he trained. Yet in all these matters the basic outlook of those times is merely a part of our inheritance. The object of these pages is to demonstrate that fact by reference to the specifically Prussian outlook of officers today.

A good many of the Brandenburg nobility were troublesome at first, but the early Electors broke their power and their old importance, while the Thirty Years' War had extinguished their wealth. This was the time when a beginning was made with a standing army. Rough as the younger noblemen often were, impetuous and unused to discipline, they applied for commissions and received them. In the many battles of those times the greatest bravery was always shown by the officers, and they set their soldiers an example just as they did to their servants. Admittedly, the officers of that day showed great self-interest too – more than at any other time – but an *esprit de corps* began to emerge none the less, a spirit of keenness and comradeship.

Frederick William I and 'the old Dessauer'* together systematised the tactics of the times, and the result was to demand wearisome, rigorous training every day, even in time of peace. As the years of peace succeeded one another the hope of seeing action, such as the officers longed for, dwindled away, though this made no difference to the manner in which the officers pursued the strict curriculum of training. They did so, however, not as a matter of obedience alone, nor even from conviction, but because a man of independent mind, who values his independence, puts up with things like that in the hope of one day seeing war and action. He does not

---

* Prince Leopold I of Anhalt-Dessau (1676–1747), Prussian Field-Marshal.

257

do it, as the private soldier does, because he must: he does it *for a reason!*

That reason was derived from Frederick William I, and it made every officer an independent judge of the orders he received. The reason was honour. In the Spanish regulation of 1726 – the true original, which the King had translated into German and gave to every officer in the Army – it says that the officer owes obedience to his superiors 'even though it run counter to his honour'.

And so the custom grew up that if an officer wanted to convey to someone that honour forbad him to serve under that man, he reversed his spontoon. The junior officer would likewise lay about him with his sabre, on the spot, often on duty too, and even in the face of the enemy, if he thought his superior officer had insulted him – and so forth.

Everything is open to abuse, and in this case particularly so at a time when many coarse, uneducated men found their way into the corps of officers, when officers got drunk every evening and speech was plain and rough. This peculiar idea of honour was bred in every officer's bone, and there is no point in my discussing whether it did more harm than good. People seem, at all events, to have felt some serious doubts about it and in the end it must have been looked on as a bar to any serious discipline, for when Frederick II revised his father's regulations in 1744 he dropped all mention of it (and from subsequent editions too), imposing the severest penalties on anything that smacked of it.

Frederick II may have held it in check, but to suppress it altogether was more than he could do. Nor has it died out even yet. It is alive, I am convinced, in our corps of officers today, whether they realise it or not, and to some degree it infects every man who undergoes an officer's training. In support of this assertion, I may quote a series of examples.

1. The mass-migration of Prussian officers to Russian service between 1807 and 1812. Shortly before the outbreak of the war of 1812, several hundred officers did this* and among them were men of the noblest name and character – men we later came to regard with the highest admiration. They did this in a spirit of independence because they did not wish to fight under Napoleon and against Russia. They preferred to fight against their own Army, against the Prussian Army, because they thought Prussia, *their* Prussia, was no longer fighting under the black-and-white flag but under the Russian.

2. The officers' attitude in March and April, 1848. Large numbers of Guards officers, especially those of the 'Czar Alexander' regiment, who had fought in Berlin, wanted to resign because they were out of

* Marginal note in a later hand: 'Wrong: only 23!'

sympathy with what was going on, and thought their honour as officers had been tarnished. The only man they trusted – wrongly, too, in all probability – was General von Prittwitz who had just given up commanding the Foot Guards to take command of the Corps. It was only due to his daily exhortations and the efforts of some other officers that very few actually resigned. Two things lent our efforts powerful support: the 'appeal' by the officers of the Danzig garrison to those of the Corps of Guards, and especially the frequent reading-out of a letter to General Prittwitz from King Ernest Augustus of Hanover.

3. The Convention of Tauroggen. This was not solely the work of Yorck. It was a dangerous thing to do and he was morally driven to it by the spirit of the Prussian officers – the officers of his own Corps just as much as those in the Russian service. They swept him off his feet and never gave a thought to the dangers they might expose the King to at that moment. What they did was prompted by their honour. They set their honour above their duty to obey. A similar Convention may be made one day. The officers are capable of doing it again and the example of Tauroggen would encourage them. Nowhere but among Prussian officers is such a thing to be imagined. Schill's withdrawal (*Auszug*) in 1809 was quite another story.

4. The officers are more royalist than the King, when it comes to the point. After March, 1848, with or without the knowledge of superior officers, there was a crop of regular conspiracies, secret meetings and assignations. Eighty officers from the Potsdam garrison very nearly went to Berlin to 'liberate' the King 'by force' and 'even against his will', and bring him to Potsdam. It had all been worked out and only the date remained to be fixed, when the King appeared among the officers in the Marble Hall of the Palace at Potsdam. Protests, indignation, sympathy and tears were caused by the officers' anger and emotion when they heard the King declare 'he was free in Berlin and felt just as safe under the protection of the citizens as in our midst, and he had come to tell us so.'

At the same time as that intrigue, another was set on foot by Major von Roon as he then was (now Lieutenant-General and Minister of War) and Herr von Bismarck-Schönhausen, now Minister at St Petersburg. The plan was that General Wrangel, then commanding at Stettin, should be persuaded to march on Berlin, liberate the King, and restore the old régime. They could think of no other man for the task, and the reason why the hope they placed in Wrangel came to nothing is that they discovered he could only put three battalions in the field.

The *Landtag* elections that were held in 1858, just after the Regent had installed the liberal Ministry, were another occasion for the officers to show themselves – with very few exceptions, whom

God forgive – more royalist than the King. They voted almost to a man against the candidates put up by the Ministry – which amounts to voting against the wishes of the Regent, misled though he was.

Again, in that year of upheavals, 1848, the junior officers acted with more royalism than the King or their superiors when, without support from most of their superiors, and in spite of disapproval and warnings, they maintained and strengthened the Army's discipline and loyalty. The men who achieved this were the company-commanders and lieutenants. To gain their end they even used improper methods; but from higher authority they got no help. Our Commanders and our Generals had lost their heads. They tried to hush everything up – not only the dangerous political activities of individual soldiers but the ordinary breaches of discipline which were very common at the time and were particularly aimed at the authority of the non-commissioned officers. It could no longer be said of the Army what the greatest of our Kings once said of it: 'I have no arguers at all'* It still cannot be said today, and it is unlikely ever to be true again; yet 'the world rests not more surely on Atlas' shoulders than the State of Prussia on the shoulders of its Army.'

5. In general, the foregoing seems to me to lead to the conclusion that in the Prussian corps of officers nowadays *there is a stronger desire for independence from above and for taking responsibility upon one's self than in any other army*. What more striking proof of it could be quoted than the total disobedience shown by General von Schlack when he illegally forbad any of his men who were 'dissenters', or were so inclined, to attend 'dissenters'' meetings and, by risking his own person, won his point? There can hardly be one general-officer commanding today who has enforced no single regulation in his Corps that differs in some respect or other from those His Majesty has promulgated. Would such practices be possible anywhere else? They are perfectly possible here.

One day when a staff-officer was duly carrying out an order he had received, a high-ranking general rebuked him, saying 'Sir, the King made you a staff-officer so that you should learn when *not* to obey.'

6. *This habit of thought has undeniably had an influence on our battle-tactics*. Prussian officers object to being hemmed in by rules and regulations, like officers in Russia, Austria and England. With officers like ours you cannot fight a formal defensive action of the kind that Wellington introduced, whereby every individual is bound by rules and procedures. We look at the way things tend to go and leave the individual more freedom to use initiative; we ride him on a looser rein, back up each separate success even if it had run

* Frederick the Great: '*Ich habe keine Raisonneurs nicht*'.

counter to the intentions of a commander-in-chief such as Wellington, who used to insist on having full control over every unit at all times. But that you cannot have if subordinate commanders, without the knowledge or instructions of their seniors, go off into action on their own, exploiting each and every advantage, as they do with us.

7. This habit, too, is peculiar to the Prussian corps of officers, and I am inclined to attribute it in the main to a cast of mind that Frederick William I bequeathed to us – I mean, the custom of resigning when passed over for promotion. Such is the tyranny of honour, and among other things it can be most inconvenient to higher authority. It can also cost the State much money and cause the untimely disappearance of many a capable officer. Nowhere else is it practised on such a scale as here. The man we serve is our Supreme Commander-in-Chief, and he has the absolute disposal of our talents and abilities. Yet, if he thinks some junior more capable than we are, if he passes us over without sweetening the pill enough to satisfy our honour, we ask permission to resign. 'The senior is the cleverer', they say. If true of nothing else, it is true of the Prussian Army. Yet again, if the Commander-in-Chief should put us out of sorts, if he should slight us in any way while saying and doing nothing to put things right with us, we go through the same performance. Here there is no appeal: the King is always right, and if any man feels his honour or his rank has been taken lightly, that is that – be it only a single time and no matter who did it. He can suffer no blot on his reputation, and he would rather leave of his own accord than risk having others point the finger of scorn at him and know they are thinking, 'there goes one more fellow who ought to clear out and find himself another job'. I have been in that position myself, and I did what the Army expected of me. At first it was badly received and permission refused. I then had to find out for myself how an injury can grow and grow, so that everything seems to inflame it even further. I no longer felt I was standing on the same solid ground as the rest of the officers. In the end I got my way, and went on twelve months' leave. Everyone else, quite understandably, took this to mean the end of my service, and so did I. Things are not the same for a Royal Prince as they are for other people; and that is just as true of my retirement, my atonement, as of my reinstatement.

Over this affair I was deeply hurt by Major-General von Manteuffel, just as all other officers in the Army have been. But I do not intend to go into that matter here, and although it really is the right place for describing the harm he has done to the Army, I shall choose some other occasion.

He is not the only one, however, from whom the essential Prussian spirit of the Army has suffered serious blows. To some extent it has now recovered and their only interest for posterity is that they show

how strong that spirit is. Some of these wounds, however, have not yet healed: they rankle still and will do so for a long time yet. The very worst of these are the following.

1. A certain type of officer, who fought in the Wars of Liberation, stayed in the Army after the restoration of peace. 'Many a strange creature' was to be found among them; men of no proper birth or upbringing, men from other armies, one-time volunteer 'Jäger', brave men promoted from the ranks, and a whole lot of pretty good rogues. Friction, duels, bad feeling and cliques were common in the corps of officers after the war, but things settled down again once the misfits had been got rid of. The Prussian officer stood next in line to the King once more and was ready to lay his life down for his Sovereign, so that any insult to the King was an insult to every officer as well – just as it always used to be. But when the last of those volunteer 'Jäger' etc. had finally – in the 'forties and afterwards (i.e. until about five years ago) – gradually risen to influential ranks such as regimental-commander and higher still, they began to show that they were not all cut from the stuff that Prussian officers are made of. In the main these were probably the men who spoiled a lot of our infantry regiments by behaving with irresponsible laxity over the acceptance of officer-candidates, so that once again 'many a strange creature' was allowed in. *Clericus clericum non decimat* would be apt as a summing up.*

2. The right type for making a Prussian officer seemed to be getting scarcer. But this was not really the case, for the right sort has never been lacking when the country was in danger – as we saw in 1848, 1849, 1854 and 1859. In time of peace, however, there were plenty of more attractive careers – more suitable, too, for those of superior education. Boyen, the Minister, had got rid of the surplus officers but then the examinations came, and they made entry into the Cadet-Corps less easy for the sons of hard-up officers and impecunious nobility which between them had always filled almost all the Army's needs. Times were hard, the cost of education and upbringing were more than that sort of people could afford, a shortage of officers began – and in brief, the corps of officers fell below strength while the demands made on officers rose with the increasing demand for training. Officers simply had to be found; and in the end they were recruited from wherever one could hope to find anything suitable: young bourgeois were commissioned in numbers hitherto undreamed of, and such aristocrats as were accepted were all too often the stupidest sons, the ones who had abandoned their education – and such like. Around this time, too, our military academies all began leaving much to be desired – and

* 'One crow does not peck another's eyes out' is the Prince's rendering into German. The point is clear.

they do so still. In the Berlin cadet-corps there was a good deal of stealing. My adjutant Jagow was the senior in the cadets' mess and in his time, I think, three cadets were thrown out for stealing in a single year. The quality of the replacements we have had in the last fifteen years must and will, alas, mean that the honour of the Prussian corps of officers will not stand so high as it has stood since 1848. An insult to the person of the King is no longer an absolute personal insult to the officer. The Old-Prussian, highly monarchist mentality of the officer-corps is nowadays a thing of the past. In many places, in the newspapers, even in the Landtag, our profession (*Stand*) can often be traduced with impunity. Honour, as Frederick William I conceived it, is being undermined at present by a certain number of senior officers who think they have been chosen to command a pack of servile knaves, not gentlemen, and who therefore treat them in a manner that is almost indecent, illbred and unbecoming to a gentleman. Boot-licking is not punished but rewarded by success, telling tales commands a hearing like the secret police, instead of being rejected with indignation – both of them being especially acceptable to General von Manteuffel – and so forth. They happen only in isolated cases, thank God, but they still have a most disruptive effect, for they do not remain secret. And so things go from bad to worse. It is happening everywhere else, and it is happening in the Army too, now that we have to put up with the declining quality of the officer-intake. Time has a loosening, disintegrating effect, not a tightening one. The consequences will not be slow to follow – however many fine exceptions there may be, or rather, however few corps of officers there may be that have not yet been infected. The really sound ones are the Guards, the whole of the cavalry, the old regiments with the exception perhaps, from what I hear, of the 4th and 5th infantry regiments. The 32nd is not too good. But all these regiments are still in better shape than some of those on the Rhine which still had some pretty peculiar officers to put up with in 1848 and 1849. In those days it was really only the worst regimental commanders who were posted to the Rhine, and most of them were men who belonged to that part of the country. And in the Rhineland, of course, things are not easy for the officers. Life there is not at all like it is in Prussia. All classes without exception consort together, and in the wine and beer-shops officers have to mix with tradesmen, etc. who are richer than they are.

3. I cannot help wondering whether the honour of Prussian officers will not suffer yet further by the imminent transfer of a large number of Landwehr officers to the regular Army. How many of these officers are there, anyway? I can only judge by the proportions in the 3rd Division which I do know. Here there are forty-one who

want to transfer, and about a quarter of these are noblemen. Some of them are young men of about thirty, in easy financial circumstances and fully independent. By last year most of them had already been a good while with the colours; they had made friends among the other officers and had found their status (*Stand*) a source of pleasure. Men of this sort are certainly not misfits; to some extent, indeed, they are an asset, just as much as a large number of others who are already *Auskultatoren*, *Referendarien* and even *Assessoren*.* These latter had already (1858) fitted in very well among my officers and they are welcomed there, for they are well – indeed exceptionally well – educated and they are not without means either. I was able to make them officers very quickly. The Army does not require examinations to be taken late in life; these men have their outfits and in the Army they draw pay. This is a welcome addition to their means, and a thing they might have had to do without, if they had remained civilians, until they reached the age of thirty, so that their transfer is welcome to both parties.

The rest, however, amount to about half the total number, and they form another category. By joining up last year they have had to sacrifice their subaltern appointments (Inspectors, etc.), but they find their life pleasanter and better-paid as officers, and so they remain with the colours. Their real opinion they keep to themselves, but some of them certainly hold the view I have described. It is bad enough that they should do so, but woe to them if they show it. This type of man is regarded with some distrust and he is not accepted willingly. It does mean, however, that they can do no harm *now*, and the staff-officers themselves say there are, after all, many officers whose upbringing and education is no better. As I put it in my speech on the 8th January (this is written on the 21st) we hope the honour of Prussian officers may still apply to them all, inspire them and exalt them, just as it has so often succeeded in doing in the past.

The nobility dominates our corps of officers, in the sense that they believe commissions are really meant for them alone and that bourgeois are only admitted on sufferance. But this was not always so in Prussia, not even in the cavalry. At Hohenfriedberg† [the prince of] Anspach-Baireuth still had four officers who were not noblemen. It was only after the Seven Years' War that Frederick II gave commissions to noblemen alone, save in the hussars and the artillery. This was one of the many French ideas which that great man blindly copied. In France and Prussia alike, it was bound up with the decay of the nobility. The nobleman offers no advantage, not even as an officer, save sometimes by his education and all that

* These were specialist technical officers.   † A battle fought in 1745.

goes with it. But the same advantage is offered by anyone who is born and brought up in wealth and comfort. The really impoverished nobility has none of it, least of all by birth. The manners and outlook that are naturally found among the well-to-do and the *grand seigneur* are what the public calls 'prejudice', or snobbery, in a fellow who is really poor, and they are not so far wrong either. *A man who is brought up in want* gets little chance to make real good breeding his model and he cannot acquire nobility of soul. A certain financial ease is a precondition. But if he has once become a gentleman in thought and action he will not easily forswear his upbringing, no matter how deep he may fall into poverty and want. But, of course, there are always exceptions.

It seems to me that it was the spirit of the officers which passed into the nobility of Prussia and not the spirit of the 17th-century nobility (of which, by modern standards, I hold no great opinion) that passed into the officers. The very most the officers derived from it were the so-called noble passions and their corresponding vices, viz. brawling and drunkenness, gambling, and that tendency to excess and the life of the 'Landsknecht' which holds such attraction for Germans generally.

One feature that constantly recurs in our corps of officers is also a form of snobbery (*Adelsstolz*) based on noble birth, the pretension of superiority over other corps and other classes, with a tendency to take it too far in all directions. The first to show this in the old days were the *Gendarmes;* then it was the *Garde du Corps*, and latterly it reached new peaks in the 2nd Guards 'Landwehr' Cavalry Regiment in 1850, and in both the Guards 'Landwehr' Cavalry Regiments in 1859. The way to infect a regiment with snobbery is that the officers should all be noble and extremely *rich*. Without this the regimental corps of officers are always better fellows and better soldiers too. Really rich men seldom make good officers and, unhappily, it is the rich ones who set the standard of living for the poor, instead of its being the other way round as it should.

The honour of the Prussian officer is honour raised to the very highest power. No prince or King can escape its influence or its dictates. It is more exalted than they are, although they may not all be aware of the fact. The man of honour takes orders willingly and needs no visible punishment. Honour alone is his task-master; conscience his judge and his reward. It is not for pay and awards that he serves. An award or decoration flatters him but adds nothing to his merit in his own eyes or in those of his equals. The Prussian officer today still thinks the most he can do is his duty. He cannot understand how people in Austria can be eager to obtain the Order of Maria-Theresa* when one of the conditions is proof that a

* Founded by the Empress in 1757, i.e. during the Seven Years' War.

man has done more than his duty. Zieten and Ferdinand of Brunswick recommended *not a single* officer for a decoration during the whole of the Seven Years' War. Their creed was simple: 'The most a Prussian officer can do is his duty: anything more is a matter of Grace.'

(*signed*) FREDERICK CHARLES

(Reichsarchiv: A.VI.)

APPENDIX 2

Statistics of the Social Origins of Pupils at the War Colleges, 1903–13, with comparative Figures for 1888 and 1899

Father's Status	1888	1899	1903	1904	1905	1906	1907	1908	1909	1910	1911	1912	1913
1. Ruling Houses, and families formerly Sovereign	–	–	–	1	–	1	1	3	2	1	1	–	–
2. Officers serving and retired	252	342	295	337	267	260	302	268	292	262	318	290	279
3. Higher civil servants, clergy, lawyers, civil and military doctors, university teachers	235	307	303	279	329	282	270	279	319	369	450	471	459
4. Landowners	147	131	96	100	99	111	93	83	95	85	93	93	107
5. Tenant-farmers and estate-managers	20	40	12	24	30	18	18	22	17	28	26	20	28
6. Merchants and factory-owners	79	122	128	161	148	146	143	155	152	184	186	182	183
7. Minor officials, non-commissioned officers, etc.	59	20	19	31	46	25	37	34	48	53	64	56	49
8. Other private persons	41	100	44	50	39	73	56	63	49	65	90	69	70
Total of pupils in War Colleges	833	1062	897	983	958	916	920	907	974	1047	1228	1181	1175

APPENDIX 3

Statistics of Reichswehr-officers of Noble Family, 1920–32

	1920		1926		1932	
	Total	*Noble*	*Total*	*Noble*	*Total*	*Noble*
Staffs	770	26·4%	767	21·8%	722	19·3%
Infantry	1692	17·6%	1480	17·6%	1481	17·3%
Cavalry	520	50·4%	567	45·0%	613	47·3%
Artillery	544	12·5%	551	10·7%	588	12·8%
Pioneers	112	4·5%	76	3·9%	82	6·1%
Intelligence	88	5·7%	75	5·3%	87	10·3%
Motorised Units	112	10·7%	70	15·7%	86	9·2%
Lines of Communication	113	6·1%	92	7·6%	78	5·1%
Medical	–	–	61	13·1%	63	12·7%
TOTALS	3971	21·7%	3739	20·5%	3800	23·8%

APPENDIX 4

The Origins and Development of Nobility in Germany

Tacitus tells us that even the original Germans had an aristocracy. It seems, however, that the aristocracy we find among the German tribes after the *Völkerwanderung** was at most only partially descended from the nobility that Tacitus reported. While bands of German warriors moved as conquerors into the northern provinces of the crumbling Roman Empire and there set up a new kind of rule, a new upper class arose from the clash of races. This class consisted of the victorious warriors and they in turn were graded in accordance with their functions. So far as our knowledge goes, it was really in this hierarchy of soldiers and officials that the new aristocracy of western Europe had its origins. The higher nobility arose from the court-officials, the counts and similar functionaries of the Carolingian imperial administration – men who were a mixture of Saxons and Bavarians subordinate to the Franks, and of members of the older native nobility partially in the service of their new masters. The 'lesser' nobility, on the other hand, who formed the great majority, sprang from the lower ranks of the warriors and to these, at a later date, the body of administrators was assimilated. One part of them lived at the courts of the kings, dukes, counts, lieutenants or vice-counts, bishops or abbots, or were in their immediate service as keepers of castles, for example, and of other fixed defences. Another part was given land to settle, with a court on an appropriate scale. This land was held on feudal terms and carried the permanent duty of obeying a summons to arms as a knight or mounted warrior.

It is the practical requirements of government, military occupation and territorial defence that account for the basis of the mediaeval feudal system. Feudal tenure should be thought of as a kind of salary for services rendered, capitalised in land; and it afforded the material means for the performance of mounted feudal service in time of war – which was the whole point and meaning of feudal investiture and at the same time its *quid pro quo*.

The function of a professional knight was thus purely military in origin, and indeed it long remained so; but starting about the twelfth century it began to depreciate in social terms against factors of pure rank and title – factors, that is, of status. The essential status of knighthood, as such, remained unaltered to the end of the Middle Ages – a period that owed indeed to knighthood and chivalry some

* The great tribal migrations.

of its main characteristics. In essentials, too, the status of knighthood suffered little from the many new creations of nobility that resulted from the *Realpolitik* of Charles IV* with its largely financial character.

Now economic activity in the early Middle Ages consisted of little else than agriculture and barter; but as production became more and more divorced from exchange, as trading-links grew ever more extensive (spread, too, by Crusades and by pilgrimages to Rome), as mining developed – especially the extraction of precious metals – and as city-guilds began to flourish, so did the importance of gold increase as a stable measure of value and facilitate other forms of development in its turn. Side by side with the simple agrarian economy there arose an urban economy based on crafts and on the exchange of goods; and barter, in consequence, gradually gave way to an economy based on money. Military knighthood had arisen from the older economy; and from the newer there emerged, with equal logic, a new type of warrior – the mercenary, or soldier – and little by little he took the knight's place or caused him to adapt himself. Mercenaries were a late-mediaeval institution that could only have developed from a money-economy; and within it lay a force that tended to annihilate all social rank. Of itself, no doubt, that force could hardly have developed into anything really revolutionary; but it did prepare the way for other and more potent factors in the technology of war that slowly but inexorably drove the older chivalry in a downward spiral to extinction.

Among the new and decisive factors was the rise, or rather the revival, of a type of infantry which was not just an auxiliary to mounted combatants, and which no longer needed the relative safety of entrenchments in order to stand up to knights on horseback. This infantry was a genuinely independent arm. It stood up to cavalry, and it proved that its tactics and leadership were superior in a series of victorious battles and campaigns throughout the fourteenth and fifteenth centuries. There were the Flemish foot soldiers, there were the Hussite Bohemians too; but it was chiefly the Confederate Swiss whose innovations in tactics and the art of war were to put an end both to feudal armies and to chivalry itself. With its military prestige in decline, chivalry found the very basis of its social standing was being undermined as well, and this process was hastened and intensified by the application of chemistry to weapons – i.e. when the energy latent in gunpowder was applied to the propulsion of missiles. His military superiority already lost to the infantry, the value of the mounted knight in war now diminished even further. This fact, when it dawned on him, was made more bitter still by the loss of social status it entailed.

The logic of events during the last two centuries of the mediaeval

* Holy Roman Emperor from 1346 to 1378.

age thus gradually robbed the feudal knights of their leading role in battle, and by the sixteenth century they had no further military justification at all. The more this process advanced, however, the more the economic aspect of their life became its dominant feature, and the more the territorial nobility that sprang from them showed a tendency to coalesce with the equally downgraded nobility of the cities, the patriciate.

Yet from the sixteenth century onwards there emerged an essential difference between the ways in which the feudal estates in the east of Germany, i.e. east of the Elbe, and those in the west and south developed. In earlier times, the possessor of a feudal estate everywhere exercised seignorial rights (*Grundherrschaft*) and for some time yet this legal relationship survived without much change in the old territories of the Holy Roman Empire. But in eastern Germany these rights became manorial (*Gutsherrschaft*), with the result that in the great majority of cases the peasant communities were dissolved. The peasant, who had once been liable only to pay the lord his dues and render him strictly limited labour-services, was now deprived of his freedom and became a labourer and serf (*subditus*) of the lord of the manor, the *Gutsherr*.* This was a fateful development, peculiar to the countries east of the Elbe. The causes that led to it are not easy to determine,[2] but several factors – some historical and some geographical – were apparently at work. In the present context, however, they need not be examined.

In this diversion of his colonising urge, his spirit of enterprise and his will to power, the eastern German knight (for all the decline of his military importance) still found it possible to maintain and practise his traditional rôle as ruler and commander. This he continued to do, and eventually he was able to put it to good military use again, from the second half of the seventeenth century onwards into the nineteenth, in the modernised Prussian corps of officers on which, indeed, he left a mark of major and permanent importance. We have, of course, already seen the dominant part that was played by the Prussian country-gentlemen from the time of the Great Elector onwards (especially under Frederick the Great) right into the reign of William I. This 'Old-Prussian officer-material' drew its recruits either straight from the feudal manors of eastern Germany or else from families of Old-Prussian officers and – rather less – of civil servants, who were often descended from the former group or related to it by blood. Sociologically speaking, it is to a large extent in the manor-houses east of the Elbe that the typical qualities of the Prussian officer *par excellence* had their roots.

On the other hand there were certain differences between the

---

* The translator is much indebted to Professor F. L. Carsten, of the University of London, for expert help with the foregoing passage.

officer-type of south-west Germany and its northern (or, more properly, north-eastern) prototype. These distinctions were not due simply to the differing social origins of the two groups of officers. If we take only the noble members of each group, the differences of type were due, on the contrary, to the fact that the two social structures differed in respect of seignorial and manorial tenures or, alternatively, in respect of the general lines along which the nobility of southern and western Germany developed. By their historical origins alone their revenues imposed on the average south-western nobleman a mode of life unlike that which resulted from the feudal estates of eastern Germany. Once the sword had been sheathed and the armour hung up to rust, Old Prussia, as we have seen, produced agriculturalists, whereas the noble of the south and west, if his lands and revenues sufficed for him to live according to his station, became a rentier, a capitalist and sometimes indeed an industrial entrepreneur. This process was favoured by one factor in particular – the increasing concentration of capital, in the form of feudal land-tenure, through the revocation of grants by the greater lords.[3] But in cases where the noble of the south and west had neither means nor inclination enough to engage in such concentration and expansion, it was always open to him to enter the service of his sovereign or *Landesherr* as an official or a lawyer.

Canon law had long since undergone the revolutionary change whereby a judge no longer shaped the law to his convictions but shaped his conviction to the law. Judgments, in other words, had become the logical subsumption of particular cases under pre-existing rules of law. As the Middle Ages gave place to modern times, this basic revision spread more and more to the field of secular jurisprudence; and with the reception of Roman law in Germany it became a general principle.[4] The ancient German tradition was thus superseded; and this was matched, when the Middle Ages were past, by the gradual secularisation of education and culture in general. There then began to appear a class of professional jurists, trained in the universities; and as territorial sovereignty became more fixed and a money-economy more general, this new class was able to gather all jurisprudence and administration into its own hands. In former centuries the judge, steward or treasurer had usually been either the lord himself or some other man of noble birth; and notions deriving from those times probably led people to give the new class of jurists, bourgeois though their origins mostly were, the social status attaching to their offices alone. After a time, indeed, the custom grew up of granting these *doctores juris* a personal status of nobility on the ground that 'as *milites legalis militiae* (or 'soldiers in the forces of the law') they stood on an equal footing with the highest and most privileged of hereditary knights.'[5]

These higher administrative officials, whose functions in the lower courts were not unlike those of the bygone lords of the manor, enjoyed a much-respected, influential and lucrative position; and such was no doubt the ostensible ground on which the hereditary nobility, the *noblesse d'épée*, thronged by preference into these, the ranks of the *noblesse de robe*.* There must none the less have been some weighty consideration to explain why so large a part of the nobility accepted with their offices a certain economic dependency, however sweetened or 'disguised'. The explanation lies in their particular mode of inheritance. No matter whether an estate was entailed or freehold, the aim of keeping it profitable always led to heavy discrimination against the younger sons (to say nothing of the daughters) and in favour of the eldest at the moment of inheritance. So grave was the disadvantage they suffered that the younger sons very often had to look round for additional sources of income if they were to go on living in a style appropriate to their rank. In the later Middle Ages, when knights were of little further military use, their younger sons were apt to seek compensation for their meagre portion by turning highwayman; but the gradual if incomplete enforcement of public peace (for which purpose the *Reichskammergericht*† was created and empowered in 1495) eventually clipped their wings.

The creation and maintenance of a system of justice required, however, a larger administrative machine. More efficient financial administration under absolute monarchy offered the sovereign, moreover, a means of multiplying offices of state beyond what was actually required so that he could use some of them as sinecures for needy noblemen. For these people (so an official reported in 1800) 'seek to live, and sooner or later to die, at the State's expense. They pester the Court so long for well-paid posts for which they are usually quite unfit, and for extra pay and pensions, that in the end they get their way – the getting of which is all the easier for the fact that the entire nobility constitutes a single whole for this purpose (whether cousins or brothers, close relatives or distant, it is all one) and while the rudder of state is in irresolute hands they contrive to swing it wholly to their own advantage.'[6]

In Prussia, with its relatively large standing army, such needy nobles and 'cadets' (i.e. younger sons) found the profession of arms, with its ancient traditions of chivalry, an easy matter. Absolutely and relatively alike, the kings and princes of the other German states maintained much smaller armies; they did not regard themselves primarily as soldiers and in consequence they did not follow the Hohenzollerns by giving their corps of officers the social standing

---

* These were respectively the first and second classes of nobility in pre-revolutionary France.

† An Imperial Criminal Court.

of the 'first Estate in the land'. For these varying reasons the civil offices in the State and at the Court were all the more sought after by impecunious noblemen concerned with keeping up their social prestige. It is this which explains why there was a decree in Bavaria as early as the sixteenth century to the effect that there should always be more noblemen than scholars in the higher offices of State. We need waste no time on the question whether a learned clerk – doubtless of bourgeois origin – was always appointed too, in order to do the work. In this historical link between the State's lawyers and the nobility we have at all events the explanation of the fact that, after the nobility and the families of officers, it was the families of the higher civil servants who kept the corps of officers provided with recruits.[7]

None the less there were snobbish, doctrinaire cranks who, if a noble accepted an office, reproached him on the ground that it brought him into close contact with the bourgeois merchant-class, most of all in the days of official mercantilism. To 'common, bourgeois trades', it was written in the mid-eighteenth century, 'only one clear rule can be applied. Without loss of dignity (*salva nobilitate*) they are not to be engaged in even for daily bread, let alone for profit and lucre. . . . Farming, the care of estates, the liberal arts and sciences. are not such professions as detract from a nobleman's dignity.'[8] In contrast to the German nobility, a quite different view of these matters were taken, at least as early as the eighteenth century, by the nobility of western Europe as well as by that section of the German aristocracy, the city nobles, or patriciate, which, in the discussion of nobility, is so often either overlooked or insufficiently distinguished from the territorial.[9]

In spite of later intermarriage and assimilation, the historical and sociological bases of the patriciate are essentially different from those of the territorial nobility, which sprang entirely from knighthood. The latter's social superiority was based in theory on military service but in practice in the main upon land. The social position of the patriciate on the other hand rested chiefly on the political function it discharged in directing municipal affairs, and on the ownership of city-property; and once the guild-revolution had unseated it politically, its prestige was maintained by large-scale trade, by finance and, to some extent, by industry as well. It goes without saying that this different type of property and even more this business-activity bred a quite different mentality, one that was to develop further in the course of the centuries. It did so by proving itself the vital element both in war and in peace; producing necessities on the one hand, less-necessary goods and luxuries on the other; running on the one hand an economy concerned with meeting simple, not to say primitive, needs, and on the other hand an economy aimed at acquisition and accumulation, with capitalist leanings that were not slow to appear. Finally, if a direct comparison of the patrician with the east-German feudal landowner is made, a very great contrast will be seen; for the business of the latter was large-scale farming while the patrician's business was large-scale operations in goods and money.

These briefly-stated contrasts contain the seeds of the whole problem of nobility and *bourgeoisie*, including the problem of the latter as a type. For while the patrician reckoned himself a hereditary nobleman from the sixteenth century onwards and induced the Emperor to confirm this claim, a mere stroke of the pen was not enough to alter a social and economic structure that had grown in the course of history out of the urban *bourgeoisie*. Ink alone could certainly not have brought about a bio-chemical amalgamation between patriciate and landowning nobility unless that 'very special liquid' called blood had gone to work by action and reaction, to create a new synthesis of the two. Apart from intermarriage it was closer social relations that forged a spiritual link between these two groups of such very different origins. They worked to the intellectual enrichment of them both, and they gradually brought about a *rapprochement* between their two worlds of ideas, or *Weltanschauungen*. The exclusiveness, moreover, that each so jealously maintained against other classes of society could not fail to create a kind of mutuality of social interest, and thus to reinforce a sense of class-solidarity between the two.

The sixteenth century, then, saw the start of a period of inter-penetration – a feudalising of the patriciate and an *embourgeoisement* of the country aristocracy. But the second of these processes is the more interesting to us because the first is to some extent a simple progression along the straight line that leads upwards from below to the creation of an urban élite; whereas the second represents a deflection of the older line of development. In Italy this process became visible in the late fourteenth century already; but not until the sixteenth century did it become plain in France and England, as well as in western and southern Germany. As regards the country gentleman the clearest outward signs were his activities in fields of commerce that had formerly been held to be too bourgeois, too 'money-grubbing', for a man of noble birth. It was not just that he was getting a substantial part of capitalist, large-scale commerce into his hands (financial business in particular) but that he was often a major participant in the development of capitalistic industry.[10] In many parts of Germany the iron and copper industries, for example, owe their development to the capital of adventurous landowners – the Silesian mining-industry almost entirely so; the glass, porcelain and textile industries likewise to a substantial degree.

At the same time the nobility in western and even in eastern Germany showed no sort of reluctance to sell its feudal estates; and such estates thus passed not only into patrician ownership but into the hands of downright bourgeois. [11] Nevertheless in the eastern part of Prussia this was still being vigorously opposed by the Hohenzollerns as late as the eighteenth century; and royal consent to the acquisition of a feudal estate by a bourgeois was only given in exceptional cases – by Frederick the Great, for example, in respect of western Prussia only. By the end of the nineteenth century, however, only one-third of the feudal estates in the six eastern provinces of Prussia was still in noble hands. [12] In terms of percentages, therefore, this reduction was numerically almost exactly the same as in the supply of Prussian officers. In such a case it is hard not to see a connection between the two curves on the graph of development; and from the social and economic point of view, in fact, the old Prussian corps of officers was based upon the feudal estates that lay east of the Elbe, where the country nobility had kept clear much longer than in western and southern Germany from close contact and intermarriage with the *bourgeoisie*, even when ennobled in the patriciate.

The Hansa cities and the other coastal trading towns form a class apart; for their position on the sea gave them an intellectual, political and social structure that was quite different from what was to be found inland, where communications were much slower to develop. But leaving them aside, where was there in the inland areas of eastern Germany any patriciate so large, so highly developed in the commercial and cultural sense, as in the numerous imperial cities, large and small, of western and southern Germany? [13] At a time when great families in such places had already reached the zenith of political power and had laid the foundations of their social standing for succeeding centuries, German civilisation in the east was only just beginning its real penetration of the country, not excepting the towns. In the east, therefore, there was nothing at all to match the urban nobility of the Old-German cities, a nobility gradually bred in the course of centuries out of the mass of the citizens at large; and this had not ceased to be the case even in the twentieth century. Things being so, it was hardly a practical possibility, even in later centuries, for the feudal landowners of eastern Germany to coalesce with a patriciate and thus take part in an urban, bourgeois world of the type that existed in western and southern Germany.

Farming, it is true, was tending to increase in scope, to turn into large-scale ownership of land with large-scale operation of it; but farming by its very nature also tends to breed attachment to the soil, to breed a rural, not to say a rustic, outlook – something quite unlike the mentality of the noble landowners of the south and west. Not that the latter did not make for conservatism too; landed property, whether in town or country, tends naturally to concentrate thought upon the maintenance of the *status quo*. Money-rents, however, were what these landowners now lived on, whether they shared the blood and outlook of the urban patriciate or not; and considerations of money led them, far earlier than the eastern Germans, towards thinking in terms of a money-economy. It brought them also into immediate personal and general intellectual contact with those who controlled the machinery of production and credit. It was no rarity if they became capitalist entrepreneurs themselves; others again were more inclined to accept a general climate of capitalist thought and activity as passively as they had accepted fusion with the patriciate. But in either case they accepted these things as part of their intellectual world or adapted themselves in a manner which Sombart's pioneering researches have taught us to regard as typical of 'bourgeois'. [14]

The centres of this modern 'capitalist spirit' were normally in the towns; and to these they were tied by internal and external factors, requirements of organisation and so forth, that would lead us far astray were we to examine them. In consequence the noble landowner himself was far more influenced by the urban mentality, by the urban spirit with its mainly intellectual civilisation, than was possible in the case of the nobleman who farmed his own lands.

The problem of nobility and *bourgeoisie* is thus a part of this division between the country and the town. The second part investigates the varying forms this polar dualism assumed in the German corps of officers, and the way in which there was a gradual shift of attitudes, individual and general, in this most important sector of the great *Kulturkampf*.

APPENDIX 5

Memorandum submitted by members of the nobility on the preparatory education of officer-candidates

UNDATED (1861)

To His Excellency, etc., Herr von Manteuffel:

Your Excellency is a man who inspires confidence in those who defended their historic rights when those rights were violently attacked, even here, twelve or thirteen years ago.

Before any regulation is issued, prescribing that only those who hold a certificate of qualification for the *Prima* shall be permitted to sit for the ensigns' examination, should one not ask one's self the following questions?

1. How will parents be able to get their sons made officers if they have had them educated privately? Is it not the old aristocratic families who will be hardest hit?
2. How will parents be able to get their sons made officers if their sons never got as far as the *Sekunda* but still succeed, by private education, in passing the ensigns' examination?
3. Will not this regulation cause a radical change in the character of the corps of officers? Instead of Dönhoffs, Dohnas, and so forth, will not the commissions in the *Garde du Corps* be given to the sons of bankers who have made fortunes?
4. Would this new kind of officer-corps show the same behaviour as was shown in 1848?
5. Why is the present ensigns' examination not enough?
6. Might it not be dangerous to alienate the nobility so gravely?

(no signature)

(Prussian Secret State Archives: Mil.-Cab. I.1.15.vol.1.)

APPENDIX 6

Memorandum from General von Manteuffel, Chief of the Military Cabinet, to the Minister of War, on the preparatory technical education of officers

(manuscript draft)

BERLIN, 25TH NOVEMBER 1861

I am more and more convinced how important it is, under present conditions, that the Army should stimulate the flow of officer-candidates of the old type instead of discouraging the entry of young men from families of impecunious noblemen and officers; further-more, how sensible it would be to give permission well in advance to young men who want to enter the Army and aim at being com-missioned, so that they can suit their preparatory education to the new requirements, etc.

I am certainly not the one to underrate the value of the efforts now being made to influence the technical training of officers; but as early as 1808 the relevant Order of the 6th August said: 'Education and technical knowledge are not the only things required for a competent officer: he also needs presence of mind, rapid judgment, punctuality, regular habits on duty and proper behaviour. These are the cardinal virtues that every officer must have.' Even in 1824–1840, I remember, young men used to be recommended for the grant of a leaving certificate by Royal Prerogative because they possessed these qualities even though they had not done well enough in the examination, and some of those thus favoured have turned out very good officers. Since those days, more and more emphasis has been laid on purely technical training, etc.

Experience, however, has shown what value is to be attached to the certificate of military proficiency (*Dienstzeugnisse*) that are generally required, etc.*

If His Majesty makes attendance at a War School obligatory, a young man must at least spend a good time with the colours after-wards, when he has passed the examination, and the officers of his regiment must train him up to be one of themselves. The corps of officers, on the other hand, takes less and less interest in bringing its juniors on. There is substance in the complaint that young officers are not properly trained for their service, and it is true that some very young ones have too little moral fibre; but part of the reason, accord-ing to my own experience, is that the young men are no longer

* The writer himself afterwards struck this sentence out.

expected to have real contact with the officer-corps while they are candidates, but must wait until they are officers themselves, so that their real formation and training is not supposed to begin until then. Another reason why the corps of officers takes less notice of its juniors than it used to is that the authorities have abolished the category of young men 'serving on approbation for promotion to officers'.

In 1848, anti-military opinion concentrated on the cadets and on the above-mentioned category. His late Majesty (Frederick William IV) had great trouble in preserving the right of the cadets to wear uniform and it was some little time before their school could be given a rather more military character again. Attacks on it continue even now, etc.

These regulations have discouraged not only the Mecklemburg nobility from entering the Army, but our own as well; and our present widespread shortages of officers mainly dates from their entry into force, etc.

It was a strict rule formerly that Landwehr-officers were only transferred to Line-regiments in exceptional cases. My predecessor in office specially recommended me to keep an eye on this, because experience had shown that each time His Majesty approved such transfers a lot of young men chose this relatively easy way of getting themselves made officers of the Line, *via* the Landwehr. His late Majesty was a strong upholder of the old rule and it is only since 1860 that His present Majesty has approved of exceptions being made in view of the great need caused by the Army's reorganisation. These transfers are now approved in principle.*

This trenches, however, upon the ancient privilege of the Prussian corps of officers which His Majesty confirmed by his Order of the 6th February 1860, viz. that each corps of officers had the right to decide by vote whom it wished to accept as a member; and it has a damaging effect on *esprit de corps*, etc.

All this, moreover, is gradually weakening the essential feature of the Prussian corps of officers – the one that has done more than any other to form and preserve its particular character, viz. the right and the duty to choose and train its own successors, etc.

The Order of the 5th November, 1854 laid it down that when dealing with recommendations for ensigns' appointments, regimental commanders were to report on candidates' financial circumstances, in particular their freedom from debt, etc. Since the 5th October these Royal Orders have been in abeyance, etc.

E. M(ANTEUFFEL).

(Prussian Secret State Archives: Mil.-Cab.I.1.15.vol.1.)

* This plainly ignores the Royal Order (AKO) of the 1st October, 1860.

APPENDIX 7

Memorandum from General von Manteuffel to King William I on the Comparison of Efficiency and Military Temperament with Examinations

Pro-Memoria

BERLIN, 18TH APRIL 1862

... His Majesty's Cabinet Order of the 31st October 1861 approved the new Regulation on the recruitment of officers for the standing Army and ordered that they be brought into force on the 1st January 1862.

Attendance at War Schools is obligatory henceforth for all, save for young men who have been to a university, as a condition of receiving permission to sit for the officers' examination, etc.

In the year previous to the mobilisation of 1859 a great many officers were pensioned off; and furthermore, when the Army was reorganised in 1860, a certain number of Captains' and First Lieutenants' appointments remained unfilled while H.M. the King ordered monthly postings so that the qualifications of those who were candidates remained subject to special scrutiny. The average age in all commissioned ranks of the Army was considerably reduced thereby. One natural consequence was that for the time being the rate of retirement was also reduced. This conjunction of a falling-off in retirements with the increase of recruitments stimulated by the emergency measures had the effect of rapidly correcting the shortage of officers that had occurred in the first years after the reorganisation. But a further fall in the rate of retirements compared with previous years cannot be relied upon, for the Army is again beginning to be over-age. Leaving aside the most senior ranks, staff-officers of fifty-six can again be found, and Captains of forty-eight or forty-nine. As the Army grows, the retirement-rate will rise again in comparison with previous years. It becomes important, therefore, to make sure of a corresponding rate of recruitment.

In 1861, so it appears from the annual report of the Inspector-General of Army Education and Training, 154 fewer young men took the ensigns' examination, and 242 fewer ensigns took the officers' examination than in 1860, etc.

These figures show there is clearly a falling-off in the number of young men entering the Army in the belief that they have chosen a regiment that will accept them. The main reason for this is that parents and guardians no longer feel they can let their boys and

281

wards enter the Army with any assurance that once they show keenness and proper behaviour they will soon be made officers.

The things that shook this confidence were the Regulations of the 7th October 1841 on the dismissal of supernumerary officers and of the 3rd February 1844 on the stiffening of the examination-requirements.

By Orders made in 1858, H.M. the King restored the situation. By the first of these, he once again consented to supernumerary appointments of ensigns and officers being proposed; and by the second he consented that a third examination should be available for those who obtained good certificates from their units and that, where good service followed, a leaving-certificate might be granted by way of Prerogative. Finally, the reorganisation of the Army called for emergency measures which indirectly brought about a more indulgent attitude towards the results of examinations.

It is certainly desirable that emergency measures should not be left in force too long; and it is undoubtedly right to continue stimulating technical training in the corps of officers and treat it as an important element in the formation of judgment, etc.

Is it really very dangerous that a few young men should pass the officers' examination without having been to a War School? etc.

The reorganisation is not yet complete; the whole Army is still to some extent in a state of emergency and the shortage of officers is still so great as to be a danger until there is a fall in the rate of retirements. Indeed it must end by making it necessary to commission non-commissioned officers.

These considerations are already present to the minds of general-officers. Experienced generals told me in the recent Military Commission that if there were a mobilisation they would have to put non-commissioned officers to doing officers' work at once and then recommend them for promotion, and that they were already ear-marking non-commissioned officers with this in mind.

Nevertheless, once people get accustomed to this sort of thing there is no stopping it – and the result will be to destroy the foundations on which the Prussian corps of officers rests.

The sole defence and remedy in this case lies in recruiting the right sort of officer-material.

I asked General von Werder what he thought should be done about it, and he answered: 'Stick to what His late Majesty King Frederick William III used to say – "I need not only scholars but fighting officers!" ', etc.

Many a young man, he said, only reached maturity at twenty-two to twenty-four, and could then become a thoroughly good fighting officer, but that under the present system he would have to be posted to the Reserve long before this degree of maturity was reached.

Recruitment to the corps of officers, training young men to be officers, the conditions that govern their becoming officers – these are all matters of the greatest importance; yet for more than thirty years no one has listened to what general-officers commanding, and other commanding-officers, have had to say on the matter, etc.

What is needed is that, parallel with the rule that the officers' examination must be approached through the War Schools, as much importance should be attached to efficiency and a proper military temperament as is given to specialised technical training already, etc.

Attendance at War Schools assures the young men of great advantages as regards technical training, and the Army itself will equip them with the right mentality for their further development. Once ensigns who attend War Schools are again assured of receiving commissions and inexpensive education, there is no need to fear that these emergency measures will jeopardise either the true function of the War Schools or full attendance at them, etc. Equally, I do not think the so-called 'officers' preparatory schools' will particularly benefit if it is left more to the units to propose supernumerary appointments, and if a more lenient standard applied when these young men are examined. It was the stiffening of the examinations that brought the preparatory schools into existence: if the former is removed, the latter will disappear too, etc.

(Prussian Secret State Archives: Mil.-Cab.I.1.15, vol.1.)

APPENDIX 8

Observations on Manteuffel's Memorandum by an un-named General-Officer Commanding

His Majesty's Regulations on the recruitment of officers to the standing Army, dated the 31st October 1861, lay down the following rules as regards the ensigns' examination:

1 In order to reduce the number of young men with inadequate preparatory education who present themselves for the ensigns' examination, admission to it is limited to those who can produce a certificate, issued by the appropriate teachers' committee, giving admission to the *Prima* of a Prussian *Gymnasium* or of a Prussian *Realschule* of the first class.

2 ... the general importance of this subject (sc. the German language) is such that anyone whose papers on German grammar and spelling are marked 'insufficient', or worse, is deemed to have failed the whole examination.

When the final decision is taken, the decisive thing is not merely the examiner's marking of the German-language papers but also the judgment of the rest of the examiners, taking account of the papers written on the other subjects.

On both these points the new regulations differ from the earlier ones regarding requirements for the ensigns' examinations.

The reasons why the standard of technical education required of young men entering the Army as unpaid volunteers has been raised are stated in the 'Memorandum on the historical Evolution of Requirements respecting Evidence of formal Education to be presented by Officer-Candidates', etc.

That interesting paper gives a survey of the various phases which military education has passed through since 1808. The subject is most important, and the paper shows the Army has always given it very serious attention. None the less it is clear that very different views have been held at various times as regards the technical standard to be required of officer-candidates – in principle and degree alike.

Up to 1828 the relevant regulations were inspired by special benevolence towards the sons of impecunious soldiers, whether serving or retired.

Their sons received free technical training and *upbringing* in the divisional schools; but these schools accepted small boys into the

284

Appendices

lower classes who had next to no acquaintance even with the elements of technical studies.

The divisional schools were often criticised on the ground that the teachers and pupils were equally ill-trained – the former for teaching and the latter for learning. Moreover, progress through these schools was slow and the burden on the officers who taught there was heavy. But in the end the corps of officers got useful material (or did the Prussian Army in those days fall rather behind-hand in any way compared with what was expected of it?)

About that time (1828) it appeared necessary to raise the requirements for the ensigns' examination in order to maintain the social standing of the corps of officers: and the main reason for this was that a higher general education was becoming necessary in the other branches of the public service. The instruction provided in the lower classes of the divisional schools was thought inadequate, and efforts were made to suppress these lower classes altogether.

It was indeed often pointed out (as the memorandum says) that a method of teaching and upbringing had been evolved for those who wanted to enter the Army which was different from what applied to other professions, but that there were various grounds for this – not all frivolous, and some of them deep-lying – such as social origins, the position of the nobility in all the newer States,* the Army's needs and the means of satisfying them. It was therefore proposed that bursaries should be created in the *Gymnasien* and the higher civil schools for sons of serving and retired officers, country gentry and civil and military officials who wanted to enter the Army.

While no action was taken on this proposal, there was a movement in 1828 to :

1 abolish the lower classes of the divisional schools as preparatory institutions for the ensigns' examination, and

2 only allow such unpaid volunteers (*Avantageurs*) to attend the divisional schools as had passed the ensigns' examination.

An attempt was made at the same time to get the standard raised for the ensigns' examination itself. None of these reforms, however, was carried out. The second class in the divisional schools continued to prepare candidates for the ensigns' examination and the proposed stiffening of the examination had to be abandoned.

It was thought that the root of the trouble had been attacked at last when a certain standard of general technical knowledge was prescribed as a condition for taking the examination. General von Luck had proposed that the standard should be completion of the *Prima*, i.e. readiness for the university; but completion of the *Sekunda*, was thought good enough. So in 1844 it was laid down that –

1 in addition to what had previously been required, more or less,

* i.e. those parts of Germany recently joined to Prussia.

285

candidates for the entrance-examination were to show the general technical level of those who had completed the *Sekunda* class at a *Gymnasium*, and that

2 candidates could take the ensigns' examination and the officers' examination only twice each.

These requirements are still in force, but they have never been applied with absolute strictness. Three and even four attempts at the examinations have been allowed, and no notice has yet been taken of all the efforts made by General von Peuker, the Inspector-General of Military Training and Education, to have the regulations more strictly observed.

The explanation, however, is not far to seek: the Army's first requirement, after all, is for suitable officers; and a higher standard of technical education cannot be demanded until this vital need has been satisfied.

Even so there are limits to what can be required, and the question arises whether any army could be run with only a lot of book-worms for officers.

The expansion of the Prussian corps of officers in 1852 and its enormous expansion in 1860 now makes it look as if it would be a mistake to demand a higher standard of preparatory technical education for officers and thus make entry into the Army harder.

People say the intellectual level of the Army is not what it was. It has been possible none the less to increase the strength of the General Staff and the adjutants, and to staff the War Schools with teachers with much higher technical attainments than before. The regulations of 1844 gave such advantages to those who had completed the *Prima* (*Abiturienten*) that they brought the Army more than two hundred of them as officer-candidates in 1860. Is there any serious reason to fear the social standing of the officer-corps will decline for lack of technical proficiency among its members? If we are really to believe the technical requirements for young men entering as unpaid volunteers must be raised, and if the present time, with its immensely swollen demand for officers, is really the right moment to do this, then the obvious way to begin is to cease applying the regulations with *indulgence* and try applying them *properly*, i.e. *strictly*, for if there is any place where *quality* counts more than *quantity*, it is in the Army. What should *not* be done, however, is to stiffen the standards of 1844 (which were anyway hard enough for the mass of officer-candidates to satisfy, even though they have never yet been applied with full vigour) by *raising* the standard in German and moreover requiring a certificate from the *Sekunda* to be produced before a candidate can sit for the ensigns' examination. There is something most objectionable in this last condition. It used to be the Military Examinations Commission *alone* which decided who should be allowed to take the examination, but now it lies *in the first place* with the *School Directors*. The worst elements in the corps of officers really are not the ones who did worst in the *Gymnasium*. It is common for the teachers there to be arrogant, hostile on principle to the better classes, and filled with conceit at the thought of their own scholastic attainments. They brutally stamp out all true sense of honour, they are steeped in the destructive tendencies of the times and most of them are rationalists to boot. Men of character are the last thing they seek to produce!

(It is legitimate, therefore, to ask which provides the later officer with more real training for his profession – the *Gymnasien* and *Realschulen* or the former divisional schools where education was in the hands of Prussian officers?)

The present writer is ready to support this assertion by quoting names of his contemporaries at the *Gymnasium* who have since had distinguished careers as officers. From all the most reliable accounts he has heard, the evils described above are very much on the increase.

Yet nothing would have been easier than to make the conditions for the entrance examination match the attainments needed for the passage from the *Sekunda* to the *Prima* while entrusting the necessary decisions to members of the Army, i.e. to the Military Examinations Commission.

Finally, the new regulations will cause quite exceptional hardship by coming into force so soon. Most of those who form the better elements in the Prussian corps of officers (namely the sons of country gentlemen) get their technical education from domestic tutors until they are confirmed. There is always some bias about such tuition and as regards the level of positive knowledge imparted it must lag behind the schools: but it will hardly be contended that a young man who has spent his first sixteen years in a decent family will be a better officer-candidate, physically and morally, than one who was put out to board at the age of ten so that he could go to a school.

If this sort of boy goes to the *Gymnasium* after his confirmation, say at fifteen or sixteen, he will generally be judged fit only for the *Tertia*, but if he spends a year or two in that class and also has private tuition, he passes the entrance-examination. It is obvious that in respect of formal education this sort of boy is behindhand compared with boys who have been at the *Gymnasium* continuously ever since they were ten (this was often the case, too, with the sons of officers frequently transferred from one garrison to another); but it is a fact, none the less, that these boys eventually developed into better officers than the others.

(Regiments could easily be asked to supply the relevant figure.)

For such young men to get a *Primareifezeugnis* would be downright impossible. To do so they would have to stay in the *Gymnasium* until they were nineteen or twenty at least, and quite apart from their coming late to military training, and from the expense, they would be at a gross disadvantage compared with those who had started their schooling younger.

Justice and the Army's interest alike therefore demand that the same procedure should be followed as on earlier occasions of this kind, and that the new regulations should not be brought into force until the young men concerned, who are preparing for military careers and relying in good faith on the guarantee offered by the previous regulations as regards the entrance examination, have reached their goal – i.e. they should be suspended for another three or four years at least* since it can be assumed that boys can obtain the *Primareifezeugnis* if they are sent to school at not more than twelve or thirteen and work properly until they are seventeen or eighteen.

(unsigned)

(Prussian Secret State Archives: Mil.-Cab.I.1.15.vol.1.)

* In fact this was done by Royal Order (AKO) of the 23rd April 1862: the regulation objected to entered into force only on the 1st October 1865.

APPENDIX 9

Memorandum from the Inspector-General to the Chief of the Military Cabinet on the general education of Prussian Officers

BERLIN, 8TH MARCH 1909

To His Excellency Freiherr von Lyncker:

. . . It seems to be a matter of general knowledge that His Majesty the Emperor and King, knowing the shortage of young officers, is graciously pleased to use his Prerogative almost every time an application to that effect is made on the responsibility of units: and it appears to me that this removes any incentive for the less talented pupils to try to obtain the *Primareifezeugnis*, as even they could do if they were to make an adequate effort. These young men then go before the Higher Military Examinations Commission where they naturally show very superficial technical preparation. In the last four years an average of 24 per cent of them have failed the ensigns' examination, compared with only 10 per cent of those who had the *Zeugnis*. They show a lack of grasp and little critical capacity, and they are often unable to arrange their ideas in logical order when writing essays on subjects appropriate to their years. These weaknesses make it plain that they are still a long way from possessing the level of education that an officer needs.

Yet at a time when greater demands for intellectual development are being made everywhere else, it is not right that a large proportion of the officer-intake should be so markedly inferior. In none of the other higher professions would a young man with so little education be accepted. Even the middle-class professions nowadays mostly require a final certificate (*Abitur*) from the *Prima*. There is no doubt that this state of affairs does harm to the standing of the corps of officers – even in the eyes of foreign countries. I have a number of press-articles, opinions published by senior French officers in 1907, which bear this out. For example General Bonnal in the *Neue Revue* speaks of the 'very low average of general education' of our lieutenants, and General Langlois likewise in his *Revue Militaire* says the general knowledge of our officer-candidates is 'normally very low'.

For the present, unfortunately, there seems to be no chance that a final passing-out certificate will be required of all officer-candidates in Prussia as it already is in Bavaria. I therefore deem it all the more my duty as Inspector-General of Military Training and Education

289

to draw the attention of Your Excellency, as principal Adjutant-General to His Majesty the Emperor and King, to the grave short-comings which I have described in the preparatory education of our officer-intake.

(*signed*) V. PFUEL

(Reichsarchiv: Mil.-Cab.I.1.15. vol.3.)

APPENDIX 10

Reply of the Chief of the Military Cabinet to Appendix No. 9

BERLIN, 24TH MARCH 1909

... At all events it is clear that in most public offices there are first-class officials who began their career as Army-candidates (*Militäranwärter*) without any special schooling but who are highly esteemed by their superiors on account of their achievements. – Now the officer's profession, more than any other, demands practical gifts. How many men there are whose strong suit is practice rather than theory, but who are in their element as soldiers! It is certainly desirable that our officer-intake should be as well educated as possible; but conditions being what they are we must accept the fact that higher qualifications cannot be demanded as long as a considerable number of lieutenancies remain unfilled. I do not regard this as a great calamity either, so long as the supply of character keeps up. Nor do I attach much importance to the French generals' opinions cited in the paper under reply. One may doubt whether these critics were so familiar with conditions in our Army as to be able to form an accurate estimate of our officers' level of education. In any case there is no comparison to be made between the level of education in the German corps of officers and that which obtains in the French officer-corps where so many captains and lieutenants have been promoted from the ranks.

(*signed*) FRHR. V. LYNCKER

(Reichsarchiv: Mil.-Cab.I.1.15.vol.3.)

APPENDIX 11

Petition to the King from the non-commissioned officers of the 2nd Bavarian Artillery Regiment asking for promotion to the rank of officer

WÜRZBURG, 21ST SEPTEMBER 1848

Allerdurchlauchtigster Grossmächtigster König
Allergnädigster König und Herr!

The Army Order of the 31st March last, which appeared on the occasion of Your Majesty's Accession, caused general rejoicings on the part of all non-commissioned officers, for it stated that claims to promotion would solely be judged by genuine merit, talent and proficiency. It thereby gave many a proficient non-commissioned officer ground for hoping that continued zeal and effort might earn him Your Majesty's favour and bring him advancement to the rank of officer.

This general joy was increased still further by the appearance of the Royal Rescript (through the Ministry of War), No. 8508 of the 12th May last, 'respecting some improvements for non-commissioned officers and other ranks', for it granted concessions of several kinds, and not financial concessions alone.

This joy, however, was much diminished again by the appearance of the Army Order of the 21st August last, which made it clear that vacancies among the officers of the Army, and in particular in your Majesty's 2nd Artillery Regiment (Zoller), would not be filled by proficient non-commissioned officers or by other well-attested persons of proven ability and zeal from the public educational establishments of the Kingdom, but were in fact partly filled by civilians so youthful that they were not required to undergo any test of their knowledge.

Far from desiring to be heard in complaint against this decision Your Majesty's most humble, obedient subjects, undersigned, still hold themselves bound to lay the following requests before Your Majesty.

It is well known what extensive attainments an artillery-officer must possess, not merely in theoretical but in practical knowledge too; and it is furthermore accepted that a non-commissioned officer of artillery, who has a variety of duties to perform, can hardly make himself a proficient gunner in his first six-year period of services. Much time will therefore be required before the newly-commissioned officers, whose technical ability is known to some of Your Majesty's humble, obedient petitioners, can complete their training in gunnery.

For a non-commissioned officer who has given several years of faithful service in Your Majesty's Artillery and has thereby gained not only the respect of his subordinates and fellows but also the esteem of his superiors and who, though perhaps not trained in theory, has abundant practical knowledge of the art of war, it is mortifying, at so serious and critical a time, to be placed under the command of a juvenile officer freshly commissioned direct from civil life who has no acquaintance with the Army yet and who therefore knows neither how to obey nor, much less, how to command.

The fact that Your Majesty's 2nd Artillery Regiment contains such non-commissioned officers and that they have been considered fit for promotion to higher ranks is doubtless clear from the personnel reports which the regimental command has submitted to Your Majesty; and that efficient officers are to be found among non-commissioned officers is attested by the fact that Your Majesty's Army contains staff-officers and others of higher rank (*Oberoffiziere*) who have worked their way up from carrying a pike and who now enjoy general esteem for their general ability.

For these reasons Your Majesty's most humble, obedient petitioners, undersigned, believe themselves justified in submitting the following most humble petition:

'THAT Your Majesty may be graciously pleased to order that
'vacancies among the officers of the Artillery be henceforth filled
'by individuals whose moral and technical education is amply
'proven and whose proficiency is recognised, to the end that every
'proficient non-commissioned officer may have a prospect of
'promotion and that less capable but no less loyal soldiers shall
'not be placed under the command of inexperienced persons.'

In the hope that the foregoing most humble petition may receive a gracious hearing, and with the deepest respect,
we remain, for and on behalf of
Your Majesty's most humble, obedient non-commissioned officers,

(*signed*) MÜLLER, *Oberfeuerwerker*
SCHULER, *Feuerwerker*
BUB, *Aud.Act.*

Würzburg, the 21st September, 1848

(War Archives, Munich: Kr.Min.Arch.Kap.III.Lit.a.XVII. No.1a, fasc.I.)

APPENDIX 12

Record of a Meeting of the Commission which considered a petition from a number of married non-commissioned officers of the 7th Bavarian Infantry Regiment, requesting promotion to the rank of officer, or other concessions.

MUNICH, 4TH JULY 1849

Present: Lieutenant-General Freiherr von Heideck, Chairman.
(the names of other members follow)

The Commission met at 9 a.m. today in Room 28 at the Ministry of War.

His Majesty's Letters Patent setting up the Commission for the purpose stated were circulated to all its members, who were thereby seized of the questions remitted by His Excellency the Minister of War for answer, to wit:

1 what moral, physical, technical and practical qualifications should be required of every man recommended for an officer's commission, whether in the infantry, cavalry, artillery or engineer-corps;

2 whether and, if so, on what conditions married non-commissioned officers too should be recommended for officers' commissions;

3 whether and, if so, how non-commissioned officers receiving officers' commissions may be provided with their outfit, either wholly or partially gratis, out of some fund;

4 how many of the vacancies occurring annually among ensigns and officers should be filled by non-commissioned officers already with the colours, and how many boy cadets graduating from the 'Pagerie'.

The Chairman, Lieutenant-General Freiherr von Heideck, then opened the proceedings with the following address:

To answer these questions will involve giving thought to the internal soundness of the Army as well as to the future standing of the corps of officers in relation to the other educated classes in the country. Duty requires, therefore, that all should receive serious study, free from preconceived ideas or biassed views. Our answers to them will determine whether appointment of ensigns and second-lieutenants should primarily be made in the light of technical and general education, allied to moral and physical soundness, and, if so, how far these factors should outweigh mere practical knowledge of the service; in other words, whether and, if so, to what extent

294

practical knowledge of the service is enough by itself to justify admitting men of imperfect technical and social education to enjoyment of an Estate whose eminence in the country's society attracts the attention and often the envious criticism of other classes and which must on that account be doubly careful that its claim upon society shall be justified by its moral, ethical and intellectual merit alone, since all other grounds, even that of superior birth, have become insecure.

It is these considerations which underly the new plan for the War Schools and divisional schools that has been laid before His Majesty, the essentials of which have already been put into effect by means of Orders. With no regard to class or religion, but solely in the light of proven moral and technical merit, these schools now offer entry into the corps of officers to students at the War Schools as well as to young men serving with the colours. Moreover they also open the way into the officer-corps for non-commissioned officers who are qualified in respect of true military merit by having distinguished themselves in the face of the enemy, even if their technical and general education is deficient.

Though lacking in general and technical education, this type of officer will, as a rule, be an honour to his class. He will also receive proper respect and esteem from previous comrades who consider themselves his equals as regards other aspects of their service, provided not so many of them become officers that those with little education or none at all will form the majority.

If, however, – moral and physical qualifications being equal – a non-commissioned officer has only his longer service in garrison or in the field with the resulting amount of practical experience to set against the store of technical and general education that a young man acquires in a military school, a *Gymnasium* or a University, the former qualifications should not as a rule decide matters in favour of the non-commissioned officer. The well-educated youth can quickly and easily acquire practical experience, whereas the non-commissioned officer can hardly be expected to make good the gaps in his technical and general education.

In the past twelvemonth, in view of recent troubles, 250 non-commissioned officers have been promoted lieutenant and 126 have been promoted ensign – a total of 376 promotions.

Since then, the non-commissioned officers have been pressing to be given not higher qualifications but higher ranks. Far from causing satisfaction, therefore, these promotions have increased their discontent and their pretensions. The reason for this is probably the fact that in most of these promotions the test was not higher qualification in all respects but greater practical experience – a test by which every man rates himself the equal of his more fortunate comrades, so that lack of promotion looks like loss of rank and is thus held to be a ground for complaint.

Even short experience of this innovation has clearly shown what sort of men achieved the honour of commissions under it and how far they showed themselves worthy of the honour. 'I am reminded,' said the speaker, 'of Field-Marshal Prince Wrede's frequent saying, viz. that he regretted most of the cases in which he was responsible for non-commissioned officers being promoted, for few of them had come up to expectations – although they were mostly only men who had distinguished themselves in battle.'

If it were a question of raising an army, or if the existing Army were short of officers with practical experience, then it would be right to make practical experience the decisive factor when commissioning officers. But neither is the case; and so the newly joined young man of education has time to acquire the necessary practical experience without diminishing his utility to the Army and will quickly make himself proficient by zeal and application. Compared with a lack of other higher qualifications for entering the corps of officers, this consideration therefore seems a minor one. In the proposed divisional schools, non-commissioned officers who lay claim to promotion already have an opportunity of matching their practical experience with the technical knowledge they most require. Those, therefore, who have a true ambition not merely to achieve the rank of officer but to be an honour to that rank in every way, are now catered for in the best way possible.

None the less it would be fair, and can be recommended, that suitable measures should be taken in the future on behalf of proficient long-service non-commissioned officers whose level of education is not equal to the higher demands made by the status of officer.

The lower posts in the public service – those which require only writing and arithmetic, punctuality, honesty and strict attention to duty – should be reserved, as they are in Prussia, for deserving non-commissioned officers; and the pay attached to them should be made adequate for the bringing up of a family.

In this way, good non-commissioned officers would remain longer in the Army; and their emoluments, like the good service which such well-proven men would be able to render to the State in their new capacity, would be appropriate to the sort of social and intellectual circles in which they, and their wives, if married, would be at home and feel happier than in unfamiliar, higher society, where they could never play any but a somewhat awkward part.

Having put forward these considerations, founded as they were on positive experience, the speaker proceeded to discuss the answers to be given to the questions put by His Excellency the Minister of War, as follows:

Question No. 1. The officer's supreme concern must be the honour of his status. He must therefore be morally irreproachable, physically fit and healthy: he must keep his body strong and supple by gymnastics, and in all physical exercise he must train his men and set them an example.

He must know his profession thoroughly. He must be familiar with the spirit and letter of all regulations, or else he will be unable to impress them on his men and ensure that they are carried out with intelligence and efficiency under all conditions.

Only a superior degree of general and technical education can fit him for so high a standard of professional efficiency.

An officer can as a rule be expected to possess a general technical education and to be conversant with mathematics, history, geography and one of the principal foreign languages. He should also have some knowledge of the arts, for if he is ignorant of them he will be bored in educated circles where nothing but knowledge will enable him to feel at home. Such knowledge will likewise keep him away from low haunts, to which boredom commonly drives the uneducated and where they often end in moral and financial ruin.

Individual weapons and their special uses require a higher training in mathematics and technology. The artillery-officer and the engineer must master their ancillary sciences too. The cavalry-officer must master the *haute école* in riding, and have a thorough knowledge of horses as well as some acquaintance with veterinary science.

Further details would doubtless be superfluous here. The qualifications required by officers of the several branches of the Army are laid down in the *curricula* for divisional schools and War Schools.

Question No. 2. In the Chairman's opinion, officers' commissions should no doubt be accessible in principle to married non-commissioned officers: but such men should only be recommended if they have not merely the qualifications above-mentioned but also those which govern the marriage of officers generally, i.e. the rule that a prior marriage affords no ground for claiming preferential treatment over officers who seek permission to marry after they have been commissioned.

Question No. 3. In the light of the foregoing, this question does not arise.

Question No. 4. Here the answer is determined by the proposals drawn up by the Commission on the War Schools and divisional schools, viz. all vacancies for officers should as a rule be filled by graduates from the War School and by those non-commissioned officers possessing exactly the same qualifications who have received professional and technical education in divisional schools. In the case of non-commissioned officers who have not attended divisional schools and have not acquired the equivalent of even the modest amount of technical training available there, the Commission considers that the sole ground for promotion should be distinguished conduct in the face of the enemy.

Having thus indicated the answers which he thought should be given to the four questions asked by His Excellency the Minister of War, the Chairman, Lieutenant-General Freiherr von Heideck, asked the members of the Commission to what extent they were in agreement.

1st Question: What moral, physical, technical and practical qualifications should be required of every man recommended for an officer's commission, whether in the infantry, cavalry, artillery or engineer-corps?

The members who had been present at the discussion of the above-mentioned *curricula* prior to their submission to their High Destination (viz. Major Fries, *Oberkriegskommissär* Frohm and Captain Malaisé) concurred in the qualifications (as outlined by the Chairman when dealing with Question No. 1 above) which that Commission thought should be required of every man recommended to fill an officer's appointment.

The other members, who had not taken part in the discussion of the new *curricula*, were none the less in general agreement with the qualifications as defined by the Chairman.

The Auditor-General, von Policzka, in particular, thought it should be left to the 2nd Section* to consider the military and technical aptitudes to be required of officers – the more so as the questionnaire was based on the above-mentioned draft for the future organisation of the War Schools and divisional schools, whereas the 2nd Section had no knowledge of that draft. In general he thought, speaking from his own point of view, that in addition to the appropriate physical and moral qualifications, a suitable level of education and intelligence should be required, and at least a general grounding in school-subjects. Where competitors were equally qualified, actual proficient service in a unit might well decide the issue. It was surely essential that an officer should be likely to show bravery in battle and hold his honour sacred, in addition to being of good moral character.

Major Passavant observed that when non-commissioned officers serving with units showed practical aptitude and demonstrably had as much technical education as was prescribed for the military schools, they ought to be given preferential promotion compared with pupils from the military institutes, since the latter had already

* Probably the personnel department.

received preferential treatment by being educated wholly or partly at the public expense.

Captain Malaisé replied that the principles on which the proposed new War Schools were to be founded meant that they would no longer be institutions for the care of boys and youths of mean ability but would make sure – instead of leaving it to chance – that the Army would henceforth always have a certain proportion of officers of proven intelligence, allied to general education and technical military knowledge. So much value had been, and was still, attached to this assurance by every régime in France, both in peace-time and under the conditions of a long war, that individuals with qualifications equal to those required by War Schools were commissioned into higher ranks than were assigned to non-commissioned officers on promotion; and the latter, moreover, seldom received commissions without having first held each successive non-commissioned rank, from that of sergeant-major upwards.

The *2nd Question* was then read out again:

Whether and, if so, on what conditions, married non-commissioned officers too should be recommended for officers' commissions.

All members concurred in the answer that had been proposed by the Chairman, viz. that officers' commissions should no doubt be accessible in principle to married non-commissioned, but that such men should only be recommended if they had not merely the qualifications set out in reply to the 1st Question but also those which govern the marriage of officers generally.

The Auditor-General, von Policzka, in particular, referred to the opinion he had earlier expressed on limiting officers' marriages in the interest of the Service and of economy.

Major Fries observed that there was still a Royal Order in force which laid down that 'a non-commissioned officer who marries shall be excluded for ever from promotion to the rank of officer', and he produced the relevant Order, dated the 15th April 1802 (Acta.10. Fasc: *Reformen beim Churpfalzbajerschen Kriegsstaat*), section 10 of which contains the above-quoted rule. He also produced the order of the 31st May 1802 (Acta II.Fasc: *Heirathsverordnung*) which laid down that 'non-commissioned officers who marry shall deliver up their bâton; thereafter they shall serve only as private soldiers and exceptions shall only be made for those who are recognised as skilled and talented non-commissioned officers and are certified as such; but even so, they shall pay a fine and forfeit their pension rights.'

The *3rd Question* was then read out:

Whether and, if so, how non-commissioned officers receiving officers' commissions may be provided with their outfit, either wholly or partially gratis, out of some fund.

The Auditor-General, von Policzka, and *Oberkriegskommissär* Frohm stated that there was no such fund: the statutes of the Officers' Assistance Fund would not permit of making such grants. At this, the other members all pointed out that to do so might also amount to malversation of the officers' contributions to that Fund, since they were meant for 'giving assistance in cases of undeserved misfortune'.

4th Question from His Excellency the Minister of War, viz.

How many of the vacancies occurring annually among ensigns and officers should be filled by non-commissioned officers already with the colours, and how many by cadets graduating from the 'Pagerie'.

The members concurred in the reply proposed by the Chairman, viz. that all vacancies should as a rule be filled by graduates of the War School and by those non-commissioned officers possessing exactly the same qualifications who had received professional and technical instruction in divisional schools, while in the case of non-commissioned officers who had not attended divisional schools and had not acquired the equivalent of even the modest technical training available there, the sole ground for promotion should be distinguished conduct in the face of the enemy.

The Auditor-General, von Policzka, while he thought a reply in that sense should be left to the sole discretion of the 2nd Section, felt obliged to adhere to his previously expressed opinion that where all requirements were satisfied and the candidates equally qualified, the preference should be given to those who were already serving with the colours; he also thought that transfer from one branch of the Army to another should be made easier – e.g. in cases where an officer lacked the private means for the cavalry but appeared well qualified for the infantry.

Captain Malaisé found himself unable to concur in the above proposal for giving preference to those already in the Army, and he referred to the observation he had made in connexion with the reply to be given to the 1st Question. He was further of opinion that to fix a ratio between the number of non-commissioned officers to be promoted each year and the number of graduates from the War School to be commissioned during the same period would conflict with meeting the Army's need for officers – a need which was unpredictable owing to the variety of causes that could lead to officers leaving the service, and to the varying prospects of war. In the previous 20 years, for example, the ratio between the number of non-commissioned officers promoted each year to the ranks of ensign and lieutenant, and graduates of the Cadet Corps and the 'Pagerie' who were commissioned, varied between 3:2 and 17:1 approximately.

Furthermore, to fix a ratio of this kind would be to fix a 'permanent' ratio between the numbers of qualified graduates of the divisional and War Schools which would, without doubt, have to be subject to annual variation.

As no member wished to make any observation, the present record was drawn up with a view to being forwarded to its High Destination.

The Commission.

(*signed*) v. HEIDECK, *Gen., as Chairman*
POLICZKA
FRIES, *Major*
SPIESS, *Major*
FROHM
PASSAVANT, *Major*
MALAISÉ, *Captain, and Secretary*

(Kriegsarchiv, Munich: Kriegsmin. – Archiv.Kap.III.Lit.a.XVII. No.1.)

APPENDIX 13

General Karl H. L. von Borstell to King Frederick William III on Honour and Duelling, with two annexes

KÖNIGSBERG, 18TH JANUARY 1821

The decision against Lieutenants [three names follow, with their units] which Your Majesty transmitted to me with Orders dated the 11th December 1820 for its execution, contains the following statement as regards the last-named, viz. that, contrary to the finding of the Court Martial, he is to be retained in service even though he has suffered unprovoked physical assault. By this decision of Your Majesty's I understand that Your Majesty wishes an otherwise sound officer who, without giving offence, has been markedly, indeed physically, maltreated should be retained in military service although, in disregard of the principles governing his status as an officer, he did not vindicate his honour in the customary way.

For me Your Majesty's orders are sacred. – The substance of this decision is new; it must be the first such decision ever issued by Your Majesty or Your illustrious Forbears; and among the officers of this garrison it has aroused feelings which I am endeavouring to combat, as a matter of conviction as much as of duty,

On the subject of the laws of honour the opinions voiced in the Army are well-nigh unanimous, yet they rest only upon individual views and on a tradition that is founded, more or less, in history.

A delicate regard for a man's own honour and for that of his peers (*Stand*) is an ideal that was transplanted, in the golden age of chivalry, from France to Germany and it spread across the whole of civilised Europe. It is one which the great majority of officers, including many highly respected officers of senior rank, accepts as binding; and closely bound up with it is the maintenance of the principle of duelling, albeit the latter is tolerated only as a necessary evil.

Such, however, is not my view of it. Ideas about a man's own honour and that of his peers may often be confused, often tangled, and too widely various to be summarised with clarity; yet they should not be allowed – and least of all when applied to so disciplined and cultivated a class as the the corps of officers – to silence the voice of conscience, the voice of the mind and of reason. Nor should they be allowed to prolong the sway of duelling (which rests upon the tottering pillars of a far-off, brutal and almost lawless age) into the cultivated law-abiding times in which we live, and even exalt it above the authority of public law.

302

More than any of Your illustrious Forbears, Your Majesty has publicly denounced duelling as an evil both needless and unlawful; yet the personal view which Your Majesty thus made known has not succeeded yet in overcoming the older, deep-rooted power of custom, or tradition.

If Your Majesty will allow me, I would observe that while the content of this important decision has squarely challenged the almost universal consensus that duelling must be preserved as a means of maintaining virtue against vice, it now becomes urgently necessary that clear and carefully-considered measures of quite different kind should be taken on this most important question.

From my earliest youth I have lived on intimate and happy terms with my brother-officers and have closely observed their life and ways. I have reached the conviction that the honourable company of officers requires not only the bond it principally finds in war and in a sacred concern for King and Fatherland, but also needs, especially in time of peace, some closer link, some form of collective conscience, that will assist its members to live in harmony with comrades, social equals and themselves, under conditions of greater leisure, greater temptations, smaller income and much more varied interests. The one certain way it finds of meeting this need lies in cultivating a delicate sense of a man's own honour and that of his fellows, and in keeping that honour spotless. In time of peace this will be more effective than the best rules of discipline as a means of keeping the corps of officers (impecunious, almost poor, as it is) in a state of unity and virtue, and of maintaining the reputation it enjoys among all classes of the population, lettered and unlettered alike.

The institution of duelling is morally good in its basic principle though morally bad in practice; and there is no denying that it has, been strikingly effective (albeit brutal, unjust, irrational, unlawful yet akin to a universal law) in maintaining morals and honourable conduct both in individual officers and in the officer-corps as a whole. Though duelling dates from the darkest anarchy of the Middle Ages, logic required the preservation of this rough and sanguinary sort of justice even in our politer age with its wise, protective legislation; and this senseless law has had to be maintained, fanatically and in the teeth of fierce prohibition by every civilised government, because the *ideal* it serves is good, and because no better instrument has been devised.

Yet experience all through the ages has shown that the immanent power of an idea, the really formidable spirit of the times, cannot be repressed or intimidated even by the severest prohibitions.

What has been lacking hitherto is some institution of a strongly moral character that could banish duelling by replacing it, and which could both warn and punish with the authority of law behind it.

An officer would then discover that, while the old method of revenge was no longer open to him, his own honour and that of his class were being jealously safeguarded – treated, indeed, as the concern of all. A single slight, therefore, would call down censure, while repeated slights, or a grave offence, would be visited by loss of the right to further membership of the corps of officers.

Results as grave and inescapable as these would more satisfactorily safeguard a man's own honour and that of his class than any thought of the uncertain, often unjust, outcome of a duel.

For me, as a friend of my brother-officers, this is a grave and important matter, and it has long been my earnest desire to be allowed to submit it for eventual decision to Your Majesty. Today that wish has become my duty.

I now submit these lines for Your Majesty's gracious considera-tion; and with them I respectfully submit two Annexes. They contain my views on duelling and on the state of the civil and military laws, which partly encourage duelling and partly threaten it with the direst punishment and are quite out of keeping with the Army's modern Constitution. I also offer my opinion of certain other military institutions, imperfectly developed yet effective, that exist in a number of regiments, humbly requesting that Your Majesty will be graciously pleased to instigate the legislative measures which this matter of such importance for the Army and for every man of honour now urgently requires.

(signed) V. BORSTELL

ANNEXES

(a) *On the Desirability of banishing Duelling from the civilised World and in particular from the Corps of Officers in Prussia.*

The King, with far-seeing wisdom, has endowed his people with a Military Constitution which provides the Army with well-tried institutions such as modern disciplinary regulations; and the latter give subordinates the assurance of treatment appropriate to differ-ences of rank while inculcating the need for promoting and uphold-ing a high level of morality in their relations with one another.

Duelling has continued hitherto because it commanded respect as a means of publicly vindicating honour; but with the Military Constitution now in force, could duelling be defended as useful or necessary for a moment longer if some other institution, clothed with sufficient authority, were there to assure an offended party of adequate moral satisfaction and give the officer-class a guarantee that proper standards would be upheld?

On closer study, duelling itself, as a means of vindicating honour, appears to emanate *solely from the idea of class-honour;* whereas with *true class-honour*, as well as with the spirit of the public law, it appears to be plainly incompatible.

The principles of honour, as hitherto imposed by *custom*, require that an officer, like any other man of honour who is his equal in birth or rank,

> shall resort to a duel in order to avenge any symbolical or verbal insult to which he attaches importance. If this minor sort of provocation to a duel does not lead to a reconciliation by way of verbal compromise or an apology from the offender, then the idea of class-honour demands that blood shall be shed in some degree, by way of expiation or punishment, according to the whim of the contending parties. If an insult generally recognised as grave is offered by way of gesture, word or deed, it unconditionally requires to be decided by the shedding of blood in a duel, even to the point of an accidental or, in extreme cases, an intentional death.

Thus the law of honour is satisfied according to the whim of the individual or of public opinion.

Even if both parties emerge from the final test with their lives, it can be argued that justice has been done. Peace, however, has not been assured, for the duellists are usually more likely to derive material for even greater ill-will from the duel and its antecedents. They then resort to fighting again, as soon and as often as they wish, and the second duel is, if possible, more sanguinary than the first.

Against this, military law contains only an ambiguous prohibition and is therefore ineffective; but civil law expressly prohibits all private revenge for any symbolic, verbal or physical insult.

The public law against duelling is strict, and prescribes the following penalties (etc.).

(b) *What provisions of law apply to duelling between persons of military status, and how have they hitherto been applied by the highest authority iu the State?*

(There follow first a study of the current service-regulations and Cabinet Orders; then a study of the anti-duelling laws issued by Frederick I, Frederick William I, Frederick II, Frederick William II and lastly Frederick William III.)

The reign of our present King is distinguished by the acute intelligence with which essential reforms in the structure of the Army and its disciplinary regulations have been made, and in general by the new, contemporary outlook now common in the cultivated world.

The 'Regulation on the Punishment of Officers' breathes the new spirit that has now seized hold of the world and of the Prussian Army too. None the less it avoids, to all appearances with care, any mention of duelling; and it does so, perhaps, on account of the conflict that is growing up between the new Constitution of the Army, the views and opinions of the modern world, and the older spirit of the officers as a class, deep-rooted in honourable concepts as it is, founded upon law and by law protected.

The fact, however, that the reigning Monarch does not consider the provisions of general public law to be applicable to officers is shown not only by the general clemency he has prescribed (with rare exceptions) in respect of penalties but, even more plainly, by the indication he gave only a few months ago that new legislation for the Army was to be expected once the review of present military law had been completed.

In the civilian world, times are now quite different. Caprice has yielded place to law, roughness and indecency to education and to feelings of a finer and more moral kind.

In such circumstances it should be not merely possible, but is surely a crying necessity in the present state of civilian morality, that the law on duelling should be re-cast in *a new and stronger* mould, with particular reference to the military, among whom the present evil is most plainly evident.

It is not, indeed, to be denied that duelling has actually been encouraged by the *present uncertainty of the law* and by the *widespread conviction that the supreme authorities in the State connive at duelling* when it takes place among officers, despite the advance of civilisation, and have even given it encouragement.

The law should therefore draw such distinctions, and prescribe such penalties for every case, as to strike each offender with full force. The sacred character of the State's jurisdiction should be upheld in all its dignity by a fresh declaration, so that the sword of justice will protect the life, liberty and honour of each and every inhabitant.

If, however, one examines more closely the particular situation of the corps of officers and the features of the present Military Constitution that give rise to it, the following conclusion appears to result. An officer of the standing Army, whatever his education, ought, within the close corporation of his own unit, to be inspired by a noble spirit of comradeship, or *esprit de corps*. In general, he should be animated, too, by an exceptionally lively sense of honour, and this should ensure his support for the objective of the law, viz. the suppression of all capricious violence by way of appropriate military institutions.

The same assumption cannot, alas, be made in respect of the

corps of Landwehr-officers as constituted since the war. The situation in the Landwehr, therefore, appears all the more appropriate for introducing such institutions as will deliberately prevent the causing and fighting of duels, though in this case duelling has almost ceased to be appropriate.

In the light of the Army's present constitution it appears in both these connexions that the following measures are highly desirable and should be put into force as soon as possible:

1 a special *review of the laws on duelling*,
2 amendment of the regulations on the constitution and holding of Courts Martial, and
3 legislation creating

    a a *Commission of Honour in every Regiment or Corps of Officers* – such as already exists in many regiments – with the object of promoting morality, settling disputes, repressing unbecoming conduct by admonitions and referring serious misconduct to higher authority for investigation; perhaps also

    b a *Commission of Honour for every Division*, to which unbecoming conduct on the part of captains and staff-officers might be referred with a view to warnings being issued. An appropriate attitude on the part of the Commission of Honour towards the corps of officers might be ensured if it were established that an officer who

        had received two or three warnings should be regarded as incorrigible and should be referred to the Tribunal of Honour for a decision whether he could continue to enjoy the status of an officer,

    and

    c a *Tribunal of Honour for every Division*, empowered to decide matters which the Commissions of Honour had been unable to resolve and had referred to higher authority.

There is another reason for creating this quasi-judicial authority for matters concerning officers' morals and honour, and for giving it a more definite legal form. The type of Tribunal of Honour set up by the 'Order on the Punishment of Officers' (dated the 3rd August 1808) did not obtain the respect required by a disciplinary power, since its decisions had to be taken by a three-fourths majority of a given corps of officers and thus did not inspire confidence. More useful results, on the other hand, were produced by the Tribunals of Honour, consisting of one captain and two lieutenants, that were set up for the Landwehr regiments by the 'Landwehr Ordinance', section 77.

From the views expressed above it follows that the latter type of tribunal should be the model for the Commission of Honour, while it should be reserved to the Divisional Tribunal of Honour to investigate and decide the question whether an officer should be allowed to retain his status. If the officer's exclusion should be deemed necessary, such verdict would be for submission to His Majesty the King himself.

Institutions of this kind will scrutinise morals, prevent honour from being attacked and, should such attacks occur, it will punish them more satisfactorily than the outcome of a duel which itself may often be unjust. Duelling is quite unsuitable to modern times and compared with former customs and standards it has degenerated, regardless of chivalry, into a caricature of what the vindication of honour should be.

The review and amplification of the present laws on duelling and discipline, and the drafting of this important new piece of legislation on honour, should be entrusted to a mixed Commission, appropriately compounded of soldiers and lawyers, under the chairmanship of a General-Officer who deserves and enjoys widespread confidence in this connexion.

May the reign of our respected King be remembered for a decision so important to the happiness of the peoples of the civilised world, by banning the hydra of duelling from all his dominions! Such a decision will light the way for the other States of Europe and the civilised world by its noble display of modern enlightenment!

May Prussian law, like that of Virginia, brand the duel as being in reality a dishonourable business '*which shows the transgressor to be unworthy and condemns him to forfeiture of his civil rights!*' There can then be no doubt but that the other governments of Europe will not be slow to do the same.

And lastly, should not the general concern and disapproval with which all civilised Europe regards this custom that usurps mankind's most precious right of security and inflicts such grievous harm on the might of the law, this lawless survival from an age of tyranny

> which in every State of Europe is still daily liable to plunge the happiest family into bitter mourning, robbing it and the State alike of their supports,

should not this matter of such moment for mankind and for all civilised Europe be deemed worthy to be brought before the Congress of Heads of State, which is still in being,* with a view to its redress by general and concrete agreement?

In these enlightened times, when the well-being of mankind

---

* The Congress of Troppau, at which the Emperors of Austria and Russia and the King of Prussia were meeting to concert measures for repressing 'revolution'.

arouses such solicitude and when the rulers of our hemisphere are zealous to regard all Europe as a *single* nation, it truly needs but a hint to bring about the triumph of Good.

(Prussian Secret State Archives: KM.,Ztr. – Dep.,gen.,V.14.2.i. vol. 1.)

APPENDIX 14

Cabinet Order by King Frederick William III on Honour and Duelling

BERLIN, 13TH JUNE 1828

I have observed with growing displeasure that duelling in the Army tends to grow rather than to diminish. In recent years this custom has claimed the sacrifice of numerous victims, sometimes on account of wretched trivialities. The Army has'thereby been deprived of promising officers, while pain and sorrow has been brought upon their families. – An officer's life is consecrated to the defence of his Sovereign and his Country, and any man who risks that life for a trifling quarrel* gives proof that he is ignorant of the higher purpose which he serves, and shows himself incapable of maintaining a proper standard of conduct, based upon morality and a true sense of honour.

I require of the corps of officers that by mutual scrutiny of one another's conduct they shall prevent improper behaviour, compose quarrels by appropriate means such as reproving the parties and, if necessary make use of the authority granted them by My Order of the 15th February 1821 respecting tribunals of honour to bring the guilty party into such a forum. A corps of officers which puts an end to duelling by the appropriate handling of these affairs of honour will acquire a claim to My favour and will prove that the true spirit of honour dwells in it. For senior officers, too, I hereby make it an especial part of their duty to counteract this pernicious habit by vigilance and precept. I shall cause the full severity of the law to be felt by any man who disregards these warnings or goes so far as to challenge his opponent to a duel with pistols; and no consideration shall be shown to any man who provokes another to a duel by a deliberate breach of manners or by some wanton insult.

I charge you to communicate the foregoing to the officers of the Army and to lay stress upon the fact that, reposing confidence in their sentiments, I count upon their efforts to enhance the well-earned reputation of the Army by suppressing an out-moded practice and cultivating a nobler moral standard.

(*signed*) FREDERICK WILLIAM

to General of Infantry von Hake, Minister of War.

(Prussian Secret State Archives: KM.,Ztr. – Dep.,V.14.2.1.vol.1.)

* On a later copy of this Order in the archives appears the following pencilled remark: 'NB! Tauentzin challenges Bülow because he, instead of Tauentzin, received the title of Dennewitz!'

310

APPENDIX 15

Memorandum by General Zieten on Duelling

BRESLAU, 10TH FEBRUARY 1829

The Royal Cabinet Order of the 13th June 1828, in which His Majesty forbad duelling, is no less wise than gracious and, if I may say so, *fatherly* in its concern for the Army. Alas, however, experience goes to show that it will not suffice to overcome this grievous evil because

> young officers often speak without reflecting, and this leads to their gravely insulting brother-officers; or else because older officers – sometimes even those of high rank – decline to admit the impropriety of duelling and fail to act with all the vigour at their command against younger officers who behave in this way.

It will, I allow, be hard to manage a whole corps of officers in such a way that the younger ones behave at all times in a manner that befits their status (*Stand*) and the education they have had. I admit, too, that without a duel I do not know how insults occurring between officers are to be put right. I have been a firm opponent of duelling from my youth up, and I have proved that a man can achieve high rank without engaging in it. I am therefore sincere in my desire to see the total disappearance of duelling from the Army, and the question is how. I take leave to offer Your Excellency, in confidence, my respectful views on the matter.

a If a commission is set up in every regiment to enquire into insults occurring between officers, it must also prescribe penalties, and the question then arises, on what principles are these to be determined? Will not dissension within a regiment lay a wide field open, and lead to the commanding officer's authority being still further limited? In these days it is limited already to the point of putting him in difficulty.

I will admit that I am no friend of commissions which transfer rights to the corps of officers that ought to belong to the regimental commander.

b It seems to me therefore that other means must be invented; and I believe they are easy to find. The *Duell-Mandat* was drawn up many years ago and is no longer suitable to present conditions. Courts Martial, of course, apply it; but their sentences are so reduced by His Majesty's Prerogative that the *Mandat* is a dead letter.

311

c It seems to me therefore that a strict anti-duelling law, suitable to present conditions, should be drafted, and that it should prescribe the penalty for him who utters the insult and forces the other party to challenge him.

d If such an anti-duelling law were strictly drawn, Courts Martial should be instructed to apply it rigidly: but no reduction of their sentences should be made.

At the outset, I realise, some officers would be punished very harshly; but the example given would be effective without question and would do more to check duelling than all prohibitions and remonstrances.

Your Excellency will have the goodness to forgive me for confidentially putting forward my opinion on a matter which is of great importance for the well-being of the officer-class, as well as for that of many a respectable family which is plunged into bitter grief by this unhappy practice of duelling.

(*signed*) ZIETEN

To the Minister of War, von Hake.

(Prussian Secret State Archives: KM.,Ztr. – Dep.,V.14.2.1,vol.1.)

APPENDIX 16

Introductory Order by William I to the Ordinance on Tribunals of Honour dated the 2nd May, 1874

It is My desire that the officers of My Army shall accept and apply the Ordinance on Tribunals of Honour, which I have signed today, in the spirit which has distinguished My Army from its very beginnings.

I therefore look to the whole corps of officers of My Army to make honour their finest jewel in future as they have always done hitherto. To keep its honour pure and spotless must be the most sacred duty of the whole Estate and of every member of it. If that duty is fulfilled, then every other duty incumbent on an officer will be fully and conscientiously performed. True honour cannot exist without faithfulness unto death, without invincible courage, firm determination, self-denying obedience, simple truthfulness and strict discretion, nor without self-sacrifice in the fulfilment of what may seem but trivial tasks. Honour requires, too, that an officer's outward bearing shall reflect his conscious pride in being a member of the Estate to which the defence of Throne and Fatherland has been entrusted. An officer should endeavour to keep no company but that in which high standards are cherished; and least of all in public places should he forget that he will be looked upon not merely as a man of education but as one who represents the honour and the higher obligations of his Estate. He should keep aloof from all dealings that may reflect upon the good name of the individual or of the fellowship to which he belongs; especially from all excess, from drunkenness and gambling, from contracting any obligation that may lead to even the slightest appearance of dishonest conduct, from speculative dealings on the Stock Exchange, from taking part in any commercial enterprise whose aims are not unimpeachable or whose reputation is not of the highest. Never should he lightly pledge his word of honour.

As luxury and good living become widespread in other walks of life, the more it is an officer's serious duty never to forget that it is not by his possessions that he gained, or will preserve, the highly honoured place he occupies in the State and society. It is not simply that his military value may be reduced if he lives in comfort; the pursuit of riches and good living involves the danger that the very foundation on which the officers' Estate is built may be brought to total ruination.

The more attention the corps of officers pays to cultivating genuine comradeship and a true *esprit de corps*, the easier will it be to prevent excess of any kind, bring comrades back if they stray from the right path, and avoid senseless quarrels and unworthy wrangling.

The pride which an officer rightly feels should never lead him astray into showing lack of respect or arrogance toward other Estates. The more an officer loves his profession, the higher he rates its aims, the better will he grasp the extent to which success and renown in the discharge of the Army's ultimate and highest task depends upon all classes having the fullest confidence in the Estate of officers.

As for the officers of the Reserve, and those former officers whom I have authorised to continue wearing the outward marks of their Estate, I am confident that, as they have not ceased to share in the honour of that Estate, they will ever be mindful that even in civilian life the preservation of that honour remains their duty.

It is, above all, the regimental-commanders, and other commanders of equal rank, who are answerable to Me for maintaining a lively sense of honour in the corps of officers of the standing Army and the Reserve. It is principally they who should find opportunities of exerting influence through the means available for training the younger officers – an influence that extends far beyond their personal range in time and space, and should aim at that spirit which alone can make an army great. Their discharge of this duty will be the more successful if they seriously exhort the younger officers to follow the friendly advice of their older brother-officers, and if they leave the latter in no doubt that an essential part of their duty is to keep a watch upon their juniors and train them up.

If proper action in this sense is taken by way of training, example, instruction, warnings and orders, it is certain that there will be a gradual reduction in incidents of the kind which call for settlement by others of the same Estate through the tribunals of honour established by this Ordinance.

The purpose aimed at by the terms of this Ordinance is to assist the officers' Estate in preserving the well-tried tradition of chivalrous behaviour, and to secure the means whereby orderly action can be taken if an officer incurs the reproach of having suffered injury to his honour, or if he has reason to fear that such a thing may occur.

For this purpose the councils of honour are to serve as instruments for commanding officers; but on the latter alone fall the duty of directing the tribunals of honour, and the responsibility for the proper handling of all eventualities within their competence. Councils of honour should moreover make their friendly advice available to any brother-officer who turns to them in an affair of honour. By leaving the officer-corps itself to choose the members of a tribunal of honour, it was not solely My intention to furnish commanding officers with a suitable instrument for use in affairs of honour, troublesome as these can be. My aim was also that these positions should be filled by men who enjoy their brother-officers' confidence in such a high degree that they can successfully function as the latter's chosen advisers in affairs of honour. I assume, of course, that no officer, when engaged in choosing another, would allow himself to be guided by principles other than those which conform to this My intention.

The tribunals of honour have, however, a dual task. Their findings must clear the individual's honour of all unfounded suspicion unless other means, acceptable to the Estate, are open to him for this purpose; and they must take action to protect the honour of the Estate from any of its members whose conduct is incompatible with a proper sense of honour and with the standards of the officers' Estate. I do not intend to provide any exhaustive list of cases in which such action might be advisable. The intention which I have expressed above should furnish sufficient guidance for them to be identified as they arise.

Likewise, I feel Myself amply assured that commanding officers will rightly value the penal authority given them for preserving discipline and maintaining their authority, and will not resort to a tribunal of honour in cases that can be dealt with as matters of discipline, lest they reduce thereby the significance and weight that should attach to such a tribunal's findings.

All proceedings of councils and tribunals of honour should be governed not only by consideration for the maintenance of the honour of the Estate but by mutual good-will. Proceedings should be limited to enquiring into the points complained of and should not be concerned with side-issues; nor should they be burdened and delayed by needless formalities. In this connection too, there is a point that should be carefully observed, viz. that the private affairs of a corps of officers should not become more widely known than is absolutely necessary.

Confident that high standards and good manners will continue to be normal in My Army and that private quarrels, like insults occurring between officers, will become steadily rarer, I have cancelled the procedure laid down in Ordinance II of the 20th July 1843. Only on an officer who finds himself in a private quarrel involving honour with another officer is it still incumbent to notify his council of honour, or have it notified by a brother-officer; and he must do so, at the very latest, when he issues or receives a challenge to a duel. The council of honour must then make an urgent report to the commanding officer; it must do so, if possible, before the duel takes place and, insofar as the usages of the Estate permit, attempt a reconciliation. If this last should fail, however, the council of honour must try to ensure that the terms on which the duel is fought

L*   315

are not inappropriate to the gravity of the case. If a duel is to be fought, the president or some member of the council of honour must be present on the duelling-ground as a witness and ensure that the usages of the Estate are observed in the fighting.

Action on account of a duel shall only be taken against an officer by way of a tribunal of honour if one or other party has offended the honour of the Estate either by the occasion that gave rise to the quarrel or by the manner of its prosecution. – Action is especially important in the not impossible event that an officer wantonly and without any provocation gravely insults another. For an officer who is capable of wantonly impugning the honour of a brother-officer is no more to be tolerated in My Army than one who is incapable of defending his own. Regimental-commanders and other commanders of equal rank are to ensure with care that this My Order is brought to the notice of every newly-commissioned officer of the standing Army and the Reserve. From time to time, moreover, the Will which I have expressed herein is to be read aloud to the assembled individual corps of officers, so that it shall be the more often in the mind of the officers of My Army.

(signed) WILLIAM

APPENDIX 17

Memorandum from the Bavarian Minister of War to the King, on Duelling and Tribunals of Honour in Central and Western Europe, and especially in Bavaria

MUNICH, 9TH AUGUST 1858

On the 24th March last Your Majesty was graciously pleased to address a Manuscript communication in the following terms to Your obedient servant, undersigned:

'I think the laws now in force on the subject of duelling are in some 'respects defective, and it would be advisable to undertake some 'amplification and amendment of them. For this purpose I think it 'will be wisest to appoint a Commission charged with considering 'how best to limit duelling; and attention should be paid to the 'situation obtaining on this subject in other German states, as well 'as in France. – It might also be useful to introduce the Prussian 'device of tribunals of honour with power to recognise a duel, or not, 'so that when a duel was recognised, the parties would escape being 'punished. I wish to see a report on the matter.'

Pursuant to Your Majesty's command the undersigned respectfully begs leave to make the following submission:

I

In the Bavarian Criminal Code of 1813, duelling is not listed as a serious crime or offence. Instead, it is only the general provisions of law on the commission or attempted commission of a crime and on culpable designs and negligence, and the provisions of law on bodily injury or homicide, that can be used, according to circumstances, against the parties to a duel.

The anti-duelling Order (*Mandat*) of the 28th February 1779, was never fully applied on account of its extreme severity: and as long ago as the 17th October 1828, the Royal Council of State decided, with Royal approval, that this Order should cease to be treated as valid and applicable even in those parts of the country where it had theretofore been enforced.

Like the previous editions (of 1822, 1827, 1831 and 1851) of the Penal Code in respect of crimes and offences, the latest edition, that of 1855, contains provisions on the subject of duelling.

The study of this text which the Legislation Committee had already started came to a provisional end as a result of Your

Majesty's decision of the 20th March last, suspending the sittings.

As long ago as 1828 a Bill on the subject of tribunals of honour was brought before the Chambers, but the Estates did not reach agreement to approve it; and the message dissolving the Assembly of Estates on the 15th August 1828 therefore expressed His then Majesty's lively regret 'that no agreement between the Estates had been reached, and that His Majesty was therefore determined to use all His strength and all the legal means at His disposal to combat duelling, as an intolerable affront to religion, moral law and civil order alike.'

2

In the Service-Regulations of 1823 for the Royal Bavarian Forces, and in other Royal Ordinances issued to the Army, there is no detailed regulation covering duels between members of the military forces.

Individual Ordinances express only the King's intention, as Commander-in-Chief, of preventing duels between officers. They strictly forbid tribunals of honour to recognise duels, and they threaten officers taking part in pistol-duels, either as principals, seconds or witnesses, with punishment by expulsion from the Army or reduction of rank in addition to any other penalties awarded: they draw attention once more to the fact that duelling is forbidden, and they contain provisions governing the competence and proper functioning of tribunals of honour.

Only in Section 482(2) do these Service-Regulations provide that attacks upon an officer's honour by word or deed are to be submitted to the judgment of a tribunal of honour, and that any man who on account of such insult seeks his own satisfaction in evasion of the tribunal of honour, or fails to obey its decision, shall be punished by dismissal. Sections 514(6) and 531 lay down how a tribunal of honour is to be constituted and function.

Nor is duelling as such made the subject of particular provisions in the Military Penal Code incorporated in the Service-Regulations, any more than it is in the general Penal Code. In the case of a duel between officers, therefore, the terms of the Penal Code are applicable according to circumstance; and in cases where satisfaction has been sought in evasion of a tribunal of honour, the usual practice of Courts Martial is to order the military penalty of dismissal in accordance with Section 482(2) of the Service-Regulations, in addition to any penalty attaching to the consequences of the duel.

For a number of years past, however, the common-law sentences passed by judges have not been served in full but have been reduced by Royal Prerogative, while the simultaneous penalty of dismissal has always been remitted by Royal Prerogative; and indeed the undersigned can recall no case since the Service-Regulations of 1823 came into effect in which the penalty of dismissal has been enforced against an officer who procured satisfaction for himself in evasion of a tribunal of honour.

3

With a view to informing Your Majesty, with all respect, on the position in other States regarding duelling and tribunals of honour, Your Majesty's humble, obedient servant, undersigned, has not failed to examine the relevant laws and regulations, and has had recourse to the diplomatic channel in order to inform himself about the latest developments.

Such information is now to hand; and it has been assumed that Your Majesty's Command of the 24th March referred solely to the situation as regards the *armies* in the other German States and not to legislation in those States on the subject of duelling in general and among civilians. Your Majesty's humble, obedient servant therefore begs leave to make the following further submission:

Austria

Tribunals of honour, as an institution for judging and composing affairs of honour between officers, have not been introduced into the Austrian Army.

Under the older Articles of War and anti-duelling Orders the penalties for duelling were corporal and capital punishment. Duelling is declared a crime by Sections 437 ff of the current Military Penal Code, dated the 15th January 1855, which mainly reproduces the provisions of the Civil Penal Code.

These Sections make duelling punishable:

a if no bloodshed results, by six to twelve months' imprisonment,

b if serious injury results, by one to five years' imprisonment and, in exceptionally aggravating circumstances, by hard labour for the same period,

c if the death of one party results, by five to ten years' imprisonment and if there was agreement to fight to the death, by ten to twenty years' imprisonment.

d Seconds incur six to twelve months', or one to five years', imprisonment, according to circumstances,

e no penalty is incurred if the parties voluntarily abandon a duel before it starts and if its abandonment is due to the efforts of those who would otherwise have been accomplices; and seconds who are of officer's Estate are not punishable in the case of a duel in which at least one of the parties was an officer, if they have made zealous efforts, however vain, to settle the dispute.

4

Prussia

The institution of tribunals of honour has been given particular attention in Prussia.

The anti-duelling Edicts of 1652 and 1688 were excessively severe, and made duelling punishable in all circumstances. Their penal provisions were repeated in the Order of 1713. Provision for the introduction of tribunals of honour was included in the general legal Code drawn up in the reign of King Frederick William II.

The first draft of the general legal Code appeared in 1785, and it was based on the assumption that it might be possible in exceptional cases to obtain the Sovereign's permission to seek satisfaction for one's self; but the Army Council was so strongly opposed to the introduction of tribunals of honour that King Frederick William II was obliged to abandon the project, and on the 21st May 1791 he made a Cabinet Order confirming the existing penal provisions.*

The severity of the laws on duelling had made it necessary for the Prerogative to be used in the direction of clemency, and the law was thus robbed of importance and respect; it was considered, moreover, that its object, the suppression of duelling, had not been achieved. Two Royal Ordinances were therefore issued on the 20th July 1843; one was concerned to enlarge the scope of tribunals of honour, while the subject of the other was their procedure when investigating quarrels and cases of insult arising between officers.

The first Ordinance gave tribunals of honour compulsory jurisdiction over all acts of commission or omission which, though not punishable by law, ran counter to a proper sense of honour or to the decencies of an officer's Estate. It clothed the tribunals of honour with authority to impose penalties, laid down rules for their constitution and that of the councils of honour which made preliminary investigations, and prescribed the procedure to be observed in each case.

With a view to the utmost avoidance of duels, the second Ordinance empowered the tribunals of honour to act as umpires in all quarrels and cases of insult arising between officers, gave guidance on how councils of honour should proceed once they had been notified of a quarrel that might lead to a duel, and how a tribunal of honour, when convened after an investigation by a council of honour, should arrive at a decision in the light of the circumstances.

This Ordinance also contains penalties for duelling between

* The important Ordinances issued by Frederick William III are ignored, strangely enough, but evidently on the basis of the Legation's reports from Berlin, which in turn were based on information supplied by the Ministry of War.

officers; and Your Majesty's humble, obedient servant, under-signed, believes he will not stray far from his terms of reference if he takes leave to summarise their contents:

If no death results, the parties incur detention in a fortress for one month to two years, according to the gravity of the injury inflicted (Section 21).

If one of the parties is killed or dies of his wounds, the survivor incurs one to four years' detention in a fortress (Section 22).

If, according to the form of the duel, the death of one party was the inevitable or agreed result, the survivor incurs five to ten years' detention in a fortress and, if no death results, two to six years (Section 23).

If the survivor causes the death of his opponent in contravention of the traditional, or the agreed, form of the duel, he incurs not only dismissal from the service, but ten to twenty years' detention in a fortress; and in exceptionally aggravated circumstances he incurs the capital penalty under ordinary civil law.

Likewise for cases in which a duel takes place in evasion of the council or the tribunal of honour, or while the affair is pending decision by the latter, or if a duel takes place without seconds, the second Ordinance of the 20th July 1843 prescribes penalties, viz. according to the circumstances of each case and to the outcome of the duel the appropriate penalty is increased by a further period of two months' to two years' detention in a fortress.

5

Authority to recognise a duel in particular cases, which means that the parties are at once exonerated, is *not* conferred on tribunals of honour in Prussia by the above-mentioned Ordinance or by any later amendment.

If a quarrel or a case of insult arising between officers does not yield to composition by a tribunal of honour, or if the parties thereto announce that they cannot accept the tribunal's decision, the tri-bunal must close its proceedings; but the council of honour must draw the parties' attention to the penalties which the Ordinance of the 20th July 1843, Sections 22 ff, prescribes for duelling.

The impression that tribunals of honour in Prussia are empowered to recognise a duel is possibly due to the peculiar provisions of Section 17 of the above-mentioned Ordinance.

That Section provides that if a council of honour learns that the parties intend to fight a duel it has the right, but not the duty, to proceed to the duelling-ground and, after further fruitless attempts at a settlement, to supervise the course and outcome of the duel in the character of an umpire, to forbid any misuse of weapons occurring in the course of the fight and to order its cessation as soon as it judges that circumstances and the usages of the Estate permit.

While it is permissive, though not mandatory, for the tribunal of honour thus to function as an umpire, its appearance in that role confers neither legality on the duel nor exoneration on the parties. On the contrary, as soon as the duel is over, the penalty for duelling takes effect on the basis of the proceedings in the tribunal of honour, unless a fresh investigation appears to have been rendered necessary by some feature of the duel or its outcome (Section 19).

In certain exceptional cases the scale of penalties prescribed for award by tribunals of honour under the Prussian laws on duelling does not go beyond the disciplinary limit of arrest (Section 31), viz. where a duel has taken place without malice and solely because of the peculiar requirements of the officers' Estate and where no evil result has followed, where both parties have behaved irreproachably and no aggravating circumstance is present.

The unmistakable spirit and intention of the second Royal Prussian Ordinance of the 20th July 1843 is that the tribunals of honour should be a means of preventing deliberate insults, keeping duelling among officers within bounds and reinforcing the prestige of tribunals of honour in the eyes of the officers' Estate. Moreover, the punishment laid down for duels of every kind (according to circumstances and outcome) are consistent with the preamble to the Royal Ordinance on penalties for duelling, and they leave no room for doubt that duelling is forbidden by law and that a commanding officer's duty is not to authorise but to prevent it.

The one extraordinary feature is the authority granted to the council of honour to be present at a duel and supervise it in the role of umpire. This amounts to taking part in something which its task is to prevent (and which the law forbids under penalties) and thereby giving it the seal of approval and legality. Yet the council of honour is to use this authority solely for the purpose of continuing its efforts, even on the duelling-ground, to prevent the duel taking place. Even so, therefore, it is still within its terms of reference; and it would be all the more unjustified to conclude that the duel has been authorised since the penalty for fighting it takes effect the moment it is over.

6

Saxony

In Saxony there are no definite rules that apply to duelling between officers, or between officers and civilians. The tribunals of honour that formerly existed were abolished a few years ago, since they were ineffective, and were replaced by a law on disciplinary tribunals for officers.

The sole duty of these tribunals is to investigate and report to the Ministry of War the acts specified in the law as being liable to lead to an officer's dismissal by Royal decision.

As for duels between officers, or between officers and civilians, it is left to the parties to settle matters however they please. But an officer who refuses to fight may expect automatic dismissal. The thing which determines the eventual attitude or intervention of the authorities is always the outcome of the duel itself.

7

Baden

In Baden the provisions of the general Penal Code in respect of duelling apply equally to military persons and civilians, with the sole difference that the penalties therein prescribed must be converted into the corresponding military penalties prescribed by the Articles of War. Even so, duels arising out of acts committed in the course of duty are governed by the special provision that if any such duel should take place between a junior and his superior officer, that fact will be held to be an aggravation and will lead to dismissal or a request for resignation, in addition to the penalties incurred.

Under the general Penal Code of Baden, duelling is punishable by a maximum of two years in prison or in the workhouse. In the event of death or wounding, the penalty (according to the gravity of the wound) is six months to six years in the workhouse for the guilty party or, if he is an officer, under detention in a fortress.

Tribunals for settling affairs of honour are unknown to the law of the Grand Duchy or to the practice of the Grand-Ducal Army Corps, and no need to introduce them has been felt. A tribunal of honour (in Baden called an '*ehrengerichtliche Commission*') is only convened when an officer commits an offence of such a kind, or behaves himself in such a manner as to raise doubt, by the standards of his Estate, whether he should not be removed from the Service at once and without previous notice. The officer concerned must appear before this tribunal on orders from the Ministry of War pursuant to the Grand Duke's command, and the tribunal's only function is to decide whether the officer may remain in the Service or should be dismissed.

8

Grand Duchy of Hesse

Tribunals of honour have not yet officially existed in the Grand-Ducal service. At the time when the Legation was making enquiries, the Government was considering their introduction, but the discussions had not then been concluded and no official information could therefore be supplied. None the less it was already clear that the proposed tribunals of honour would merely have the duty of giving an opinion whether, in a particular case, an officer had offended against the honour of his Estate. It was also the Government's intention to model these tribunals of honour on those which already exist in Prussia, Saxony, Baden and other German States.

Since then, the creation of tribunals in the Grand Duchy of Hesse has been decided.

Provision for creating them was included in a bill for the reform of the military establishment, but this particular section was resisted by the Second Chamber with every weapon available. It was denied, first of all, that the honour of the military Estate had any distinct existence; it was then objected that tribunals of honour would give officers less protection against persecution than the ordinary courts-martial; and it was further asserted that without the concurrence of the Estates the Government had no authority to promulgate regulations for the convening and procedure of tribunals of honour. When it came to the vote, the whole bill was defeated – mainly on account of the section on tribunals of honour.

In consequence the Government could not proceed to create tribunals of honour empowered to pronounce in favour of dismissing officers found unfit for further membership of the officers' Estate. Tribunals of honour have therefore been set up by Ordinance. Their findings cannot lead to dismissal without pension, but if they find that an officer has offended against the honour of his Estate he will be stripped of everything to which he has no legal claim.

By the relevant Ordinance of the 2nd July [1858] it is laid down that officers and military officials are to be brought before a tribunal of honour when accused of acts of commission or omission, or of utterances, that are incompatible with the honour of the Estate, provided that the law does not make these acts, etc. punishable by dismissal or by such other penalties as must entail dismissal.

Duelling between officers, or between officers and civilians, remains subject to Article 154 of the Grand-Ducal Military Penal Code, which makes duelling punishable in accordance with civil law.

9

Wurtemberg

The general military ordinance for the Royal Wurtemberg Forces, dated the 7th February 1858, contains provision for tribunals of honour. The tribunals have two main fields of activity:

1 They pronounce on the question whether an officer's behaviour

has been such as to offend against the honour of his Estate and has thus rendered him unfit for further service as an officer.

2 In cases of insult to honour occurring between officers the tribunals must act in a mediatory capacity and, if unsuccessful, they must act as umpires.

In the latter capacity the tribunal is to omit no possible means of bringing a reconciliation about, provided such a thing is still permissible by the current standards of the Estate; and contravention of its findings will entail the offender's dismissal. – If, however, the tribunal concludes that reconciliation is not permissible, it is to release both parties, stating that they are to settle their affairs of honour as the honour of their Estate requires.

Duelling between officers is governed by the special provisions of the Penal Code of the Kingdom of Wurtemberg, dated the 1st March 1839; and the penalty is determined by the facts of the case or by the outcome of the duel.

In ordinary cases, i.e. when, without previous agreement to that effect, the death of one party has resulted, the penalty is detention in a fortress for two to six years. In the case of injury involving danger to life or permanent damage to health, the penalty is detention in a fortress for one to five years; and when minor injury has been caused, or none at all, the penalty is detention in a fortress for two to twelve months.

In themselves these provisions are not too severe: but in the special cases of officers they lead, at least in theory, to undeniable hardship, inasmuch as members of the officers' Estate have no other choice whatever but to fight once the tribunal has found in a given case that a compromise is not permissible and has declared 'that the parties are to settle their affair of honour as the honour of their Estate requires'.

In practice, however, this hardship is avoided as far as possible. According to the report from Your Majesty's Legation at Stuttgart, the Minister of War has officially stated that the regulations governing tribunals of honour are no different from those contained in the published general Articles of War, and that within these limits the tribunals are to act with full independence. But from less official (and thus perhaps more impartial) sources Your Majesty's Minister-Resident at Stuttgart received confidential information to the effect that when a tribunal of honour thinks it will have to issue a finding in a duelling-case it must always make a confidential report to the Minister of War, and that the latter at once seeks His Majesty's instructions. If the Monarch consents to the duel he thereby assumes to some extent the moral obligation of using the Prerogative if a culpable offence should result, provided always that the duel was

correctly fought by the rules. In that event a Pardon always follows
in a relatively short space of time.

10

Hanover

Under the terms of the Military Penal Code (Sections 223 ff) for the
Kingdom of Hanover, issued in 1841, the penalties laid down in the
general Penal Code apply to duelling between officers, save when the
duel originated in an insult which, by the standards currently held
by the Estate on the *point d'honneur*, can be removed by no other
means, and provided the duel is fought in the traditional manner,
viz. in the presence of two seconds and a surgeon.

Even in these cases, however, the officer whose fault made the duel
necessary is to suffer detention on account of his fault if it arose from
lack of foresight or excess of haste; and if malicious intent is present
he is to suffer detention in a fortress or loss of his appointment.
Officers whose intolerant or quarrelsome temperament is the cause
of frequent trouble and disputes, or provokes others thereto, are to be
sentenced to dismissal if punishment has already been proved
ineffective.

So far as the undersigned is aware, Hanover is the only State
whose laws provide that duelling in certain cases is not a punishable
offence.

In general, what effect this provision has had since it came into
force; whether, in particular, it has not gone too far for the so-called
'honour laws' to be respected as a whole and to the very letter;
whether, in brief, some amendment has not become necessary in this
respect – these are matters on which the undersigned has no
information.

11

Oldenburg

The Military legislation of the Grand Duchy of Oldenburg dates
from 1841 and makes no mention of duelling among officers. Duelling appears, therefore, to be a non-military offence, cognisable and
punishable only by the civil courts.

On the other hand, Appendix 2 of the Military Laws contains
several Articles dealing with tribunals of honour. Their function and
powers, however, extend only to acts of commission and omission
by officers which appear to involve an offence against the honour of
their Estate, e.g. if an officer's behaviour and habits are such that
they seem in any way to offend against the honour of the Estate, the

326

tribunal is to investigate the matter, once seized of it, and pronounce whether the honour of the Estate has suffered.

Should such be the tribunal's finding, the papers are to be submitted to his Royal Highness the Grand Duke for consideration and decision whether the accused should be deprived of his military rank and status, and of the right to wear uniform.

In affairs of honour which seem likely to lead to a duel the tribunal of honour has no competence.

12

France

According to information obtained by the Legation from the Imperial French Ministry of War, there is no particular law against duelling nor is there any institution corresponding to the German tribunals of honour. While French law does not recognise duelling, the Army none the less regards it as necessary if a soldier receives an insult to his honour. The question whether a duel shall take place is decided by unit-commanders themselves when it is brought to their notice, although military regulations do not oblige them to do so.

If the military authorities are unable to intervene before a duel is fought, they impose a disciplinary punishment on the party which gave the first offence; and a duel only gives rise to criminal proceedings if it is fought in disregard of the rules of honourable combat.

If an officer disgraces himself on the occasion of a duel or by the circumstances that gave rise to it, that officer's conduct is examined by a court of inquiry; and in the light of the court's decision the officer may be deprived of his status as such.

These courts of inquiry are not, however, tribunals of honour such as exist in Bavaria. They are only called upon to give their opinion when there is any question of an officer's dismissal from the Army.

In general, striking differences of opinion have been shown by the French Courts on the penalisation of duelling. Some of them have adopted the principle that duelling is not an offence in itself but that if a duel leads to a death or to wounding the penalty to be imposed is the one prescribed by the ordinary law for killing or wounding. Other courts have let duelling go unpunished, partly because the law is silent, partly on account of what they deduce from legislative expressions to be the legislator's intention.

In 1837 the Court of Cassation declared that a death caused in a duel fell under the penal laws on killing and was to be punished accordingly. Several courts of appeal, however, held to the view that duelling was not to be subsumed under the penal laws on killing; and when prosecutions were begun in lower courts the jury acquitted the accused. No action has yet been taken in France on any demand for a special law on duelling.

In the Palatinate, the French penal code is in force; and in 1844, a duelling case in which one party was wounded, the Prosecution Division (*Anklage-Kammer*) of the Court of Appeal at Zweibrücken declared the laws on wounding to be inapplicable. The Court of Cassation, however, held the opposite view. As recently as last June [1858] in a case at Zweibrücken, the accused (a lawyer named Jung who had mortally wounded a Lieutenant Rauh of the Engineers' staff) was acquitted by the jury with the assertion that duelling was not punishable under the *Code Pénal*.

13

England

While no enquiry was made by the Legation as regards the procedure now followed by the British Army in respect of duelling, the undersigned begs leave to submit herewith some information on the subject derived partly from the General Military Journal for the year 1843 and partly from the records of criminal jurisprudence for the year 1850. They illustrate the attitude to duelling that has latterly been growing commoner in England, and they also give some indication of military penal law on the subject.

As long ago as 1843 an association was formed in England for the suppression of duelling, which it described as sinful, contrary to reason and an offence against the laws of God and man; and its members pledged themselves to combat the continuance of duelling by their influence and example.

At that time the association already counted 416 members: among them 38 Lords and sons of Lords, 18 members of Parliament, 20 baronets, 35 admirals and generals, 56 naval captains, 32 colonels, 26 majors, 42 captains, 26 lieutenants and 28 barristers; and in 1850 the association's numbers were still growing.

They select a certain number of gentlemen to arbitrate in affairs of honour. Three suffice to constitute a court; and if the friends of the parties cannot effect a reconciliation, they are bound to bring the matter before these arbitrators, whose award the parties must accept.

In the Articles of War of 1844 it was plainly stated that the Queen approved the conduct of any officer who, if he had the misfortune to offend someone, voluntarily expiated the offence either by withdrawing his words or by making a declaration on his honour, etc, or who, if he was the offended party, accepted such declarations frankly and sincerely or, if a friend of the offended party, did his best to settle the matter by effecting a reconciliation.

Officers who challenge others, fight duels, or provoke or encourage others thereto are, if brought before a court-martial, to be cashiered or otherwise punished at the court's discretion.* According to the above-mentioned association's Reports, the War Office closely watches the working of the new regulation, and takes the view that it is always easy to bring about a reconciliation if the brother-officers of the offended party really desire it.

The association's Report for 1850 states that duelling in England has already become a rarity.

14

It cannot altogether be denied that the tribunals of honour, as they exist at present in the Bavarian Army, have done some good. While their existence has not quite put an end to duelling, it has reduced it, especially in cases in which the insult rested primarily on a misunderstanding or on a biassed and strained interpretation, or was trivial in itself, or was easy to settle by a legally permissible form of satisfaction or by agreement, or where the findings of a tribunal of honour sufficed to put an end to its prejudicial effects.

It must be admitted, on the other hand, that the tribunals enjoy limited scope and authority, while their pronouncements and the other effects of their proceedings are still closely confined to mediation and reconciliation. They are therefore not always in a position to give direct and effective protection to the offended officer's honour in the eyes, or in the teeth, of public opinion; nor are they able to undo the harm which the honour of an officer who has been insulted must inescapably suffer as regards his utility to the Army and his standing in the eyes of his brother-officers.

The insufficiency of the tribunals' limits is shown up very sharply by affairs of honour occurring between an officer and a civilian or a foreign officer. As constituted in Bavaria the tribunals have no jurisdiction over a civilian or an officer of another State; and it will always be rare for a civilian to submit himself voluntarily to the verdict of a military tribunal composed exclusively of officers. The Royal decision of the 3rd February 1834 extended the competence of military tribunals of honour to cover the case of officers insulted by civilians; but the officer concerned is bound to submit to the proceedings and findings of the tribunal within the limits of its competence, whereas the tribunal is only competent as regards the civilian if he voluntarily submits himself to its proceedings and findings and does so to a degree that makes its arbitration a reality.

* Article 98, as amended in April, 1844, says that 'every person who shall fight or promote a duel, or take any steps thereto, or who shall not do his best to prevent a duel, shall, if an officer, be cashiered or suffer such other penalty as a general court-martial may award'.

If, in a mixed case of this sort, an officer places the affair in the hands of a tribunal of honour in accordance with His late Majesty's command, he is at a disadvantage. The tribunal cannot secure him any full and appropriate satisfaction for the insult offered him: all it can do, if the insult appears to have been unprovoked, is to protect him against further harm by reaffirming his honour and suggest that he seek satisfaction from the courts.

But, short of a considerable change in the conventional standards of society, such an affirmation will rarely strike either the officer concerned or his brother-officers as a fully adequate means of removing the stain upon his honour; nor is a favourable judgment by a court of law, though set forth with all legal learning and acumen in the light of more than exhaustive hearings, by any means able to erase a slur from a man's honour, either in the eyes of a public opinion reluctant to bow to a penal code of law, or by the standards of honour held by the Estate.

In Prussia, a Royal Ordinance of the 27th September 1845 laid down that in the event of a duel between an officer and one of non-commissioned rank or a civilian, the officer concerned and the officers who acted as his representatives, seconds, etc. should incur the penalties prescribed for a duel between officers.

Infinitely difficult as it is for the legislator to reconcile the regulations on duelling and the penalties therefor with the principles of law and ethics, with public opinion and the deep-rooted convictions on honour held by the Estate, it is no less hard to create soundly based tribunals of honour which shall take account of all aspects of opinion in the Estate and be fully able to assure ample satisfaction for an insult without recourse to duelling, command general approval, and achieve the object of reducing the number of duels with certain success.

(Further exhaustive discussion of the question whether and, if so, what amendments might be made to Bavarian military law on the subject of duelling and tribunals of honour are here omitted).*

(*signed*) MANZ
(Major-General, Minister of War)

(Bavarian Kriegsarchiv: A XIII.3.fasc.3.)

* On the 10th January 1860 it was decided in the Ministry of War that this subject must be left in suspense, since it was not known whether, when, or to what extent the new Penal Code would be ready and would pass through all legislative stages into law.

APPENDIX 18

Circular from the Supreme Command of the Army. Subject: 'Challenges to Duels and Rules for Duelling'

BERLIN, 22ND FEBRUARY 1937

A challenge to a duel is the ultimate means for the defence of honour. It is only to be employed if personal honour has been gravely injured and if a superior officer is powerless to restore the situation.

Misuse of challenges is to be avoided in all circumstances. Duelling is no child's play and is no general remedy for affairs of honour. An exaggerated sense of honour must be firmly repressed.

In affairs of honour between officers, measures taken by superior officers, and decisions taken by the commander-in-chief subsequent to the proceedings appropriate to such matters, can provide satisfaction for the offended officer. Even in a grave case, the offended party can forgo a duel if the offender is dismissed either summarily or without the right to wear uniform, once the appropriate proceedings have taken place. No officer is open to reproach if he refuses to fight a duel with a man who has been dismissed either summarily or without the right to wear uniform.

If a duel is to take place, the following general points are to be covered:

(1) The type of duel. (2) Issuance of a challenge. (3) Participation of the council of honour. (4) Persons to be present at the duel. (5) The role of impartial persons. (6) Seconds. (7) Position of the surgeon. (8) Members of the council of honour as observers.

(Printed as Annex 4 to circular No.2500.38.P.A.(2) from the Commander-in-Chief of the Army: subject 'Defence of Honour': signed: von Brauchitsch; Berlin, 1st March, 1938.)

(From the Bundesarchiv – Militärarchiv.)

APPENDIX 19

Report on the liberal Opinions of a Bavarian Officer

WÜRZBURG, 6TH JANUARY 1822

From Lieutenant-General (acting Commandant-General) Count Beckers to His Majesty the King of Bavaria.

Subject: Secret meetings by certain officers at Würzburg.

.. As regards Your Majesty's further command – to investigate the accusation made by Colonel H. against Lieutenant-Colonel O. – I feel bound to start by giving Your Majesty some account of the characters of each of these staff-officers, for they are relevant to the matter at issue.

In addition to an unshakable loyalty and attachment to his Most Gracious Sovereign, Colonel H. has high abilities, though without any great reputation for achievements in the Army. He also has a weakness for writing; and it may be that this, with his lively sense of self-respect and his passionate nature, was what led him astray into writing to Field-Marshal Prince Wrede (I respectfully return that document herewith) and making accusations against Lieutenant-Colonel O. On the subject-matter of that document (which I did not mention) he made me the following statements in reply to my persistent questioning:

'Lieutenant-Colonel O. certainly had many qualities; but he was very reserved and his ideas were very confused; he would not be a good man to serve and advise His Majesty at a time of imminent danger. At a public military dinner a few years ago he had proposed a toast to the Constitution of the Kingdom and in general he was full of liberal ideas. Colonel H. could neither assert nor prove Lieutenant-Colonel O.'s connivance at the officers' meeting; nor did Colonel H. or any other officer dream of saying he would serve with Lieutenant-Colonel O. no longer. He had certainly said one could not reveal everything one learned about other officers, but this did not refer to the present case which, indeed, the two had not really discussed.'

Lieutenant-Colonel O. is an educated man, especially in technical matters. He has never incurred censure for neglecting the duties of his profession or his appointment; but he is reputed to hold the most liberal views – which go very strangely with his reserve and taciturnity. Without mentioning his colonel's complaints about him, I felt it necessary to question him about various matters that were disturbing good relations among the staff-officers in the regiment. In reply he repeatedly assured me of his devotion to the Army, saying he was in fullest agreement with the colonel on everything to do with the interests of the service.

I also judged it necessary to collect detailed information about this man. All of it was to his credit and yet, without attaching decisive weight to Colonel H.'s accusations, I think it my duty to observe, with all respect, that there is something strange about the man's whole nature – his persistent liberalism, the toast to the Constitution, his journey to France and the Low Countries, his proposal to visit Italy (not at his own expense but with money from some dubious source), the fact that Lieutenant-Colonel O., who was then commanding the regiment, allowed Lieutenant Sch. and the two seconds to go on leave only a few hours after the former's duel with Auditor N., the ease with which contacts that are currently dangerous to the State can be made – chiefly on the premises of a high school – these things all make the man an object of suspicion and, if he is personally angered, dangerous. The principal ground is that the art of secret machination is so skilfully practised by disaffected persons that States have been plunged into revolution in recent years before the most wide-awake Governments could seize the threads of the conspiracy and break them.

I doubt if the man ever had such contacts; and I would certainly not suggest that enquiries be made, for he has shown he is a clever man and he would undoubtedly defeat them. But with the deepest sense of duty and of intimate attachment to Your Majesty's Person and Throne, I beg leave to express my conviction that it were well if Your Majesty should be graciously pleased to have Lieutenant-Colonel O. transferred away from this garrison without his suffering disadvantage thereby; and the same is urgently necessary in respect of the officers whom the Commission of Enquiry found guilty.

I remain, with the deepest respect,
Your Majesty's
humble, obedient Servant
(*signed*) BECKERS, *General*

(War Archives, Munich: A.XII., 3.fasc.4.)

APPENDIX 20

Report on the persistent liberalism of a Bavarian general staff-officer.

MUNICH, 12TH DECEMBER 1852

To His Majesty the King of Bavaria
from the Quarter-Master General,
 Major-General Anton von der Mark.

Subject: Political Intrigues.
Allerdurchlauchtigster Grossmächtigster König
 Allergnädigster König und Herr!

... It would be easy to conclude, at least from first impressions, that Captain Max Count B. has not yet fully renounced the ideas which the year 1848 brought with such vehemence to the fore. The undersigned is far from having any positive charge to make against this officer; yet his reserve, and his avoidance of other officers (Captain A. is his only companion) do much to bring his earlier tendencies back to mind. When the disturbances were rife he long nourished the hope that the people would elect him a Deputy – a thing which, after all, could only have come about as a result of his making his opinions known. With a view to putting a rapid end to all this, the undersigned recommended he be appointed general staff-officer for 1849–50 to the 2nd Army Corps, and this received the Highest approval. The poetry he wrote at that time showed very liberal leanings too. It was only natural that he should have been strengthened in such views by the intrigues of the '*Freischaren*' in Schleswig-Holstein.

In contrast to the rather unmannerly behaviour of Captain A., the impartial observer who knows of Captain Count B.'s antecedents is much more likely to be led into silent suspicion of his political attitude by his dark and taciturn demeanour and his peculiar, unbalanced look.

Though he is better equipped than Captain A. from the technical point of view, he lacks any real inclination to work. He has to be spurred on and constantly watched or he will be very slow to finish any task. His character being what it is, regimental duties would be much more suitable as well as being very necessary for his career.

Such duties would bring the two of them into daily contact with their superior officers and with the other officers of the regiment, and it would then be quickly and easily seen whether their ideas were straying from the path prescribed by duty and honour. They were

334

transferred to the general staff after the first campaign in Schleswig-Holstein in August 1848 but did not come up to expectations. It would be better for Your Majesty's service, therefore, as well as for these officers' personal position, and careers that they should revert to their former branch of the Army.

In submitting the foregoing to Your Majesty's consideration.

the undersigned remains, with the deepest respect,

Your Majesty's humble, obedient Servant,

(*signed*) VON DER MARK, *Major-General*

(War Archives, Munich: Kr.Min.Arch. A.XII. 1a. fasc.17.)

APPENDIX 21

Request by King Max II of Bavaria for a Report on Officers' political views.

VORDERRISS, 3RD NOVEMBER 1858

(To the Minister of War)

Herr Kriegsminister! I have no intention of bringing up old political aberrations or of penalising those concerned; and still less do I intend to institute some sort of political Inquisition. But with the object of obtaining an impression of the political reliability of My Army based on facts already known to you, I wish you to give Me, *in the strictest confidence* and in your own hand, accurate information about the present political attitude of those officers (such as Major Count B., the then Lieutenant von B., since resigned, and several others) who revealed a certain instability in their political attitude in the years of revolution, 1848–49.

Your King and well-wisher,
(*signed*) MAX

(**War** Archives, Munich: K.M. – Archiv A.III.1a.fasc.17.Nebenakt.)

APPENDIX 22

Report by the Bavarian Minister of War in Response to No. 21

MUNICH, 5TH NOVEMBER 1859

Subject: Political Opinions of certain Officers.

By the attached manuscript communication of the 3rd inst. Your Majesty was graciously pleased to instruct the undersigned to provide Your Majesty with an indication of the political reliability of the officers of Your Majesty's Army by reporting on the present political opinions of those officers, such as Major Max Count B. and others, who showed themselves unreliable in 1848–49.

Basing himself on the files of the Ministry of War, as well as on information obtained in the greatest confidence, and upon his own judgment, the undersigned, in obedience to Your Majesty's command, has the honour to report that those who behaved discreditably in those days were a very small proportion of Your Majesty's corps of officers, and that the majority of them have since left the Army – for example 2nd Lieutenant Freiherr von B., (who was named in Your Majesty's communication), Lieutenants Z., B., T. and 2nd Lieutenants D and D.

The others have meanwhile been promoted; and that fact shows that they must have furnished ample proof of reliability in all respects for it would not otherwise have been possible for them to be recommended to Your Majesty for the favour of advancement. Among these are Majors Max Count B. and Max A., of the Quarter-Master General's staff, Captain Johann F. of the First Chevauléger Regiment 'Czar Alexander of Russia', Captains Karl Sch. of the Seventh Infantry Regiment 'Hohenhausen' and Ferdinand K. of the First Jäger Battalion. Moreover, the latest confidential personal reports (*Sitten- und Fähigkeitslisten*) on these officers give not the slightest ground for doubting that they have abandoned an attitude which to a large extent only resulted from youthful lack of reflection in times which were very different from those of today. Major A. in particular has a lively sense of the especial favour shown to him by Your Majesty, and is wholly loyal. In the case of Major Count B., his reticent nature makes it difficult to feel perfectly sure he has altogether given up his former leanings and could be relied upon not to revert to them should the occasion arise. At the same time his generally honourable character gives warranty that as regards his military duties, which he has always performed in a satisfactory manner, he can be counted on to give efficient service.

337

It is always a hazardous thing to say what political leanings might, in critical times, be revealed by individuals – either out of vanity or out of intellectual or emotional excitement. Nevertheless the undersigned feels able to express to Your Majesty a firm conviction that there is at present no occasion for the slightest misgiving as regards the loyalty and attachment of the officers of the Army to the Throne and to Your Majesty's sacred Person. If, contrary to expectation, a few isolated individuals among the large number who form the corps of officers of Your Majesty's Army, should (were the case to arise) deviate from the path of honour and duty, a vigorous use of the means available would certainly be enough to render such few aberrations harmless. Your Majesty may therefore have full confidence in the political reliability of the officers of the Army.

With the deepest respect,
(*signed*) M(ASSENBA)CH

Munich, 5th November 1858

(War Archives, Munich: Kriegsmin. – Archiv A. III.1a.fasc.17. Nebenakt.)

APPENDIX 23

Circular by General von Eichhorn (G.O.C., 18th Army Corps) to his officers on the subject of lecturing to their men

FRANKFURT AM MAIN, 19TH SEPTEMBER 1909

In the course of the past year I have listened to educational courses given in various units. Some of them were excellent, but I have not been able to avoid the impression that in many cases this form of activity does not receive all the attention it deserves.

Its prime objective is to improve training and increase the efficiency of troops in war. . . .

The only really valuable thing about it is when the instruction is given by officers. For all the respect due to our admirable non-commissioned officers, my experience is that they are not cut out for the task of giving fruitful instruction on such matters, or of widening the men's horizons. Moreover, it is often the senior and most proficient non-commissioned officers who are the least effective for this purpose. Routine is the bane of all understanding, and can have a fearfully deadening effect. This leads me to believe that instruction given by even the most junior officer is of far more use; and I should be glad if you would let the younger officers know that this is the view I hold. . . .

Like any other kind of instruction, however, its aim must be to enhance the men's general understanding, enlarge their field of vision and open their eyes and senses to the world around them. We need intelligent soldiers. At the same time this instruction must fulfil another aim, inseparable from the first: it must arouse and strengthen the men's sense of honour, their loyalty to the Crown and their patriotism, and implant in them for life the spirit of duty, honour and self-sacrifice for the Fatherland.

This is a high and sacred task, and it lies on even the most junior officer. Officers, as I know very well, often regard this instruction as an exceptionslly tiresome job. I can understand that: but if officers really understood the worthwhile nature of the task they have to do, they would see it in another light.

I will not conceal my belief that the officer of today has a political duty as well – the duty of training his subordinates to be loyal subjects and of making them proof against the deleterious influence of Social-Democracy.

The man who has the greatest opportunity of doing this is the young officer in charge of recruits.

The young soldier's mind is normally like a piece of wax on which

M 339

every sort of impression can be made. Many, of course, have already been infected by Social-Democracy before they were called up; but they are still young, their sickness is only superficial and their service with the colours must work like a healing spring, and wash the sickness out of their system. Even men who have lived for years as tramps, in and out of prison all the time, men who can hardly remember when they last heard a friendly word from a decent person – even that sort of man is not impervious if spoken to seriously but kindly, in a way he may not have been spoken to since he was a child.

The vital thing, the essential condition of success, is that officers must win the confidence of their men. The men must be convinced that the officer is their best friend, and that what he says is true and right.

Here I should like to make a digression. Once an officer has really gained the confidence of his men, I consider it quite impossible for a non-commissioned officer to commit the offence of systematically maltreating his subordinates for long. If this were to happen, any recruit who felt brow-beaten and maltreated would certainly go to his lieutenant and tell him his troubles. The Articles of War that deal with cases of persistent maltreatment may not contemplate an officer being culpably negligent in exercising control, but for my own part I could not exonerate him. He has not done what he should, for he has not won the confidence of his subordinates.

On duty or off it, an officer has countless opportunities of winning this confidence; but nowhere can he and his men get to know one another more easily than in the instruction-periods. No other time gives an officer a better chance of close contact with every individual, or an easier way to get possession of a man's whole mind. All he has to do is talk to the man, get him to talk about himself, show interest in what interests him, and use all this to establish his superior position through the superiority of his own knowledge and character.

If he then talks to the man about the Imperial Family, about regimental history, the history of Germany, about great men of the past – it is appalling how few of the men have even heard of Bismarck or Moltke – success is sure to follow. The one thing he must not try and do is to put his points over like the points in the catechism, and make the man learn them by heart. His job is to open the man's mind to greatness of every sort. The more intelligent men will soon be able to ask questions, and answer them too, and the duller ones will at least show interest and enjoy listening to the lecture. The men may not be able to reel the facts off afterwards, but the general impression will remain with them. The instruction-periods will then be a continuation of the primary school – or rather a reinforcement of it, for the primary schools seem less and less equal to their task, which is not merely to implant facts but to train their pupils' minds and character.

A part I have always found particularly hard is instructing soldiers on their duties under the Articles of War. Officers endowed with wit and enthusiasm can achieve a great deal even with the groundwork of theory, as I have often had occasion to observe. Others are better advised not to spend too much time on the subject, or they will bore the men and stifle their imagination with incomprehensible jargon. It will be like in *Hamlet**:

> My words fly up, my thoughts remain below:
> Words without thoughts never to heaven go.

A better way is to take any and every opportunity that offers a suitable pretext for talking about one or other of the soldier's duties. Older officers, such as company commanders, should not hesitate, either, to talk about public affairs, the merits of the social reform laws (accident and sickness insurance, etc.), the soldier's duties when he returns to civil life, Social-Democracy, and so forth. But I must repeat: only on one condition can we count on success – but then with certainty. The man, who has pretty sharp eyes for such things, must see and recognise that his own welfare is the object of great and serious effort on the officer's part. He must have confidence in his officer.

One mistake the officer must avoid at all costs: he must not bore his men. For that reason he must enjoy a certain liberty in choosing what to talk about and how to do it. The great thing is to hold the men's attention.

It can be nothing but stimulating, therefore, if the lecturer takes any suitable opportunity of deserting his real subject to talk about some incident or other in history, some recent event that has been much discussed (such as the Russo-Japanese War or German South-West Africa) and goes on from there to tell his men about the moon and the stars, new inventions, foreign lands and strange peoples, etc.

This is the way to arouse interest; this is how to widen the men's field of vision, and get new ideas into minds that are all too often sluggish. By the same device an officer can sometimes even make some progress with the theory of ballistics, provided he takes care not to treat it simply as a sort of text that has to be mastered for an examination. If the officer can work it the other way round, and get the men to tell him about their lives and experiences on the farm and in the workshop, a link will be set up between the men and their officer, and bit by bit it will become unbreakable.

In all this, I know, I am making great demands; but I am sure the

* Act III, Scene iii, 97–98.

officers of this Army Corps realise the importance of this subject and will act on these suggestions freely and willingly. Company-commanders, in particular, I earnestly recommend to take especial care that their men shall not be weary and tired when they have to attend their officers' lectures.

This circular is for officers' eyes only.

(*signed*) VON EICHHORN

(Reichsarchiv: KM., Armee-Abt., I.9.1.No.3, Heft 6.)

APPENDIX 24

Bavarian departmental Report on the Abolition of Corporal Punishment

REICHENHALL, 16TH AUGUST 1848

The types and methods of punishment are always related to the level of intellectual and moral education of the several classes of people who compose the Army.

Flogging, therefore, which was still employed in German armies at the start of this century even for minor breaches of discipline, is now treated as follows:–

a In *Austria* and *Wurtemberg* it must be ordered by a court-martial:
b In *Prussia*, the Grand-Duchy and Electorate of *Hesse*, and *Saxony* likewise; but the court-martial must also order the soldier's transfer to the second punishment-class.
c In *Bavaria* it has fallen almost entirely out of use.
d In *Hanover* and *Baden* it has been entirely abolished.

The view is now firmly held that corporal punishment injures a soldier's self-respect and thereby undermines his sense of military honour.

That sense, however, is the foundation of discipline, and the surest warranty of an army's loyalty and reliability.

From the moral point of view and in the interest of the efficiency of the Service, therefore, it would appear advisable:
to abolish punishment by flogging immediately and indeed totally, since close confinement would undoubtedly have the same disciplinary effect.

(*signed*) J. VON HARTMANN, *Colonel and Aide-de-Camp*

(War Archives, Munich: KM-Archiv A IV.1.fasc.57.)

APPENDIX 25

Report by General von Lesuire to the Bavarian Minister of War in favour of the total Abolition of Corporal Punishment

MUNICH, 31ST OCTOBER 1848

Hochwohlgeborner Herr
hochgebiethender Herr Minister!

I have the honour to acknowledge receipt of Your Excellency's communication of yesterday's date.

In order to answer the question contained therein conscientiously and in a manner corresponding to my deepest convictions, I must at once declare that I took, and still take, His Majesty's Rescript No. 18202 of the 13th inst as having abolished the penalty of corporal punishment once and for all. It is hard to say at this moment whether an amendment can still be made to it, but I am more inclined to wait and see whether the abolition of corporal punishment has such an effect upon discipline as to make it seem advisable, appropriate and practicable to re-introduce this penalty. Being myself thoroughly convinced that forms and methods of punishment must depend on the way in which the young soldier's superiors have trained him in his duties and broken him in to discipline since the day he joined (and there can be no doubt that he must be formally and systematically *trained* for these things), the decisive point is how his commanding-officer and the other officers of the unit generally discharged their duty in this respect. The older method of breaking a soldier in and giving him orders will no longer do. In those days a categorical imperative was enough. Nowadays, those to whom His Majesty has granted his commission must use not only the categorical imperative but prove themselves by word and deed. But word and deed again are not enough by themselves; the heart and soul must be mobilised as well. In brief, troops must be trained, led and disciplined by the methods of a *father;* and even disciplinary punishment must only be ordered when the accused himself has been convinced that he is guilty and that the interests of discipline and the Service require his punishment. This may well look like a very round-about business; but I always employed it in my seventeen years in command of troops and in practice it turns out to be very brief and effective.

Your Excellency will doubtless recall the time when the birch was abolished as a punishment, and unimaginative officers said it was the end of everything. How wrong they were! Did we not go on to fight the brilliant campaigns of 1813–14?

But, of course, it becomes more and more necessary every day to take great care in selecting officers and the best possible regimental-commanders. The latter choice, indeed, is so arduous that Napoleon once said *Avec cent bons colonels je vaincrai le monde!* It is not advisable, either, to leave non-commissioned officers in their old regiment once they have been commissioned, for they usually treat their former comrades with exceptional severity in the quite erroneous belief that this will earn them respect. On the contrary, their former comrades are jealous and put up with less from them than from anyone; and this gives rise to endless friction and bad blood – all of which can be avoided if these men are always posted to some other regiment where their antecedents are unknown.

After these tiresome disgressions – which are solely due to my zeal for the matter in hand – I have the honour to summarise my views as follows:

1 I regard corporal punishment as having been totally abolished.

2 I should regard its re-introduction as extremely dangerous and retrograde.

3 I am utterly convinced that, given good officers and command-ing officers, the best discipline can be maintained without corporal punishment, and that the purpose of the latter can be attained by other means.

> With the expression of my deepest respect,
> I remain,
> Your Excellency's most obedient Servant,
> (*signed*) VON LESUIRE, *Lieutenant-General*

(War-Archives, Munich: KM-Archiv A IV.1. fasc.57.)

* 'Give me a hundred good colonels and I will conquer the world.'

APPENDIX 26

Circular by General von Falkenhayn, Prussian Minister of War, on increasing the Penalties for the Maltreatment of subordinates

BERLIN, 25TH MAY 1914

The cases of maltreatment of subordinates that recently received publicity have rightly caused widespread indignation and have brought the Army and its institutions under heavy attack.

In such circumstances it is the duty of the Army Command to remind all concerned that this serious state of affairs must be tackled with vigour.

The lenient punishments commonly ordered by military courts are not in accordance with the Sovereign's wishes as expressed in Cabinet Orders. In an Order dating as far back as the 1st February 1843 it was laid down that maltreatment of subordinates, or their treatment in contravention of regulations, amounted to disobedience to an order from the Supreme Commander-in-Chief and that this would be taken into account in determining punishment. The same thing is said in the Sovereign's Orders of the 6th February 1890 and the 17th September 1892.* Nevertheless it is striking that minor cases have been coming before the courts in proportions that increase with every year. The assertion, too, is commonly made that the victim's health has suffered little permanent harm or none at all. It has also been observed that those who are sentenced for maltreatment of subordinates are often charged with lesser offences and thus receive the minimum punishment or else, when a cumulative sentence is imposed, it is one that hardly exceeds the minimum.

If the offences are treated with such leniency, the effect is to weaken confidence in military justice and thereby to lower respect for military courts; nor is such leniency calculated to discourage maltreatment itself. What is required is severer sentences and, where appropriate, removal of the guilty party from his position.

In cases that come before the courts, therefore, it is the presiding officer's duty to see that the prosecution requests a punishment proportionate to the offence in accordance with the Sovereign's wishes. In cases of undue leniency, or of incorrect formulation of the charge (e.g. 'treatment in contravention of the regulations' instead of 'maltreatment') it is the presiding officer's duty to apply the legal correctives in the interest of the Service. There can be no possible

* See the following Appendix for the latter.

doubt that the only suitable way to suppress the grave offence of systematic maltreatment is that the courts should, without hesitation, apply the full rigour of the law.

... Copies are attached for distribution to the higher and lower military courts.

(signed) VON FALKENHAYN

To
all General Headquarters
the Governor of Berlin
the Imperial Governor at Ulm.
(Reichsarchiv: KM. V.14.3. No.21, Heft 9.)

APPENDIX 27

Minute by the Emperor William II to the Minister of War on the Maltreatment of Subordinates

POTSDAM, 17TH SEPTEMBER 1892

From the reports submitted to Me by General-Officers Commanding giving statistics of the punishment awarded for the maltreatment of subordinates, I have noted with satisfaction that there has been a general reduction in the number of cases of ordinary maltreatment. I have, however, gained the impression that part of the maltreatment attributed to non-commissioned officers could have been avoided if supervision of them – at least while engaged on more personal duties – had been more continuous and thorough. Proof is to be found in these very reports, indeed, that most cases of maltreatment occur during cleaning-periods and instruction-periods, in quarters and in the stables, and that it is not unusual for non-commissioned officers to go beyond their authority and order extra drill, reporting and so forth, which in turn are often a source of maltreatment. Many a case, moreover, could have been prevented if the officer had stepped in at once with a suitable disciplinary punishment in the minor cases of improper treatment that so often lead on to maltreatment, properly so called. I request General-Officers Commanding to draw their subordinate commanders' attention to these points in accordance with My Order of the 6th February 1890, and I hereby make it known that I expect them to reduce still further the frequency with which maltreatment of subordinates occurs. It is the duty of officers of all ranks to contribute to this end, primarily by example and precept. Should these measures not be enough, the guilty must be made to answer for it and left in no doubt that I shall not tolerate any negligence as regards the maltreatment of subordinates. You are to take the necessary action.

(signed) WILLIAM R

To the Minister of War.

(Reichsarchiv: KM., Ztr. – Dept., V.14.3.21. vol.3.)

APPENDIX 28

Circular from the Chief of the Heeresleitung, General von Seeckt, on the Principles of Training

BERLIN, 1ST JANUARY 1921

The Principles of Army-Training

The Reichswehr exists. A new chapter of German military history begins.

Instead of expressing good wishes for the New Year and the future in general, let us take a solemn vow to stand together, dedicated to our profession. The sword must be kept sharp, the shield bright.

I am confident that the new Army as a whole, like every member of it, will preserve and cultivate the old sense of honour as a precious legacy from the great days of the past. True honour cannot exist without faithfulness unto death, without invincible courage, firm determination, self-denying obedience, simple truthfulness and strict discretion, nor without self-sacrifice in the fulfilment of what may seem but trivial tasks.*

Our calling is the defence of the Fatherland; our country, therefore, the Army and every soldier in it must feel the most intense affection and be ready, in accordance with his oath, to give his life itself in the fulfilment of his duty.

The Army is the prime expression of the power of the State. Every member of the Army must remember, therefore, that on duty or off duty he represents the power of the State and forms a part of it as well. His bearing and the whole of his visible life must show he knows that fact and the responsibility that flows from it.

In the eyes of the public a soldier's profession (*Stand*) makes him one of the group, more than membership of any other profession does. Outstanding efficiency and irreproachable conduct on the part of an individual quite rightly enhances the standing of the rest, while an individual's shortcomings are a charge upon it. Every officer and every man must feel at all times that he represents the whole Army and is responsible for keeping its reputation spotless.

If the new Army is filled with this sense, the true sense of honour and responsibility, and with love for the Fatherland, it can hope to rival the old in fitness for battle.

As an active, living part of the nation's body it will prove itself worthy of respect, affection and concern on the part of all. It will earn these things and value them. Even though universal military

---

* Taken, like several other passages and phrases, from William I (Appendix 16).

349

service is no more, the Army will be what it should be – truly an Army of the whole people.

All sections of the Army must be bound together by a strong sense of comradeship which must spread downwards from above, upwards from below and be equally distributed throughout. Comradeship is seen at its finest in mutual support, in the care shown by the higher ranks for the welfare of the lower, and the latter will requite it with their confidence. This sense of comradeship will forestall excesses on the part of individuals, bring back comrades who have strayed from the right path, and prevent senseless quarrels and unworthy wrangling. The older and more experienced officers and men should feel responsible for the younger; and the latter should accept their guidance willingly and gratefully.

Strict discipline is and remains the corner-stone of all military training. Example is far more effective than exhortation or punishment. The sacred right of every superior is to make himself a model of self-discipline and devotion to duty.

It is not in outward honours but in the inward satisfaction derived from duties done that a true soldier seeks his reward. He shuns all pursuit of personal gain and an easy existence. In simplicity and dignity of life, as befits the gravity of the times, in selfless labour for the good of all, the soldier, whatever his rank, should be a pattern for every section of the populace.

It is every soldier's duty to improve himself unceasingly, to strive to reach the highest pitch of military efficiency for which his nature fits him; and the special duty of every superior in this connection is to help and encourage his subordinates, first and foremost by his own example. Knowledge should not be confined to military matters; it should serve to enhance education in general and make a soldier into a valuable, useful member of society for the rest of his life. But what a man knows and what he can do are less important than what he is, and the strengthening of character takes precedence over the improvement of the mind. Only by this means can we reach the high objective we have set ourselves, namely to train not just a small band of professional soldiers but men who will lead the people in the hour of danger.

The prime responsibility for training the corps of officers rests upon the regimental-commander, and on company-commanders, etc. for training non-commissioned officers and men. The historic, traditional position and responsibility of regimental-commanders should be maintained to the full under the guidance of their superior officers. With the scattered distribution of regiments, the contribution made by staff-officers to training becomes all the more important, but it must be made under the regimental-commanders' guidance and responsibility. On the other hand, the demands of training and instruction in all fields have so expanded by comparison with the past that there should be no decrease in the contribution made by battalion-commanders to the relief of over-worked company officers.

Regimental-commanders have a special responsibility for ensuring that the corps of officers is guided by a proper sense of honour, true comradeship, selfless dedication to the Service and decorous style of living. He must take the newly-assembled elements and hammer them into a single whole, inspire them with a corporate sense and lay the foundations for new regimental traditions and a new regimental history. He must be his officers' closest friend and adviser, the natural man to resolve any doubt or difference of opinion. In the difficult task of training his men he should be able to count with confidence on the help of his older officers and should make it his aim that the juniors can always turn to them for friendly help and advice.

The tasks of a company-commander, etc. in respect of his non-commissioned officers and men is the same. The demands made upon him are different from what they were in former times, and they are heavier too. The longer term of service* will enable him to bring the men under his command up to a far higher level of military efficiency, but it also lays on him the duty of not letting his company or unit be staled by monotony. He must therefore pay attention to the training of each individual man. Experience alone will teach us how best to cultivate the rich field of activity which is hereby opened to us. If we set our target high we shall find that twelve years' service is not too long for the achievement of our aims, and the harvest we shall reap will richly reward us for our labours.

Officers of every rank must keep it constantly in mind that in all aspects of the Service, intellectual or physical, it is their duty both to teach and to set the example. This requirement will make great demands on the devotion and self-sacrifice of every one of them. But only by meeting these demands to the full can an officer be of real assistance to his responsible superiors and earn a claim to succeed them in due course. Nor can anything but superior ability, firmness of character, self-sacrificing care for his men and a warm-hearted interest in their affairs bring an officer a degree of confidence from his men that will stand up to the stiffest testing from within and without.

The non-commissioned officers and men of a company, together with their officers, form a single unit in which comradeship and a sense of coherence must be fostered, and a feeling of tradition developed and preserved. The days are gone when the task was to train recurrent annual intakes of recruits in a short space of time.

* Twelve years.

Today it is the individual who must be taught and trained, so as to develop him to the utmost of his capacity. Such work demands that all should collaborate and that the best and maturest elements should be mobilised to help in that great educational institution which is the Army. If this is done we shall succeed in our aim, and make every member of the Army, in character, skill and knowledge, a man and a leader of men: self-reliant, self-respecting, devoted and eager for responsibility.

(*signed*) VON SEECKT

(Reprinted in Karl Linnebach: *Deutsche Heeresgeschichte* (Hamburg 1935) pp. 384 ff, from the *Heeresverordnungsblatt*, No. 79 of 1920.)

APPENDIX 29

Letter from Lieutenant Leist, 3rd Infantry Regt. No. 12, to Lieutenant-Colonel Freiherr von Hammerstein

MUNICH, 22ND OCTOBER 1923

Hochzuverehrender Herr Oberstleutnant!

I sent you the following telegram today: 'Request guidance. Leist'. This request may have seemed rather puzzling [to you] in Magdeburg, and in order to account for it I beg leave to explain the grave dilemma of conscience that has faced me here as an officer of the Reichsheer [sic.] The first official news of the revolt in Bavaria reached us this morning through the promulgation of General von Seeckt's circular. The School-Commandant, General v. Tychowitz [sc. Major-General Tieschowitz von Tieschowa] also announced that he had sent all Bavarian members of the school (every one of whom, an hour before, had promised allegiance to the Bavarian Government) on indefinite leave, since he could no longer bring himself to work with such people. All non-Bavarians, he said, must of course be guided by the views of the Army Command. Courses would be continued so far as possible and he himself was going to Berlin this evening to seek instructions.

Lively, sometimes needlessly heated, debates had already taken place among those in the Weapons School, especially among the officers; but the speeches now became more than vehement. I myself had firmly taken the very line from the start that the only problem for us was whether or not to observe Army discipline, and that if we lightly set aside our oath to the Government of the Reich we should bring discredit to the corps of officers. I fear I found little support for this view: most of the others were carried away by childish enthusiasm for Bavaria and the popular (*völkisch*) movement,* they never stopped singing the '*Ehrhard-Lied*' and they hoisted black-white-and-red cockades. I and one or two others who agreed with me were called (behind our backs, I admit) red dogs and supporters of government by Jews. We were sometimes met with dirty looks even on quite ordinary occasions.

During lunch the Commandant of our year's class, Colonel Leupold, appeared (though as a Bavarian he had been sent on leave) and made a long speech in favour of the Bavarian point of view, i.e. on the theme of 'Nationalism vs. Marxism.' He ended by urging

* i.e. National-Socialism.

353

those who wished to give allegiance to the Bavarian Government to enter their names on a list – but he did not say whether this exhortation was addressed to us all or only to the Bavarians. He gave us to understand, however, that if anyone disagreed he would regard him as an international Marxist and a downright filthy swine. As a matter of fact several Prussian officers afterwards said they would 'naturally' give their allegiance to the Bavarian Government. During the afternoon's work, the senior instructor, a Lieutenant Teichmann of the 13th Inf. Regt., told us he had reported to Colonel Leupold that with a few exceptions the instructors were solidly with him and not with General v. Tychowitz. He said he had asked the Colonel to tell the General this before the latter left for Berlin.

I refused to accept this attempt to speak for me, and this afternoon I had a long interview with the General and his adjutant. The General was disgusted with the behaviour of Colonel Leupold, for the latter had promised to abstain from all propaganda; and he was thinking of a fresh attempt to give the officers full account of the situation.

This sequence of events has placed me in a thoroughly false position. The great majority of those whom I still think of as my comrades regard me as a traitor to the cause of patriotism, especially as I have become the spokesman for our small group. In actual fact I regard the popular movement, if sensibly run, as the only hope for the Reich; yet I am bound to treat it as something to be resisted by every means, along with mutiny and perjury. My conception of honour requires me to do everything I can to defend a Government I would gladly send to perdition.

I have no means of judging how things will now develop. According to a story that was being busily put about today, but which strikes me as unlikely, the popular movement will break out all over the country in a few days, supported by the Reichswehr. The II Army-Group HQ was specially mentioned as having officially come out for [General] Lossow. Until further notice I regard this sort of thing as a piece of rumour-mongering intended to confuse public opinion – which has anyway been almost criminally misled already. There is nothing I more ardently desire at this moment than to be able to take the popular side with honour and decency, but as an honourable officer and soldier I see not the slightest possibility of doing so for the present.

It was the faint hope that you, Colonel, might perhaps be able to show me how this could honourably be done which prompted today's telegram. In present circumstances it would give me the utmost pleasure to revert to my battalion, and if this should be at all possible I respectfully request you to take the necessary action as soon as you can. The thing that worries me most is that if it comes to

354

an armed conflict with Bavaria I shall not be able to get away in time.

I hope, Colonel, that you will be kind enought to forgive me this long screed and will understand my desire, in this unhappy confusion, to see a little more clearly ahead.

With the warmest good wishes to the corps of officers of the 3rd (Prussian) Bn., Inf. Regt. No. 12 and to everything else that is soundly Prussian, I remain,

with great respect, Colonel,
your obedient Servant,
HANSJOCHEN LEIST, *Lieutenant*

NB All the ensigns from Inf. Regt. No. 12 are solidly behind me, so that the Regiment already has the reputation of being totally Jew-ridden, red and Spartacist. I should never have expected to hear myself described in such terms.

Magdeburg, 24th October 1923

Colonel Schniewind

Submitted for information. On the 22nd October I telegraphed as follows in reply to Lieutenant Leist's telegram: 'Obey Prussian superiors'.

v. HAMMERSTEIN

Halberstadt, 25th October 1932

Lieutenant-Colonel Frhr. von Hammerstein

Noted. I have privately sent an extract from the letter to the Divisional Commander. I shall tell Lieutenant Leist I appreciate his behaviour.

SCHNIEWIND

(Reprinted by Th. Vogelsang in the *Vierteljahrshefte für Zeitgeschichte*, 5th Year (1957), pp. 95–97. Original in the Bundesarchiv at Coblence; Schleicher Papers, vol. 17/1,fol.9f.)

APPENDIX 30

Circular dated the 6th October, 1930, from General Groener, Reichswehr Minister, to all Officers of the Reichswehr, following the Trial of Reichswehr-Officers at Leipzig

On the 4th October 1930, the Reich Court at Leipzig pronounced the following sentence upon the former Lieutenants Scheringer and Ludin and Oberleutnant (retd.) Wendt*:

The accused are sentenced under Section 60 of the Reich Penal Code to eighteen months detention in a fortress, with food-costs, for conspiracy to commit treason. Six months and three weeks already spent under detention during the investigations will be taken into account in each case. Ludin and Scheringer are to be dismissed from the Army. Scheringer is acquitted on the other charges. When announcing the Court's decision, the President of the Fourth Chamber of the Reich Court expressly emphasised that in committing the offences for which they had been sentenced the accused were actuated by honourable motives and a passionate love of their country. The Court none the less rejected all extenuating circumstances and emphasised that it was wholly impossible for the German Wehrmacht to allow lieutenants to go about recruiting, no matter what political party they worked for.

I have the following very serious observations to make on this affair:

1 The Reichswehr is, and must by its very nature remain, patriotic (*national*) to the highest degree. Astounding presumption, however, and a most deplorable lack of respect for authority are shown when young officers, who have no credentials but their youth, bring charges of insufficient patriotism (and presume that they alone know what patriotism is) against their most senior officers, including von Hindenburg, Commander-in-Chief of the Reichswehr and President of the Reich, to whom the decision of all questions involving patriotism falls.

2 It is perfectly correct to say that the main purpose of the Reichswehr is the external defence of the Fatherland, and it is obviously the duty of the High Command to make every possible preparation for discharging this obligation. It is, however, an impertinence and an astonishing piece of conceit for young officers to talk of inadequate measures for national defence, and criticise those measures in public, when they have no means whatever of

* See Note 13 to Chapter 24 (Part 4).

judging the possibilities of the situation in the light of foreign policy and finance.

3 The Reichswehr is above all parties, and it serves the State alone. It must hold itself absolutely clear of party-strife and of day-to-day political pressures. There is thus no question of its leaning to the right or to the left. All military measures and regulations are governed by this consideration alone. It amounts therefore to a total misunderstanding of the facts, and to almost insurpassable conceit, for young officers to think they must oppose what they imagine to be a leftward inclination on the part of the High Command.

If there are regulations or measures which they do not understand they can always go to their commanding officer, or lay a complaint. Generally speaking it is one of the worst features of the post-war climate that every young officer feels entitled to criticise his superiors' decisions and to demand that every measure be explained and justified to him.

4 The soundness of any Wehrmacht rests upon unreserved, unlimited obedience. Soldiers who want to see whether an order suits their own ideas before they carry it out are absolutely worthless. Thoughts of that kind lead on to mutiny, to the dissolution of the Reichswehr and eventually to a war of all against all. The day when officers were to be heard talking in this strain before the Reich Court was one of the very blackest for the Army.

5 It is obvious that officers holding views of this kind can not remain in the Wehrmacht. I therefore expect any officer with a sense of honour and the courage of his convictions to resign from the Reichwehr at once if he harbours similar opinions.

6 This Order is to be communicated in full to all officers.

The completion of action is to be reported through official channels to the Reichswehr Ministry by the 1st November 1930.

(*signed*) GROENER

(Johannes Hohlfeld: *Dokumente der deutschen Politik und Geschichte von 1848 bis zur Gegenwart*, vol. 3: *Die Weimarer Republik 1919–1933* (Berlin 1952), pp. 350f. From *Deutscher Geschichtskalender, Inland*, Oct. Dec. 1930, pp. 417f. Reprinted by Otto Ernst Schüddekopf: *Das Heer und die Republik. Quellen zur Politik der Reichswehrführung 1918–1933* (Hanover and Frankfurt a.M., 1955), pp. 290–2.)

APPENDIX 31

*Special Circular from General Groener to Senior Commanders and
Regimental-Commanders, arising out of the Leipzig Trial*

(OCTOBER, 1930)

In the statements made by the junior officers before the Reich
Court, no little part, I am sure, was played by a certain sense of
solidarity, by the desire to conceal an inward insecurity under a
brash exterior; and something was also due to the conceit and arrogance so common among young people in these times. For these
reasons I am equally sure that in spite of this affair discipline and
unconditional obedience are intact. We should not deceive ourselves,
however. This behaviour on the part of a few young officers has done
considerable harm to the Reichswehr's reputation. Ill-wishers and
anti-military circles will present us with the bill at the next opportunity.

Our well-wishers and those who are closest to us have been
shocked, and their faith in the Reichswehr as an unshakable rock of
obedience and devotion to duty, on which is founded the whole
edifice of the State, has been rudely shattered. We should have
escaped this sort of crisis of confidence if all commanding officers had
paid more attention to the spirit and the opinions to be found in the
corps of officers. But alas, I must be brutally frank for once. There
are commanding officers who avoid political talk of any kind with
their subordinates – either because they feel an inward uncertainty
or because they lack the courage of their convictions. Again, they
have refrained from openly contradicting this sort of talk and have
thereby let their juniors suppose they were in agreement with it,
perhaps because they are afraid someone might think them un-
patriotic or that they might make themselves unpopular with their
officers. There is no other way of explaining how such totally false
ideas could have taken firm hold of these young men – doubts about
the patriotism of the High Command, rubbish about the Reichswehr being handed over to the left-wing parties, obedience only on
conditions, and so forth. If commanding officers had done their duty
and always pointed out what enormous obstacles at home and abroad
the High Command has had to overcome to make the Reichswehr
the strongest element in the State, a factor that no political decision
can ignore, the corps of officers would not have allowed the growth
of opinions which, to say the least, are all too liable to destroy the
position in the State which the Wehrmacht enjoys. It would have

358

sufficed to teach the young men a lesson and make them see the stupidity, the emptiness of their opinions, if even a slight effort had been made to familiarise officers with the arguments I have used again and again during the past twelve months – in speeches and circulars, in the battle for the defence-estimates, and in other debates with hostile organisations and people of unsympathetic views.

The conclusion to be drawn from this state of affairs is that in future the only men we can place in command of a corps of officers are those who have the courage of their convictions and enough intellectual vigour to train their young men properly; for the latter possess great arrogance and extreme sensitivity, but likewise a highly developed sense of honour, intelligence well above the average and, what is finest of all, a streak of high idealism.

All officers are to be made familiar in suitable ways with the views I have expressed in this circular.

(signed) GROENER

(This Order was first published by a newspaper of the 'Staatspartei' from which the *Völkischer Beobachter* (*Reichsausgabe*) of the 17th March 1931 copied it. See also Dorothea Groener-Geyer: *General Groener, Soldat und Staatsmann* (Frankfurt a.M. 1955) pp. 271–2.)

APPENDIX 32

Record of evidence taken after the attempt on Hitler's life on the 20th July, 1944: *General Hans Oster on the intellectual outlook of officers*

Hans Oster spoke with greater clarity than any of the others involved about the intellectual and political outlook of the older, professional officers. What governed their attitude, he said, and made it exceptionally complicated, was the fact that in the space of thirty years (1914–1944), i.e. a bare generation, they had served three entirely different political systems, viz. first the monarchy, then every sort of government under the 'System',* and lastly the National-Socialist State. In a statement on the officers' attitude, Oster says:

'Under the monarchy it was really a sort of boyish enthusiasm for soldiering that sent us into the Army. It never even crossed our minds that the whole régime might collapse one day. Politics meant nothing to us. We were in uniform and that was all that mattered. It was "not done" to read the *Berliner Tageblatt* or the *Frankfurter Zeitung* in the "Kasino".'

The collapse of the monarchy on account of the revolution in 1918 had been a fearful shock and surprise to the officers, for they were all monarchists at heart.

'It was like being hit on the head with a hammer – the collapse in 1918 and the way the monarchy ended in a rickety affair of political parties.'

The State that emerged then faced the older officers with a fresh decision. 'After the gravest struggle with ourselves we finally decided, against our inclinations, to serve the socialist Republic and under a new flag. What we hoped and intended was to help the country get over the worst of it.'

General von Seeckt, he said, had forbidden the Reichswehr of the day to engage in any political activities whatever. Even under the monarchy the officers had deliberately paid no attention to current politics or political movements, but now they were ordered to ignore current politics by the law, so to speak, itself.

'When the Army was only 100,000 strong the system of training made us into non-political soldiers in the crucial years of our military development, and we learned that we were to obey the Head of the State.'

In his written statement Oster says:

* 'The System' was the standard Nazi term of abuse for parliamentary democracy as practised under the Weimar Republic.

'We were all quite sure that under the political conditions of the times this was the only road to our objective, viz. getting the troops under discipline again, and making them the foundation and preparation for building up the Army later on into the Wehrmacht of today. The words "party" and "playing politics" had an unpleasant ring for us.'

With the upheaval (*Umbruch*) of 1933, says Oster, the soldiers felt released from the strain which the 'System' had laid on their consciences. The return to a vigorous patriotic policy, the rearmament, the re-introduction of universal military service – to the officers, this all meant a return to older traditions. Under the 'System' soldiers had done their work because it was their duty: but these features of the National-Socialist work of reconstruction had warmed their hearts. 'All the same, as professional soldiers, we too had to come to terms with this upheaval. Some managed it quicker than others.

'Not everyone, for example, understood the identification of "Party" and "State". After all, we had never had any use for the word "party".

'We had to swallow a good deal, too – some things that really stuck in our throats – the "Storm Troopers' Song" – reaction – shootings. The Röhm-Putsch – Schleicher – Bredow – the Blomberg affair – the Fritsch trial – the Waffen-SS being made the élite of the Wehrmacht. In my opinion the Blomberg business was the worst of all because it did terrible damage to the reputation of the corps of officers. Putting up with all that was pretty hard for some of us.'

Ever since 1933, in Oster's opinion, certain sections of the corps of officers had remained totally impervious to National-Socialism as a *Weltanschauung* that embraced the whole of life. There were still men here and there in the corps of officers who had never grasped, or had already forgotten, the fact that National-Socialism had brought forth a revolution in the true sense of the word – a revolution entailing reforms that had become necessary, painful adjustments and the renunciation of much that used to be dear.

At the end of his statement Oster makes this admission:

'We were not born into the world of politics; we are not political fanatics fighting to get power in the State for one party. That is not what we were taught to do. In November 1923 we did not march in a solid mass to the *Feldherrnhalle*: on the contrary, my General gave me the unwelcome job of disbanding a brigade of the Reichswehr that was among the units that had joined Kapp.'

The foregoing amounts to an admission on Oster's part that to some extent he still subscribes to the ideal of the non-political officer (see also the report dated the 20th August 1944). The account he gives is true of a whole section of the older officers, and it shows that in fighting the ideological battle and carrying out a socialist revolution, the National-Socialist Reich was obliged to use a certain number of officers who so far from realising the historic nature of that revolution were politically more inclined to watch and wait, or else would really rather have sided with our opponents.

(From a photographic copy supplied by Dr H. A. Jacobsen, original in the so-called 'Kaltenbrunner Papers' on the attempted assassination of the 20th July 1944. Microfilm, Washington.)

APPENDIX 33

Proclamation by Field-Marshal von Hindenburg, President of the Reich, on 'The Duties of the German Soldier'

BERLIN, 25TH MAY 1934

1 The Wehrmacht is the sword-arm of the German people. It protects the German Reich and the Fatherland, as well as the people, who are united in National-Socialism, and the people's *Lebensraum*.* It draws its strength from a glorious past, from German national feeling (*Volkstum*), from German soil and German toil. Service in the Wehrmacht is a service of honour to the German people.

2 A soldier's honour requires him to pledge the whole of himself for his people and the Fatherland, even to the sacrifice of his life.

3 The highest military virtue is the will to victory through battle. It demands inflexible determination. Cowardice is disgraceful; hesitation, unsoldierly.

4 The Wehrmacht is founded on obedience and on trust. True military leadership rests upon eagerness to take responsibility, superior ability and tireless concern for the welfare of subordinates.

5 Great achievements in war and peace can only result if officers and men form an indissoluble band of warriors.

6 Such a band demands comradeship; and the latter proves its worth above all in time of need and danger.

7 Self-confident yet modest, upright and faithful, God-fearing and truthful, reserved and incorruptible, the soldier should offer the whole people a pattern of manly strength. Achievement alone justifies pride.

8 The soldier seeks his highest reward and his greatest joy in the consciousness of duty cheerfully done. It is character and achievement that mark out his path and measure his worth.

The President of the Reich
(*signed*) V. HINDENBURG

The Reichswehr Minister
(*signed*) V. BLOMBERG

(By a decision of the Reichswehr Minister dated the 1st June 1934

* 'Living space': the word used by Nazi propaganda to justify Hitler's expansionist policies.

363

this proclamation was to be read out before an oath was taken, and every soldier was to learn it by heart. The Minister recommended that it should be posted up in barracks, etc.)

(Reprinted in Berlin (Verlag Mittler), 1936. From the publications (*Bücherei*) of the Bundesarchiv-Militärarchiv.)

APPENDIX 34

Directive from the Supreme Army-Command (OKH) on National-Socialist Leadership in the Army

HEADQUARTERS, OKH, 28TH MARCH 1944

With effect from the 14th March 1944, the Führer has appointed me Chief of the National-Socialist Leadership Staff (Active Forces and Reserves) at the Supreme Army-Command. I am directly responsible to him. The task the Führer has given me is to 'organise the formation and stimulation of the Army's political will by means of a unified direction of politics and *Weltanschauung*.' To remove all possible ambiguities I issue the following guidance:

Purpose of National-Socialist leadership.

This is a war of *Weltanschauungen* and is correspondingly bitter. The fate of our people is at stake. Wars fought on this scale are not won by the weight of numbers or material. The only decisive things are a people's highest qualities: bravery, iron discipline, honour and the consciousness of upholding and fighting for a noble idea. In a war of *Weltanschauungen*, above all, the decisive weapon is the militant idea.

To mobilise these qualities for victory, to stimulate political education so as to make every man a fanatical National-Socialist soldier – that is the task of the NS Leadership Officers. The longer the war lasts, the more sharply the front-lines between the two *Weltanschauungen* are defined, the more important that task will be.

The critical point is that every soldier – in slit-trench or in the rear – must be conscious at all times that he is responsible for the safety of his race, and must act accordingly. Day in, day out, his superiors must impress this on him. If he is fully conscious of being a militant for the National-Socialist *Weltanschauung* and of carrying the final responsiblity for his homeland in its time of trial, each soldier will be inspired to put up the fiercest resistance even in the most hopeless situation. Firm faith in the superiority of the idea and the justice of the cause is the sharpest sword there is for use against the enemy and his threadbare morale. A German unit inspired by that faith is superior to anything. It will overcome any crisis, even if supplies of arms and munitions break down.

The officers' tasks.

It is the Führer's wish that in the formation of the Army's political will the lead should be taken by the officer. It is he who leads his men in battle. The pre-condition is that he must train them properly. Their political attitude being the fundamental part of their training, the responsibility is fully his. Any separation of military and political tasks would be contrary to National-Socialist principles of leadership, and must be rejected. This requires that every officer must speak and act in such a way that his National-Socialist convictions are absolutely plain. His faith in victory and his loyalty to the Führer must know no bounds. He must show that his readiness for self-sacrifice as a soldier and his political convictions are one and the same thing. Correct behaviour as regards National-Socialism is not enough for an officer in a struggle as fierce as this.

It goes without saying that an officer in the National-Socialist Army must frankly and firmly counter any criticism. In times of crisis especially, the officer's faith and confidence in victory must shine out like a beacon to his men, and fortify their morale. An officer must do this for his men at every opportunity.

The NSFO. (National-Socialist Leadership Officer).

In all these tasks, his right-hand man and constant adviser is the NSFO; and the NSFO himself must be an experienced front-line officer. . . .

The NSFO is a Leadership Officer. He is not there to see to the men's supplies, nor to look after their welfare. His job is a militant's not a chaplain's; and the job is no less important than tactical command and training. . . .

The NSFO must possess the unlimited confidence of his commanding officer and of the men. He must therefore give not the slightest ground for being mistaken for a 'political commissar'. His task is to bring into being a close-knit, indissoluble National-Socialist fighting unit, not to split it into National-Socialists and others.

To stimulate National-Socialist education, the NSFO must reach and influence every single man. This part of a regimental NSFO's task is exceptionally important. The officer and the NSFO must be always on the job, combatting every sort of slackness or incipient indifference. Even in isolated units the NSFO's work goes on, and in such cases it is more important than ever.

If this work is properly done, a commanding officer will soon see the effect that political education has upon the spirit of his men and their qualities in battle. In general the NSFO should only work in a positive way and contribute to the unit's fighting quality. On no account is he to think he can do his job by staying at headquarters. In choosing my NSFOs I shall have no use for anyone who is not an activist and a fanatical National-Socialist militant. . . .

(*illegible*)	In the Führer's name
1st Lieutenant	(*signed*) SCHÖRNER
Certified true copy	General, Mountain Troops

(Partial reprint of the full text given by H. A. Jacobsen: 1939–1945. *Der zweite Weltkrieg in Chronik und Dokumenten* (5th edn., Darmstadt 1961) pp. 653–6.)

APPENDIX 35

Secret Circular from General von Blomberg on 'The Wehrmacht and National-Socialism'

No. 455. 34. J. Ch.

25TH MAY 1934

Since the 30th January 1933 the National-Socialist State has continued to accord the Wehrmacht the position to which its unswerving patriotism, its strong cohesion and solid discipline entitle it. The truth of that statement is proved by the repeated appreciation of the Wehrmacht expressed by the Führer, Adolf Hitler, and by the respect in which the Wehrmacht continues to be held by all unbiassed sections of the German people.

Patriotism is the obvious foundation of everything a soldier does. Let us not forget, however, that the *Weltanschauung* which inspires the new State is not only patriotic, or 'national', but national-*socialist*. National-Socialism deduces its law of action from the vital needs of the people as a whole and from the obligation of working in common for the good of all. It derives from the bond of blood and fate that binds all Germans together. The same law must form, and always form, the foundation for the whole of a soldier's service. Soldiers and National-Socialists each have a store of ideas derived from their common experience of the Great War.

This law, however, must not be allowed to govern us only when we are at work and on duty: it must rule our lives off-duty, our social lives, as well. I wish to see the corps of officers retain its leading position in social life wherever it is stationed, especially in the smaller places – the position it had gained for itself before the war, the position it has kept even in the difficult post-war years. But for this purpose it needs a new outlook under modern conditions and with the new structure of society: it needs to take in a wider cross-section than in the past. It is right and even necessary to give official receptions if they serve to create closer private and official contacts with the leading representatives of the Germany of today, especially contacts with the authorities and organisations. They should be kept simple, and they can show in their own way that the Wehrmacht combines tradition with progress. The old practice of seeking company within a particular social class is no longer any part of the duty of the corps of officers. Our social habits must be permeated by the realisation that the whole people forms a single community. There is no warrant for preferences based on nothing but social origins and education. If this means our dropping a few individuals who cannot rid themselves of their traditional social outlook, it may be hard on those affected; but it must be done. Anyone who has still not fully adapted his thinking to the concept of the people as a community (*Volksgemeinschaft*) has ruled himself out. The Wehrmacht has no reason to take any further notice of him. I do not intend, nor is it possible, to define exactly what sort of personalities it is desirable to win over, or to lay down a pattern for social occasions. I expect commanding-officers to take the fore-going guidance to heart and find the right way.

It remains as important as ever that a spirit of friendship should be cultivated within the corps of officers, for the training of the younger officers is closely bound up with it.

When non-commissioned officers and men take part in any festivity, care must be taken that the officers do not all sit together. They belong, just as much as the non-commissioned officers do, either to the men or to the guests, according to the type of festivity concerned.

I request that this guidance be given the most serious attention. On the way in which it is put into practice depends not least the opinion that will be formed of the Wehrmacht by those sections of the German people to whom the chance of seeing us at our daily work is still denied.

The text of this Order is to be communicated immediately to all officers and is to be made the subject of regular instruction in the Weapons Schools and analogous training establishments for officers.

(Reprinted from Part II of the secret 'Political Handbook', printed in 1938 in the 'Reichsdruckerei' in Berlin. – Militärarchiv.)

Notes

Introduction

1 Infra., p. 77 (all page references are to this book)
2 Ibid., p. 278
3 Ibid., p. 87
4 Ibid., p. 89
5 Ibid., p. 291
6 Ibid., p. 49
7 Ibid., p. 349
8 Ibid., p. 58
9 Ibid., p. 263

PART I SOCIAL ORIGINS

1 Prussia: Before Jena

1 Max Lehmann: *Scharnhorst*. Vol. II (Leipzig, 1887), Annexe 4, pp. 644ff., 11th Supplement to the *Mil. Wochenblatt*, 1909.
Extracts from the *Archiv des Kgl. Kriegsministeriums*, 1899, Part 1.
Robert Frhr. v. Schrotter: *Das Preussische Offizier-korps unter dem ersten König von Preussen*. In *Forschungen zur brandenburgischen und preussischen Geschichte*, vol. 27, part 1. (No date.)
Kurt Jany: *Geschichte der Kgl. Preussischen Armee*. 3 vols. (Berlin, 1928–29). This comes from vol. 1.
2 E. v. Frauenholz: *Das Heerwesen in der Zeit des Dreissigjährigen Kriegs*. Part 1: *Das Söldnertum*. (Munich, 1938), p. 34.
3 Max Lehmann: *op. cit.*, pp. 55ff.
4 Recounted by Frederick the Great in his *Oeuvres*, vol. 1, p. 192.
5 From Jany, *op. cit.*, p. 725.
6 Original in the Reichsarchiv: A VI.
7 See R. Koser: *Friedrich der Grosse*, 4th and 5th edns., 4 vols. (Stuttgart, 1912).
Also Elsb. Schwenker: *Friedrich der Grosse und der Adel*. Diss: (Berlin, 1911).

Notes

For the attitude of the other Hohenzollerns see Otto Hintze: *Die Hohenzollern und der Adel* in the *Historische Zeitschrift* 112 (1914), pp. 494ff. Gustav Schmoller: *Die Preussische Wahlrechtsreform von 1910 auf dem Hintergrunde des Kampfes zwischen Königtum und Feudalität*. In *Schmollers Jahrbuch* 34 (1910), pp. 1261ff.
Felix Priebatsch: *Die Hohenzollern und der Adel der Mark*. In *Historische Zeitschrift* 88 (1902), pp. 193–246.

8 W. Gembruch: *Vauban*. In *Klassiker der Kriegskunst*, ed. by W. Hahlweg. (Darmstadt, 1960) p. 160.

9 *Oeuvres*, vol. 6, p. 95.

10 From the *Minerva*, 1807, vol. 4, pp. 422ff.

2 Prussia: Reform and Reaction

1 1806. *Das preussische Offizierskorps und die Untersuchung der Kriegsereignisse.* Published by the Prussian General Staff. (Berlin, 1906.)
The basic accounts of these events as regards non-military history are almost all of rather earlier date. Compare also: von Altrock: *Jena und Auerstedt*. In the Supplement to the *Militär-Wochenblatt*, 1907.
Colmar Frhr. v. d. Goltz: *Rossbach und Jena*. (Berlin, 1883 and later edns.)
Hans Delbrück: Discussion of v. d. Goltz' above-named book in the *Preussische Jahrbücher*, vol. 52 (1883), Part. 6.

2 Compare Max Lehmann: *Frhr. vom Stein*, vol. 1 (Leipzig, 1902), pp. 292ff.

3 *Friedrich August von der Marwitz, ein märkischer Edelmann im Zeitalter der Befreiungskriege*, ed. by Friedrich Meusel. 2 vols. (Berlin, 1908–13). This is from vol. 1, pp. 319ff.

4 Here I deliberately adopt the views of a respected military writer who tried to put the failure of the Prussian army in 1806 in the best possible light:
Colmar Frhr. v. d. Goltz, *op. cit.*, and see the monograph thereon by Hermann Teske (Göttingen, 1957).

5 The main works on the reorganisation of the Prussian Army in 1807ff are:
Scherbening and von Willisen: *Die Reorganisation der preussischen Armee nach dem Tilsiter Frieden*, 2 parts: in Supplement to the *Militar-Wochenblatt*, 1854–56 and 1862–66.
G. H. Pertz: *Das Leben des Feldmarschalls Graf Neithardt von Gneisenau*. 3 vols. (Berlin, 1864–80).
Hans Delbrück: *Gneisenau*. 2 vols. (Berlin, 1882).
Max Lehmann: *Scharnhorst*. 2 vols. (Leipzig, 1886–7), especially vol. 1.
Friedrich Meinecke: *Das Leben des Generalfeldmarschalls Hermann von Boyen*. 2 vols. (Stuttgart, 1896–99).
Later works are listed by K. Demeter: *Scharnhorst*, in *Klassiker der Kriegskunst* ed. by W. Hahlweg (Darmstadt, 1960), p. 227.

6 B. Poten: *Geschichte des Militär-Erziehungs- und- Bildungswesen in den Landen deutscher Zunge*. (Berlin, 1889ff).
Meinecke: *Boyen*. Vol. 2, pp. 113ff.

7 From v. d. Osten-Sacken: *Preussens Heer*. Vol. 2 (Berlin, 1912), p. 260.

8 Cp. Meinecke, *op. cit.*, p. 49, and Prince Frederick Charles of Prussia's MS essay in Appendix 1 to the present work.

9 Cp. on this point J. F. Benzenberg: *Ueber Preussens Geldhaushalt und neues Steuersystem*. (Leipzig, 1820), pp. 4–12.

10 From Meinecke, *op. cit.*, p. 313.

11 Cp. *inter alia* Meinecke: *Weltbürgertum und Nationalstaat*. (6th edn.: Munich, 1922), also his *Das Zeitalter der Restauration*, in his *Historische und politische Aufsätze* (Munich and Berlin, 1918), pp. 167–77. The essay quoted first appeared in 1906. See also K. Demeter, *op. cit.*, pp. 211ff.

12 There is a great lack of monographs on these matters. For the present, therefore, it must remain an open question, on the one hand, to what extent the bourgeois officers in the Prussian army in the thirty or forty-odd years after the Stein-Hardenberg reforms came from large-scale landowning and farming families (since this was the time when so many large estates were passing into bourgeois hands) and on the other hand how far the nobles in the corps of officers were drawn from noble families who were large landowners and how far from the noble element in the civil service (*Beamtenadel*).

13 On Prince Frederick Charles see also the 2-vol. work by Wolfgang Foerster (Stuttgart, 1910) and compare also the essay reprinted in Appendix 1 which should be regarded as the Prince's reply to his critics, given an historical disguise.

14 Gustav Schmoller: *op. cit.*, Note 7 above.

15 *Aus dem Leben Theodor v. Bernhardis*, ed. by his son Friedrich: part 2, p. 231.

16 Private letter dated 'Berlin, 29th January', 1855 to an unnamed correspondent – probably the Minister of War. Akten Mil.-Kab.I. 1. 15, vol. 1, in the Prussian Secret State Archives.

17 Dated 'Berlin, 26th September 1954' and attached in the Archives to the letter referred to in the preceding Note.

3 Prussia: Expansion and Dilution

1 Max Lenz: *Geschichte Bismarcks* (Leipzig, 1902), surely goes too far in his view (pp. 116ff), that the reorganisation of 1860 was effected wholly in the interest of the nobility, alleging that territorial (*Landwehr*) officers and bourgeois cadets were carefully held back or turned aside, and the senior classes of the Cadet-Schools commissioned *en bloc*, to ensure that the new posts went to the sons of military families. Unfortunately the documentary sources on which this judgment is founded are not named.

2 Letter of the 19th May 1862.
Akten Mil.-Kab. I.1.15, vol. 1.

3 Prussian Secret State Archives: Akten Mil.-Kab. I.1.15, vol. 1. I have confined myself here to the totals, omitting analyses into those who (a) underwent examination from the Cadet Corps: (b) entered from units for the ensigns' examination; and (c) passed out with

certificate (*Reifezeugnis*): and also analysis according to separate years. The clerk here made a mistake over the percentage of officers' sons in the righthand column. He wrote 23: I have corrected this to 33.

4 Compiled by the 'Allgemeines Kriegsdepartement' in Prussian Ministry of War, dated Berlin, 21st March 1870; and comments thereon by the 'Militär-Kabinett' dated 28th March. Prussian Secret State Archives: Akten Mil.-Kab. I.1.15, vol. 1.

5 Letter from Werder to Manteuffel, from Königsberg: 13th May 1862. Prussian Secret State Archives: Akten Mil.-Kab. I.1.15, vol. 1.

6 Order to the Ministry of War, dated 24th February 1870. Prussian Secret State Archives: Akten Mil.-Kab. I.1.15, vol. 1.

7 Royal Order (AKO) of the 15th November 1870 from Versailles to the acting G.O.C., 9th Army Corps. Prussian Secret State Archives: Akten Mil.-Kab. I.1.15, vol. 1.

8 Royal Order (AKO), of the 23rd April 1872, to the Ministry of War. Reference as for Note 35.

9 Unabridged draft, not intended for publication. Reichsarchiv: Akten Mil.-Kab. I.1.15, vol. 2.

10 Cp. conversations with von Einem, Minister of War, and with General Friedrich von Bernhardi on the 10th December 1904, and the 11th February 1905 respectively, published by the latter in his *Denkwürdigkeiten* (Berlin, 1927), p. 263, also notes for a report to the Minister of War; Reichsarchiv: Akten Mil.-Kab. I.1.15, vol. 3.

11 Observations on the shortage of officers, reproduced in a communication of the Military Cabinet to the Minister of War, dated the 15th February 1902. Reichsarchiv: Akten Mil.-Kab. I.1.15, vol. 3.

12 So phrased in notes for a report in March, 1909 to the Prussian Minister of War; this corresponds moreover with the documentary evidence.

13 Werner Sombart: *Die deutsche Volkswirtschaft im 19. Jahrhundert* (7th edn.: Berlin, 1927) pp. 358ff.
Theodor Frhr. v.d. Goltz: *Geschichte der deutschen Landwirtschaft*. 2 vols., (Stuttgart, 1903) appendix.

14 On the question of the 'good' stations, see also Alb. Benary: *Das deutsche Heer. Ein Buch des Stolzes, ein Buch der Hoffnung.* (Berlin, 1932) p. 282ff.

15 cp. especially: *Nationalzeitung* of the 10th January 1904; (article on 'Der Adel im Offizierskorps' by General leutnant z.D. Litzmann); *Vossische Zeitung* of the same date (unsigned article on (*Adelige und bürgerliche Offiziere*); *Tägliche Rundschau* of the 8th March 1910 (article on *Die diesjährige Kadettenverteilung* by General Litzmann; *Deutsche Tageszeitung* of the 16th April 1910 (article on *Die Junker, das Militärkabinett und Herr Gädke*, replying to an article in the *Berliner Tagblatt* headed *Militärkabinett und Adel*); and the *Frankfurter Zeitung* of the 7th July 1912, 4th morning edn. (article on *Preussens Bürgertum und Adel Militärische Betrachtungen eines alten Offiziers*. This last was actually entered in the files of the Mil.-Kab. and of the Ministry of War, and discussed in written minutes.

16 Reported 'on the best authority' on the 8th April 1909, by the Bavarian military plenipotentiary in Berlin, Ludwig Frhr. von Gebsattel. Cp. his

Notes

Politische Berichte, pubd. by K. Demeter in *Preussische Jahrbücher*, issues for January and February, 1933.

17 Files of the *Offiziers- und Unteroffiziers-Ergänzungsabteilung* I.3.4, No. 3, Pt. 1.: Reichsarchiv.

18 In an unpublished draft for a newspaper-article by Scheuch who was a 'Referent' in the Ministry of War about 1910.

19 According to the *Militär-Wochenblatt* of the 3rd and 5th March 1910. See also General Litzmann's article in the *Tägliche Rundschau* of the 8th March 1910.

4 Saxony, Bavaria and Wurtemberg

1 See generally O. Schuster and F. A. Francke: *Geschichte der Sächsischen Armee*. 3 parts (Leipzig, 1855) and H. A. Verlohren: *Stammregister und Chronik der Sächsischen Armee*. (Leipzig, 1910.)

2 Cp. the *Sächsische Rangliste* for 1785 under the heading: *Geschichte und gegenwärtiger Zustand der Kursächsischen Armee* (Dresden, 1785). In an appendix the book also gives a list of the staff officers serving in 1730 in the regiments encamped at Zeithayn.

3 H. Meschwitz: *Geschichte des Kgl. Sächsischen Kadetten- und Pagen-Korps* (Dresden, 1907).

4 See especially Karl Staudinger: *Geschichte des kurbayerischen Heeres, insbesondere unter Kurfürst Ferdinand Maria, 1651–79* (Munich, 1901) which is the first volume of the *Geschichte des bayerischen Heeres unter Kurfürst Max II Emmanuel, 1680–1726*, 1st half-vol. (Munich, 1904).

5 Ernst Kemmer: *Entwicklungsgeschichte des Königlich Bayerischen Kadetten-Korps*. ('Festschrift' in honour of the 150th year of the Cadet-Corps: 14th July 1906; Munich, 1906.) As a supplement see V. Hellingrath and Koerber: *Das bayerische Kadetten-Korps 1906–20*. (Munich, 1920.) The authors were both officers: one a lecturer at the institute and the other its commanding officer
Also: Annual Reports on the Bavarian Cadet-Corps from 1899 to 1913.

6 I compiled these figures from the printed reports on the 'Oeffentliche Prüfung der Eleven in der kurfürstlichen (bayerischen) Militär-akademie zu München' for the years 1791 to 1802. From 1789 to 1805 'Militärakademie' was the name of the Bavarian Cadet-Corps.

7 Cp. especially du Moulin-Eckart: *Bayern unter dem Ministerium Montgelas, 1799 bis 1817*. (Munich, 1895).

8 Royal Rescript of the 8th August 1805. See also: *Nachricht über einige Einrichtungen des Königlich Bayerischen Kadetten-Korps für die Eltern usw. gedruckt*, (Munich, 1825).

9 The files are in the Bavarian 'Kriegsarchiv': (1) Kriegs-Minist.-Archiv. Kapitel III Lit. a XVII Nr. 1 and Nr. 1a fasc. I. (2) Kapitel III Lit. b XIII Nr. 2. (3) A. IV. 7.

10 By way of illustration I quote a passage from a pamphlet named *Die deutsche Centralgewalt und die preussische Armee* that appeared anonymously in Berlin in July, 1848. It asserts that in the Bavarian Army, 'in the interest of the Valhalla, the Pinakothek, the Glyptothek, etc., scarcely a promotion has been made for twenty years'.

Notes

11 From statistics given by the *Pagenhofmeister* August Frhr. von Müller in his *Geschichtliche Entwicklung der Königlich Bayerischen Pagerie von 1514 bis zur Gegenwart* (Munich, 1901).

12 I compiled the figures for 1799 from the surviving *Offiziers-Konduitelisten* of each regiment (twenty in all); those for the nineteenth century come from the printed *Ranglisten*.

13 From the Annual Report dated the 23rd March 1884, in the Bavarian 'Kriegsarchiv': files on *Offiziersprüfungen*, A III 1f. fasc. 1. Page 10 of this MS report is exceptional in giving a summary of the social origins of the 103 pupils taking the current course.

14 At irregular intervals, mostly of several decades, when the old book could no longer be kept up to date, a new one was started on the basis of the latest establishment. An incomplete collection of such books is preserved in the Bavarian 'Kriegsarchiv'. For Prussia, with her far larger army, a set of random examples might easily give an unreliable picture of the whole.

15 *Offizierstammliste* of the Bavarian Foot Guards (Inf.-Leib-Regiment) 1814–92 (Illing, Berlin: 1892).

16 Cp. Karl Demeter: *Zur Soziologie der sozialpolitischen Begriffsbildung in Schmollers Jahrbuch*, 50th year (1926), part 1.

17 G. v. Niethammer: *Geschichte des (1. württ.) Grenadier-Rgts. Nr. 119.* Continued by J. Seybold (Stuttgart, 1897) Pfister: *op. cit.*
Rud. Menzel: *Geschichte des (2. württ.) Infanterie-Rgts. Nr. 120, 1673–1909* (Stuttgart, 1909).
Schempp, Luschka, Hardegg and Horn: *Geschichte des (3. württ.) Infanterie-Rgts. Nr. 121, 1716–1891.* (Stuttgart, 1891).
Herb. Müller: *Geschichte des (4. württ.) Infanterie-Rgts. Nr. 122* (Heilbronn, 1906.)
Fromm: *Geschichte des (6. württ.) Infanterie-Rgts. Nr. 124, 1806–1906* (Weingarten, 1901).
Marx: *Geschichte des (1. württ.) Infanterie-Rgts. Nr. 125, 1809–1895* (Berlin, 1895).
Griesinger: *Geschichte des (1. württ.) Ulanen-Rgts. Nr. 20,* (Stuttgart, 1889).
Gleich: *Die ersten hundert Jahre des (2. württ.) Ulanen-Rgts. Nr. 19,* (Stuttgart, 1909).
Starklof: *Geschichte des württ. 2. Reiter-Rgts.* (Darmstadt, 1862).
Starklof: *Geschichte des württ. 4. Reiter-Rgts.* (Stuttgart, 1867).
v. Neubronner: *Gechichte des (2. württ.) Dragoner-Rgts. Nr. 26,* (Stuttgart, 1905).
Gessler, Tognarelli and Ströbel: *Geschichte des (2. württ.) Feldartillerie-Rgts. Nr. 29,* (Stuttgart, 1892).

5 Germany: Collapse and Continuity

1 The figures are taken from the study by E. O. Volkmann (Major, rtd., of the staff of the 'Reichsarchiv'):
Soziale Heeresmisstände als Mitursache des deutschen Zusammenbruchs von 1918. Second half-vol. of vol. II of the Report of the Reichstag's

Commission of Enquiry into the causes of the German collapse in 1918 (Berlin, 1929). The other contents of this study should be compared with the previous study of the same question by Martin Hobohm: ref. as above; 1st half-vol. of vol. II (Berlin, 1929).

2 Unimpeachable evidence on the point is furnished by Groener's entry in his diary for the 13th September 1917, quoted in Dorothea Geyer-Groener's *General Groener, Soldat und Staatsmann*. (Frankfurt, 1955), p. 74.

3 Dorothea Geyer-Groener, *op. cit.*, p. 74.

4 Gustav Noske (b. Brandenburg a.d. Havel, 1868), son of a modest weaver, became a woodworker and basket-maker. Joined the SPD (German Socialist Party) and though self-educated worked his way up to being an editor of the Party's papers. Elected to the Reichstag in 1907 and soon became a specialist in military and naval questions. Died at Hanover, 30th November 1946.

5 Quoted by Fritz Ernst: *Aus dem Nachlass des Generals Walther Reinhardt*. (Stuttgart, 1958), p. 50.

6 From the essay by Franz Woertz: *Die Verschwörung der Offiziere* (about the Reichswehr trial at Ulm) in *Die Tat*, 22nd. Year, part 8 (November 1930), pp. 610ff. The essay is undoubtedly based on authentic material from the Reichswehr Ministry at the time.

7 Gustav Adolf Caspar: *Die sozialdemokratische Partei und das deutsche Wehrproblem in den Jahren der Weimarer Republik* (Supplement 11 to the *Wehrwissenschaftliche Rundschau*). (Frankfurt, 1959) pp. 51ff.

8 Otto Völcker: *Der französische Soldat. Wesen und Haltung*. (Berlin, 1939) pp. 51ff.

9 The full text is printed as an appendix in Caspar, *op. cit.*

10 On Seeckt and Gessler, see generally:
Friedr. v. Rabenau: *Seeckt. Aus seinem Leben, 1918–1936*. (Leipzig, 1940.)
Otto Gessler: *Reichswehrpolitik in der Weimarer Zeit*, with a foreword by Theodor Heuss. Published by Kurt Sendtner (Stuttgart, 1958).
H. Meier-Welcker: *Deutsches Heerwesen im Wandel der Zeit*. (Arolsen, 1954). Section IV, pp. 91ff.
Otto-Ernst Schüddekopf: *Das Heer und die Republik. Quellen zur Politik der Reichswehrführung 1918–1933*. (Hanover-Frankfurt, 1955.)
Harold J. Gordon: *The Reichswehr and the German Republic, 1919–1926*, (Princeton University Press, 1957).
Wolfgang Sauer: *Die Reichswehr*, in K. D. Bracher, W. Sauer and G. Schulz: *Die nationalsozialistische Machtergreifung*. (Cologne-Opladen, 1960), pp. 229–84.

11 Rabenau: *op. cit.*, p. 239.

12 See *inter alia* Groener's *Gedanken über die Entwicklung des Kriegswesens*, a lecture given before the *Mittwochs-Gesellschaft* in 1928: quoted by Dorothea Geyer-Groener, *op. cit.*, pp. 367ff.

13 See Note 6 above.

14 From the personal records (II) for the province of Nordrhein-Westfalen, the files of the 64 Reichswehr officers were selected who were either commissioned between 1921 and 1933 or who at any rate were cadets (Offizieranwärter) before 1933. The figures calculated thus apply only

to one part of the Reich but are useful for comparing the whole period of twelve years with the figures for the whole of the Reich for 1926 and 1927 given by Woertz.

Dr W. Sauer of the Free University of Berlin most generously placed at my disposal his unpublished MS on 'The nobility's share in the Reichswehr's corps of officers', having been able to use only very little of it in his chapter on the Reichswehr in Bracher's book on the dissolution of the Weimar Republic (*Die Auflösung der Weimarer Republik:* 3rd edn., 1961). I am thus most grateful to him for these statistical data which seem to me to round off the picture of developments very aptly. As regards Woertz' figures the following should be noted. The two years 1926 and 1927 were Seeckt's last year as head of the Army Staff and the first year after his departure. They are thus very interesting for our purposes. Moreover, compared with the old Army of 1912–13, the figures for the small Reichswehr of the day were of a very minor order of magnitude: and for this reason it is important to have figures for two successive years, since the figure for a single year might easily have some exceptional feature and thus lead to a false conclusion.

15 From Wilhelm Karl, Prince of Isenburg: *Zur Statistik des Deutschen Adels* in the *Deutsches Adelsblatt*, 55th year, part 2, of the 9th January 1937, pp. 33ff.

16 From Hélène, Princess of Isenburg (using the same sources) in the *Archiv der Sippenforschung*, 1935, reprinted in the *Deutsches Adelsblatt*, 1936.

17 W. Sauer's frequently-cited MS lists the following names for 1932: six times v. Arnim, v. Schwerin; five times v. Bülow, v. Kleist; four times v. Blomberg, v. Both, v. der Chevallerie, Frhr. v. Uckermann, v. Witzleben; three times Frhr. von und zu Aufsess, v. Boltenstern, v. Dewitz, v. Krebs, v. Engel, v. Frankenberg und Prochlitz, Frhr. v. Hammerstein, v. Hillebrandt, v. Horn, v. Hülsen (incl. one Count v. Hülsen), v. Klitzing, v. Kunowksi, de Ondarza, v. Prittwitz und Gaffron, Frhr. v. Schleinitz, v. d. Schulenburg, v. Seher-Thoss, v. Stülpnagel, v. Tippelskirch, Frhr. v. Uslar-Gleichen, Frhr. v. Waldenfels, v. Wintersheim, v. Winterfeld.

18 Essay on *Der Offizierberuf im Reichsheer* by Capt. von Kortzfleisch (1st Inf. Regt.) in the *Deutsches Adelsblatt* 39th Year, part 22, of the 30th November 1921, pp. 338ff.

19 The figures in Sauer's MS are arranged by years, based on the printed lists of officers for the 'Reichsheer'.

20 As Sauer did in the MS mentioned in Note 14 above.

6 The Third Reich

1 Frido v. Senger und Etterlin: *Krieg in Europa* (Cologne, 1960), pp. 429ff.

2 From Hans Mundt: *Das Offizierkorps des deutschen Heers von 1918–1935*, in *Führungsschicht und Eliteproblem*, Jahrbuch III der Ranke-Gesellschaft, 1957: pp. 115–26.

3 Frido v. Senger und Etterlin: *op. cit.*

Notes

7 Summary: The Two Mentalities

1 This was repeatedly brought out at the German Historians' Congress at Treves (Trier) in 1958; but a change of approach has long been taking place, eg Hans Delbrück: *Geschichte der Kriegskunst*, vol. 3 (Berlin, 1907), pp. 235ff., and vol. 4 (Berlin, 1920).

Georg v. Below: article on *Adel* in the *Handwörterbuch der Staatswissenschaften* (3rd. edn., 1909). The article was unfortunately dropped from the 4th. edn., of 1923.

Georg v. Below: *Die unfreie Herkunft des niederen Adels* in the *Historische Zeitschrift*, vol. 135 (1926), pp. 415ff.

C. H. Frhr. Roth v. Schreckenstein: *Die Ritterwürde und der Ritterstand. Historisch-politische Studien über deutsch-mittelalterliche Standesverhältnisse auf dem Lande und in der Stadt.* (Freiburg i. Br., 1886.)

G. Köhler (General): *Die Entwicklung des Kriegswesens und der Kriegführung in der Ritterzeit.* 3 parts. 1886–9.

See also Eugen v. Frauenholz: *Entwicklungsgeschichte des deutschen Heerwesens*, vol. 1: *Das Heerwesen der germanischen Frühzeit, des Frankenreiches und des ritterlichen Zeitalters.* (Munich, 1935.)

Herm. Conrad: *Geschichte der deutschen Wehrverfassung*, I. (Munich, 1939.)

W. Schlesinger: *Burg und Stadt*, and Karl S. Bader: *Reichsadel und Reichsstädte*, both in *Festschrift für Theod. Mayer*. (Lindau-Konstanz, 1954.)

Karl Schib: *Das Mittelalter*. (Zurich, 1956).

PART II EDUCATION

8 The Two Principles: Character and Intellect

1 Gustav Schmoller: *Das Wesen der Arbeitsteilung und der sozialen Klassenbildung*, in *Schmollers Jahrbuch* 14 (1890), has this sentence on p. 84: 'The basis of the capacity of the body social is that the most important places should always be given to those who have similar training and upbringing; in all situations, therefore, that have no particular systems for these matters there is really no choice but to make status and profession hereditary in principle.' In the course of the essay, this important idea is unfortunately lost to sight amid the welter of historical detail.

2 Cp. B. Poten: *Geschichte des Militär-Erziehungs- und Bildungswesens in den Landen deutscher Zunge*, especially vol. 1 with its general survey. (Berlin, 1889.)

9 Prussia: The first Military Schools

1 From Gerhard Oestreich in the study referred to in Note 3 to Appendix 4.

2 The old-style German establishments for the education of young noblemen (*Ritterakademien*), which used to exist in every German State,

admitted no distinction of nationality. The last to survive (though converted into a national institution) was the Bavarian 'Pagerie' which lasted until 1918. – The word 'cadets' comes, of course, from France where it designated the 'younger' sons in a noble family, who would inherit the least. They sought their fortunes in the army where, after 1682, they were formed into special 'cadet-companies'. The French example was imitated after 1700 in Germany, and notably in Prussia, after the Revocation of the Edict of Nantes, for the sons of émigrés. Along with the name 'cadets', Prussia took over the thing itself, but soon gave it a different content by converting the 'cadet-companies' into Cadet-Academies which were then developed into officers' educational establishments (*Offiziererziehungsanstalten*) for the sons of needy Prussian noblemen. For details of the gradual transformation of the Prussian 'cadet-companies' into a school, the so-called 'Cadet-Corps' see Jany: *op. cit.*, vol. 1, pp. 543f. and 726ff.

3 Kleber: *Von Schlesien vor und seit dem Jahre 1740*, part 1 (Freiburg, 1758). Preface, p. 22. Quoted from Kurt Jany: *Geschichte der Königl. Preussischen Armee*, vol. 1, p. 735.

4 Cp. Jany *op. cit.*

5 See supplement to the *Militär-Wochenblatt* 1854–55, p. 154.

6 R. Koser: *Friedrich der Grosse*, vol. 2, p. 406.

7 From Delbrück: *Kriegskunst*, vol. 2, p. 406.

8 *Op. cit.* (Meusel's edn.) vol. 1, pp. 41ff.

9 K. Demeter: *Die soziale Schichtung des deutschen Parlaments seit 1848*, in *Vierteljahresschrift für Sozial- und Wirtschaftsgeschichte* 39 (1952), pp. 1–32.

10 Prussia: Scharnhorst, Examinations and Resistance

1 Cp. Lehmann: *Scharnhorst*, vol. 1, pp. 227f. and 298.
K. Demeter: *Scharnhorst*, in *Klassiker der Kriegskunst* (published by W. Hahlweg, Darmstadt, 1960), pp. 211–27, with a bibliography of the latest literature. Also H. Meier-Welcker: *Gerhard von Scharnhorst*, in *Grosse Soldaten der europäischen Geschichte* (published by W. v. Groote, Frankfurt, 1961).

2 *Militärische Schriften Kaiser Wilhelms des Grossen* (Berlin, 1897), vol. 1, p. 61.

3 *Ibidem*, vol. 2, p. 258.

4 Memorandum of the 3rd January 1836 (quoted from Meinecke: *Boyen*, vol. 1, p. 469).

5 Meinecke: *Boyen*, vol. 2, p. 510.

6 Letter to Boyen, dated Berlin 9th May 1844, in *Militärische Schriften Kaiser Wilhelms des Grossen*, vol. 1, pp. 489ff.

7 Reprinted from the brochure printed in manuscript-facsimile in December, 1848, in *Militärische Schriften Kaiser Wilhelms des Grossen*, vol. 2, pp. 1ff. Who actually drafted these 'Observations' is not made clear in the new edition, but in all probability it was the Prince himself. The style is very like his; and the contents are obviously very much his thoughts.

8 Emphasised in the edition mentioned.

Notes

9 Royal Cabinet Order (AKO) of the 30th May 1848, in Akten Mil.-Kab. I.1.15, vol. 1 (Prussian Secret State Archives).

11 Germany: Expansion; The Die-Hards at Bay

1 Felix, Count von Luckner, has this delightful passage in his book of worldly-wise memoirs: *Aus 70 Lebensjahren* (Biberach/Riss, 1955): 'I don't mind a bit if a man muddles "I" and "me" up, but if a man confuses "mine" and "thine" I don't like it at all!'

2 Delbrück: *Geschichte der Kriegskunst*, vol. 4, pp. 298ff.

3 Order of the 10th December 1861. In Akten Militärkabinett I.1.15, vol. 1 (Prussian Secret State Archives).

4 Communication from the 'Allgemeines Kriegsdepartement' of the Ministry of War, dated the 30th June 1869: in Akten Mil.-Kab. I.1.15, vol. 1.

5 Communication from the 'Personal Affairs Section', signed 'von Tresckow' and dated the 31st January 1870. The draft, marked to be fair-copied, is with it in the files.

6 In another communication (*ibidem*) connected with the subject, dated the 28th March 1870, signed 'von Tresckow' and initialled by von Albedyll, Chief of the Military Cabinet.

7 In a communication of the 21st March 1870 (*ibidem*).

8 From the report of the Inspectorate of War-Schools to the Emperor (Akten K.M. Offizier- und Unteroffizier-Ergänzungs-Abteilung X. 1.1b.2. vol. 8, in the Reichsarchiv).

9 From the 'Instruction for the Execution of His Majesty's Order of the 13th November 1890.' In this Order William II decreed that '. . . to permit a greater flow of officers into the peace-time establishment for the next few years', shortened courses would temporarily be introduced in the War Schools, with a partial lowering of the entrance-requirements. The Order itself, as well as the decree on its aims and the manner of its execution which was printed as a manuscript-facsimile, are in Akten Mil. Kab. I.1.15, vol. 2 (Reichsarchiv).

10 From the Akten K.M. I.3.4, No. 3, part 1 in the Reichsarchiv.

11 Royal Cabinet Order (AKO) of the 28th March 1899. Akten Mil.-Kab. I.1.15, vol. 2, in the Reichsarchiv.

12 In a confidential communication of the 3rd February 1910, the Minister of Education (von Trott zu Stolz) had observed 'that out of the 2,739 pupils in private preparatory establishments who in 1901 to 1909 inclusive were examined by the Higher Military Examination Commission, 803, or almost 30 per cent had been excused from producing a *Primareifezeugnis*'. On the other hand the Ministry of War (Akten Mil.-Kab. I.1.15, vol. 3, in the Reichsarchiv) calculated that the figure for the period named should be 'only' 638. By this, however, it meant only the number of those who, after dispensation from the *Primareifezeugnis*, actually passed the ensigns' examination and were accepted as ensigns (but see the table in the text!). The Ministry of Education, on the other hand, was giving the number of those who, after dispensation, had been examined – including those who in the

event were ploughed. These account for the difference of 165 between the two figures.

13 Minute on a private letter of complaint about the misconduct of the 'crammers'.

14 According to a Minute of the 28th September 1909, in Akten Mil.-Kab. I.1.15, vol. 3, *ibidem*. In the 1907 Service Instructions for the Naval Staff, Commander Hollweg had written: 'In time of peace the object of education is simply and plainly to raise the quality of the whole corps of officers – at any rate of the keen ones – as much as possible; but an immediate effect can only be made on a few of them.' K. Hollweg: *Der Admiralstabsdienst*. (Berlin, 1907) Secret.

15 Cp. O. H. von der Gablenz: *Das preussisch-deutsche Offizierkorps* in *Schicksalsfragen der Gegenwart, Handbuch politisch-historischer Bildung*. (Ministry of Defence – 'Innere Führung') vol. 3. (Tübingen, 1958), pp. 47–71. Also R. Stadelmann: *Moltke und der Staat* (Krefeld, 1950).

16 K. Demeter: *Scharnhorst, op. cit.*

17 Details will be found in Erich Wagner: *Goethe und die Generäle der Freiheitskriege*. New edn. 1959.

18 E. A. Nohn: *Der unzeitgemässe Clausewitz*. (Supplement 5 to the *Wehrwissenschaftliche Rundschau*: Berlin-Frankfort, 1956.) Also Clausewitz: *Moralische Grössen*, in the book *Vom Kriege* and in an unsigned contribution to the *Neue Bellona*, 1801. In *Historische Zeitschrift* 186 (1958), pp. 35–64.

19 Cp. *inter alia* Walter Görlitz: *Der deutsche Generalstab* (Frankfurt, 1953).

20 From the appendix to a communication of the 11th January 1905, from the Ministry of War to the Military Cabinet. Source as in Note 14.

21 To the 'Allgemeines Kriegsdepartement'. Akten Mil.-Kab. I.1.15, vol. 3, in the Reichsarchiv.

22 From E. O. Volkmann: *Der Marxismus und das deutsche Heer im Weltkriege* (Berlin, 1925), p. 155.

23 In a letter to Leopold von Gerlach, dated Frankfort-on-the-Main, 19th December 1857, Bismarck called the Military Cabinet '*die Mördergrube hinter dem Marstall*' ('the assassination-pit behind the Mews').

12 Bavaria and Saxony

1 Ernst Kemmer: *Entwicklungsgeschichte des K. B. Kadetten-Korps*, in the *Festschrift zur Feier des 150jährigen Bestehens des Bayerischen Kadetten-Korps* (Munich, 1889) give systematic prominence mainly to the externals of the matter, and to the educational side. It is illustrated.

2 Ep. E. von Schelhorn: *Die Königl. Bayer. Kriegsschule in den ersten 25 Jahren ihres Bestehens*. (Munich, 1883.)

3 On the 20th March, 1848 King Lewis I had handed power over to his son Maximilian. On the very next day after his accession King Max II approved a proposal to fill up the officers' and non-commissioned officers' posts which, under the Army Act of 1825, were to be left vacant in time of peace: in April and May he approved the raising of a third battalion for each infantry regiment, a fourth division (i.e.

two companies) for each rifle-battalion, a seventh squadron for each cavalry regiment, the increase of each artillery regiment by three batteries, and the raising of a regiment of horse-artillery.

4 Report by Section 3 of the War Ministry dated the 28th July 1847. In the Bavarian Kriegsarchiv, A VIa 6. Fasc. 7: quoted from Rudolf von Xylander: *Geschichte des (bayer.) Feldartillerie-Regiments*, vol. 3, (Berlin, 1909), p. 6.

5 Decision of the 4th December 1855. In the Bavarian Kriegsarchiv, General R. Dienstvorschrift I. Teil fasc. III: quoted from the copy in the Kriegsministerial-Archiv Kap. III., Lit. b. XIII. Nr. 2.

6 MS letter of the 31st July 1859: in the Bavarian Kriegsarchiv: K. M.-Archiv Kap. III., Lit. a XVII, Nr. 1.

7 From the report of the Inspectorate of Military Educational Establishments on the results of the current year's officer-examination (i.e. of the final examinations in the War Schools): textually reproduced in a communication from the Zentralabteilung des K.M., 15th May 1878. Bavarian Kriegsarchiv A III -1f. fasc. 1.

8 Dated Dresden, 15th January 1835. King Frederick Augustus II's papers in the Saxon 'Hauptstaatsarchiv' at Dresden, Fach 405. For reasons of space the quotation has been abridged, but without alteration of the sense or text of the original.

13 *The Reichswehr and the Third Reich*

1 Friedrich von Rabenau: *Seeckt. Aus seinem Leben*, 1918–36 (Leipzig, 1940). Compare herewith the attitude of Hans Meier-Welcker, who questioned the sources, in his study: *Die Stellung des Chefs der Heeresleitung in den Anfängen der Republik. Zur Entstehungsgeschichte des Reichswehrministeriums*, in *Vierteljahrshefte für Zeitgeschichte*, 1956, April. As regards the origins of the book, see the essay in memory of Rabenau by Strutz in the periodical *Der Archivar*, 1956, cols. 133–44. From both these appreciations it is clear that Rabenau, who was chief of the 'Heeresarchiv', wrote at the desire, but also under the political supervision, of his National-Socialist superiors; in other words, he wrote with only limited academic freedom and therefore had to adjust the objective truth in many places. (After his retirement he studied evangelical theology and met his death in connection with the plot of 1944 against Hitler's life.) Despite some critical reserve about his account, including many quotations, it remains the basic, comprehensive source-book about Seeckt and his achievements in connection with the Reichswehr.

As a complement it is worth mentioning the very fair and well-documented book by the American historian, Harold H. Gordon: *The Reichswehr and the German Republic, 1919–1926*. (Princeton U.P., 1957.)

2 Rabenau: *op. cit.*, p. 478.

3 Textually quoted from Fritz Ernst: *Aus dem Nachlass des Generals Walther Reinhardt*. (Stuttgart, 1958), p. 58.

4 This is no reason to treat as objectively accurate the novelettish account of the Cadet-School at Plön which is given by the writer

Notes

Fritz von Unruh (a former cadet) in his autobiographical book *Der Sohn des Generals*. (Nuremberg, 1957.)

5 Cp. Julius Deutsch: *Abrüstung, Heeresreform und Democratie* in '*Gesellschaft*', 1926.
In general, see K. Demeter: *Das Hochschulstudium in der Reichswehr, Eine Betrachtung um Clausewitz* in *Deutsche Wehr*, 1931, pp. 1101f, and G. A. Caspar: *Die sozialdemokratische Partei, op. cit.*, p. 56.

6 From Gessler: *Memoiren*, published by K. Sendtner (Stuttgart, 1958) p. 287.

7 Beck's papers in the 'Bundesarchiv-Militärarchiv' in Coblence (Blatt 91 a).

8 In his book of reminiscences: *Soldat unter Soldaten*. (Constance, 1951), pp. 26ff.

9 *Inter alia* in a letter to Brauchitsch from Colonel-General W. Ritter von Leeb, dated the 31st October 1939: quoted in full by H.-A. Jacobsen: *1939-45* (5th edn., Darmstadt, 1961), pp. 604f.

10 Waldemar Besson: *Zur Geschichte des national-sozialistischen Führungsoffiziers* (NSFO), with 15 documents, in *Vierteljahrshefte für Zeitgeschichte*, part 1, January 1961, pp. 76–116.

PART III HONOUR

14 *The Dual Nature of Honour*

1 Georg Simmel: *Einleitung in die Moralwissenschaft*, vol. 1 (facsimile of the 1892-3 edn., Stuttgart, 1904) pp. 191ff. Also by Simmel: *Die Selbsterhaltung der sozialen Gruppe*, in *Schmollers Jahrbuch No. 22* (1898), pp. 596-640. Similar in tendency but less extreme in wording: Franz Eulenburg: *Über die Möglichkeit und die Aufgaben einer Sozialpsychologie* (Inaugural Lecture at the University of Leipzig) in *Schmollers Jahrbuch No. 24*, (1900), pp. 201-37.

2 Cp. also Clausewitz: *Vom Kriege* (annotated by W. von Scherff: Berlin, 1880), Book 1, Chap. 4, *Von der Gefahr im Kriege:* also later edns.

3 On the subject of honour in general, see also Friedrich Paulsen: *System der Ethik*, vol. 2. (7th and 8th edns., Stuttgart, 1906), pp. 94ff.
Paula Kronheimer: *Grenzglieder des Standes* in the *Kölner Vierteljahrshefte für Soziologie*, 6th Year (1927), pp. 248-68.
Rolf Kluth: *Preussische Ehrauffassung. Der Ehrbegriff im preussischen Heer des 18 Jahrhunderts* (Berlin, 1941). Loses himself in confusion of thought by trying to make impossible distinctions between the honour of knights, warriors and soldiers. Contributes nothing to the history of the Prussian concepts of honour, etc. Hans Reiner: *Die Ehre. Kritische Sichtung einer abendländischen Lebens- und Sittlichkeitsform* (Darmstadt-Frankfurt, 1956). Takes insufficient account of the problem that faced the officers. The following are also worth mention:
Ulrich Mann: *Lorbeer und Dornenkrone. Eine historische und theologische Studie über das Wehrverständnis im deutschen Soldatentum* (Stuttgart, 1958). See also the refutation by E. A. Nohn in the *Wehrwissenschaftliche*

Notes

Rundschau, 1960, Part 8. (See also Chapter 15 Note 2 for literature on duelling.)

15 Duelling: Origins and Early Efforts at Suppression

1 Excellent examples are to be found in pure literature: e.g. the character of Imstetten in Theodor Fontane's novel *Effi Briest* which is set in the late nineteenth century; and Arthur Schnitzler's *Leutnant Gustl* (Berlin, 1900).

2 H. Fehr: *Der Zweikampf* (Berlin, 1908).
Georg v. Below: *Das Duell und der germanische Ehrbegriff* (Kassel, 1896) and Georg V. Below: *Das Duell in Deutschland* (Kassel, 1896).
Also the review of the last-named in the *Preussische Jahrbücher* No. 84 (1896), pp. 375–9, by 'D' (probably Hans Delbrück) and also A. von Boguslawski (Lt-Gen. retd): *Die Ehre und das Duell* (Berlin, 1896).
The term *duellum* is frequently met with in mediaeval legal writings; but it there refers to the judicial duel that was often tolerated, and even ordered, by authority. The Emperor Frederick II, for example, admitted it in cases of *lèse majesté*, homicide and alleged witchcraft. In civil cases, too, the litigants were ordered to fight a *duellum;* the victor was judged to have been in the right, and he who refused to fight was found guilty. When kings', princes' and noblemen's daughters had more than one suitor, duels between suitors took place as 'ordeals' and the victor won the daughter's hand. 'But', writes the Brandenburg councillor and auditor-general, Johann Friedrich Schulze, in his *Corpus Juris Militaris* (Berlin, 1693), 'since such trials are not only a defiance of GOD but often, as historians tell us, cost the innocent man his life while the guilty man may triumph and thus the course of justice be perverted: all ecclesiastical, secular and natural law as well as the law of nations declare such evil practices to be inadmissible, indeed unchristian, forbidden and totally abolished.'
Nevertheless it seems that some trace of this practice of 'ordeal' survived in the notion of a right of vengeance and in the formalities of jousting, and may have contributed something to the later customs of duelling; but the origins of duelling have not yet been accurately established.

3 The following passages from the anti-duelling Edicts of the seventeenth century are quoted from the *Corpus Juris Militaris* mentioned in the previous Note.

4 *Corpus Juris Militaris:* commentary by the author on Article XLIX of the Brandenburg Articles of War.

16 Prussia: Tribunals of Honour Introduced

1 A departmental minute in the Prussian Ministry of War, most of which reappeared in a secret 'Memorandum on Duelling and on the amendment of the Regulation on Tribunals of Honour of the 2nd May, 1874' (printed in Berlin, July 1896) contends that the Service Regulations of

Notes

1714, 1718, 1726 and 1743 indirectly recognised an officer's duty to demand and to give 'satisfaction'; but impartial study of the relevant passages will hardly bear this contention out. It obviously sprang from a desire to show that duelling had been officially countenanced by royal Orders back in the eighteenth century, and thereby to buttress the arguments being used at the end of the nineteenth.

2　Meanwhile Section 77 of the Landwehr-Ordinance prescribed that on annual manoeuvres there should be a tribunal of honour for each of the two battalions, chosen by the officers of both together. Its function was to settle all outstanding matters involving officers that had arisen during the year, as well as 'any irregularities in the conduct of individuals'. This system was also applied to 'the other parts of the Army' (i.e. to the Regular officers as well) by decision of the Minister of War, dated the 28th December 1817. In the following year the King set up a Commission to revise Military Law (including tribunals of honour and duelling-regulations) and placed it, by letters of the 18th April 1818, under the Minister of State, von Beyme, and Major-General von Grolman. On their proposal, Major-General von Thile was appointed to assist them. The Commission was to work in conjunction with the Department of Military Justice. On Grolman's resignation Major-General Rühle von Lilienstern joined Thile as Beyme's assistant (20th April 1820). On the 31st October 1825 the King transferred responsibility for the Commission to the Minister of Justice, von Danckelmann, personally, exhorting him to bring the work to the earliest possible conclusion without scamping it. Danckelmann reached final agreement with the Minister of War, von Hake, on the 30th December 1825, and completed his task. (Prussian Secret State Archives, Ministry of War, Central Dept., Akten, V.14.2.1.,vol.1.)

3　C. von Altrock: *Zur Geschichte des preussischen Offizierkorps* (in the work *Vom Sterben des deutschen Offizierkorps* (published by the author, Berlin, 1922) pp. 9ff. The assertion here quoted rests upon 'regimental histories and personal memoirs'.

4　Karl Heinrich Ludwig von Borstell made an important contribution to the victories of Grossbeeren and Dennewitz in 1813 but was sentenced to four years' detention in a fortress for disobeying Blücher's order to burn the colours of the mutinous Saxon regiments and shoot the ringleaders. He was pardoned in 1815. For his work as an army-reformer, see Meinecke: *Boyen*, vol. 1, pp. 171ff., and vol. 2, p. 87.

5　Under the Order (AKO.) of 1821 only subalterns and captains were subject to the tribunal of honour. Another important provision was that when the tribunal voted, the junior member should vote first, so as to preserve a maximum of independent judgment.

6　An unofficial but highly authoritative piece of guidance to officers on questions of honour, which also gives a picture of current ideas on the subject, is to be found in a lengthy communication, dated the 12th May 1828, from Duke Charles of Mecklenburg, general-officer commanding Guards Corps, to his officers. (Printed by A. v. Boguslawski in *Der Ehrbegriff des Offizierstandes:* Berlin, 1897.) This writer states that the Duke's memorandum was still being read again and again as a model

386

Notes

to all officers by regimental-commanders in the 'fifties and 'sixties in every Prussian unit.

I do not wish to make this part of my account still longer than I fear it is, lest I weary the reader. I shall therefore refrain from quoting this document. Besides, it largely consists of platitudes and artfully avoids the really awkward points.

7 The Commission was composed of Kamptz, Thile I, Rühle, Duncker and von Müller.

8 Cp. Meinecke: *Boyen*, vol. 2, pp. 514ff.

9 In addition to Boyen, the Commission now consisted of Knesebeck, Müffling, Natzmer, Stolberg and our old acquaintance Borstell.

10 Meinecke: *Boyen*, vol. 2, pp. 515f.

17 Prussia: Further Efforts, Councils of Honour and Reaction

1 Boyen's drafts were communicated on the 26th June 1842 for observations to the following general-officers commanding; Count Dohna (Königsberg), von Wrangel (Stettin), von Weyrach (Frankfurt-on-Oder), Count von Brandenburg (Breslau), von Pfuel (Münster), von Thile (Coblence), von Grolman (Posen), as well as to the brigade-commander Prince Radziwill (Berlin), the Inspector-General of the Engineer Corps, von Aster, the Inspector-General of Artillery, Prince Augustus of Prussia; to Prince William and Prince Charles of Prussia, and to the Minister of Justice, Mühler. Written observations by all the addressees, save Prince Charles and Grolman, are in the files. (Prussian Secret State Archives, Ministry of War, Central Department, V.14.2.1., vol. 2). Aster's observations, for example, include the remark that the *Offizierstand* partly owed its position and dignity in the State to prejudice, but that he had more respect for that prejudice than for an humanitarian outlook.

2 See also the Emperor William I's *Militärische Schriften*, I., pp. 442 ff.

3 The range of those subject to tribunals of honour could therefore now be extended without misgivings to staff-officers; but they were to have special 'benches', composed of staff-officers too; and this extension also covered gendarmerie-officers, reserve-officers, unemployed officers and officers retired with the right to wear uniform. Landwehr-officers were covered already. Loss of promotion was removed from the list of penalties which tribunals of honour could inflict: as the Prince of Prussia rightly observed, there was something rather unpleasant about junior officers voting for this penalty to be imposed on their seniors. But of course this reduction of the tribunal's powers entailed reducing the importance and authority of the institution as a whole, and it was no substitute to revive lesser penalties such as admonition, withdrawal of the uniform, and such like. One improvement, however, was the stricter regulation of procedure.

4 From a communication dated the 3rd September 1845, from Lieutenant-General von Neumann, Adjutant-General to the King, to the Minister of War, von Boyen. (Prussian Secret State Archives, Ministry of War, Central Department, V.14.2.1., vol. 2.)

Notes

5 From an undated and unsigned document in the Prussian Secret State Archives, Ministry of War, Central Dept., V.14.2.1., vol. 2, which bears only the registry-stamp for 1851. It is obviously a brief for the representative of the Prussian Minister of War to be used in the Berlin Constituent Assembly.

6 Stenographic reports of the National Assembly at Frankfort, published by Wigard (Frankfort-on-the-Main, 1849) 8 vols.

7 Letter written at Compiègne, 2nd August 1871, published in A. Dove's *Ausgewählte Schriften* (Leipzig, 1898) pp. 237f.

8 Orders (AKO) of the 6th August and 14th December 1872. The members of the Commission (see Akten, Reichsarchiv, V.14.2.1., vol. 4) were: Lt.-Gen. von Podbielski (Chairman); Lt.-Gen. von Pape, cmdg. the 1st Guards Infantry Div; Maj-Gen. von Danneberg, cmdg. the 4th Guards Infantry Bde; Col. Frhr. von Loë, cmdg. the 3rd Guards Cavalry Bde; Col. Bronsart von Schellendorf, cmdg. the 1st Guards Dragoon Regt; Major von Haugwitz, attd., Personnel Section, Ministry of War; Major von Derenthall, of the 'Kaiser Franz' Guards Grenadier Regt. No. 2; Major von Lettow of the Ministry of War; a representative of the Navy; the Auditor-General, Fleck; one Bavarian, one Wurtemberg and one Saxon staff-officer, and Col. von Caprivi also representing the Ministry of War at that Ministry's special request.

9 Von Werder, von Fransecky, von Manteuffel and von Tresckow.

18 Germany: The Gradual Victory of Personal over Collective Honour

1 On the 11th May 1912 in the 33rd session of the Budget Committee: stenographic report, p. 2.

2 In the *Reichstags-Drucksachen* No. 1, 13th Parliament, 1st Session, 1912–1913, there is a documentary summary of the 'previous debates in the Reichstag on the question of duelling' as 'Material for the XVIth Commission for preliminary examination of motions for solving the question of duelling'. The Commission had had this summary prepared by a deputy of the Centre Party named Werr; however, it records only the text of the motions and what became of them, but not the debate on them. The debates are preserved in the stenographic records only.

3 See Heinrich Dietz (Counsellor of the Court-Martial at Rastatt): *Disziplinarstrafrecht, Beschwerderecht, Ehrengerichtsbarkeit für Heer, Marine und Schutztruppen. Grundriss.* (Rastatt, 1916), part 3. On p. 81 we read that the sentence of a tribunal of honour 'under modern law is the Emperor (*der oberste Kriegsherr*). In Bavaria the King is partly replaced by the Ministry of War.' As regards the legal position there is an important passage on p. 84: 'The Regulations on tribunals of honour are to be regarded as military and naval orders, not as regulations on discipline. In Prussia they were issued without the counter-signature of a responsible Minister. In his capacity as supreme commander, the King was and is entitled to issue them. Their legal basis is Art. 46 of the Prussian Constitution.'

4 In Fontane's novel *Effi Briest*, which is set in the late nineteenth century, the Privy Councillor Wüllersdorf has this to say to Imstetten on the

Notes

question of duelling: 'That grandiose stuff you hear about 'God's tribunal' is rubbish, of course, absolute rubbish. It's the other way round. Our cult of honour is idolatry; but we have to submit to it as long as men believe in the idol.'

5 In the 76th Session of the Budget Committee of the Reichstag, 9th April 1913.

6 Akten, Ministry of War, Central Dept., V.14.2.1, vol. 2 in the Prussian Secret State Archives.

7 In a later memorandum of 1894 (Ministry of War, Central Dept., V.14.2.1, vol. 4. in the Reichsarchiv.) it is stated nevertheless that in 1817 to 1829 twenty officers lost their lives in duels.

8 The political upheaval of 1848 resulted in a reform of Bavarian criminal procedure by the law of the 10th November 1848. Under this law, Orders (AVO) were made on the 14th April 1856, 7th July 1862 and 31st March 1863, introducing a system of criminal procedure, applicable also to the Army, which adopted – albeit still within narrow limits – the principle of publicity on the military side, whereas unrestricted publicity had already been admitted for the civil courts. Officers and military authorities were allowed full access; access for non-commissioned officers and private soldiers was at the discretion of the commanding officer. There was no access for civilians. From 1862 onwards, however, access to the main proceedings was allowed to relatives, relatives-in-law and guardians of the accused. It was only with the Military Criminal Proceedings Order of the 29th April 1869 (in force from the 1st January 1870), that full civilian and military access to Bavarian military courts was permitted. (Information supplied by the staff of the Bavarian War Archives.)

9 Akten of the Prussian Ministry of War, Central Dept., V.14.2.1, vol. 5 in the Reichsarchiv.

19 The Reichswehr: The Third Reich

1 Wolfgang Foerster: *Generaloberst Ludwig Beck* (Munich, 1953), pp. 20ff.

2 From Reinhardt's account, *Der Aufbau der Reichswehr*, written in 1929–30 at the request of Friedrich Meinecke (who was then President of the Reich Historical Commission) for the Reichsarchiv in Potsdam. Quoted from Fritz Ernst: *Aus dem Nachlass des Generals Walther Reinhardt* (Stuttgart, 1958), p. 77.

3 This was pointed out, in particular, by Ernst Buchrucker in his critical pamphlet *Die Ehre des Soldaten* (Stollhamm: Oldenburg, 1953).

4 As described, convincingly, by Gessler himself in his memoirs, viz. Otto Gessler: *Reichswehrpolitik in der Weimarer Zeit*, ed. by K. Sendtner (Stuttgart, 1958) p. 304.

5 As recorded by Siegfried Westphal: *Heer in Fesseln. Aus den Papieren der Stabschefs von Rommel, Kesselring und Rundstedt* (Bonn, 1950) p. 79.

6 *Vor dem Sturm.* (Standard-Verlag edn., Hamburg, 1961) pp. 230–3.

7 Cp. Karl Demeter: *Tauroggen. Zur Problematik von Gehorsam, Eid, Verantwortung*, in *Veröffentlichungen des Instituts für Staatslehre und Politik*, Mainz: vol. 4. (Munich, 1954) pp. 415–25.

Notes

8 Moritz von Faber du Faur: *Macht und Ohnmacht. Erinnerungen eines alten Offiziers* (Stuttgart, 1955) p. 158. Likewise, *inter alia*, Ernst Buchrucker, *op. cit., passim*.

9 Quoted from Percy Ernst Schramm's introduction to the *Kriegstagebuch des Oberkommandos der Wehrmacht*, part 4 (Frankfort, 1961) pp. 1500f.

10 General Weygand: *Conférence Prononcée à l'Ecole Supérieure de Guerre*, 23rd February 1959 (no imprint), p. 4.

PART IV THE STATE

20 Relationship with the Sovereign: 'Liberalism'

1 *Das politische Gespräch* and *Die grossen Mächte*, last edited by Th. Schneider (Göttingen, 1958) p. 50 in that edn.
The substance of Ranke's historical judgment was elaborated by Hans Delbrück in his *Geschichte der Kriegskunst* and in the *Weltgeschichte* which he based thereon, as well as by Otto Hintze in his lecture on *Staatsverfassung und Heeresverfassung* (*Ges. Abhandlungen*), ed. by Fritz Hartung, vol. 1 (Leipzig, 1941) pp. 42ff. Ranke's basic thesis was overstrained and distorted in the National-Socialist interest by Ernst R. Huber in *Heer und Staat der deutschen Geschichte* (Hamburg, 1938): 2nd edn., enlarged 1943). Hans Herzfeld's contribution *Staats-, Gesellschafts- und Heeresverfassung* to the *Schicksalsfragen der Gegenwart* (see Note 34 to Ch. 2 herein), vol. 3, p. 10, recalls and continues the intellectual evolution of the idea.

2 Cp. *inter alia* Kurt Woltzendorff: *Der Gedanke des Volksheeres im deutschen Staatsrecht* (Tübingen, 1914). This book was written before the first World War and, as the title indicates, it deals with the Army as a whole. Only part of it, therefore, is relevant to the present enquiry. The same applies to the biographies, already quoted, of Stein, Scharnhorst, Gneisenau, and Boyen; but the relevant parts contain many a useful detail for our purposes, seen from the general aspect of the Army's constitution. Cf. also Fr. Meinecke: *Landwehr und Landsturm seit 1814*, in *Schmollers Jahrbuch*, 40th Year, part 3; and the same writer's discussion of *Boyen und Roon* in the *Historische Zeitschrift*, vol. 77 (1896). Also Also Richard Höhn: *Verfassungskampf und Heereseid*, 1938.

3 On this point, of Jany *op. cit.* and Wilhelm Rohr: *Die militärische Bestände des Preussischen Geh. Staatsarchivs und ihre Bedeutung für die Personen- und Familienforschung* (Leipzig, 1927).

4 Frederick William IV's class-conception of the State made a typical appearance when the Order on Tribunals of Honour was in draft. When they were discussing a regulation to govern disputes between officers and civilians, the King expressed a wish 'that students should be excluded, but that owners of feudal estates as well as civil servants should be covered' (Communication of the 6th July 1844 from the Ministry of War to the 'Allgemeines Kriegsdepartement': Prussian Secret State Archives, K.M.Zentraldepartement V.14.2.i, vol. 2). At a

Notes

period when the delimitation between public and private law had been put into effect in almost all other countries, in Prussia it was still possible to place the *Rittergutsbesitzer*, the owner of feudal property (a person of private law although exercising important public functions) in the same legal category as the civil servant (whose functions were entirely governed by public law).

5 M. Lehmann: *Stein*, vol. 2, p. 545.

6 Textually as recounted by the Saxon general, Gustav von Schubert, in his *Lebenserinnerungen*, ed. by Prof. Hans von Schubert (Stuttgart, 1909) p. 59.

7 This tale is told in full by Moritz von Süssmilch, who was present as a lieutenant. (Papers now in the Saxon Staatshauptarchiv in Dresden.)

8 Records of the enquiry in the Bavarian War Archives, A.XIII.3 fasc.4.

9 In Bavarian official language 'Reich' (the word the witness used) meant the Kingdom of Bavaria. Cp. for example, the name 'Allgemeines Reichsarchiv' which was still being applied to the Central Archives of the Bavarian State several years after the first World War.

10 Original in the Bavarian War Archives: A.IV.7. fasc.5.

11 This emerges from the hundreds of periodical reports on the attitude of individual regiments which I have examined in the Bavarian War Archives.

12 An officer who was appointed to the General Staff at the same time proved his earlier 'liberalism' in later years when, as a regimental-commander at Würzburg, he was the first to undertake large-scale measures for the relief of needy dependents of officers killed in action, and thereby put his progressive ideas to practical use within the limits set by his official position. For this information I am grateful to the late President of the Reichsarchiv, Mertz von Quirnheim.

12 Th. von Bernhardi: *Leben*, vol. 2, p. 168 and p. 355.

14 Friedrich von Bernhardi: *Denkwürdigkeiten*, p. 91.

15 In his report of the 15th February 1908. See K. Demeter: *Politische Berichte, op. cit.*

16 Edited by Friedrich Freiherr Hiller von Gaertringen (Göttingen, 1957) pp. 59f.

17 Adolf Stöcker (1835–1909) founded the *Christlichsoziale Partei* in 1878 and later introduced anti-semitism into German politics – though it was not based on race.

18 Cp. Lothar Wilfred Hilbert: *The Role of Military and Naval Attachés in the British and German Service, 1871–1914* (Doctor's Thesis, Cambridge, 1954) 392 pp. Reviewed in the *Historische Zeitschrift*, vol. 181 (1956) p. 726.
H. O. Meisner: *Militärattaches und Militärbevollmächtigte in Preussen und im Deutschen Reich* (Berlin, 1957).

21 Military Journalism: The Press, Politics, Civil Liberty

1 Friedrich von Berhardi's book *Der kommende Krieg* was not widely read in Germany itself, so far as can be ascertained; but it was very much

391

exploited abroad for purposes of propaganda against Pan-German militarism. Cp. *inter alia* the section on 'Germany before 1914' in Otto Gessler's memoirs, as regards the 'idealisation' of the war in a wide range of European countries.

2   This was the reason the General, a bachelor, gave his nephew for refusing to write any account of his life – according to the foreword to Thilo Krieg's biography of him (Berlin, 1903).

3   Circular from the Military Cabinet to all general-officers commanding; dated the 4th March 1876 and signed by von Albedyll.

4   From the text of the Order (AKO) of the 28th June 1877.

5   From the Military Cabinet's 'interpretation' (dated the 11th February 1908, signed by Count Hülsen-Haeseler and addressed to all general-officers commanding) of the Cabinet Order of the 4th March 1876. Akten, Mil.Kab.II.XXX.2. vol. 2 in the Reichsarchiv.

6   Cp. the account of the affair, and of the ministerial differences that arose from it, in Field-Marshal Count Waldersee's *Denkwürdigkeiten*, ed. by H. O. Meisner, vol. 1 (Stuttgart, 1922) pp. 257f.

7   Order (AKO) of the 13th June 1894.

8   Order (AKO) of the 23rd January 1897.

9   Opinion dated the 7th March 1914 and addressed to the Prussian Ministry of War. Reference as above.

10 So described in a communication of the 9th December 1911 from the Prussian Ministry of War to the Bavarian Military Plenipotentiary. Original in Akten der Z.1. des K.M., V.8.6. No. 1. (Reichsarchiv).

11 Alexander von Kluck: *Wanderjahre – Kriege – Gestalten* (Berlin, 1929) p. 41.

12 Notes for oral use at a meeting on 'Discussion of Questions of social Policy in Lectures to Troops', dated the 24th November 1906. Akten K.M., Armeeabteilung, I.9.1.No. 3, Heft 6 (Reichsarchiv).

13 Circular (*Erlass*) of the 5th April 1907.

14 Cp. Erich Otto Volkmann: *Der Marxismus und das deutsche Heer im Weltkriege* (Berlin, 1925) pp. 170f.

15 W. Groener: *Lebenserinnerungen* (Göttingen, 1957) p. 377.

22 Leadership, Discipline and the Humananitarian Spirit

1   On the problem of leadership as such (ignoring its racial and materialist hypertrophy under National-Socialism) the basic work is still Friedrich von Wieser's *Das Gesetz der Macht* (Vienna, 1926). See also various publications by Theodor Geiger, especially his short essay on *Führer und Genie* in the *Kölner Vierteljahrshefte für Soziologie*, 6th Year (1927), pp. 232ff. A survey which includes other points of view and theories, as well as a bibliography, is contained in the article *Führer* in the *Wörterbuch der Soziologie*, ed. by Wilhelm Bernsdorf and Friedrich Bülow. (Stuttgart, 1955) pp. 142–7.

2   Marmont: *Esprit des institutions militaires* (1845). The young Prince Frederich Charles wrote to Captain von Zastrow that the fourth and last part, 'The Philosophy of War', was written with rare beauty and truth and had greatly impressed him. Later, in 1874, he said it was this

book that had aroused in him a greater interest in his profession than the parade-ground had ever done. Cp. Wolfgang Foerster, *op. cit.* In this connection the following also deserve mention: Ernst van den Bergh: *Die seelischen Werte im Frieden und im Kriege* (Supplement to the *Militär-Wochenblatt*, 1906, pp. 205–36). Sperling: *Von Heer und neuer Zeit* with a preface by Friedrich Meinecke (Stuttgart, 1917). Kurt Hesse: *Feldherr Psychologos* (Berlin, 1922) and the answering brochure by F. von Rabenau: *Die alte Armee und die junge Generation* (Berlin, 1925). Reinhard Höhn: *Der Soldat und das Vaterland während und nach dem siebenjährigen Krieg* (Weimar, 1940).

Erich Schwinge: *Die Entwicklung der Mannszucht in der deutschen, britischen und französischen Wehrmacht seit 1914* (Berlin, 1940).

From the last post-war period, *Der deutsche Soldat in der Armee von morgen*, vol. 4 of the publications of the 'Institut fur Staatslehre und Politik' at Mainz (Munich, 1954). See therein especially Section IV: *Innere Struktur und Erziehung*, pp. 293–384.

H. von Böckmann: *Die Wandlung des deutschen Soldaten* (Berlin – Frankfurt a.M., 1956) and lastly

Rolf Elble: *Vom künftigen deutschen Offizier* (Bonn, c. 1956) especially Section 6: *Der Offizier als Führer.*

3 Gustav Schmoller: *Die Entstehung des preussischen Heeres von 1640–1740*; in *Deutsche Rundschau* 1877, pp. 248–73. H. Delbrück: *Geschichte der Kriegskunst*, vol. 2 (Berlin, 1920) pp. 299ff.

Eugen von Frauenholz: *Entwicklungsgeschichte des deutschen Heerwesens* (mainly documents) vols. 2 and 3 (Munich, 1936–39).

4 Cf. G. Droysen: *Beiträge zur Geschichte des Militärwesens während der Epoche des Dreissigjährigen Krieges:* in *Zeitschrift für deutsche Kulturgeschichte*, N.F., 4th Year, 1875; and Frauenholz, *op. cit.*, vol. 3.

5 Delbrück: *op. cit.*, vol. 3.

6 Details of the early history of modern methods of drill are now available in Werner Hahlweg's probationary treatise (*Habilitationsschrift*): *Die Heeresreform der Oranier und die Antike* (Berlin, 1941).

7 From Delbrück, *op. cit.*, vol. 4, p. 300.

8 Meinecke: *Boyen*, vol. 1, pp. 30ff.

9 E. M. Arndt: *Staat und Vaterland. Auswahl aus seinen politischen Schriften.* Ed. with an introduction by E. Müsebeck (Munich, 1921) pp. 10ff.

10 Meinecke: *Boyen*, vol. 2, pp. 541f.

11 *Handbuch für die untersuchungsführenden Offiziere und Beisitzer der Kriegs- und Standgerichte der Königlich-Preussischen Armee*, containing *Die ersten Begriffe und Grundsätze des Criminalrechtes*, by E. Erhard, 'Brigade-Ober-Auditeur' (Merseburg, 1818) p. 39.

12 According to Edwin von Manteuffel in a letter of the 27th July 1877 to Ranke. The letter is printed in A. Dove's *Ausgewählte Schriftchen* (Leipzig, 1898) p. 288.

13 Foerster, *op. cit.*, vol. 1, pp. 106f.

14 Draft regulations on Promotions in the Bavarian Army. Bavarian War Archives: K.M.-Archiv. A.III. 1a. fasc. 16a.

15 Akten, Bavarian War Archives, A.IV.1.

16 Essay of 1815 on '*Die Aristokratie*'. Müsebeck, *op. cit.* (see Note 10).

Notes

23 Maltreatment of Subordinates

1 Cp. Karl Demeter: *Der Geist der deutschen Sozialpolitik vor dem Kriege* in *Preussische Jahrbücher*, 1924, pp. 67ff.

24 The Weimar Republic: The 'non-political' Reichswehr

1 Sallust: *Catilina* II, 4. *Nam imperium facile iis artibus retinetur, quibus initio partum est.*

2 Quoted from Otto-Ernst Schüddekopf: *Das Heer und die Republik. Quellen zur Politik der Reichswehrführung 1918–1933* (Hanover, 1955) p. 48.

3 Fritz Ernst, *op. cit.* (Stuttgart, 1958).

4 Major Fleck, in a memorandum to be found at p. 54 in Ernst, *op. cit.* Reinhardt himself wrote a memorandum in 1930 on *Aufbau der Reichswehr* for the *Historische Reichskommission beim Reichsarchiv. Ibidem*, p. 80.

5 Reinhardt, in the commemorative volume issued by the Reichsregierung on the tenth anniversary of the Constitution – 11th August 1929 (Berlin, 1929) pp. 177–82.

6 According to Schüddekopf, *op. cit.*, pp. 266f. relying especially on Herman Rauschning: *Die Revolution des Nihilismus* (Zurich-New York, 1938), 5th edn., pp. 209ff.

7 From Gustav Adolf Caspar: *Die sozialdemokratische Partei und das deutsche Wehrproblem in den Jahren der Weimarer Republik* (Supplement 11 in the *Wehrwissenschaftliche Rundschau*) 1959.

8 These and many of the following points are fully expounded in Wolfgang Sauer: *Die Mobilmachung der Gewalt*, Part III of the book by K. D. Bracher, W. Sauer and C. Schultz: *Die nationalsozialistische Machtergreifung* (Cologne, 1960). The same writer has expanded his views in chapter IX (on *Die Reichswehr*) of K. D. Bracher's *Die Auflösung der Weimarer Republik* (2nd edn. Stuttgart-Düsseldorf, 1957). See also Thilo Vogelsang: *Die Reichswehr und die Politik, 1918–1934* (*Schriftenreihe der Niedersächsischen Landeszentrale für Heimatdienst. Zeitgeschichte – Heft 1*) 1959.

9 How far these matters still are from being finally cleared up was shown by the large number of well-informed letters that were sent to the *Frankfurter Allgemeine* in the weeks following its issue of the 1st March 1961 in which its *Dokumenten-Beilage* had published an article on the 'Kapp-Putsch' by Dolf Sternberger.

10 From Rabenau, *op. cit.*, p. 470.

11 On this point, cf. *inter alia*, Hermann Teske: *Die silbernen Spiegel. Generalstabsdienst unter der Lupe* (Heidelberg, 1952). It contains the writer's important personal account of the complicity of graduates of the *Offiziersschulen*. See also Thilo Vogelsang: *Die Reichswehr in Bayern und der Münchener Putsch 1923*, in *Vierteljahrshefte für Zeitgeschichte*, 5th Year (1957) pp. 91ff.

12 This period is thus described by Helmut Krausnick in his study *Vorgeschichte und Beginn des militärischen Widerstandes gegen Hitler* in *Vollmacht des Gewissens* (issued by the '*Europäische Publikation*' *e.V.*, Frankfurt a.M., 1960) p. 184.

Notes

13 According to Schüddekopf, *op. cit.*, Note 685, p. 268, the following people were concerned:

Lt. Richard Scheringer, b. 1904, only son of a regular officer killed in 1915. Said to have tried to stop a Separatist printing-plant during the struggle in the Ruhr. Finished his education in 1924 and later became an officer. Later still he joined the Communist Party.

Lt. Ludin, son of a professor at the 'Realschule' at Freiburg i.Br., brought up in an artistic, non-political atmosphere. In 1924 he too became an officer. Later he became a high-ranking Storm-Troop leader, and from 1940 he was German Minister in Slovakia.

Ober-Lt. (retd.) Wendt then belonged to Otto Strasser's 'Black Front'. From the fortress where he was confined, Scheringer wrote an open letter on the 28th October 1930 to Groener, in which he said, in part: 'The Herr Minister quotes General von Seeckt, saying he too was attacked by political parties and had to "compromise" also.' This is not the place to discuss the political views of the former Chief of the Army Staff; but General von Seeckt and the Reichswehr Minister Gessler never swerved from the basic military principles of discipline, comradeship, honour and fighting spirit. In those days the troops felt themselves high above all political parties; they felt themselves the nucleus of a future army of liberation, an unassailable pillar of the Reich. No one had any doubts then. Later, things changed. The struggle between the fighting soldier and the bureaucrat began.... (Quoted from Schüddekopf, *op. cit.*, pp. 302f.)

14 To make this mental process clearer, let me quote part of an article by a Reichswehr officer on 'Reichswehr and National-Socialism' that appeared in the *Berliner Börsenzeitung* on the 23rd November 1930. '...The "national" parts of National-Socialist thought have found whole-hearted support in the Army; but there are the most serious misgivings about National-Socialist aims. They cover the whole social field and they leave no room for an officer to say "but". The average officer is poor himself and he normally comes from a class with a modest income, so that he knows enough about most people's financial worries to understand them. For a true officer it has always been a matter of honour and duty to help other people who were hard up. But the word "socialist" has an unpleasant ring in officers' ears.' (Quoted from Schüddekopf, *op. cit.*, pp. 320–2.)

15 According to Dorothea Groener-Geyer's life of her father: *General Groener, Soldat und Staatsmann* (Frankfurt a.M., 1955) p. 273. Mention must also be made of Franz Woertz: *Die Verschwörung der Offiziere.* '*Tat*', 22nd Year, (1930), pp. 610–19.

25 The Impact of National Socialism

1 Quoted from Geyer-Groener, *op. cit.*, pp. 276f.

2 According to W. Sauer: *Mobilmachung der Gewalt*, p. 738, which gives sources from publications and from written evidence in the Munich 'Institut für Zeitgeschichte'.

3 A photographic copy of this document (Appendix I to the so-called

Notes

'Kaltenbrunner Report' of the 25th August 1944) was supplied to me by Dr Jacobsen, to whom my sincere thanks are due. The text seems generally authentic. It is only in the wording of the passages which do not give a *verbatim* account of Oster's statements that the editor has obviously injected a Nazi tinge.

4 Schüddekopf, *op. cit.*, p. 275, which names further sources.

5 The original is in Beck's papers in the 'Bundesarchiv-Militärarchiv' at Coblence. On Beck's resistance-group, see *Vollmacht des Gewissens, op. cit.*, pp. 427ff.

6 *Generalfeldmarschall Keitel – Verbrecher oder Offizier? Erinnerungen, Briefe, Dokumente des Chefs OKW*, ed. by Walter Görlitz (Göttingen, 1961) p. 393. For comparison see P. E. Schramm's introduction to vol. 4 (which he edited) of the OKW's War Diary (Frankfurt a.M., 1961) esp. p. 73.

7 Görlitz, *op. cit.*, p. 51.

8 From Beck's papers: first printed by Friedrich Hossbach: *Zwischen Wehrmacht und Hitler 1934–1938* (Wolfenbüttel-Hanover, 1949) pp. 68–72. The important entries are printed fairly accurately, as I have been able to establish by comparing them with Beck's papers now in the 'Bundesarchiv-Militärarchiv'. The notes should be compared with *Vollmacht des Gewissens, op. cit.*, p. 226, note 122.

9 See Hermann Teske: *Die silbernen Spiegel*, p. 32, and W. Sauer: *Mobilmachung der Gewalt*, p. 739. Mertz was the only son of the first President of the 'Reichsarchiv' at Potsdam.

10 Details about him will be found in the *Geschichte der Ritter des Ordens Pour le Mérite im Weltkrieg*, p. 307. Hitler later appointed him *SS-Obergruppenfuhrer* and awarded him the '*goldenes Parteiabzeichen*'. He died at St Blasien on the 19th May 1939. For these facts I am much obliged to Col. Teske of the 'Bundesarchiv-Militärarchiv.'

11 Letter from Halder in Beck's papers; printed in part by Wolfgang Foerster: *Generaloberst Ludwig Beck. Sein Kampf gegen den Krieg* (Munich, 1953), pp. 27ff. According to a note by Foerster, Beck showed Halder's letter (which touched on other political problems as well) to Fritsch, and also brought it to the notice of the chief of the counter-espionage service.

12 Quoted from Hossbach: *Entwicklung des Oberbefehls 1655–1945* (Würzburg, 1957), p. 105. Cp. also Hermann Mau: *Die 'zweite Revolution' – der 30. Juni 1934* in *Vierteljahreshefte für Zeitgeschichte*, 1st Year (1953), pp. 119–37.

26 The Oath to Hitler's Person and its Consequences

1 His letter of the 15th January 1952 was addressed to Wolfgang Foerster. See the latter's above-quoted book, pp. 26f.

2 This comes from a carefully documented article in the *Frankfurter Allgemeine* of the 26th July 1956 written by Dr Karl Otmar Freiherr von Aretin, of the staff of the 'Institut fur Europäische Geschichte' at Mainz.

3 Cf. Siegfried Westphal: *Heer in Fesseln*, p. 42.

Notes

4 Görlitz: Keitel, *op. cit.*, p. 112.

5 According to Gerald Reitlinger: *The SS, Alibi of a Nation, 1922–1945* (London, 1956) pp. 76–79. Using German sources he tabulates the origins and previous history of the Waffen-SS officers, both the professional and, in part, the sociological points of view.

6 Printed issue of the Order *Zwischenfälle zwischen Wehrmacht und SS* in the publications of the 'Bundesarchiv-Militärarchiv', B.23. No signature.

7 Erich Raeder: *Mein Leben*, 2 vols. (Tübingen, 1956–7) vol. 2, pp. 116f.

8 Sources are given in W. Sauer: *Mobilmachung der Gewalt*, p. 740.

9 See for comparison, and on the differences between the three arms of the Wehrmacht, Erich von Manstein: *Aus einem Soldatenleben, 1887–1939* (Bonn, 1958) p. 269c.

10 Printed issue of the Regulation in the publications of the 'Bundesarchiv-Militärarchiv': printed without signature.

11 Texts of both documents in H.-A. Jacobsen: *1939–1945. Der zweite Weltkrieg in Chronik und Dokumenten* (5th edn. Darmstadt, 1961).

12 Quoted textually from notes by General Blaskowitz for an oral report to the Commander-in-Chief of the Army on the 15th February 1940. *Ibidem:* pp. 606ff.

13 The phrase is from W. Görlitz' postscript as editor of the book on *Keitel, op. cit.*, p. 416.

14 Jacobsen, *op. cit.*, pp. 571 and 573.

15 Full text *ibidem*, pp. 578f.

16 Printed by Waldemar Besson, *NSFO, op. cit.*, pp. 76 ff, Doct.3.

17 *Ibidem*, p. 81.

18 *Ibidem*, Doct. 14.

19 H. R. Trevor-Roper: *The Last Days of Hitler* (London, 1946) p. 38.

20 *op. cit.* (see Note 4 to chap. 25) p. 28.

21 See especially Hans Rothfels: *Die Opposition gegen Hitler* (2nd edn., Krefeld, 1951) and also the *Vierteljahreshefte für Zeitgeschichte* which he had edited since 1953.

22 In his novel *Vor dem Sturm* (collected edn. of Fontane's works: Standard-Verlag, Hamburg) vol. 7–8, p. 230.

PART V SOCIETY

27 Introduction: 'Community' and 'Society'

1 See the relevant articles entitled *Anpassung, Gesellschaft, Masse* and others, in the *Wörterbuch der Soziologie* (Bernsdorf and Bülow, Stuttgart, 1955), also Arnold Gehlen: *Sozial-psychologische Probleme der industriellen Gesellschaft*, 1949.

28 The Churches, the Sects, the Freemasons

1 On these aspects of Protestantism, see also Ernst Müsebeck: *Schleiermacher* (Berlin, 1927).

2 Cf. Joh. B. Kissling: *Geschichte des Kulturkampfes im Deutschen Reiche*,

vol. 1 (Freiburg i.Br. 1911), also Georg Franz: *Kulturkampf* (Munich, no date, but recent).

3 Royal Order (AKO) dated 26th January 1895.

4 Akten Mil.-Kab. *betr. Offizierersatz*, I.1.15., vol. 3 (Reichsarchiv).

5 Cf. M. Buchner: *Kaiser Wilhelm II, seine Weltanschauung und die deutschen Katholiken* (Leipzig, 1929).

6 For details see *Vollmacht des Gewissens*, p. 277, note 139.

7 Bernhard Vollmer: *Volksopposition im Polizeistaat. Gestapo und Regierungsberichte, 1934–1936. (Quellen und Darstellungen zur Zeitgeschichte)*, vol. 2 (Stuttgart, 1957) pp. 139 and 156.

8 Erich Raeder: *op. cit.* has a pretty full account of these things in vol. 2, pp. 136–48, part of which covers the Army too. See also Friedrich Hossbach: *Zwischen Wehrmacht und Hitler*, p. 53, Siegfried Westphal, *op. cit.*, p. 21 and *Vollmacht des Gewissens*, pp. 277–82.

9 Helmut Krausnick, *op. cit.*, p. 281.

10 From Besson, *op. cit.*, pp. 8off. These facts come from the files of the *Arbeitsstab NSFO (Ruder)* in the Party Headquarters. The papers include a draft by Ruder entitled *Ein Jahr NS-Führungsarbeit in der Wehrmacht* according to which the *NS-Führungs*-staffs comprised 96 officers in OKW, of whom 14 were regulars and 82 reservists, while 74 were Party-members and 57 *Gottgläubige*; 20 officers in the Army, of whom 12 were *Gottgläubige*; 38 officers in the Luftwaffe; 32 officers in the Navy, of whom 19 were Party-members and 19 *Gottgläubige*.

11 See Lenning's *Allgemeines Handbuch der Freimaurerei*, 3rd edn. (2 vols.: Leipzig, 1900–01): also Lennhoff and Posner: *Internationales Freimaurerlexikon* (Vienna, 1932).

12 *Volksschöpfung* is the title of his reminiscences of the years 1919 to 1925 (6th thousand: Munich, 1940) dedicated to his 'wife and companion Dr Mathilde Ludendorff, who showed the way to the German idea of God'.

13 Order by the OKH, dated the 2nd December 1939: Subject – Transfer of personnel from regular units to the Medical Corps (Army). (*Heeresverordnungsblatt – 1939 A.B.* pp. 357–60). It was therein laid down that an applicant who had left a Lodge or anything of the sort must submit either a certificate of dismissal or some other paper from the Lodge showing the date of his final cessation of membership, as well as a certificate of 'no objection' from the Party.

14 Beck's papers, *op. cit.*, folios 73 and 73a. Also Wolfgang Foerster, *op. cit.*, pp. 20–22.

29 *The Jews*

1 A case which formed an exception to this rule is recounted by Prince Bülow, the former Chancellor, in his memoirs, viz. when the Prince of Prussia had to leave Berlin on the 20th March 1848 and flee to England, he was lent a carriage as far as Spandau, and thence a boat to the Pfaueninsel, by a strongly monarchist Jewish banker named Mossner. In the 'sixties the Prince, then King, commissioned Mossner's son, despite serious opposition, into one of the most 'feudal' of Prussian

Notes

cavalry-regiments. After distinguished service in two wars the son became a general and was ennobled by William II.

2 *Das jüdische Bekenntnis als Hintergrund bei der Beförderung zum preussischen Reserveoffizier* (Berlin, 1911). See also the brochure by Dr Max J. Löwenthal (on behalf of the *Verband der deutschen Juden*): *Jüdische Reserveoffiziere* (Berlin, 1914).

3 Secret order by the Prussian Minister of War, 14th December 1895. Acta Gen. des K.M.Zentraldepartement V.8.6. No. 1, vol. 3 (Reichsarchiv).

4 Akten des preuss. K.M., Armee-Abtlg., Geheim I.9.1. No. 3, Heft 7 (Reichsarchiv).

5 This excellent definition comes from Siegfried Westphal's memoirs, p. 21.

6 See the *Kriegsbriefe gefallener deutscher Juden*, first published in 1935. New edn., Stuttgart, 1961, with a preface by the Federal Defence Minister, Franz Josef Strauss.

7 Letter of the 3rd November 1918 to his wife announcing his transfer from General HQ to the Ministry of War in Berlin (from Fritz Ernst, *op. cit.*, p. 5).

8 Reich 'Law on Citizenship', and 'Law on the Protection of German Blood and German Honour', adopted at the *Reichsparteitag* at Nuremberg, 15th September 1935).

9 Erich Raeder, *op. cit.*, vol. 2, p. 132.

10 Léon Poliakov and Josef Wulf: *Das Dritte Reich und seine Diener. Dokumente* (2nd edn., Berlin, 1956). Part III deals with the Wehrmacht. The documents mainly come from the great archives of the *Centre de Documentation Juive Contemporaine* in Paris, and most of them were published for the first time in this book. Others are from the archives of the International Military Tribunal at Nuremberg.

11 Jacobsen: *Der zweite Weltkrieg* (5th edn.) p. 581, document No. 195.

12 From Poliakov and Wulf, *op. cit.*, p. 460.

13 Frido von Senger und Etterlin's memoirs: *Krieg in Europa* (Cologne-Berlin, 1960) p. 434 in the section *Die Niederlage Hitler-Deutschlands und ihre Ursachen*.

30 Morals, 'Materialism', 'Militarism', Manners

1 According to an Order from the War Minister, von Kameke, to all general-officers commanding, dated the 27th June 1879. Akten K.M., Nachr.-Abt., II.2.1. No. 3. vol. 1 (Reichsarchiv).

2 Order by the War Minister, dated the 15th October 1896 (*ibidem* vol. 3).

3 Rescript of the 14th July 1832. Draft in the K.M.-Archiv Kap. XIV No. 2 in the Bavarian Kriegsarchiv.

4 Rescript of the 25th November 1810. Bavarian Kriegsarchiv, A.IV.7., fasc. 5.

5 Dated Berlin, 19th February 1841. Akten, Mil.-Kab.I.1.15., vol. 1. Prussian Secret State Archives.

6 This is quoted from an Order by the Saxon Minister of War, dated the

9th February 1900 (Reichsarchiv, Zweigstelle Dresden: Archiv des K.M., *Abt. für die pers. Ang.*, lfd. No. 160) which also pointed out that it was the duty of regimental-commanders to keep themselves posted at all times about the private life of their officers. But the same attitude to such matters is to be found outside Saxony too, almost identically worded. There is no need to quote other examples.

One special problem that is relevant was whether officers' commissions could be granted to those who were either illegitimate or born before their parents' marriage. As regards Bavaria the not infrequent appearance of such persons in the *Offiziersgrundbücher* shows that throughout the nineteenth century such cases presented no difficulty. The Prussian corps of officers, however, seems to have been 'stickier'; but the archives of the Military Cabinet for the last years before 1914 mention cases in which one such young man was commissioned into the regular Army and another into the Reserve. In the case of the first, the officers of the regiment raised such objection that the Emperor had to intervene on the young man's behalf, while proposing transfer to another regiment. In the end the ensign resigned in order to transfer to the Bavarian Army.

7 Cp. Major-Gen. (retd.) Paul von Schmidt: *Das deutsche Offiziertum und die Zeitströmungen* (Berlin, 1892).

8 This particular importance of the 'onlooker' as regards group-psychology was also pointed out by Alfred Vierkandt in his *Gesellschaftslehre* (Stuttgart, 1923), especially in chapter 5 on *die Kollektiv-phänomene und die Gruppe*.

9 On this point cp. also Vierkandt, *op. cit.*, p. 370.

10 A similar line of thought is suggested by Oldwig von Uechtritz in his instructive book: *Das deutsche Offizierkorps und seine Bedeutung für Königtum und Gesellschaft* (Heilbronn, 1887).

11 W. Sombart: *Die deutsche Volkswirtschaft im 19. Jahrhundert* (7th edn., Berlin, 1927) pp. 358ff.
Theodor Freiherr von der Goltz: *Geschichte der deutschen Landwirtschaft in Preussen und Deutschland, 1800–1930* (Würzburg, 1960).

12 Order of the 2nd December 1841. Akten Mil.-Kab.I.1.15, vol. 1 in the Prussian Secret State Archives.

13 Mentioned by Bismarck in a letter of the 22nd June 1851 from Frankfurt to Leopold von Gerlach (*Bismarckbriefe*, ed. by Horst Kohl, 6th edn., Leipzig, 1897, pp. 70f.).

14 Royal Order (AKO) of the 9th December 1845. (For source see Note 12.)

15 On a memorandum by General Freiherr Roth von Schreckenstein, dated Münster, 12th July 1856, on ways and means of preventing junior officers from getting into debt. (Source as above.)

16 Akten des Kriegsministeriums, Zentraldepartement, *generalia betr. Ehrengerichte*, vol. 3 (Reichsarchiv).

17 See von der Osten-Sacken: *Preussens Heer*, vol. 3 (Berlin, 1914) p. 330.

18 The impression is often given that the foundation of the new German Empire and the injection of a few milliards from France had launched the German people into materialist ways. I think my account of the

relevant state of affairs in the Prussian corps of officers during the previous thirty years has incidentally shown that this process had begun much earlier. The *Gründerjahre* only hastened it.

19 Gustav von Schubert, *op. cit.*, p. 447.

20 Major-Gen. Freiherr von Wechmar, for example, sent the Crown Prince a similar memorandum suggesting improvements. The Prince was especially struck by his suggestion that the councils of honour might be empowered to act in these matters too as an independent, *ex officio* advisory body to regimental-commanders. On the 30th March 1876 the Crown Prince sent the whole document to the Military Cabinet intending that the latter should, at its discretion, submit extracts from it to the Emperor for consideration.

21 Royal Order (AKO) of the 17th June 1886. Amplified by William II in a Cabinet Order dated at Abbazia, the 27th March 1894.

22 Electoral Decree of the 17th September 1753. Münich: *Geschichte der Entwicklung der Bayerischen Armee* (Munich, 1864).

23 The details of the transplantation of Prussian institutions and principles to Bavarian soil needs much closer investigation. As a matter of intellectual history they would be of interest in connection with current problems too.

24 Communication to the Ministry of War, dated Munich 17th April 1827. Bavarian 'Kriegsarchiv', A.XII.3, fasc. 2.

25 On this, see Kauffmann's polemical work: *Die Vorrechte der Offiziere im Staate und in der Gesellschaft* (issued anonymously; Berlin 1883) which was provoked by one section of the book by Colmar Freiherr von der Goltz: *Das Volk in Waffen* (Berlin, 1883). In its turn it gave rise to several rejoinders and counter-rejoinders and was thoroughly discussed both at home and abroad. See also the small book by Felix Priebatsch, the Prussian historian: *Geschichte des preussischen Offizierkorps* (Berlin, 1919) which devotes some attention to the way in which the modern Prussian officer was treated in light literature (e.g. the *Gartenlaube* and in caricature.

26 A useful guide here is Hans Herzfeld's essay: *Zur neueren Literatur über das Heeresproblem in der deutschen Geschichte* in *Vierteljahreshefte für Zeitgeschichte*, 4th Year (1956), pp. 361–86.
See also pp. 21 ff. of Gerhard Ritter's public lecture to the 22nd Conference of German Historians in 1953, published in the *Historische Zeitschrift*, vol. 177 (1954); and later, with far-ranging arguments, in his book *Staatskunst und Kriegshandwerk. Das Problem des 'Militarismus' in Deutschland*, vol. 1 (2nd revised edn., Munich, 1959), vol. 2, 1890–1914 (Munich, 1960). Vol. 3 (1914–1945) is in preparation. See also the review in the *Zeitschrift für Politik*, N.F.I/1954 pp. 379–85, and Ludwig Dehio's unfavourable review: *Um den deutschen Militarismus*, in the *Historische Zeitschrift*, vol. 180 (1955), pp. 43–64. See also Karl Kautsky: *Sozialismus und Krieg* (Prague, 1937), p. 383: 'The influence of the soldiers on policy is the test of what can be described as militarism. That influence is not to be measured simply by the size of the army. A militia-army' (the pet scheme of the German Social-Democrats' defence-policy) 'will be far larger than a standing army but will never

let its corps of officers dominate politics.' The book gives no references whatever.

27 Some references to books on the subject are given on p. 238 of Wolfgang Sauer's *Die Reichswehr*. See in addition O. H. von der Gablenz: *Das preussisch-deutsche Offizierkorps*, in *Schicksalsfragen der Gegenwart, op. cit.*, pp. 47ff.

28 Recounted by Dr Richard Jaeger, vice-president of the German Bundestag at Bonn, in his lecture *Heer und Staat in der Bundesrepublik*, published in *Schicksalsfragen der Gegenwart*, vol. 3, p. 207.

29 Franz Karl Endres: *Soziologische Struktur und ihr entsprechende Ideologien des deutschen Offizierkorps vor dem Weltkriege* in the *Archiv für Sozialwissenschaft und Sozialpolitik*, vol. 58 (1927), part 2, pp. 282–319.

31 The Reichswehr: National Socialism

1 Rabenau: *Seeckt*, p. 508.
2 Dietrich von Choltitz, a former cadet at Dresden, spent most of his service in eastern Germany and ended the second World War as military governor of Paris. His memoirs, *Soldat unter Soldaten*, aim at throwing special light on 'the human side of things'.

32 German and other Ideals of Conduct

1 See in particular the following:
W. Dibelius *England*, vol. 1 (Stuttgart, 1923) pp. 127 ff.
Agnes von Zahn-Harnack: *Die Schule der grossen Welt. Eine Goethe-Studie* (in *Preussische Jahrbücher*, August 1928).
Friedrich G. Kleinwächter: *Der deutsch-österreichische Mensch und der Anschluss* (Vienna, 1927), sections on *Der Aristokrat*, pp. 71ff., and *Die Bürger*, pp. 104ff.
R. N. Count Coudenhove-Kalergi: *Adel*, 1923.
Franz Oppenheimer: *System der Soziologie*, vol. 1, pp. 702ff., and vol. 2, p. 669.
Werner Sombart: *Der Bourgeois* (Munich, 1913).
Joachim H. Knoll: *Führungsauslese* (Stuttgart, 1957).

Appendix 4

1 Werner Sombart: *Krieg und Kapitalismus* (Munich-Leipzig, 1913).
Hans Delbrück: *Geschichte der Kriegskunst*, vol. 4. (Berlin, 1920).
2 The various views that modern historians have put forward on the factors that gave rise to manorial rights (*Gutsherrschaft*) in eastern Germany were collected and reviewed, but only partially refuted, by G. v. Below in *Territorium und Stadt. Aufsätze zur deutschen Verfassungs-Verwaltungs- und Wirtschaftsgeschichte.* (Munich, 1900: not the 2nd edn. of 1923), sections 1 and 2. Cp. also the relevant chapters in Richard Schröder: *Lehrbuch der deutschen Rechtsgeschichte.* 6th edn., continued by Eberhard Frhr. v. Künssberg (Berlin, 1922) and see also

inter alia W. Wittich: *Die Grundherrschaft in Nordwestdeutschland* (Leipzig 1896) and

G. F. Knapp: *Grundherrschaft und Rittergut*. (Leipzig, 1897), especially pp. 77–100.

3 Characteristic evidence is provided by a critical paper written in 1609 by the ruling Count John VII of Nassau. On grounds of sociology and development-policy he complains that 'the patricians (*Geschlechter*) are waxing and the knights (*Reutter*) are waning'. In support he observes that 'great nobles', contrary to the laudable custom of the past, 'grant no more land in fee, but call grants in'. Quoted from his *Discurs das itzige Teutsche Kriegswesen belangendt* in the 'Hauptstaatsarchiv' at Wiesbaden, Abt.171K938. Other interesting passages are quoted and the whole document carefully assessed by Gerh. Oestreich: *Eine Kritik des deutschen Heerwesens am Vorabend des Dreissigjährigen Krieges*, in *Nassauische Annalen*, vol. 70 (1959) pp. 227–36.

4 Cp. Franz Oppenheimer: *System der Soziologie*. (Jena, 1922–26) vol. 2, pp. 597ff. and

G. V. Below: *Die Ursachen der Rezeption des römischen Rechts in Deutschland*. (Munich, 1905.)

5 From Stintzing and Landsberg: *Geschichte der deutschen Rechtswissenschaft*. (Munich, 1880–1910) I, p. 61. Reprinted in 3 sections and 4 vols., 1957.

6 Printed in Hans Schmelzle: *Der Staatshaushalt des Herzogtums Bayern im 18. Jahrhundert*. (Stuttgart, 1900) p. 197 and see also pp. 24f.

7 There is need for a closer study of the reasons why the higher civil service in Bavaria had, at least as early as the last quarter of the eighteenth century, provided so much larger a part of the officer-intake than was the case in contemporary Prussia. There are regrettable lacunae in the constitutional, administrative, military and social history of Bavaria, particularly for the nineteenth century. As an introduction to the matter, Walter Schärl's *Die Zusammensetzung der bayerischen Beamtenschaft von 1806–1918* is worth mention (Kallmünz Opf. 1955: Münchener Histor. Studien, Abt. Bayer. Geschichte. Hrsg. von Max Spindler: Band I.). Cp. my own review in the *Vierteljahrschrift für Sozial und Wirtschaftsgeschichte*, 45/1 (1958), pp. 109f.

On the above-mentioned general postulates see also Karl Alexander v. Müller: *Probleme der neuesten bayerischen Geschichte* (1799–1871). *Probe-Vorlesung an der Universität München*, in the *Historische Zeitschrift* 118 (1917) pp. 222ff.

8 Kreittmayr: *Anmerkungen über den Cod. Maximilianeum Bav. civilem*. (Munich, 1758–66) Pars 5, Cap. 22, S. 14. Quoted from Schmelzle, *op. cit.*, pp. 26f.

9 There has been little study of the patriciate's history after the guilds had driven it out of municipal government. The major work is the one by Roth von Schreckenstein mentioned in Note 1 to Chapter 7, though he will not command assent on every point; see also his earlier study of *Das Patriziat in den deutschen Städten* (Freiburg, c. 1865). A useful supplement to this is Siegmund Keller's essay *Der Adelsstand des süddeutschen Patriziats*, pp. 741–58 of the *Festschrift zum 70. Geburtstag Otto Gierkes*. (Weimar, 1911) also H. F. Friederichs: *Das mittelalterliche*

Patriziat. Neue Erkenntnisse und neue Probleme, in *Nassauische Annalen* vol. 69 (1958) pp. 312ff. The discussion continues.

10   On this point see especially the summary by Werner Sombart: *Der moderne Kapitalismus*, vol. 1 (1st and 5th edns.). In general, alas, there is still a great shortage of detailed investigation of the personal aspects of modern German economic history.

11   Typical documentary evidence will be found in Max Lehmann: *Stein*, vol. 1, pp. 88ff. and also in Otto Hintze: *Preussische Reformbestrebungen vor 1806*, in the *Historische Zeitschrift* 76, pp. 422ff.

12   From J. Conrad: *Agrarstatistische Untersuchungen*, in *Conrad's Jahrbücher*, N.F., vol. 16 (1888) pp. 138ff, and *ibidem*, 3rd series, vol. 2 (1891) which contains a special study of east- and west-Prussia only.

13   According to Jastrow: *Die Volkszahl deutscher Städte zu Ende des Mittelalters und zu Beginn der Neuzeit* (Berlin, 1886). Berlin, an Electoral capital, had at most 14,000 inhabitants in about 1500, whereas Nuremberg had 40–50,000 already.

14   Werner Sombart: *Der Bourgeois. Zur Geistesgeschichte des modernen Wirtschaftsmenschen.* (Munich, 1913 and 1923). As its sub-title says, the book is, of course, primarily concerned to elucidate matters of economic history; but it contains exceptionally valuable material on the intellectual history of the *bourgeoisie* and this naturally entails giving a good deal of attention to its opposite, the landowning aristocracy. In this context, see also

Max Scheler: *Der Bourgeois*, in his collected essays *Vom Umsturz der Werte* (2nd edn., Leipzig, 1919) vol. 2, pp. 245–79; and *ibidem* also *Der Bourgeois und die religiösen Mächte*, pp. 281–317. Quite different in kind, but well worth reading are the witty essays by Count R. N. Coudenhove-Kalergi: *Adel* (Leipzig, 1923) and *Held oder Heiliger*, (Vienna, 1927). Only a general reference can be made here to the latest and very extensive literature on the problem of an élite.

Index